Dear Mom

Why Raising Four Boys Was Neither Boring Nor Monotonous

Jean Willett

Goblin Fern Press
Madison, Wisconsin
www.goblinfernpress.com

Copyright ©2005 by Jean Willett

All rights reserved. No part of this book may be reproduced in any form without written permission from the publisher, with the exception of brief excerpts for review purposes.

Published by Goblin Fern Press, Inc., Madison, WI, 1-888-670-BOOK (2665)
www.goblinfernpress.com

To order additional copies, contact your local bookstore or the publisher. Quantity discounts available.

ISBN 1-59598-003-2

Library of Congress Control Number: 2004112510

Book design and typography by Crocker Design

Printed in the United States of America
First edition
10 9 8 7 6 5 4 3 2 1

Publisher's Cataloging-In-Publication Data
(Prepared by The Donohue Group, Inc.)

Willett, Jean.
  Dear mom : why raising four boys was neither boring nor monotonous / Jean Willett.

  p. : ill. ; cm.
  ISBN: 1-59598-003-2

1. Mothers and daughters---Correspondence. 2. Motherhood. I. Title.

HQ759 .W54 2004
306.874 / 3   2004112510

A portion of the proceeds of the sales of this book will be donated to the University of Wisconsin Comprehensive Cancer Center.

Cover photo: Florence Hibbard (Mom), with, left to right, Andy, Jay, Mike, and Tim

Dedicated to Mom who inspired me to write Wednesday morning letters in response to hers written every Sunday, for years. Her last words to me were, "I've had a good life and done many things. The only thing I really regret is that I didn't get to read your book." I hope she's reading it now.

And to my husband Dann without whom, for many reasons, none of this would have been possible.

Contents

Prologue vii

1 Home is Where You Dropped Your Hat 1

2 On My Honor 17

3 When It Rains, It Pours 46

4 But When She was Bad 78

5 In Sickness and in Health 143

6 The Family That Plays Together 187

7 This Land is My Land 238

8 Bugs and More Bugs 270

9 The North Woods 317

10 New Horizons 365

11 Dear Tim 377

12 Scamper Camper 388

13 A Revolving Door 430

14 Subtracting or Adding? 455

Epilogue 468

Prologue

SUNDAY, JULY 9TH, 1950

Heat waves shimmer throughout the church vestibule where we stand. Damp spots are spreading across the back of cousin Catherine's floor-length dress.

Every time the flower girl shifts feet, petals cascade over the rim of her basket. I can't stand still either and shift my scarlet roses back and forth from one arm to the other. The usher has seated Mom in the front pew. Muffled strains of my brother's tenor solo drift through the closed door. Many friends and relatives are here waiting for the ceremony to begin.

What am I waiting for—what lies ahead? Years ago I commented to Mom that being a housewife must be "boring and monotonous." At the time, I wasn't sure why she thought that was funny, but she never let me forget it. I'm not promising to be a wife to a house. I'm not even going to let anyone call me that. I want to be a homemaker—whatever that entails. The man waiting for me at the front of the church—what does he expect and can I live up to his expectations? Questions flit helter-skelter through my mind.

As the soloist finishes, the vestibule doors swing open. The organist pulls out the trumpet stops and changes the tempo to the quick time of the processional. One by one the bridesmaids start down the aisle. Catherine gives a gentle shove to the flower girl and walks close behind her so that she cannot stop to play. Finally Dad and I stand alone, waiting. Every pew is packed. My eyes scan the backs of the waiting congregation and then jump to the seven people up front, also waiting. Dann, standing in the center, has eyes only for me. When he smiles, my gaze locks on his. I glide down the aisle hanging on to Dad. No more wondering. No more frantic questioning. Best of all, no more waiting. Whatever the future holds, we'll face it together.

1 Home Is Where You Drop Your Hat

November 15, 1956

Dear Mom,

I can't believe the tomb-like stillness in our apartment today. The baby is sleeping in his crib, Timmy is still napping and Andy won't be home from kindergarten for an hour.

Dann spotted an intriguing house for sale in his multiple listing book. We need space. Existing with three small dynamos in a four-room apartment bounces us against each other like balls in a hardball court. Dann's Mother came with us to look at the house. The ad had sounded like an estate, but it turned out to be

a fifty-year-old farmhouse covered with cracked, orange stucco, located in the middle of two acres of woodland. The 44 foot, narrow living/dining room felt like an empty bowling alley decorated with peeling walls done in hot pink and slate gray. Piles of soiled mattresses and broken furniture, topped with broken glass, filled each corner, and we counted 21 broken window panes. The thermostat setting kept the house colder than outdoors. Upstairs, we meandered through six huge bedrooms, one with a fireplace. The house offered space, that's all. Dann and I stared, but my mother-in-law strolled through the house with a running commentary. "What a spot to raise boys! Think of the memories it would create." An appropriate remark for one who raised six boys. Going home, absolute silence reigned in the car. That night our apartment seemed even smaller. Toys belonging to a five-year-old, a three-year-old and a six-month-old were strewn everywhere.

Why is my honey butter runnier than yours? Do I need more margarine?

December 15, 1956

Dear Mom,

Navy blue for mittens would be fine as the dirt doesn't show.

For seven days neither of us dared to mention that old house. I visualized two houses — what is and what could be and thought about the gruesome stucco, the trash and the ugly peeling walls. Six bedrooms would provide a playroom for the kids, an office for Dann and a sewing room for me. The old-fashioned kitchen would have to be remodeled. If we removed those puppy-stained black blots on the floor and resanded, the golden oak would be stunning. Wild flowers abounded in the woods under limitless tree fort possibilities. Dann and I scribbled lists all week: what has to be done, what we'd like to have done, cost estimates for both and submitted a $12,000 offer which they accepted! The house had been on the market for five years, and the executor wanted the estate settled. We have one month to work before moving. When can you come up? We're eager to show you our new home.

January 5, 1957

Dear Mom,

    We're delighted you liked the house and appreciate Dad's offer for rewiring. You have a good imagination to see through that dirt. This is Dann's slow season so we have laid out a schedule. He works mornings in the Realty office. At noon, when Andy comes home from kindergarten, we shift to the new (old) house. Our card table with the Coleman stove sits by the living room window where I make lunch. That picture window frames a woodsy view making us forget we're in the city. A clipped, small, green lawn, a terraced wall of worn glacial boulders that fit together like the dry walls of Scotland, and a weedy abandoned garden meet the eye. Giant oaks, black cherry and shagbark hickory stand behind surrounded by prickly blackberry bushes making the woods nearly impenetrable. The mammoth black oaks, like liveried English butlers, bow stiffly over the old garden as they reach for the almost non-existent sun.

    I placed Jason's crib and two air mattresses next to the fireplace. Andy thinks five-year-olds don't nap but he rests—under protest. Tim still sleeps, allowing Dann and me a few hours of freedom. Of necessity, the beds stay next to the fireplace because the cold seeps into our bones even though the burning trash makes a blazing fire.

    This old house doesn't have cold air returns so it resembles a drafty old barn. The wastebasket overflows with discarded kitchen plans from the University Extension Home Agent. She eliminated the kitchen stairs to make room for an eating area. That second set of stairs to the landing must have been for a maid. From now on the maid uses the main stairs and the master bedroom! We replaced the small kitchen window with six Andersen windows and a new peninsula sink allows me to oversee the play-yard.

The tiny metal plate in the center of the dining room floor mystified us until someone identified it as a plug-in. A cord from there to the hostess's lap allowed her to squeeze a bulb that alerted the kitchen help. There won't be anyone in the kitchen either to answer that bell.

Walls, painted with calcimine paint and then covered with wallpaper, have to be cleaned. We rented a backpack water tank that looks like fire fighting equipment. We aim the attached tube towards the trouble area and shoot, hoping to soak the wall. Everything else gets soaked, too, including Andy and Timmy. They love this great game, so leaving an unguarded tank is dangerous.

January 12, 1957

Dear Mom,

For every job that gets done on our old house, we discover two more. A house with all this personality deserves a name. Sitting on a hill surrounded by woods, we chose Arbor Heights.

We can't possibly get all the work done before moving in. With a house this large we can shift around the working messes. I asked to have a finished kitchen before moving and then agreed to tolerate the rest of the mess. We split the big bathroom into two. Last night I crawled into the new tub to rest for one moment but Dann woke me when he wanted to go home. The days are speeding away too fast.

Home Is Where You Drop Your Hat

January 20, 1957

Dear Mom,

The hardest way to move must be bit by bit. A few boxes travel with the car every trip and nothing gets thrown away. We set a final moving date. Final means that the real beds move and we sleep in the new place. We have hooked the furnace to the new cold air vents, have three working bathrooms, new wiring throughout (thanks, Pop), all the floors refinished and three bedrooms painted. The kitchen remains a shell. We're going anyway.

If houses could talk, Arbor Heights could spiel fascinating tales. Although the house was built in 1907, we are the second owners. The first owner, a University agronomist professor, planted trees of every available species. When he died, his wife sold the land along the perimeter. She couldn't bear to give up his special trees, so the survey lines jog around the trees. Most of those trees are gone, but the perimeter jags like a shard of broken glass. The house hides amongst the trees. Only our long, narrow driveway touches the street.

One of the professor's teenagers took an overdose of medicine which reduced his mentality. He often wandered between the houses at night, carrying a shotgun and whistling, which frightened the neighbors. We can visualize the ghost of Arbor Heights, the boy who never grew up and who probably still whistles in the dark.

After the professor's widow died, the heirs put the house on the market. It stood vacant for years with occasional renters. This old house must have shuddered during those neglected years when nobody administered any tender loving care. I think of it as a battered house—cold, forlorn, unloved. If houses had feelings, this one must now be bursting with joy as we've restored its glory and filled it with the sounds of happy little boys.

I'm reading The Five Little Peppers aloud. Although this intrigued me as a child, I don't see anything remarkable about it now. It's just a story about another family without enough money to go around. Dann howled over that, but the boys found the story fascinating.

FEBRUARY 1, 1957

Dear Mom,

We did it! We're here! If there is anything more stupid than getting married in the heat of July, it must be moving in the wintry blasts of January. Many journeys back and forth between the apartment and the house made many trips up this long driveway and the car struggled through deep snow every time. A new house feels unfriendly because nothing is familiar, most everything doesn't work yet and a three and a five-year-old don't help much. You would laugh at my still empty kitchen. The card table sits in the dining room with an electric fry pan that heats water to warm Jay's bottle. The refrigerator stands in the living room next to the playpen. I had to concede to an unfinished kitchen, but enjoy living at just one address.

We transferred Andy to the Crestwood kindergarten. Our house backs up to the schoolyard so he runs across the backyard. If he starts late, running doesn't do it as there is no travel time to take up the slack.

Thanks for the old toboggan. Everybody slides down Battlefield Hill at the back of the schoolyard. Exciting when all of us pile on.

Please give me the size again for the quilt squares?

Home Is Where You Drop Your Hat

February 15, 1957

Dear Mom,

We succumbed to some bugs. Dann spent Saturday in bed with a cold, and he shared with me. Every morning I have an exhausting headache. Jason woke up Monday with swollen neck glands. Apparently a cold infection had settled there. Yesterday a red swelling appeared at the corner of his eye and he felt hot to my touch. His temperature read 104 degrees. He didn't cry, just lay listlessly. I stripped off his clothes and laid him across my shoulder in hopes that air on bare skin might cool him. Rummaging in the medicine closet with a free hand, I mixed a 50/50 solution of water and alcohol and patted this over him in a desperate effort to reduce that temperature. A second reading registered 106 degrees. I stared in disbelief and took it again. Still 106. I called the clinic and was put through immediately.

"Forget about the 50/50 solution," the doctor ordered. "Use pure alcohol. Don't dry as evaporation reduces heat. Don't put his clothes back on. I will order a prescription. Have your husband pick it up immediately." His final shot was, "If we don't get that temperature down quickly, he'll convulse."

Continuing the alcohol baths with the phone cradled on my shoulder, I called Dann's office. As I started to explain to the secretary she interrupted, "Just hang up. I'll find him."

Back to the baths and thermometer—107 degrees. The gleaming red mercury inched up with every reading. Ten minutes passed before Dann called from the East side and listened grimly. Then, "I'm on my way," and the phone went dead.

More baths, administered as I paced the 44 feet from one end of the living room to the far end of the dining room. Still 107 degrees. More baths—more pacing—more prayers. How long would it take to drive across town through traffic? Fifteen minutes elapsed before tires growled up our gravel driveway. Continuing the baths while giving him the antibiotics, Jay's temperature slowly inched down. Dann said he had driven University Avenue at 60 mph hoping to pick up a police escort, but they didn't spot him until he was two blocks from home and then followed him up our driveway.

What frightened me most was how quickly a year-old baby can get ill. What amazes me is how quickly he's back to normal. Today our roles are reversed—he is alert and crying, while I am limp and exhausted.

July 25, 1957

Dear Mom,

We thought an announcement of that magnitude warranted a phone call. I hope the powers-that-be take notice that we have ordered a girl this time. I am feeling fine. With three lively boys underfoot, no time is left for morning sickness, but I'll have to take extra precautions because of the blood clot during my last pregnancy.

I'm tired of telling people that we have a six-bedroom house. The inevitable comeback is "looks like you're going to fill it up". Saying three bedrooms, study, playroom, and sewing room is less embarrassing.

October 1, 1957

Dear Mom,

I enjoyed my finished kitchen for two days. I had just put shortening to melt, in preparation for bread making, when the gears of a big truck came growling up the driveway. We've waited a long time to get on their blacktop schedule and worried that they might not squeeze us in before the temperature dropped.

Blacktop comes as a hot mix and gets laid rapidly. I went out to watch, absorbed by their speed until I momentarily looked back and saw flames reaching for the kitchen ceiling. I screamed, and both of us bolted for the back door. As a ball of orangish-blue flames shot out of the shortening pan, Dann grabbed the handle and raced outside. The minute he moved forward, flames fanned backwards covering his hand and forearm.

With the source of the fire removed the danger was past, but I wept over the damage. The fire had charred the spice cupboard directly over the stove, had burned the Formica backsplash, ruined the counter and turned the walls and ceiling smoky gray. The worst damage was Dann's hand. I treated his burns with ice, but it will be a long time before he can use that hand comfortably. We learned our lesson with that expensive bread. When carrying fire walk backwards, so the flames will lean away from you.

See you for lunch on Monday.

November 5, 1957

Dear Mom,

I have an ultra-conservative obstetrician who has changed my style of living because she says it's easier to prevent a blood clot than to deal with one. She limited my stairs to four times daily, down in the morning, up at night, and one up-and-down of my choice in between. The two pairs of small legs at my disposal are indispensable. They run errands willingly, but this taxes my memory to the utmost to tell them where to look for whatever I sent them to find. During the day piles accumulate by the stairs—one waiting for an up-elevator, one waiting for a down ride. Each morning I have to wrap my legs in ace bandages. Walking is okay, standing is not. Washing dishes and ironing get done awkwardly, as I perch on my kitchen stool.

Dann wants to be his own boss. He resigned from the office, applied to the state for the Arbor Realty name and will work here in the study. It may be difficult for us to accept that, though Dad is home, he is working. The bookkeeping is my chore after he shows me how. I feel that I am working, but on my own time. As my primary career of Occupational Therapy seems to be on hold, keeping books classifies as a secondary one. I'm practicing the valuable things I learned at the University—diversify and keep learning.

We restored the kitchen to mint condition and invited the church choir families for a potluck. I'm not sure whether the boys will be an asset or detriment for this undertaking.

Supper company from last week called to say that their children have the mumps. How long does it take to reach "breakout" day?

I know you are laughing again about that crack I made years ago that a housewife's days must be boring and monotonous. Probably next year things will quiet down.

December 10, 1957

Dear Mom,

No mumps yet, and our choir party was a howling success. Andy drew pictures for you. One shows our driveway with 13 cars. The other picture shows our living room filled with card tables and 43 people. They didn't sit under the tables like he drew them. He just didn't have any more room on the paper.

I lectured Andy and Tim on being good hosts, what not to do, how to take care of the children who were their special guests and suggested that after answering the door they should take coats upstairs. Andy looked dubious and remarked, "I don't talk to people very well but I could say gimme your coat so I can put it somewhere." Yes, I kept a straight face.

At 6:00 we sat waiting, but nobody came. The boys checked outside at 6:02. Nobody. It was 6:10 before the first car drove up. Eyes opened wide as a stream of cars rolled by the front door.

We divided people into eight teams, passed out puzzles and made this a race. We had planned a scavenger hunt that would get the yard picked up and show off the house. Requirements were: one catnip plant with roots (we have so many we should have required a dozen plants from each team), a piece of broken glass, the number of windows in the house (37), dates from the Britannica's, the number of harnesses on my loom (attic), a yardstick from the screen porch (omitted mentioning that we referred to the second-floor screened porch), and the model number of the garbage disposal (to show off my new kitchen). By the end they had toured all three floors of the house and circled the yard. We wondered what the neighbors thought about 43 people dashing in and out, digging up plants, and running around counting windows.

My kitchen filled with working women, but when I walked through I never found the area blocked, which surely proves a well-planned kitchen. Everybody had a good time, especially the four of us. Now we can quiet down and wait for the mumps.

When you come to freeze chickens, Dann's Mother will help. Could three of us do 26 in a day?

Andy just came down for a piece of string because Dann told him the fairies would be out tonight. The tooth is out, under his pillow and he is worrying how the fairies are going to get into the house.

Timmy has been sick again. His stomach pains act like flu. I had to take him out of church yesterday and around the block to his other Grandma's where I put him to bed. He's fine today.

January 7, 1958

Dear Mom,

The boys must have missed the mumps. Just as well because Dann has been ill. The newspapers warned that Madison was about to have an epidemic of Asian flu and the next day Dann collapsed with high fever and lung congestion. Our doctor was out-of-town, but I found a young doctor who agreed to home-visit during his lunch hour. A little Volkswagen bug chugged up our driveway and a six-foot-plus man unwound himself from inside that tiny car. He does think Dann has Asian flu. The doctor glanced at my protruding stomach. "You have a choice, either the hospital, or care for him here if you're able." Dann was too sick to care, so I decided we could cope if the boys would be runners for the necessary liquids. All Dann wanted was to sleep, but both Andy and Timmy were good at waking him up every hour for his drink. This is called nursing by remote control because I couldn't trudge upstairs to check. He has improved, but will be tired for months.

We want to adhere to the Willett family tradition to use Bible names and are studying the Bible every day searching for an appropriate name. Picking a girl's name is easy as we've had either Sarah Jean or Martha Jean waiting for three times now.

January 30, 1958

Dear Mom,

I am relieved to be home again. That was a bad idea for Dann to leave us with you for a week. Timmy obviously suffered great pain. He has experienced severe side aches so many times, but this is the first time that I have gotten him to the doctor while he was still hurting. Timmy's high white blood count obviously signified appendicitis to your doctor. He looked at my protruding stomach and asked if I could stay for two weeks if necessary and when I said no, he made it clear that I should leave for home immediately and get another medical opinion upon arrival. Thanks, Pop, for taking us halfway. Meeting Dann on the road meant that we got to the doctor's office in an hour-and-a-half. They ran tests immediately, but by then Timmy's blood count had dropped to normal and the side ache had disappeared. We had expected to be in the hospital for surgery by nightfall. Instead we have an apparently well child. This upsets me when the pains have occurred so often. We just don't know what to do.

Thanks, anyway. We had a great time for the first half of the visit.

February 15, 1958

Dear Mom,

Dann is doing fine. In fact, we are all well. The boys are looking forward to having you stay during my hospitalization. The four-piece knitted outfit you made is impressive. A cape, doubling as a blanket, is ingenious but is the soft pink positive thinking on your part?

Auntie Beth sent a pre-baby present, six heirloom spoons that belonged to your grandmother. She wrote that these had been handed down the female side of the family, that she had planned on giving them to me after the first baby, waited for the second, hoped to do it for the third, but was now tired of waiting so was sending them before the baby arrived and to keep them if we get a boy.

The language around here gets pretty descriptive. I heard the boys talking about the washer and "wiper." I explained we call it a dryer, now I hear them talking about the dryer and the "wetter."

I'm praying for no blizzards for the next couple weeks. At least we live on a hill so we can always get out of here in a hurry—on the toboggan, if necessary.

February 27, 1958

Dear Mom,

Were you shocked to get a call from my hospital bed? We weren't surprised as we had foretold a boy. It's relaxing to know that you and Pop are holding down the fort for us "back at the ranch". I trust they won't give you too much trouble. Expect Timmy to be sick. He always is when I enter the hospital—sympathetic feelings I guess. Don't be insulted that the boys asked if you knew how to make pancakes. Michael and I will be delayed coming home. I have been so careful for the last couple months wrapping my legs and limiting my stairs and thought we were home free. The doctor put me on Warfarin when the birth was imminent to prevent blood clots. He also stood me up an hour after delivery for the same reason. If the circulation keeps moving, the chance of a blood clot forming reduces, but it didn't work.

Dann probably didn't fill you in on the details of that frantic rush to the hospital. When he came home for supper I said, "It's time, but we'll eat first to make sure." After supper I reaffirmed, "It's a go."

We started to call his Mother to come stay with the crew when Dann rebelled, "I don't dare leave you alone to go get her!"

"It would only be thirty minutes."

"With you, that's too long," he muttered, remembering the two prior times when he had left the hospital to eat and came back each time to find a new son.

I fussed, "You should have thought about this earlier."

He called his brother, Don, to pick up their mother. Dann told him that we would wait if possible, but that if anything changed we would leave the boys knowing that Don was enroute. We did wait and arrived at the hospital to find Dr. Tomason pacing the floor. Having delivered three babies for me, she knew this was taking too long. Everyone's concerns were legitimate as the baby arrived two hours after we entered the hospital.

After a birth, the mother must be in a state of euphoria. I lay on the delivery table reflecting that things were taking a long time. Nobody had unstrapped my legs, but this didn't worry me. Nobody attended to me, they were all working frantically in the corner. Nobody bothered to explain. I thought it strange they would call my pediatrician in the middle of the night. If I turned my head I could see the doctor giving mouth-to-mouth resuscitation to the baby. The fact that these were not things one would expect following a normal delivery finally registered.

When the baby cried, the doctor straightened up, smiled and explained. Because Michael's lungs had filled with mucous he hadn't been able to breathe. Mouth-to-mouth as a primary emergency measure followed by suction as soon as the equipment was in place, removed the obstruction. By this time the expectant father was grimly striding up and down the hospital corridor. He knows that I breeze in and out of a delivery room. When the time stretched to an hour, he realized something was wrong. It was a bad time for him.

In many ways having just boys will be easier. All that matters is that they have the proper number of arms, legs and other parts. I'll send this letter home with Dann when he comes to visit tonight. You and Pop take it easy. Don't let our little terrors wear you out.

March 2, 1958

Dear Mom,

Glad you got home safely and are rested. Many thanks from all six of us. The boys think you're special.

Things have settled back into routine. That "boring and monotonous" living that I commented on years ago still eludes me.

This old house is going to change our lives, allowing us space to be ourselves without being on someone's lap. When we are all active simultaneously we simulate a three-ring circus. The needs of the house are endless. All its life and ours we'll be fixing things, but we get satisfaction from seeing something worn or ugly and turning it into something beautiful and functioning. Renovations cut down on our TV watching time. The house must enjoy being noisy again from the first door slam in early morning to the last radio snapped off at night. When we show off Arbor Heights people invariably comment, "Trust a realtor to grab the good buys."

We reply, "Where were you all the years this house sat on the market, deserted and broken?"

Mom Willett was right. The house is going to provide us with endless memories. We've added two major changes to our lives this last year—a country house in the city, and one more son.

Thanks, Mom, for helping and for listening.

2 On My Honor...

SEPTEMBER 19, 1959

Dear Mom,

    Andy's approaching eighth birthday marks a drastic change in our lives. The discussion around the supper table every night centers on Cub Scouts. Andy needs eight more days to that magic birthday that makes him eligible. When I volunteered to be den mother for Andy's den, it shook up the Cubmaster as he usually has to coerce people. Cubmaster Jim is a friend of Dann's and he asked Dann to be committee chairman. "It doesn't require any real work," he teased. "Just a name on the charter and a mailing address for the scout office to use." Dann agreed to do it. Handling my eight new Cubs should be easy as I've always enjoyed kids, starting with my work as an Occupational Therapist in Pediatrics.

    We had company for supper last night, people Dann had sold a house to—strangers to all of us except Dann, which made me uneasy. All of us were uneasy. When Andy and Timmy saw girls, they dove under the bed. Jason and Mike must have felt they were missing out and promptly followed. I had neglected to dust there, but it's not necessary now.

I can see why you think raising four boys is challenging. Yesterday they were still eating breakfast when I went upstairs to lay out Sunday clothes. When I returned they were joyously pelting each other with orange peels. Little girls don't do those things, do they?

October 21, 1959

Dear Mom,

We have a registered, six-week old, sable, female collie pup. We can't raise boys without a dog. Our first priority was to find a breed that would love kids no matter what they did. She does. They're inseparable. At family conference we chose her official name, Twinkletoes of Arbor Heights, using the full 25 letters the registry allows. She sleeps in the basement. About 5:00 a.m. she and Dann argue over that location. He tried hot water bottles, alarm clocks in her bed, and a folded newspaper until she finally got the message that she cannot sleep with us. She has us housebroken—whenever she wakes up or finishes eating, the next step is to take her outside immediately.

A high school girl sits with the younger boys during den meetings. This isn't as easy as I had anticipated. Either the den meeting goes smoothly and my own boys run out of control, or three sons are gainfully occupied and the Cubs run wild. Andy seems to be the leader of the pack. If your mother is den mother, you need to show the others all the no-no's, such as using the living room furniture for a trampoline.

Quit lecturing Mom, I know I'm trying to do too much.

The boys complain about piano lessons. Those lessons used to be a drudge for me. Every time I asked about quitting you'd answer, "After a while." I resolved my boys would not have this uncertainty hanging over their heads and announced a five year duration for each one. They still complain. Two get dropped at a time which translates to a full hour before pickup—about right for the other two and me to cope with weekly grocery shopping. Twelve years of chauffeuring for weekly piano lessons now hangs heavy over my head. The chauffeur needs to see the end of the tunnel also.

The boys love coming to Grandpa's house. Me, too. Planning and building the house of your dreams was a great retirement project for Dad. Jay and Mike consider sleeping on the studio couch, in the corner of your large bedroom, a special treat. I'm not so sure about the other two. Sharing a double bed with a brother must be demeaning. And not peaceful even with Sam, the rolled-up blanket dummy, between them.

Grandpa's workshop and honey house intrigue them. They figured out that anything that enters his workshop comes out fixed, but the honey-house end worries them. They demolish your honey butter, but are unsure about bees buzzing around in the pear trees that they are always climbing.

Life doesn't break even around here with the daily disorder and destruction. By the time I reached the supper table last night, a coating of pepper dusted the fruit salad. Mike can now reach and loves the pepper shaker. Tim and Jay made beer in the bathroom yesterday using sink cleanser for foam and water for base. They filled the tub half full, the sink and all their toys full, soaked their clothes, and sloshed water all over the floor.

FEBRUARY 1, 1960

Dear Mom,

Dann has decided to run for alderman. Andy and Timmy asked: what is an alderman, how do we acquire them, and how does Dad get his name before the public? We plan to take them to

City Hall on election night. I wonder why we do this. It looks like a thankless, friend-losing, time-consuming job. Maybe we just feel a need for more honest politicians.

We have had guests from India. Dann rented them an apartment, which was not available for four days so he brought them home. They were two days from their home when they arrived. To be their first impression of Americans, especially American kids, appalled me. After two days I would have dumped the whole deal if that had been possible. Increasing my discipline didn't help as it made my four model children more rebellious, rambunctious and noisy.

Hindus eat no meat. Even Andy started to question eggs three times a day. The children intrigued the guests, and after two days the boys suddenly improved and the guests intrigued them. Six house servants in India meant she had never done housework and she followed me constantly. She learned how to wash dishes and make sandwiches. She spoke only when spoken to if a man or boy was present, but an amazing personality opened up if we were alone. What do you suppose her husband thought of me who never keeps her mouth shut? The last morning she gave me a gold-embroidered, green, silk sari, and taught me how to wrap it around me. I was thunderstruck. The boys were, too. Dann's Scottish background causes him to worry about where I will wear that stunning sari.

I, and my eight Cubs, have an appointment with the fire chief.

March 9, 1960

Dear Mom,

Jay slipped and fell in the bathtub and a swelling the size of an egg developed on his groin. This appears to be a hernia and requires surgery. I dread putting a three-year-old in the hospital, even for two overnights.

March 15, 1960

Dear Mom,

I did a lot of psychological preparation on Jason and should have done it on everybody, as Timmy had an upset stomach from the night before Jay left until the night he returned. Jason has already forgotten the awful afternoon following surgery and told his brothers at great length about his bed that cranked up, breakfast in bed, milk through a straw, Disneyland life-size pictures on the walls, the playroom with TV, wheelchairs that he and his new friend raced up and down the hall for hours, the new book he received every time Mother came to visit, new slippers and all the mail. After listening to this, there isn't one brother who wouldn't willingly go to the hospital. Jay received a card with a dollar enclosed and Andy complained, "This just isn't fair!"

When we come for Easter, would you like some of us for longer? The boys and I could stay a few extra days and go home on the train. Let me know if this is a good or bad idea.

March 30, 1960

Dear Mom,

Dann lost the aldermanic race, but we rationalize that it was a good experience. We will now always be more aware of whom we vote for.

Being just a mailing address for the Scout office hasn't worked that way. Keeping these Cubbing activities running smoothly requires a committee meeting every month. After each pack meeting we all rush home, put kids to bed and reconvene at somebody's house. We rehash the mistakes and problems of the past month and start planning the next one, reminding me of that expression—the king is dead, long live the queen. There is no time between the old and the new. Dann would never have accepted this job if he had realized what it entailed, but we've been surprised. It's great fun. We have become close friends with many of the adult Scouters and enjoy the hilarious committee meetings with accompanying food and chitchat.

Jay survived fine, Dann's turn comes next. A cataract has been giving him vision problems in one eye and will require surgery as soon as his vision gets worse.

Jason, who never lacks for questions, is thrilled with the wonders of the outdoors in the springtime. After a long period of "but why" questions I thought I had him stumped by answering, "Because God wants it that way." I underestimated him.

"But why does God want it that way, Mommy?"

April 10, 1960

Dear Mom,

Thanks for a lovely Easter. The boys unloaded 40 golf balls from their pockets when we got home. Searching for balls kept them occupied for hours. A cornfield next to a golf course seems like a bad idea to me as nobody but boys could find the balls once they disappear.

I forgot to check the dollhouse in the basement and hope the boys put everything back. That dollhouse makes as good an attraction now as 20 years ago when I packed it away to wait for my daughter. I didn't realize that it's a unisex toy.

We survived the train trip home. Highlights of the trip were: passing over Monona Bay suspended high above the water, a window for each boy and a drinking fountain with paper cups. The boys weren't aboard long enough to discover that trains have johns. How do Moms retrieve boys from the men's room? They were crestfallen when the porter walked through calling, "last call for breakfast" and I was immovable.

Cousin Georgianna reminds me that, as a teenager, I wanted to have a football team. I have no recollection of this. Are order changes allowed?

June 13, 1960

Dear Mom,

The boys are envious that you kept their cousin Valerie for two weeks while her Mom was hospitalized. They don't wish me to be in the hospital, but almost.

Last weekend we visited my college roommate. The kids disappeared into the haymow the moment we arrived and we're still pulling hayseeds off their coats. Fourteen new piglets provided live entertainment. Not at a convenient hour.

My time melts away like hot butter. It depresses me to think of the canning, freezing and yard work done last year and the lack of it this year. Summer child guidance rates top priority. We go to the beach for daily swimming lessons, to vacation Bible school, or out in our woods to gather material for leaf collections. Each boy is starting a stamp collection and my supervision is required with their garden plots, daily chores, and practicing.

Setting up chores in an impartial, foolproof way defeats me. The older boys have six daily chores, the younger ones less. Every two weeks, the lists shift so no one gets permanently stuck with the least favorite jobs. Andy, Timmy, and Jason have a room to vacuum each day, which they do with precise timing. No one wants to be first, as that guy has to take the vacuum out of the closet. No one wants to be last, as that guy has to put it away. Everyone strives for the middle. One of my biggest problems has been getting one-on-one time. Dish wiping accomplishes this as everyone who can do so vanishes, and the chosen boy and I share time together. One boy clears the supper table sometimes precipitating crises as boys and adults don't eat at the same speed. Often Dann has laid down his fork, spoken to someone and turned back to his plate to find it had been cleared before seconds, or his tea cup was snatched before he finished dessert.

They are supposed to pick up their things strewn around downstairs. Each child has a step to pile belongings on until he goes upstairs. Mike, being the littlest, rates the lowest step with Andy claiming the fourth step up. In desperation, I resorted to color coding. All socks and underwear get marked with thread. Green denotes Andy. Timmy has red, Jason blue and Michael yellow. The mitten and hat shelves are also painted in those colors.

In theory, every day the house gets vacuumed, kitchen floor swept, dog fed and brushed, newspapers put away, bathroom sinks cleaned, trash burned, table set, cleared, dishes wiped, beds made and belongings picked up. In practice, it doesn't work like that. Not getting chores done on the proper day rates a checkmark and five checkmarks rates an extra dish wiping.

Andy has started a postmark collection. Each page of his scrapbook denotes a state with a miniature cutout of that state in one corner and a place for the capital and largest city. Andy pastes the printed postmark on the proper page. Please send him a card whenever you are away from Wisconsin. Great geography lesson.

We patronize the corner bookmobile with any leftover time. We've gone from ABC's to dinosaurs, Indians to ships, and Treasure Island to Swamp Fox. My dirty house and uncompleted work annoy me but I can't complain, as working with children takes precedence every day.

July 15, 1960

Dear Mom,

    We've just returned from the Willett summer cabin at Lake Nebagamon. In 1923 Dann's father bought some burned over land, which faces beautiful beachfront and has boggy swampland behind. On this he built a small cabin with a sleeping porch. A place where six barefoot boys in overalls ran free all summer, their time divided between the land and the water. The cabin makes a wonderful place for our summer vacations as we can't afford to travel with six of us, but here our boys learned to swim and sail, and how to exist happily without running water, bathrooms or TV. They hike in the woods, hunt for blueberries in the swamp, chop firewood and learn to enjoy that wondrous feeling of doing nothing.

    The cottage is a marvelous place to relax if one can survive the effort to get there. Just packing wears me out. If we didn't have a nine-passenger station wagon with luggage rack on top, we'd never fit. Twinkle sits under my feet. Dann ties the canoe on top of the luggage rack and prays that I won't need something from up top before we arrive. By the end of seven hours of driving the kids have emptied the diversion bag, devoured the picnic lunch except for the remains on people's pants, exhausted my patience and given me a headache.

    Mass confusion reigns upon arrival. No one is allowed to even look at the lake until the car is unloaded. Twinkle hates traveling. We pushed and shoved to get her into the car, and upon arrival I pulled and tugged to get her out. In the confusion of unpacking, minutes passed before we noticed she was missing. I have trained her to come to two blasts of a whistle. I blasted twice—and twice again—and twice again. No dog. Knowing how much she didn't want to get into the car, I worried that her collie homing instincts might take her home. 315 miles! Everyone stopped unloading and whistled and called and then we discovered Michael was missing, too. We raced down to the lake but saw no sign of him anywhere. Finally, standing on the back road and listening, I heard faint crying. Michael had slipped out of the car, crossed the road and wandered into the tamarack swamp and Twinkle followed. She couldn't bring him back, but she could stand in front of him when he tried to go deeper which made him cry in frustration. She must have heard the double blasts on the whistle and recognized the return command, but disobeyed and stayed with Mike.

The swim lessons are paying off, giving us many delightful hours on the beach. Dann has been teaching Andy and Timmy to fish and he quickly learned the necessity of taking a small can along in the boat as the excitement mounts so high that the resulting call of nature comes quick and sure. We enjoyed blueberry-picking on the sand barrens after dispersing big floppy hats to keep off the sun and the ticks, plenty of mosquito dope, and a pail. Sometimes not too many berries make it into four of the pails, but the other two produce enough for a couple juicy pies.

Dann is teaching me bookkeeping so I can help with Arbor Realty. Nothing ever happens the same way twice and I cannot figure out where to list the pig that he took in lieu of some of the cash on his last house sale. Dann likes being his own boss. It makes a difference having him around much of the time.

September 2, 1960

Dear Mom,

We cleaned the garage during that nice weather. Dann used gasoline for cleaning brushes and had placed the can on a pile of bricks. When we turned around Mike was drinking from the gasoline can. Dann grabbed him and ran. Holding him over the kitchen sink he forced his finger down Mike's throat until he threw up while I phoned for help. The doctor told us to force liquids for dilution and hope that the gasoline had bypassed his lungs. We did all the proper things, but frequently, during the day, Mike would burp and a powerful gasoline smell would roll out. Otherwise, no after effects, no pneumonia. He must have gotten little, but we couldn't tell. Dann is rebuilding the garage to two-and-one-half spaces. The old garage was so narrow that this pregnant wife could neither enter nor exit from the car. Six bicycles park in the half. He needs the roof finished before winter and the boys eagerly help, chalking up experience with a hammer. Andy and Timmy stride along those wobbly ceiling rafters without fear.

Wednesday Timmy had an upset stomach just before school time so I kept him home. He lounged on the couch all day with severe side pains. This worries us as it keeps reoccurring.

We are reorganizing the Cubs for the new school year. Having one's Mom for a den mother for one year is enough. One of the other mothers volunteered for Andy's den and I took a new bunch.

October 2, 1960

Dear Mom,

Having you and Dad baby-sit all day made a special birthday present. For eight years Dann has asked me to go bow and arrow hunting and I never could. Necedah is beautiful in the fall and just to be there is a delight — usually. It was our bad luck that rain poured by the bucketfuls. Murphy's Law must have been in effect. (Everything that can possibly go wrong will do so.) It was good that; we learned we were in a no-hunting part of the refuge before a warden discovered us, good that when the transmission jammed as we were driving the fire lane and had to walk out to the highway in the rain that we found a tow truck right as we exited, bad that the brakes on the tow truck didn't work making a scary ride out with our Rambler on tow, bad that his chain broke so that when we retied the short tow on the Rambler mud splashed on the windshield so Dann couldn't see to steer the malfunctioning car, good that when we got out and Dann tried the transmission once more the shifting worked perfectly. Towing had moved the gears just enough to get off that dead spot. Dann stopped at used car lots all the way home to work off his frustration. Thanks again.

October 12, 1960

Dear Mom,

There's no end to this Cub Scout stuff. I have acquired the dubious title of chief den mother and six new boys that need to be placed in dens. Unfortunately, these six don't live in the same area. Two joined my den, giving me nine. Ten is my limit. All the others made up a new den with a new den mother plus two boys from an overloaded den. We did her first meeting together at her house, and my boys stayed home by themselves. Andy was responsible for Mike and the phone, and Timmy was in charge of Jay and Twinkle. They used their emergency phone number three times. Andy complained that Timmy wasn't doing his chores and that Timmy wasn't letting Jay play with him. Timmy complained that Andy was roughhousing, verboten with braces. I should have taken one of the older boys with me. Inasmuch as one of the new Cubs came down with chickenpox the next day, it's good that I didn't. They wrestled before the meeting so that whole den will probably be absent soon.

DECEMBER 15, 1960

Dear Mom,

The eye doctor has been concerned about the reason for Dann's cataract as they don't usually occur in so young a person. He admitted Dann to Veteran's Hospital for a two-day physical. Their decision was that the severe swimming injury Dann received 20 years ago, when he was in the Army, might have caused the cataract. While he was hospitalized the rest of us went to the mall and visited Santa Claus. Santa set each boy on his lap and asked what he wanted for Christmas. Timmy answered gravely, "I just want my Daddy home from the hospital for Christmas." Two big tears pooled in Santa Claus's eyes. We'll be down early Christmas morn.

DECEMBER 30, 1960

Dear Mom,

Christmas Eve at home is our time, but Christmas Day at your house is special. I hope you never get tired of our commotion. We just had to bring that electric train. They've asked for a train for so many years that we couldn't leave it. Dann, Uncle Frank and Grandpa had a lovely time all day long setting it up in the middle of your living room floor. Valerie played too, when she could squeeze her way in.

We brought the piñata so she could join in the breaking. Piñata making has become our annual tradition. Even Michael gets involved as the only damage anyone can do is to get thoroughly pasted up. The wiener balloon that we used for a base made a natural dachshund. We don't want the piñatas breaking too soon, but everyone plops layers on so enthusiastically that even a direct hit with the bat doesn't always split it.

This year my Christmas sewing didn't get squeezed in until five days before Christmas. Using red corduroy I found on sale last summer, I made five matching red shirts in five days. The sixth one, mine, lies on the sewing machine missing its sleeves.

Trying to master this bookkeeping gives me headaches especially when closing the books for the year.

My "boring and monotonous housewife" remark didn't include bookkeeping either.

January 5, 1961

Dear Mom,

Last week Dann's 96-year-old step-grandmother fell and broke her hip. Taking Aunt Myrtle along, we drove to Platteville to visit the invalid. We had been on the road an hour, with Mike sleeping in the back, when Timmy voiced an urgent request. Dann quickly turned off the highway into a wayside with outdoor plumbing. Tim hopped out and took care of himself. Then Jay asked to go and then Andy announced that Mike needed to go, too. Dann took Michael, but returned to the car disgusted. Mike didn't really need to go, still being half asleep, but in the trying his little fur cap had fallen in! Dann stalked off into the woods and brought back a long branch. He needed to see down there and we all turned out our pockets, but no matches. I discovered a trouble light in the glove compartment which plugs into the cigarette lighter. Dann backed and turned the car squeezing between the trees until that cord would reach. Andy held the light and Dann hooked the hat with the branch. Thanks to Wisconsin's cold January temperatures, everything was frozen solid and the cap was retrieved in pristine condition.

January 16, 1961

Dear Mom,

    We're preparing for the annual Blue and Gold banquet. Each den makes and decorates a cake using the monthly theme. Committee-men judge the cakes before we devour them. My den created a six-layer teepee-shaped masterpiece decorated with sign language. Can you picture me doing this with nine eager, howling, restless kids helping? Just the process of getting nine boys' hands washed takes a mammoth effort, but essential when you see the condition of the fingers that get dipped in the cake batter if they think I'm not watching.

    At this week's appointment, Andy's orthodontist discovered the bands have come loose again. The doctor groaned, "He must have gotten bumped somewhere." He doesn't realize how many times Andy gets bumped in spite of our peacemaking efforts.

    I am deluged with winter doldrums. My car goes on vacation in this cold weather and often doesn't start. I skipped choir practice in order to balance my cash account, but instead supervised a spelling assignment, listened to everyone's piano lessons and to Timmy's reading, read to the younger two, and checked Andy on Indian signs he's learning for his Bear badge.

    This messy, old house depresses me. All the effort of picking up only lasts a few hours. I cleaned the upstairs yesterday, but after school four Indians and a sheriff on the loose tracked each other for an hour and the chase went through the entire upstairs.

Timmy was thrilled with your note. We are surrounded by mumps, chicken pox, colds and flu. Otherwise we are fine.

February 1, 1961

Dear Mom,

Sock sizes would be eight and eight-and-one-half. Don't make them smaller as socks shrink. As these are for Jay and Mike there are no hand-me-down options if we miscalculate. Mike needs a new jacket so we went shopping for Andy. Now everybody has a new-to-him jacket. We invited our other Grandma to a birthday dinner. I roasted a turkey and baked a cake, which we decorated communally with candles staggering across the top. Jay made a looper potholder, his first. He bubbled with excitement. "I just can't stand it because Grandma is going to like this so much." I don't encourage four-year-olds to do finger dexterity projects like loopers, but he tried so hard by himself that I finally showed him how. It's almost a full time job teaching him things because he wants to learn everything. Within the last couple weeks he mastered checkers, how to operate the children's phonograph, and he does any errand if I drop a hint. He calls this getting ready for kindergarten. But it's seven months before kindergarten starts.

Another new Cub Scout makes my tenth so now my den splits. Den meetings have been bedlam with nine plus Timmy, whom I have been including and Jason who can't see why he's not.

We cleaned the playroom yesterday throwing out anything broken, subject to vote first, with the guy claiming ownership getting double vote. The boys really got in the spirit and threw out their own broken treasures. If someone else did it and they found their stuff in the trashcan they would lug it back. Jay found the pile of throw-away books and demanded, "Mommy, what are you doing?"

"I am throwing out these beat-up ones."

"This is my favorite book," he replied with tenderness, "and it isn't beat up to me, Mom, just to you." Yep, he got to keep that one.

Timmy is making up prayers again. Several years ago he came out with, "Thank you God for arms, legs, and for being able to run and for being so rich." As I had run out of grocery money and meals had been coming from the garden and the freezer, that bit about being rich made my day. This time it went, "Thank you for everything and for all the things I didn't want, too." I should have asked what those things were.

Dann is helping with projects tonight. We have two dilapidated desks in the basement which Andy and Tim have been gluing, sanding and refinishing. Andy is also working on his Cub Scout genius kit. Each Cub received a bag containing doweling, corks, pipe cleaners, string, thumbtacks, and piece of paper, nails, board, glue, coat hanger, tin can and cloth. They can make whatever they wish from the bag, not necessarily using everything, but adding nothing. Dann explained patiently, "It isn't necessary to have a sail, paddlewheel, smokestack and a parachute on the same boat." Before long he pulled out the junior encyclopedia to back him up.

FEBRUARY 16, 1961

Dear Mom,

Dann and Timmy finished his desk and Tim has spent considerable time in his room proudly sitting there.

One hundred and two people attended the Scout banquet last night and I am exhausted. The creativity of the cakes and the 58 genius kits floored us. The boys' imaginations, using scrap materials, recognize no limits.

February 20, 1961

Dear Mom,

Thank you for the cookies and the aprons.

My splitting headaches have quit at last.

The chickenpox has arrived. Timmy monopolizes the couch. He seems pleased at being the plum in the pudding—no piano lessons, extra TV privileges and I heard him tell Jay this morning that he would play with him all week whenever Mom wasn't reading to him.

Stopping at our other Grandma's last night, we began to put on coats when Mike, with lower lip quivering and tears in his voice, stammered, "But we didn't get no cookies." I hastily shushed him.

Jay rushed up, took Mike by the hand and pulled him into the privacy of the kitchen. He threw both arms around his little brother in a big consoling bear hug. "Just be quiet and wait, Mike," he confided. "You'll see. This is easy." I thought Grandma was going to have a spasm, but Jay had called it correctly. As we left, she passed the cookie jar around much to Michael's delight.

February 25, 1961

Dear Mom,

Our Sunday afternoon goal was to remove that old bowling pin game machine from the playroom. Do you remember when Dann brought it home? It's the kind of thing you might see in a dark corner of the neighborhood tavern. It stood table height with a flat top, had four legs and measured two feet wide to twelve feet long. When you pulled the lever back at one end, lights flashed and a flat black disc was released which shot down the length of the monster. If you were lucky the disc knocked over varicolored bowling pins at the far end. It is unfortunate that our playroom is on second floor because that 180 degree landing turn proved deadly. Dann recruited as much manpower as he could, but the bowling game had no bend or give and was not compatible with that landing. Many slivers and cuss words later, everybody arrived upstairs at the playroom along with an announcement by Dann that he would never take that thing down again. Thereafter, the game was always referred to as the thing.

The thing proved an instant and noisy success. Boys stood in line to snap that lever and see how many bowling pins each could flatten.

This lasted a week. Suddenly nothing we could do would make the disc fly down the shoot or flash the lights. The old thing must have lived out its natural life and one week of concentrated boys was the last straw. Like the grandfather clock that was too long on the shelf, it stopped, short, never to go again. It sat undisturbed for a couple days but then I discovered that the imagination to create toys from very little extends all the way to our youngest. With the help of two blankets, thrown over the flat surface, the thing changed into a military fort. Soldiers banged away inside while Indians stealthily circled the perimeter with their bows and arrows. The following week the thing, with the same borrowed blankets, became a castle ringed by a moat as knights in armor attacked all day long. The next week the Empire State Building emerged, then Mt. McKinley. Next, objects piled under the blankets altered the roof line so that it became an Indian teepee, then an Eskimo igloo, the QE 2 crossing the Atlantic, a life raft and on and on.

Now we faced the problem of how to get the thing out. The easiest solution seemed to be an attack. Dann and his team of boys approached it with saws, hammers, screwdrivers, and axes. Dann whacked off two front legs when he was interrupted by the telephone. When he hung up 20 minutes later, sounds of great glee and whoops of laughter bellowed from the playroom. The boys had discovered that with two legs missing and one end now resting on the floor, they had a perfect slide IF they could just shinny up the tail end which was no trouble at all. Obviously the thing has earned a reprieve.

March 1, 1961

Dear Mom,

During breakfast we looked out the window and discovered that our young collie female, who hasn't been in heat before, should have been watched. Dann rushed out with a pail of cold water, too late. Four little boys hustled to vie for the best window and pelted us with obvious questions. As school departure time loomed, we covered the topic briefly but they're expecting puppies by the time school dismisses. Looks like our first litter will be just plain puppies.

March 8, 1961

Dear Mom,

Michael broke out with chicken-pox Friday, Jason on Saturday. Both were sicker than Timmy and kept us busy for several nights. Mike's sunny disposition disappeared. Instead of settling for kisses for every bump, he yowled over anything. When we went to bed late last night, we found him sitting on the stairs scratching. Even soda baths didn't help. Both boys found fault with everything and especially with Mommy who refused to put Band-Aids on all the hurts. Timmy was well broken out with one even on his navel, but Mike counted five there. Several in his mouth put him on a starvation diet.

With two sick kids, the older two had to travel on their own to piano lessons on the city bus. They started visiting with a boy they knew and rode past their stop. They didn't get off but Andy talked to the driver who suggested they wait until the bus came back around. They rode around the square, out to the East side, around the capitol square once more and the driver dropped them where they should have gotten off. They had to cross the avenue in late afternoon rush traffic and arrived for their lessons late, but unworried. Good that I didn't know about it while this was in process.

We're buried in snow, thrilling Andy and Timmy who started shoveling before breakfast — useless as the blizzard was only half spent. Jay is heartbroken that he can't go out and hopes that the storm will continue until his chickenpox abates. The city schools closed at noon and the kids came jubilantly home.

The next day dawned with a cobalt sky making the yard a fairy wonderland. Each tree trunk showed up half white, half gray and every branch and twig staggered under a burden of ice. The weight caused trees and shrubs to gently lean over, creating a stageful of ballet dancers humbly taking their last curtain call. That mammoth spotlight high in the azure sky changed the snowflakes into diamonds nestling on the trees. Nothing moved. The snowdrift on the birdfeeder stood taller than the feeder. Snow on the picnic table drifted two feet high and the drift in front of the garage piled higher than my waist.

The second day Andy had a 9:15 a.m. appointment with the orthodontist. We got up early and three of us shoveled for an hour-and-a-half which cleared only the beginning and the end of our long driveway. The car plowed through the rest which was deeper than the undercarriage. This works only with a downhill driveway.

It's late, whiffs of my baked bread are wafting through the house, and my husband is half-finished painting in the younger boys' bedroom. I hope Dann quits soon, as helping to create two snow forts this afternoon has exhausted me.

MARCH 16, 1961

Dear Mom,

Sorry Pop has not been feeling well. Tell him to take it easy.

We didn't finish painting the boys' bedroom until the weekend. We varnished the woodwork, did the closets and waxed the floor. After everything was back, Jay observed, "It looks like a new room, except the same old stuff is still here." Jay and Mike slept in the big bed in the guest room for five nights and raised a rumpus every night.

We took the Cubs on a train ride to Stoughton. Riding herd on so much energy in public takes a special skill. My car arrived at the depot last. By that time, wiggling, noisy, excited, uniformed boys filled every corner. A line formed in front of the ticket office long enough to cause anyone else to miss the train. The station master toured us through the diner, mailcar, roundhouse, the repair and piggyback loading yards and the ticket office. Jim, the Cubmaster, counted as we loaded the Scouts. We filled one coach with three boys per seat. The Cubs did not discover the rest rooms nor the drinking cups in the 17 minutes we were aboard. When the train arrived in Stoughton, Jim again counted as the boys leaped off. The driver of my pickup car said that the people there to meet the train looked thunderstruck as passengers leaped out of the rear coach.

The next day was monthly pack meeting. Dann was working on the City Board of Review and unavailable so I was stuck with all four of our boys. The movie on railroading didn't materialize. One minute before meeting time, Jim tracked me down. "Could you organize something to fill in?"

I asked Andy's den mother to watch my den and my extra sons while I dashed home for suitcases and large-sized clothes for a train trip relay. Dividing the Cubs into two teams, the first boy in each line held the suitcase. On the GO signal, he rushed to the end of the gym, opened the suitcase, put on the man-sized clothes and staggered back, usually holding up loose parts of his outfit. Much clothing fell off in transit necessitating a stop to redress. The audience howled. My ingenuity has advanced in leaps and bounds since Andy turned eight.

Today Andy came home after school and proudly announced, "Mom, here is David. Today is his birthday." You may not grasp the unspoken sequence. If today is David's birthday, he must be eight years old. He probably wants to be a Cub Scout. Tonight is pack meeting night and as it was then only 3:30, maybe Mom could fix him up quick. With the added attendance we have attracted this year, we don't need such an avid salesman to help our cause.

March 22, 1961

Dear Mom,

A speaker we heard on Wisconsin State Parks has turned us into camping enthusiasts. I can't recall, as a child, our doing outdoor activities such as camping. However, Dann seems to be an avid outdoorsman and he is gently initiating me into his favorite hobbies—hunting, fishing and camping. We picked up a secondhand tent that sleeps six. This seems like the only way, outside of the cottage, to take vacations with four, active youngsters. We just don't have money for expensive trips.

Dann says absolutely not, the playroom will be painted last because it is worst. I still hope to do Andy and Tim's room. Do you have any yellow or brown rags I could use for crocheted rugs?

March 28, 1961

Dear Mom,

Nothing works this week. When I had planned to clean, we went to the orthodontist instead because Andy knocked his bands loose again. The doctor took them out earlier than scheduled and now Andy wears a retainer.

Pulling into the middle three lanes of traffic around the capitol square on the way home, my engine killed. There is no worse place to get caught with a non-functioning vehicle. My car was filled with boys and Timmy was due home in 30 minutes with two friends that I had promised to baby-sit. There we sat. (At suppertime Michael gave an excellent animated version of the whole episode.) I floored the gas pedal like Dann had taught me to do when it floods. No go and I was ready to desert the sinking ship when a man pushed me and it started. Later that same afternoon I dropped two boys for piano lessons and went grocery shopping. This time the boy who loads groceries came to my rescue and started the engine by fiddling with something under the hood. It's a brave woman or a dumb one that takes four kids out in a car that she knows won't make it home. I have learned that to survive Wisconsin winters the car doesn't go out without everyone dressed to walk home if necessary. When Dann took it to the gas station they found nothing wrong.

How can each week be so different? I'm still looking for that "boring and monotonous" I anticipated!

April Fool's Day

Dear Mom,

I woke at 4:00 a.m. to find Andy crawling under the beds collecting shoes. He wanted an early start. Timmy bragged all through supper dishes that he had done more April fool jokes than anybody else because he did 18 without going outside. I hesitated to go to bed. The bed was there but practically nothing else. Somebody stacked a high pile of chairs, rugs, lamps, radio, clocks, and the telephone from our bedroom into the small bathroom.

Art Linkletter's House was interviewing seven-year-olds on his "Houseparty" yesterday. His standard question was, "What do you think is the most beautiful thing in the world?"

Andy was listening and without hesitation, looked straight at me and said, "You". I needed that.

One of my greatest tribulations is the constant accumulation of dirty clothes. I hate to find all those surprises that shouldn't be there when opening the washing machine so have trained myself to check pockets carefully. I found the following in just one of Timmy's pants pockets: one small rubber ball, seven bottle caps, five pegs, 1/2 nutshell, two postage stamps, one jack, one green apple, six stones, pieces of string, two plastic cars, cash register slips, three electrical slugs, marble, washer, squirt gun, six broken balloons, twelve acorns and a handful of rusty nails. Little girls without pants pockets must grow up inhibited.

April 13, 1961

Dear Mom,

There is no longer any doubt about Twinkle. She bulges. We got a book from the Bookmobile to help with details. Big dogs may have as many as 12. Some of us hope not. We set up a betting pool for litter size—three, four, five, six, seven, or two.

With a PTA meeting for me last night and Dann unavailable due to another Board of Review meeting, two boys had to stay up to baby-sit. They watched TV, read how to have puppies, played Monopoly, drank orange pop and read my Saturday Evening Posts. Only one emergency, Twinkle's accident on my good rug. She probably asked to go outside and they didn't notice.

I took my den, plus Timmy, to the airport control tower and had just walked into the tower room when a plane flew over the runway. All the vehicles were flashing lights and the tower informed us an emergency had been declared. A military transport enroute from O'Hare Field to Minneapolis had lost one engine and was requesting permission to land. Smoke rolled out when the plane finally stopped and crash trucks rushed onto the field. Three scheduled flights came in by instrument and radar because of the overcast sky. Quite a show.

I'm glad you're enjoying your library work. A part-time job with flex hours must be ideal.

April 19, 1961

Dear Mom,

Jason has been announcing to all the neighbors who will listen, "We'll probably have a girl someday, but we're awfully busy right now. We have a lot of work to do at our house."

I have just been out six nights out in a row. I can't understand how this happened as we set ourselves a limit of three nights out per week for each of us.

Dann started building a whelping bed for Twinkle. He should hurry. She is suspicious of new things and it may take awhile to teach her that she's supposed to lie there.

April 25, 1961

Dear Mom,

Another quickie letter while I wait for the red paint to dry on my Indian Chief neckerchief slide.

Twinkle reached the top of our priorities this week. We calculated her due date as next Monday, but we're expecting anytime. She provides my excuse for not going out. This works better than having a baby. Dann finished her bed. By the size, it looks like he expects an army. She sleeps there nights, so I hope she gets the idea that this is where puppies are supposed to be born. The entire Cub pack, plus the neighborhood, relatives and friends, have been alerted and are waiting to rush over. Our other Grandmother suggested that we shouldn't announce for 24 hours so that the new mother can relax before the onslaught.

Our East Indian friends invited us to an Indian supper. After much hesitation I decided my lime-green and gold silk sari was appropriate wearing apparel. I asked Dann if he was enough of a gambler for me to wear it. The gamble was whether it would stay on long enough for me to get back home. The meal was delicious, which I had not anticipated, and edible. And I arrived home safely.

For Jay's birthday we planned a zoo theme party using cardboard boxes and cutting bars on one side. We put each small guest in a cage and if he growled loudly my zookeepers, Andy and Timmy, fed him animal crackers through the bars.

May 1, 1961

Dear Mom,

Boxer, Pet, Sunday, Socks, Little Twinkle, Soot, Steps (for the one who was born there) etc., etc., and etc. arrived during Sunday dinner. Although they didn't come that way, they now look very cute. Twinkle stopped eating Saturday morning, which the book had warned us to watch for. We filled up her whelping bed with hay and went to bed ourselves expecting interrupted sleep. Poor choice of nights as Dann had gotten up at 2:30 a.m. that morning for opening day of trout season, but she was fine in the morning. With difficulty, we talked everyone into attending church. When we came home Twinkle asked to go out and Andy put her on the chain. I should have known better, but so should she. Andy rushed through dinner because his friend was waiting to do bow and arrow practice in our orchard. Immediately after finishing, he and Joey rushed out the back door and came right back in again, screaming, "There's a puppy on the front steps".

A cold, forlorn pup hunched over on that top step. We carried him down to the whelping bed and turned on the heater. Our no visitors for 24 hours rule was broken within five minutes. The boys kept busy on the phone so people streamed by endlessly. Twinkle birthed six and then stretched out and relaxed as the book said she would do when finished. Dann cleaned the bed, but she had four more. I sneaked five away this morning settling them in a box by the heat and switched every two hours. I suggested meekly that we could eliminate two so she would have enough equipment to go around but I was outvoted.

Dann wants to plow Pop's garden. Could we come on Saturday? All 17 of us? We could put them in a big box for transporting. If you don't want us for ANY reason just say no. We'll not stay overnight.

May 18, 1961

Dear Mom,

We had a wonderful time camping at Devil's Lake, even with 17. The rainy weather held off until we were home and unloaded.

We expect to freeze when camping in May, but our sleeping bags kept us toasty. We hiked the cliffs, fished, and swam. Rather the boys did. Dann and I walked in over our ankles but retreated when our legs ached from the cold.

Our puppies look like drunken sailors and tip over on their noses when they try to walk. When offered warmed milk in a muffin tin this morning, they stuck their noses in without even hesitating.

Remember the story about the guy who let his camel put his head inside the tent door and then found to his surprise the whole camel was inside. Our camel's head was when Dann agreed to let Jim use his name on the Scout charter for a mailing address. We shouldn't be surprised now to find the whole camel in our laps. Cubmaster Jim is resigning and can't you guess who the new Cubmaster will be next year? I hope we're capable of this. Competent or not, the year will be exciting.

The poison ivy is gone, thank you. We'll expect you Sunday morning. Bring a casserole, if you'd like, and we'll go on a picnic.

3 WHEN IT RAINS, IT POURS

June 5, 1961

Dear Mom,

We are applying to become a licensed foster home. I can feel your horror at the thought of adding to our frenzied existence. We have thought about this a lot, Mom, and keep coming back to two unarguable tenets: both of us enjoy children and are fine-tuned to child activities and secondly, this old house has ample space for a large family. A third point might be, as I am obviously not free to re-enter the working world, perhaps we can bring it here. We requested a girl, rationalizing that comparisons and competition might be less between a girl and our boys.

Summer activities line up thusly: Vacation Bible School, swimming lessons at the beach, day camp for Andy and accordion lessons, which allows reprieve from piano lessons. I persuaded the instructor to take two boys at the same time for the price of one. They share the half-hour lesson, share the accordion and she gave us an accordion with long straps to adjust to my height so I could share also. That accordion is so much in demand that my turn waits until everyone goes to bed.

I'm taking my Cubs to the Arboretum this afternoon and am struggling to set up a nature scavenger hunt.

June 10, 1961

Dear Mom,

We certainly enjoyed your visit. The assault of 200 species of lilacs at blossom time in the Arboretum stuns my senses. Thanks for the food you brought. I hope Dad's baby chicks didn't get too hungry while you were gone.

We had two more interviews with the social worker and hope we're through. There is not another thing that they could ask. They covered Dann's first marriage, asked how many of our children were planned, even what reaction you and Dann's mother have to this idea. The worker comes next week to inspect our house and our boys.

Keep us informed about the state of Pop's honey, and we'll arrange it so Dann can help with the lifting.

June 20, 1961

Dear Mom,

I told our interviewer that you weren't sold on this because of Dann's upcoming surgery. That brought more questions. We may have to wait months for his surgery. Five kids shouldn't be any more problem than four. The interviewer volunteered, "The fifth one might be an asset."

Unhappily we have sold only two puppies. They cuddle, romp, chew and wet and we need to sell them now. Twinkle developed a skin condition necessitating separation so we tied her on the other side of the house. Only two days elapsed before the pups galloped around the house and discovered her.

My goal tonight is to dispatch two weeks of ironing, an endless job. Fashion should change to the wearing of wrinkled clothes. The ironing loses out to the appeal of luxuriating in the tub with the June Readers Digest.

June 27, 1961

Dear Mom,

I have been hassling Dann to buy sod for the small yard between house and driveway. An ad, at two cents per square foot, caught my eye. Dann agreed and we drove and drove searching for that address. Each mile frustrated Dann more as we could have bought sod on the Beltline for three cents per foot and saved considerable time.

The man came out of his house and looked over our station wagon. "You can't carry sod in that without breaking the springs. You'll have to make two trips." I didn't realize sod is heavy. Piling it in anyway caused the old Ford to lower its muffler dangerously and we drove home at the speed of the proverbial turtle. By careful figuring before laying it out, one load did suffice.

I sold one puppy after you left and the last two the next day. Now all is quiet. We made $45, IF we don't count expenses. Adding it to some stamp money we've been hoarding, we splurged on a used canoe and have already been out paddling. It's a bronze 18 foot Old Town freighter in prime condition, with a canvas-covered wooden frame re-covered with Fiberglas. The double rib-bed floor provides additional strength and weighs 105 lbs. It will hold six of us, in life preservers, plus one collie dog. We'll use it on our long camping trip this summer.

When the boys were playing on the school grounds next door, they discovered the janitor had just finished end-of-the-season housecleaning. Scrounging in the incinerator, they retrieved: 30

marbles, a beat-up blackened charm bracelet, two rings, a pair of scissors, and a penny. They weren't allowed back in the house until they had dropped their outer layer of clothes. They are disgusted that they couldn't go back, and we now have new rules pertaining to the school playground. Privately Dann objected, "Don't get too mad. They're just taking after their old man."

July 5, 1961

Dear Mom,

"Yes, Pop, I'm watering my new sod four hours a day."
The nursery man had warned, "It's impossible to drown it."
Dann insists, "Nothing will grow there. You are wasting your time."
Now it's a matter of principle to make it grow after all that hauling and adverse advice.
This weekend I darned 44 pairs of socks. My second fashion request would be for barefoot boys that wear wrinkled shirts.
Michael just showed me a picture of what he calls Daddy's wishing pole. Very apt.

July 13, 1961

Dear Mom,

Peter and Joel, Dann's nephews, visited this week. Their family is enroute from the east to the west coast. The two oldest boys and their parents are staying with other cousins and we kept the two younger ones who are close in age to ours. They worked out a rotation system for the bunks. From night to night, I never know whom to expect where. The night before last Dann had to go to work leaving me the only person on duty. The cold war got so intense upstairs after they were sent to bed that none dared go to the bathroom without a roommate along riding shotgun with pillows for ammunition. I caught Joel red-handed in the hall and the look on his face poignantly reminded me of a night many years ago when I was staying with cousins and Aunt Eleanor caught me out on the roof. I softheartedly sent Joel back to bed without scolding and he never knew why he got off so lightly. There is nothing quite like cousins one's own age.

We all spend hours each day picking peas and raspberries. Things are so dry that the sprinkler runs all day—especially on my sod.

Last week I found over-ripe bananas for five cents a pound and treated the family to banana cream pie. When the pie appeared, Timmy announced triumphantly, "That's where all those rotten bananas went to." I didn't realize they kept such close tabs on my kitchen.

July 18, 1961

Dear Mom,

The house bursts with so many kids today that I cannot even keep track. Children challenge me ninety-nine percent of the time, but I'm rapidly reaching that last one percent. Four children, aged three to seven, are here because their sister and father are having eye surgery today.

When we took Jason for a checkup they found a lump on his throat. Although this is probably minor, the doctor insists the cyst be removed. Jason has been waiting so long for kindergarten that we don't dare interfere with his momentous first day, so we have squeezed this surgery between the end of our camping trip to New Jersey and before the opening day of school.

We camped at Castle Rock County Park last weekend. Andy and Timmy each took a friend, neither of whom had ever camped. A fact I didn't appreciate until later. We arrived late, starved, and tired. Halfway through supper the mosquito spray truck blasted through the campground spreading a thick fog. This hampers eating. I had heated canned hash when Sam, Timmy's friend, declared, "I don't eat anything out of cans."

I said, "That's too bad. That's what we eat when we're camping."

Dann added, "We always taste everything." He had dished small quantities, but Sam's plate went untouched. When Dann saw this, he filled a large spoonful, put one hand on the top of Sam's head, announced, "Open up," and shoveled it down. Dann lost his point when Sam lost the hash. That finished supper. No more house rules with guests. They can eat or starve. We don't care which.

Next Andy broke the new air pump after inflating the first mattress. Dann objects to blowing up good mattresses by mouth as this gets moisture inside, so our tired little cherubs got tucked into sleeping bags without mattresses. By the time our bed hour arrived, we had found someone we knew and borrowed their pump. Andy's friend Dale, who lives with his mother, announced, "My father gave me a tent. Andy and I can sleep in this." "This" turned out to be mosquito netting, but he was so proud of it that Dann strung it between some trees and hung canvas over for protection. It rained, of course, during the night. We got up several times but as Andy and Dale weren't getting drenched yet, they didn't want to change tents.

On Saturday all six boys arose early when Dann and I were still trying to sleep. I overheard Sam conversing with the neighbors.

"I'd like this place fine if they only had decent food!"

However, all ended well. Sunday, when we were breaking camp, I again cooked a quick meal. Sam came around to check, "What's that?"

"Dinty Moore beef stew."

"You know I don't like canned food," he muttered, "but it

smells good so I'll taste it." He did. Five helpings. Isn't it wonderful what the outdoors does for one's appetite?

Dale followed Dann around all weekend wanting to help with whatever Dann was doing. The first night I handed Sam a dishtowel. This scandalized him and it looked as though he'd never wiped dishes, but the next morning he volunteered to do it again. The longer we stayed the more things improved.

Were you serious about wanting Timmy for the week that you are keeping his cousin Valerie? For the whole week? He is an enthusiastic berry picker.

I need to either iron OR take my entire crew of eight children for a walk as soon as I decide which is more urgent. We have been so busy that we rarely meditate on what looms ahead for us. When I did stop to think last night, it depressed me terribly. Dann's eye gets steadily worse.

August 29, 1961

Dear Mom and Pop,

Thanks for taking Michael during Jay's hospitalization. Everything goes easier with Mike gone. Jay is doing well tonight, uncomplaining and cooperative. I can't find time for anything but to lay out food or collapse in bed and haven't even unpacked our camping equipment. Many friends have brought food.

Jay went into surgery at 8 a.m. yesterday and didn't return to his room for five hours. We had expected minor surgery. After being on vacation, Dann needed to be in the office and it seemed as though I could handle the hospital without him. I have often said I worry when I needn't and don't when I should. I should have. The surgeon told me afterwards that the cyst was wrapped around the jugular vein and the carotid arteries causing great difficulty when they tried to separate them. In the recovery room

Jason exhibited facial weakness on one side of his mouth and cried lopsidedly. "A child's nerves running through there are the size of a hair," the surgeon went on, "and I searched painstakingly for that nerve and never found it. The lopsidedness indicates that we damaged the facial nerve which might be temporary or permanent. Jason is also having cardiac difficulty. We probably irritated the nerve in the neck that goes to the heart. I have given him a shot of atropine to knock out that nerve for a few hours and we're giving him oxygen. Now it's wait and see."

Realizing that we had miscalled the severity of this operation, I wanted reinforcements and walked the two blocks to Dann's mother's house with tears streaming down my face. What a bulwark of strength! She set me down in her kitchen, put the teakettle on and called Dann's office. A short time later, with my face washed and hot tea in my stomach, Dann and I walked back to the waiting room, hand in hand, to face the rest of the day together.

For quite a while they took Jay's pulse every five minutes and blood pressure every half-hour. The oxygen tube stayed in all day. By evening the facial nerve had recovered. Although he neither cried nor smiled, both sides of his face did move slightly. I feel guilty for putting him through this agony and hope his turn is up for a while. Andy and Timmy spent that day at Uncle Don's, today they are invited across the street, and tomorrow they go to the neighbor around the corner. They soak up this popularity.

A friend commented this morning, "I don't suppose you got much sleep last night."

"I must be a hard-hearted mother," I responded. "The hospital efficiency impressed me so much that I slept soundly all night."

Our camping trip, just prior to the surgery, did turn out great. It was raining when we left, raining when we came home, and raining half the time in between. I have often said, "A truly good camper enjoys himself whatever the weather." The Lord must have been testing to see if I really meant that. We drove through the Chicago Loop to the Skyway anticipating the panorama over Lake Michigan, but solid sheets of rain blocked out even the front of the hood. Racing ahead of the storm, we stopped to stretch at the Indiana sand dunes and were climbing dunes a half mile from the car when the storm caught up and drenched us. The men of the family voted to give me the one dry shirt. Everybody else stripped and dangled their shirts out the windows as we sped along the toll way.

Traveling leisurely we explored the mountains of Pennsylvania and looked at the crack in the Liberty Bell in Philadelphia. We enjoyed ourselves a bit too much because, although Charles and Jean expected us Saturday night, we were still driving at midnight. Maneuvering on one of those New Jersey traffic circles, I became confused trying to figure out how to peel off. The Saturday night traffic spilled in fast worrying me, and I never saw the lady on my inside, who also didn't know where she was going.

It must have startled Charles to have his sister call at midnight. "We're going to be a bit late because we've just blocked one of your traffic circles." He asked where we were. I knew this was a local call and after a description of the traffic circle, he recognized where we had come to grief. All the boys had been asleep. The crash dumped Andy and Timmy on the floor and dropped camping gear on top of them. Timmy bumped his head and cried, necessitating a call to the first aid emergency unit. They checked Tim over meticulously until they discovered Michael stretched out immobile in the back of the station wagon. Even shaking him at both ends elicited no response. Dann walked over, tickled his feet and Mike turned over and grinned. Charles came to take the kids home, but by that time the officers released us all. We had smashed the headlight, dented the fender and broken the car top, but the car was still drivable. We didn't have time to get all that fixed in New Jersey, but Dann and Charles pounded out the headlight, put in a new one and braced the car top.

It's neat to have a brother on the seacoast. We walked down to the docks and watched the fishing boats come in. Dann bought a big blue which Jean cooked. We strolled on the beach where great rollers dashed in and threw the boys up on the beach—much to their delight.

Leaving the two younger ones with other cousins, eight of us (four adults, four boys) spent the day in New York City. For five cents apiece we boarded the Staten Island ferry and steamed past the Statue of Liberty. We took the subway to the Empire State Building and each of the many transfers delighted the boys. Charles and Dann would industriously study the map and with no warning announce, "We have to get off," and we'd each grab a boy and run.

We chose the automat for lunch. That intrigued the boys so much that they went back repeatedly for desserts. When we asked the cop on the corner how to get to the United Nations Building, he counted noses and muttered, "You have too many kids to take a cab," and directed us to a bus stop.

We couldn't resist adding, "Half of them stayed home."

Then we reversed: supper in the automat, rode the subway and ferried back home.

The next day friends in Marblehead took us sailing on the ocean. When we went beyond the harbor breakers and the boat charged through the waves tilting continually, I fussed, but the kids loved it. Fresh grilled swordfish completed our day.

At Bar Harbor, Maine, we camped again, the only campsite where we didn't have rain. Bar Harbor National Park lies on a huge, mountainous island. We drove completely around the island, climbed in the sea cave at low tide, swam at the sand beach where the water temperature was 56 degrees and canoed on an inland lake.

In the White Mountains of New Hampshire, our tent backed up to a dry mountain creek bed filled with enormous glacial boulders. The boys had an exhilarating time clamoring over the rocks, but before bedtime the heavens dropped. Water seeped up through our tent floor. I bailed continually with a sponge and a #10 can. By morning, a torrent raged down that no-longer dry creek bed.

After crossing the Canadian border, we drove to Ottawa to watch the changing of the guard and on to Algonquin Provincial Park, setting our tent so close to the lake that the boys could swim just outside our door. We packed a lunch, swimming suits, fishing gear, sweat shirts, life preservers and boys into the canoe and spent all day exploring islands. The next day, in drizzling rain, we packed a lunch, carried fishing poles and hiked 3/4 mile to an interior lake. At dusk we went out hunting and spotted 22 deer with fawns, one who ate from our hands.

The last night we stopped just across the Canadian border at a picturesque roadside area on the riverbank. The sky had cleared and Dann remarked, "Think how much time it would save if I don't have to put up or take down the tent. I've been wanting to sleep in the open."

He had just laid six bedrolls side by side on the ground when a porcupine strolled by. My enthusiasm waned rapidly, but it was too late to change our minds. We told the porky to scat and scrambled into sleeping bags. A full moon beamed down and the sky twinkled with stars, but when I woke at midnight the moon and stars had vanished and storm clouds chased each other overhead. Dann says I am now a seasoned camper as I thought I might as well sleep as long as possible and went back to sleep. The rains came in the morning but only after we were packed and ten minutes down the road.

Many trials and tribulations filled this trip, but also fun things crammed our days. We all passed the test that a truly good camper will enjoy himself no matter what.

Give Michael a kiss from all of us. We miss him.

SEPTEMBER 15, 1961

Dear Mom,

We have survived the first week of school. Andy and Tim departed after breakfast Monday morning. Jason dressed with school clothes before breakfast and then had to sit and wait until 12:15. Mike delights in having Mommy to himself. Timmy's side ached again. We thought it might have been caused by the stress of opening day. Not knowing what triggers these side aches worries me.

Dann's eye remains the same so the wait continues. Thanks for Andy's socks and for Jay's get well card.

SEPTEMBER 27, 1961

Dear Mom,

Thank goodness you got home before the storm struck. We gave Andy his birthday present from you at breakfast. He likes to get money because he never manages to have enough. For the first time, he earned babysitting money. I had an Extension Homemaker meeting when Dann was working, so I put three boys to bed, gave Andy my phone number and a book and paid him ten cents an hour. We gave him a Timex for his 10th birthday and consequently he announced the time at five-minute intervals all during supper. Last year he thought he was too big to take school treats. This year he made a double batch of fudge.

Sometimes he acts grownup. Sometimes not. For the last two days he has spent all his time from after school to bedtime doing homework, piano, or cello, except for a wee bit of time out to climb my mulberry tree to pick the tame grapes that escaped and are reaching for sunshine on top. The wild grapes switched to the grape arbor.

Andy received his cello on Monday and faithfully plucks away. At first, he lugged it around practicing where the most people could watch him. As nobody stands still in this house for long, he gave this up.

Jay, Mike, and I spent the morning outside winterizing (potting plants). Trouble is coming as, in addition to the nine house plants which I put out last spring now needing to come inside, we also have Andy's 19 airplane plants (for 18 friends), four Jerusalem cherries (one for each boy), Jay's marigold, Timmy's grapefruit tree and his three cacti. I decided I had better not propagate my red geraniums this fall.

More Cubs signed up Friday so our count hovers around 100. Timmy joins officially and I'll take his den.

October 5, 1961

Dear Mom,

What a discouraging week! I hit rock bottom last night when I was still washing supper dishes at 10:30 p.m. Sometimes I cannot keep everybody on track. When we stopped to see our other Grandma after church, Timmy ran into the street in front of an oncoming car. Monday Andy laid his cello on a chair and it slid off, cracking all the way down the bridge. Dann's allergy pills didn't work, leaving him miserable. Tuesday all the women we asked to be new den mothers said no. I have spent my evenings redoing my bookkeeping because three months ago I neglected to enter the last third and then threw away my figures. Some little boy probably talked to me at a crucial moment. Now things look better. Timmy wasn't touched, just scared and rightly so. Me too, when I heard the tires squeal and saw the car so close to him. He ran across in the middle of the block because he wanted a window seat and forgot to look. None of the boys said a word the whole way home. We've established a new rule — no more rushing. Seats move by weekly rotation.

Andy's cello teacher had the cello repaired at school expense. Dann's allergies have subsided and we found two new den mothers. We only need two more.

I am reading my picture edition of the Bible aloud. Andy wants to know how come there are so many girls if Adam and Eve only had sons. I read about the patience of Job and asked Tim what patience meant. He shot back, "That's when you ask for the honey butter and if you have to ask a second time, you don't have any." That's what I don't have any of now. Going out to the garden for a handful of mums, I tripped in the boys' rabbit trap (a camouflaged hole!) and am not a very cheerful rabbit.

Mike's infected big toe looks better, thank you. He soaks it in hot Epsom salts twice a day for half-an-hour. That's a long time to sit still. I scooted upstairs to make the bed and he must have wiggled around on the chair and fell off, splashing water all over.

Jay's questions are getting me in deeper and deeper. "What is love?" and "Who made God?" His definition of a preacher is that guy who does all the handshaking at the church door.

DECEMBER 4, 1961

Dear Mom,

This sounds like a tremendous job for you physically and emotionally. Keep telling yourself how much better off Auntie Beth will be in a nursing home. Probably hard when it's your sister. A ten-room house with 42 years of living is going to be a mammoth job to close. It's my turn to lecture. If you continue to miss sleep, you are bound to get one of your sick headaches making it impossible for the rest of us to work without your decisions. Quit early some day and drive the 50 miles home to your own bed. Does being in a strange house wake you early, or does your subconscious keep organizing things around the clock? I have this trouble when Cub Scout things don't function as they should. After a busy day of thinking, the thought processes don't stop at bedtime. Why don't you try aspirin? You need to sleep. Don't worry about Dann if he drives back after dark. That deserted back road won't bother him as he won't be facing oncoming car lights much. Dann is worrying about Pop doing that heavy lifting.

Would you see if you could sneak out the Yankee drill and buy it for me? Pop will know which it is because he and Dann priced it for the sale. Be careful, I think he will look for it to buy for himself. Maybe you and Pop could think up some little white lie if Dann asks. When we help you, the boys are intrigued by what they think is going on. They have the theory that if we don't want kids along, it must really be exciting and were captivated with the boxes that came home with us. Andy announced, "This is the best stuff you ever brought us."

But Tim questioned, "What did you throw out?" Obviously he would have liked to double check the trash pile. The things they enjoy most are the old postcards. Did you know some are leather? Take care, Mom.

December 11, 1961

Dear Mom,

Dann's mother is doing okay after her hysterectomy. Dann's brothers have been here visiting her and Andy said, "Gee Mom, aren't I lucky Grandma had such a big litter so I get so many uncles?"

I'm reading a book on nutrition and following up with experimental cooking. My young men would like it if I never tried anything new. I did a rolled tuna fish pastry with caraway seeds and cheese sauce. Going on the theory that united we stand, all four of them kicked up a terrible fuss before Dann even dished up.

"I don't like it."

"How do you know? You haven't had any yet?"

"I just don't. I saw what Mommy put into it."

"I don't want any. Why do I have to have so much?"

"Do I have to eat all that on my plate? I tasted it. Now can I quit?"

"This bite has an onion and the next bite has a worm (caraway seed) and it's wiggling!"

At this point, Jason turned sickly green and dropped the bite halfway to his mouth. He stood up on his chair trying frantically to see Timmy's worm. If you look at anything long enough, it will wiggle obligingly. This is pretty strong opposition when every boy knows the rule of the house is that any dislike announced before one sample is cause to receive more immediately. Dann relished his delicious supper, but that recipe got thrown out.

High protein breakfasts came next. That meant two eggs apiece to provide more energy. I was dubious about producing more energy in four of us, but Dann asserted, "That's okay because they go to school after breakfast. Perhaps it will produce straight As."

Already I am tired of eggs scrambled, eggs fried, and eggs soft boiled day after day. One morning I beat up yolks, powdered orange juice and milk adding beaten egg white with nutmeg sprinkled on top. Timmy pleaded mournfully, "Mom, please stop reading that book."

They have found that some good comes with the bad. This morning I offered sliced ham and eggs which they demolished and yesterday they devoured grilled liver and bacon.

Thanks for the luscious meals and for keeping Jay. I keep hearing all about his lovely time. Thanks, Pop, for the squash and popcorn from your garden. The popcorn has been spread out to dry in the guest room. Yesterday we popped some and found that it's just right and we rolled into mass production shelling. At this rate, they should be done in one week. I hope. It's impossible to walk through the kitchen without skating on stray kernels. I have been teaching my young salesmen to always give more than expected, so we're packaging 17 ounces into the 16 ounce bags that they will sell.

Jay could use new mittens, the rest still fit.

December 20, 1961

Dear Mom,

The boys have a week of vacation before Christmas, which allows time for handmade gifts. We frantically made looper potholders, Christmas candles, candy, cookies, popcorn balls, crepe paper planters, decorated soap and bow ties. In spite of the "frantically" (who can do anything with four helpers and not do it frantically,) I enjoyed it. They like giving homemade presents best.

Every year we add more decorations because I can't stand to throw away last year's productions and so this barn-size dwelling turns into a Christmas fantasyland. We made a snowman for the front door using plastic dry cleaning bags, hung glittery red bells, made from shelf paper, up and down the banisters and cut a new Advent wreath base from a birch log. One boy gets to light candles for each of the four Sundays of Advent.

Dann and I rejuvenated two beat-up tricycles that he snitched off the curb and they look like new. We found what must have been the largest cardboard box (45" square) in the city of Madison. We cut a door and windows and painted our house number over the door. It holds four warm bodies simultaneously and should make a great playhouse.

December is almost over. Jason has finally stopped asking daily how big Santa's little people are and Mike has outgrown the haircut which he gave himself in your living room at Thanksgiving while the rest of us were eating.

I hope that Auntie Beth is settling down in the nursing home. We are thrilled with the white marble top dresser and antique bedroom set that she gave us. It blends perfectly with our old house and high ceilings. If it came from a Belmont hotel when Belmont was the first state capital, that makes it at least one hundred years old. I have scrubbed twice to remove the accumulation of grime, and plan on redecorating around that seven-foot, ornately carved headboard. I don't know what to do with the old wooden flute, but  am pleased with the antique sea chest full of English Dalton china that belonged to my grandmother. See you Christmas afternoon.

January 5, 1962

Dear Mom and Pop,

What an awesome Christmas we had with you. You did a neat job on the boys' presents. We hung their shoe bags on closet doors and they filled them immediately—hope now the boys will pick up their clothes also. They wore their new outfits to church looking deceptively angelic and are half-way through the honey butter. You made a slight error on the younger boys' jars when you wrote their names. Jason insists, "Grandma scribbled on mine."

I keep telling him, "That is truly your name but in writing."

"Then writing is just scribbling."

Pop, they loved the junior size workbench you made. It found a home in the corner of the basement and already collects projects from the new jigsaw.

It must be the librarian instincts in you Mom, for the boys love all the books you picked which we are reading aloud. Thanks also for the knitted mittens.

As it is now a new year, Dann suddenly needs all the bookkeeping done and I am behind having finished only two of the three months that I threw away.

January 10, 1962

Dear Mom,

I can't get anything done in the evenings. After looking at the events of last night I can see why. After supper dishes, I listened to piano lessons, drove with Dann to look at bunk beds which had been advertised in the paper, and constructed a king's costume that Timmy needed for school, using my old bathrobe, a strip of fur, some dangly gold chains, colored construction paper (for the crown), glitter, glue and absorbent cotton for a beard. I removed the paint from Jason's school pants before it set permanently, taught Andy how to braid rope for his Scout achievement, and by the time four boys were tucked into bed and read to, the evening had vanished.

We had trouble driving to piano lessons. It had rained the night before and the last kid out of the car hadn't latched the door, so when the temperature dropped, the door froze open. If there is anything worse than car doors freezing shut, it's freezing open. I did everything but swear, to no avail. Finally I tied the door shut, anchored it to the steering column, packed the kids into the back seat and departed. We need one warm day for that to unfreeze.

A gigantic snowstorm dumped on us last weekend. We shoveled out and then trooped over to the school hill for our first tobogganing. Light snow swirled over glistening ice and we descended like the wind with Twinkle running alongside, barking furiously. For the first time, we don't have anybody that is afraid. The more snow in their faces the louder they yell.

For our skit for the "Knights of Yore" theme, we made helmets with movable face visors (cardboard sprayed with aluminum paint), tunics, shields, swords and two magnificent horses. Upending big cardboard boxes, I cut holes in the topside for the rider to slide into. Dann built a pair of wooden jousting boards for a mock tournament.

In between the knights, the king costume, the tobogganing, and the program on Alcoholism I gave at church, I have managed to read three of the novels from Auntie Beth's house. Reading is vital so that I can unwind and think about somebody else's problems.

January 16, 1962

Dear Mom,

Today is odds-and-ends day and your letter is first. My day started off wrong with the next chapter of The Case of the Wandering Boot. This began last Friday when Tim came home from school with only one boot. He had looked all over with no success and came home distressed. On Monday, his Dad went to school with him and they searched all over including the lost and found. No boot. Finally we heard via the grapevine that

David (one of my Cubs) had worn one of Tim's home. I called his mother. She checked, "Yes, it's here. I will send it up to school."

Timmy brought it home last night arguing, "It's not mine. It's too small."

This was nonsense so I laid both boots together to prove that he's wrong, but he's right. This boot has his name in it in my writing, but it is two sizes smaller than the boot he is wearing this year. If this is a boot we lost earlier, where is ITS mate? I am in a quandary what to do next. Grandmother Willett chuckles over this. It must bring back memories of when she kept track of six boys.

Next, using my iron, I tried to smooth Dann's ruffled feathers by repairing the damage to his suit coat so he could leave for work. When he came downstairs for breakfast, he apparently laid the coat across the glass on the top of the aquarium and when somebody fed the fish, the sleeve of the coat dropped in all the way to the elbow. Either that child didn't notice or thought it the better part of discretion not to have this brought up until he was safely in school.

Next, I wiped up half of the kitchen floor where my fifth grade scientist came in last night in tears because he can't dig any dirt, which he needs for his conservation project. Of course he can't dig dirt in Wisconsin in January. I should have pointed out that if we had saved what he tracked in, we would have a good start. He was so disappointed that I am now waiting for the proper psychological moment to coerce Dann into helping Jay dig. Continuing with odds and ends, I took the turkey neck bones which I have been boiling, pulled off the bits of meat and laid the bones out to dry for Scout neckerchief slides.

Lastly, I wanted to mount a head on the horse for the upcoming skit and needed a boy to stand in the horse while I measured. Jason eagerly obliged. We have created a spectacular looking horse. Jay was enthralled. He didn't wiggle, only grinned, "Gee

Mom, aren't you lucky to have boys so you can do all this stuff?" He's right, of course. Our costumes and horses are so unique, that considering all my den mother experiences, this one rates as my masterpiece.

On Saturday Dann set up the new antique bed and we slept in it. One coat of varnish made it look really good. It surprised me to see how high the bed stands when assembled. When I called the boys for breakfast all four were curled up on that mammoth thing listening to Andy read.

January 25, 1962

Dear Mom,

This week my nervous and emotional capabilities bottomed out almost before we started. Dann bought a secondhand Ford on Monday and then we got a frightful cold spell. The combination of a new car and a cold spell didn't give us a chance to work out the kinks. Every morning both cars refused to start. Usually by noon we would call the service station to come push or pull. My old Ford never starts in cold weather. Dann figured out that it wasn't the weather, but a bad generator in the new Ford. Nothing puts him in a foul mood faster than a car that won't function. On the day of my program, Dann and the service station man got the new Ford going again. Much to Dann's horror I announced, "Now we can push mine with yours to start it, as I have no intention of going out at night with a strange car that I haven't driven yet, on slippery roads with no snow tires, to an address that I'm not familiar with, when my mind is overflowing with facts for the program I'm presenting."

This resulted in considerable discussion and I have decided no man can understand those reasons. Dann never agreed, but he did concede. At 15 below zero, we tried everything possible to start that car. We couldn't even pull it down the driveway using the other car. My turn to concede. The new car performed perfectly, my program evolved into a lively discussion, and coming home I gratefully swallowed an aspirin and dropped into bed.

The pack meeting also went smoothly. Four mothers helped me dress my knights. We lined them up, and using that old record you threw out of Napoleon's Last Charge complete with hoof beats, the knights trotted out and paraded up and down. Instant applause. One Scouter exclaimed, "Ye Gods, they're getting applause and they haven't done anything yet." One horse lost his head the first time around (which Dann had predicted) and when we tried to change riders on the other horse, that Cub was wedged in tight with full armor and he stuck. I had to grab him under the arms and yank him out.

The Welfare Department has asked for another interview. It takes longer to get a child this way than enduring nine months of pregnancy.

This morning crimson spots covered me head to toe, so abundantly that in some places I turned solid red. I sit reluctantly, my knees and elbows bend with difficulty, my arms are hot and swollen, and I itch. I have pills which are supposed to help. Last week when all of us were sick, I developed such pressure headaches that I took some decongestant syrup to clear my sinuses. After three days I developed a slight rash under my clothes, but thought that it might be caused by the fever. Another dose yesterday finished me off. Apparently I have developed sensitivity to pseudoephrine found commonly in decongestants. The cure was worse than the problem.

Did you know that Helen is a Biblical name? "Our Father, who Art in Heaven, Helen be Thy Name..."

February 6, 1962

Dear Mom,

I'm sorry to hear that Pop has been sick. Maybe he has the flu. There has been much around.

Saturday Timmy complained of a headache and being cold. By Monday morning, I chalked off five of us below par. First thing in the morning I make the rounds with my thermometer and then decide who can go to school. The rest get dressed in warm clothes and take their pillow and blankets and stretch out anywhere in the living room. Only Mike has felt okay and has been delighted to wait on everybody. Dann, too, had chills and headache and works in his office here with a heater on his feet.

Yesterday the Department of Public Welfare called about a 13 year-old girl. When we discovered she was Catholic, I said no, as it's hard enough getting six of us to the Methodist church on Sunday mornings. I just don't think we could split in two directions. A couple hours later they called again with a 10-year-old girl. We're waiting to hear more.

Time to try again to get rid of that $100 surplus that mysteriously appeared in my bookkeeping.

February 13, 1962

Dear Mom,

My flu patients didn't recover as rapidly as they should have. Andy lasted in school only one day. Timmy hasn't gone back yet. What do working mothers do when they have sick kids? My invalids didn't invoke much sympathy from me as they didn't act sick. They couldn't be in the same room without picking a fight or poking. In desperation on Saturday afternoon, after they had recouped somewhat, we took them ice skating to release some of their energy before ours gave out.

When I realized that my ironing was piled high, vacuuming undone and no dinner prepared, I called a friend to cheer me up and then Andy spilled grape juice on the new carpet. I mopped it up, decided this was beyond me and called Gulessarians Dry Cleaning Establishment. The lady who answered pulled out a book and read to me exactly what to do. Using my low suds detergent and vinegar, I scrubbed for an hour before laying towels and heavy weights across the spot. That appalling spot was in the middle of the room, but at the unveiling the next morning it had vanished. Both Andy and I were relieved.

Our Blue and Gold Banquet comes next week. We'll stencil with cocoa across the top of our cake using profiles of Washington and Kennedy.

I hope Pop feels better. We appear to be better also. It's hard to be split into so many different directions.

I am still forlornly trying to get rid of that extra $100 in my bookkeeping. The senior bookkeeper of the firm is getting impatient as the books should have been closed last month.

February 20, 1962

Dear Mom,

When it rains, it pours. Dann's eye has become so clouded with that cataract that if he closes his good eye, he cannot recognize which son is sitting across the table. The doctor scheduled Dann's surgery, with ten days hospitalization, for March 6th.

The Department of Public Assistance has resurfaced. After one year, they have completed our licensing and have a girl for us. Lisa is 10 years old, the same as Andy. Contrarily, she does not come from the usual, deprived background but from an upper class family. Her adoptive parents are divorced and she has been caught in the midst of bickering and stress. Lisa has the beginnings of myriad problems. She will arrive two days after Dann comes home from the hospital. Because Dann will have lifting limits, we are readying everything now. We repainted her bedroom in sky blue, hung ruffled curtains and switched the furniture, putting in appropriate girl stuff.

I'm sorry that Pop still feels poorly. What does the doctor say? Wish we could come down.

MARCH 8, 1962

Dear Mom,

Your phone call shocked me. I cannot imagine Pop in the hospital. I cannot even imagine him sick. Do they think that he had the heart attack after he was admitted or while he was still home?

You already know, of course, that Dann is okay. The hardest part was waiting all day for 3:00 p.m. surgery. We both got weary of walking the corridors. The day after was tedious when he had both eyes bandaged and no movement was allowed. The boys and I tried to alleviate this with the gift of a transistor radio—they pitched in from their piggybanks. Dann called early this morning. As they have taken off one bandage, he can use the phone, sit up and walk gently to the bathroom.

I started out getting good cooperation from the kids. The first day they behaved great, second day fair, by last night everybody whined and complained. I laughed and told them they should know better than to think they could get by with such slipshod behavior when I needed them so much and sent them all to bed. Andy wept bitter tears because he knew he had disappointed me, but I made the rounds kissing them goodnight and we're off to a fresh start. They're glad to have me around long enough to discipline.

Now that Dann can use his phone, I will visit him less. Ten days in the hospital seems dreadfully long.

Jason drew a picture for his Dad showing Daddy lying in the hospital bed with arms and legs straight out, a nurse standing at the foot of the bed with what looks like a hula skirt, and a patch covering one of Dann's eyes but not obscuring a big smile. There really will be a big smile on Dann's face when he sees this graphic art.

It surprises me to find out how many friends one has when one needs them. I spend all my time answering the phone when home. Dann's mother came yesterday and cooked a chicken from our freezer. The hamburger diet was getting to me. The boys think hamburger is unbeatable although they did demolish her chicken dinner rapidly.

You must be worried about Pop. I feel awful that I cannot be there to support you but my brothers will arrive soon. Please call anytime that you need to talk.

Likewise, this is the first time when I've had problems that you haven't been here holding my hand in some supportive way, but try not to worry about us. We are okay. Many friends help in many ways, not quite the same as you, but indispensable and appreciated.

I still have bureau drawers to empty before Lisa comes. We send prayers and will call again soon.

March 12, 1962

Dear Mom,

It's great that Pop is home again noisying up your house.

We are expecting Dann home tomorrow. They spoiled him in the hospital, but not to the point that he wouldn't rush to come home. While I visited there this afternoon, five sets of company dropped in. That's about all he can do besides hassle the nurses. I took warm, homemade donuts and found he had already received homemade cookies, candy and cheese.

This winter weather does not cooperate. We finally succeeded in getting the babysitter's car unstuck in the driveway, but my station wagon sits imbedded in the drifts. I just drive the other car and park on the street.

This is tedious for the boys too, so I allowed the two older ones to have overnight guests, let them get thoroughly tired before bedtime, and then fouled them up by going to bed myself at the same time with a book. Even so, they talked until 11:00 p.m. and were up by 6:00 a.m.

My neighbor took all four for Saturday afternoon and supper. She said I could come too for supper, but wouldn't I rather go and do something else? Boy is that special! I went over to Grandma Willett's and the two of us enjoyed a quiet peaceful supper.

Once a day Dann calls the boys. They rush to the phone when it's their turn as this provides a unique opportunity to talk without competition.

Dann is on the eye and neurology floor, all long term patients. Now that he is allowed up he wanders all over entertaining the other patients, sometimes the nurses too. He and his roommate tease anyone available. His roommate had the same cataract operation, the same afternoon. They asked someone to pick up a trick novelty for them, a plastic imitation of the result of an upset stomach. Every time the shift changes they lay it on their supper trays or their bedclothes. The nurses all tried to scrub it up, in vain. The guys particularly waited for one nurse who they claimed hadn't cracked a smile all week. Much to their satisfaction, she laughed. The floor nurse told me that it's good for the other patients to have him wandering around.

I spent the morning trying to shovel our long driveway. As soon as we are allowed, I will bring my convalescent husband down to visit your convalescent husband. It seems ages.

March 18, 1962

Dear Mom,

I was so sorry to hear about Pop. I wondered if he might have a setback when he came home. I hope his good nights continue and I am relieved that Frank and Lois are there again. I know this discourages you and wish I could be there. Anyway here's a long letter to lighten your day.

Dann actually came home a day early. We managed quite well in his absence. His real estate business came to a standstill and the apartment buildings ran smoothly. The difficulties all occurred at home, both from his absence and mine as I was gone so much. By the time he arrived, I was struggling with five blown fuses, one loose tooth ready for pulling, a crib falling apart, a ceiling light burned out and one car still stuck. The night before he came home I had accidentally stepped on the sweeper cord, jerking it and it quit. All the living room lights went out but as it was bedtime, I left it. The next morning the kids got up early and were doing chores so they wouldn't have to do them after Daddy arrived. When Andy got out the sweeper I called down, "The sweeper won't work because the fuses are blown in the living room. Try a kitchen outlet."

When I came downstairs, he was standing there blankly with the cord in his hand, "Gee Mom, every time I plug the cord in it sparks like this, see?" and immediately showed me. He had already gone around the kitchen trying each one. Remember when Pop rewired he put each one on a separate circuit? Andy hit them all. We made our toast in the study that morning. When Dann came home he changed the fuses, Jason pulled his own tooth with great glee, the missing screw for the crib turned up and enough snow melted so that the car was no longer stuck.

Dann asked the doctor what he could and could not do. "You can get dressed in the morning and sit in a chair." Then he relented and agreed that if the weather is okay and the walking not slippery, Dann could go to church or to his night class if I chauffeured. He gets pretty restless and needs to get out. Perhaps we can drive to Delavan when the kids are in school.

Lisa arrived last Saturday. She is anxious to create good impressions, eager to please, excited with everything, and enjoys playing with the boys and they with her. She shows no reluctance at leaving home nor homesickness, expresses no hostility towards her mother although I have been told hostile feeling exists. We expect a couple weeks of good behavior before we start running into problems. We have started her in school, taught her some prayers, cut her allowance in half, and presented her with her fair share of chores, which delighted her. Last night for the first time she came and gave her Uncle Dann a goodnight hug and kiss.

March 25, 1962

Dear Mom,

I feel so much better now that Dann, Michael and I visited with you and Pop for a couple hours. Pop seemed quiet, but he obviously is delighted to be home again. He surprised me with all the questions he asked about Lisa. Perhaps next time we can bring everybody, but that seemed a bit much for this visit. It's great that Frank can come again. Is Charles flying home to see Dad also? You are a good nurse.

April 11, 1962

Dear Mom,

I am enclosing money which I received from my Extension Homemakers for Dad's memorial. I have seen or talked to you so much over the last three weeks, but I still have sundry thoughts to express.

I am glad for many things: that my brother visited that weekend so that you weren't alone when Dad had his second heart attack and that Pop died at home with you and not in the hospital. I am glad for the one last visit we squeezed in. Those two hours meant a lot to me. I am glad that Charles flew back from New Jersey so that you had all three of us with you. I was glad, but not surprised, to see so many Hibbard cousins and aunts and uncles at the funeral. Do you realize, Mom, how much you mean to the whole clan? It must be because you are always interested in everyone and such a good listener. You are obviously the matriarch of the tribe. It was vividly brought home to me the day of the funeral how much you and Dad are special to all of them. I was glad that I could spend those three days with you after everybody left. You and I haven't had any time alone together since our boys were born.

I was especially pleased with the card which Dann's younger brother sent ending with, "Life is a series of hills and valleys. Without the valleys there would be no hills." Such a simple thought, but you and I certainly would never have been content with just plains. You and Dad have shared much together and I pray that before long your valley will lessen and the hills rise again.

We had an uneventful trip home Sunday night. The children played games the whole way, and Lisa repeated to me three times, "Gee aren't you glad to be home again?" Do you suppose that she missed me?

She and I are having tough sledding. She didn't feel like studying last night. It must be hard when she knows the boys are playing because they've finished their homework. She did her fractions all wrong. I helped her do them over, but she wanted to quit and call her Mother. I said she had to do her work first so she left it unfinished and went to bed. She just needs to be ornery for a while. She was cheerful again in the morning. We had a heated discussion at the breakfast table. Dann insisted, "She just doesn't understand the principle of common denominators in fractions."

"She does too," I argued. He bet me a nickel and gave her a problem to do at the breakfast table. She was ecstatic when she caused him to lose his nickel.

It took us a long time to get our girl and I wonder what we've got. She is so lovable and so ornery. It saddens me to think of the turmoil and underlying distress there must be for a child to be willing to leave her mother, and worse yet for the mother to be willing for her to go. She needs to be loved no matter what she does, and that no matter what scares me. We wanted a girl and a challenge. We clearly have both. May the Lord give us strength and wisdom for what I am just beginning to realize lies ahead of us.

We'd like to come down again Sunday afternoon barring blizzards. Is this okay? I grow increasingly grateful that we do not live in some far away place and am sorry for those that have to grow up without guidance from Mom.

It has been a long traumatic winter, but now Dann's eye is back to 20/20, we will tackle Lisa's problems day by day, and we have many special memories of Pop to cherish. Hopefully spring is just around the corner and perhaps some of that "boriing and monotonoous" living I keep expecting.

4 But When She Was Bad

APRIL 25, 1962

Dear Mom,

    Dann helped me tune bottles this morning for my hillbilly band. Eight Cubs hold eight bottles and I make music by touching their heads when it's their turn to blow which requires absolute concentration on everybody's part.

    We could come Sunday and bring a picnic lunch.

    Spring vacation is over and I'm pooped trying to keep up with the kids. They're doing odd jobs to earn extra money. They painted two park benches, the grape arbor and a dressing table, dug and washed parsnips, raked and hauled leaves along the driveway, chopped and carried off dead brush, scrubbed the porch floor, polished silver and straightened kitchen cupboards. This sounds good on paper, but in practice it takes a small miracle to get things done efficiently with three or four working simultaneously. I went shopping at Sears for drapery material and took Timmy along to look for basketballs he is saving for. Dann took Andy to his office where he simultaneously worked and oversaw Andy's Scout whittling. In the wee hours on Saturday Andy and

Dann went fishing for opening day of trout season — no fish, only rain. Andy was thrilled anyway.

May 9, 1962

Dear Mom,

I'm sorry we didn't have time to talk when we visited you. Lisa causes ripples continually. She didn't actually break the promise she made when I sent her to the store, but she short-circuited some of the change. I monitor these things and asked if she didn't think I would find out. She muttered, "Well yes, I thought you probably would." Maybe she's testing. Her social worker says her insecurity causes this and it should lessen as we surround her with routine, restrictions, and affection. She took flowers to her teacher, got upset that nobody took any to Andy's (they are in different fifth grades) so she returned to school with apple blossoms which we agreed should come from both Andy and her. She displays a sweet, thoughtful disposition.

Her Scout troop is putting on a play. Lisa insisted on inviting her Mother although we cautioned not to be disappointed if her Mother didn't come. I have never seen Lisa so excited. Her allotment was 40 cookies so I taught her to make my special chocolate peppermint bars. I'll be glad when today is over as I am afraid that what goes up comes down.

P.S. Her mother didn't come — of course.

May 9, 1962

Dear Mom,

We visited friends at Pine Lake Camp, slept in a cabin and offered grateful thanks for dry beds. The weather turned nice eventually so although we didn't have swimming suits, everybody, but me, improvised. Lisa misbehaved all day. I couldn't figure out why. She asked if she could go wading and I told her to wait until after dinner, but when the rest of us walked around the lake, she and Timmy stripped off shoes and socks and waded in. Consequently neither could go when the rest did. She sulked and I told her, "If you feel like crying, go ahead," whereupon she burst into tears. She never cried at home and we think she needs to occasionally. But for most of the afternoon she couldn't open her mouth without shooting nasty little digs towards the boys. We finally told her if she couldn't say something good, say nothing at all.

Last night she got angry at Andy and tromped on his bike. She repented later and although the Cub committee was convening here, I left the meeting for a while and talked to both Andy and Lisa before tucking them in. I am more than ready to have her visit her Mom again for a weekend.

On the cheerful side, Lisa came home ecstatic. "Crestwood puts on a spring concert in two weeks. The music teacher listened to me sing, said she needed someone to lead the sopranos and if I could learn the music quickly, I could sing in the festival!" She learned the notes rapidly, but we are struggling with the Italian words.

Andy and Timmy participated in the space rocket derby race. Timmy's rocket worked until the trial runs when it refused to take off. Like all rockets, these are sometimes difficult to launch. Andy's rocket stayed in until the finals when he was eliminated.

I went out to lunch with my friend Allison. Neither of us could afford to take the time, but we parked our kids with a co-op babysitter and discussed our mutual foster girls over lunch. The night before when I had been baby-sitting for them, Faith, their teenage Indian foster girl became upset and retired to her bedroom. I sent the other children to bed and when the house quieted down Faith reappeared, asking for help with trigonometry. I couldn't help, but she knew all the answers anyway and we talked. "I heard you have adopted a girl."

"That's an incorrect choice of words which makes Lisa mad."

Faith replied indignantly, "I don't blame her." She cried, telling me between hiccups why she had blown up at her foster parents. This constitutes my top level baby-sitting and it obviously relieved them that I was the one who was co-op sitting.

Dann pulled Andy's tooth and gave him a quarter. Now Timmy has figured out that only four teeth stand between him and his basketball.

Yesterday I took my Cubs for a hike in the Arboretum. I piled them, plus Jay and Mike and an extra mother, into my station wagon and drove to a fire lane entrance. The boys ran frantically, searching for dead bugs, worms, leaves, nuts, etc. for their scavenger hunt. I finally managed to get them to quit and pile back into the car only to have it stall at the first stop. They pushed me onto an incline, but we had to call for help making us late for supper.

May 24, 1962

Dear Mom,

Mike and I are planning lunch in front of the TV so we can watch Carpenter land on the moon.

Today Tim reached the $4.49 necessary for his basketball. He has done a marvelous job skipping candy and doing extra jobs to save money so after school we're going to go buy it.

"It's all in your head," Dann sighed when I related my car problem to him.

After dropping Andy and Timmy off for piano lessons, Jason, Mike and I drove to the grocery store. Trouble again! It was 5:45 p.m. so I called both home and the office, but no Dann. As I thought he might be enroute coming down University Avenue (where we were stranded in a parking lot), the three of us stood on the curb. In 10 minutes he came tootling along and we waved frantically. This is nerve-wracking for a driver in late afternoon traffic in an inside lane. It upset Jay that Daddy didn't immediately stop. In fact, it took quite a bit of maneuvering for him to get back to us. We swapped cars for the rest of the week so he could figure out the problem. It's working fine for him, of course.

Yes, the boys would like your oatmeal boxes.

June 14, 1962

Dear Mom,

We took only Andy and Lisa canoe camping with the Four Lakes Campers on the Wisconsin River and started out in pouring rain. Although we carried extensive foul weather gear, it makes one apprehensive to watch the cars depart on the shuttle and know that camp might be four rain-hours away, but in half-an-hour the rain stopped. We peeled raincoats, then sweat shirts, next shoes and socks and lastly, the long pants for those foresighted people that had worn swimming trunks. Even with a cloudy sky the glare off the river scorched us. We tried to follow the channel of the river but often had to negotiate shallow water over sandbars. Needing to change drivers in the middle of the river, Dann and I jumped out on one sandbar, ran around the canoe and popped in at the other end. This is called changing horse power in the middle of the stream. Once we got stuck and had to get out and push. The four-hour trip turned into six. Everyone else had motors on their boats or canoes and when they started the motors they would put hands out and tow us alongside.

June 19, 1962

Dear Mom,

We have switched cars again and this time during piano lessons the younger two boys and I drove to the Midvale Shopping

Center. When I backed out of the parking space, the wagon gave one feeble spurt and died. I tried to locate Dann and called Andy and Timmy at their piano teacher's and told them to walk to their Uncle Don's. I wasn't sure they knew the way, but guessed they could figure it out together. The rest of us found a drug store and guzzled cokes until Dann showed up and pushed us.

The next day I had promised to drive a load of Girl Scouts to their campout. I tried desperately to get Dann to switch cars, but he insisted we would be all right. And we were — going out. This time three hours passed before Dann showed up. The Scouts were short one leader and were delighted to have an extra adult for three hours to help set up camp. They accepted Jason and Michael enthusiastically, but we fouled up supper again. Dann has taken the car to the garage and they have found some things wrong. The question is did they find the right wrong things?

We took everybody to an all-you-can-eat chicken dinner after church. They made money on Jay and Mike, but not on the rest of us. Timmy and I started with seven wings apiece. This cost sixty cents per child, $1.25 per adult.

Lisa is back from another home visit and things are always rougher then for awhile. She asked how long she had to stay with us as her Mother told her that when she, Lisa, could get out of here, she would take her to Nantucket. That's no help.

July 31, 1962

Dear Mom,

We took Timmy's birthday party guests and all of us plus Lisa's friend, totaling 12 children, to the rodeo. Bancroft issued free rodeo coupons on their chocolate milk which put 12 quarts of chocolate milk in our refrigerator. The kids liked it best when the broncos threw their riders.

Sending Jay and Mike to get ready for bed I found them fishing in the toilet with their toothbrushes. When I scolded, Jay burst out, "Why did you have to do that, Mommy? We flushed it first!"

Lisa curled up on her bed this morning and read for two hours. I have been trying to instill an enjoyment of reading in her. Today was peaceful. Most days are not, as she is so restless and I scold constantly.

August 14, 1962

Dear Mom,

My cleaning lady came only once all summer. Usually she calls to say she's tied up. Last week she didn't even call. Unfortunately we had company coming for supper. I wept and decided I don't belong to the class of people who hire help because I get so annoyed at the time I spend making arrangements and could do the work quicker. Dann was working at home, rose to the occasion and called the employment office securing someone for the next day. That didn't solve my immediate problem, but it improved my state of mind. I cleaned the dining room, straightened the rest, and then blithely thought of other matters.

Lisa is finally intrigued in a book and is reading an Elsie Dinsmore type of drama called The Little Princess. For two days she spent every free moment curled on her bed reading, instead of heckling somebody, an art she has mastered. She behaved horridly when she came back from summer camp. For the first time I'll be glad to see school start as I am petered out.

Andy needed a physical, a requirement for Scout camp. The doctor found what he thought was undescended testicles and today the urologist confirmed this. We should have caught this earlier because each year increases the likelihood that body heat might destroy reproductive capabilities. Andy received a shot of hormones. If this doesn't correct the problem, he'll need surgery. Andy would willingly go through anything to avoid a shot. I took him to Westgate for a coke to soothe his battered feelings and told him that any boy getting a shot where he did should be spanking-exempt.

This just isn't our year. Not only the summer, but the whole year needs to be crossed off as a bad deal. Perhaps a good night's sleep will help what ails me. I need to plan another camping weekend so all these other worries have to wait until next week.

August 21, 1962

Dear Mom,

We camped in the northern Kettle Moraine, fished, canoed, swam and sunbathed. Coming home we stopped to see Winnie and Don on their farm. She and I were fixing supper when Jason rushed into the kitchen yelling, "I saw him! That guy out there just laid an egg right there in the open and I saw him." He was given the egg to take home.

Each day we look to see what change those hormones might have produced on Andy, but nothing changes. But this afternoon when he went to take a bath I heard a delighted yelp, "Mom, come look!" I never really hoped. I should have had more faith, as both testicles have dropped. We need to watch for another week to see if they stay down.

A University girl is helping with my housework and I have gotten rid of that other one or she's gotten rid of us. This one worked six hours today and while I straightened the house ahead of her, made meals and chauffeured, she cleaned the whole house and did the ironing.

My new suit is tan tweed. What do you mean "now throw out an old dress"? They're just coming back into style.

If you would like two boys for a couple days, we could work it out between us and Greyhound. Yes, I could use some grapes. We shouldn't have pruned ours so severely.

August 29, 1962

Dear Mom,

Lisa visited her Dad and stepmother last weekend, quite different from visiting her other parent. Her stepmother raved about improvements in attitude.

I have been sorting, throwing and mending clothes to get ready for school. Next I'll shop for what is missing. In desperation I concocted the following inventory form. Each child fills out one!

Inventory

This is a count to help the buyer anticipate seasonal demands. Please go through your drawers and/or closets and get as accurate a count as possible on the following items. Right now you have nothing in the ironing or mending baskets. If anything does not fit, lay it on my bed. Include in your count anything which looks dirty and throw it into the dirty clothes. Include in your count anything which needs mending and make a pile on the pillow of your bed. Anything which you are positive is yours but does not have your mark, place in a pile at the foot of your bed. Please return peacefully any clothes which belong to someone else. Make sure your socks are really yours. If you have read through these entire directions you may now unobtrusively go get a cookie.

Sunday pants	____	school jackets	____	gym shorts	____
suit coat	____	play jackets	____	sweatshirt	____
white shirt	____	good sweaters	____	ties	____
school pants	____	long johns	____	belts	____
school shirts	____	under shorts	____	rubbers	____

blue jeans	____	under shirts	____	raincoats	____
play shirts	____	socks	____	shoes-good	____
pajamas-summer	____	pajamas-winter	____	shoes-gym	____

Thank you for your cooperation.
Signed *The Management*

See you Saturday, Mom. Please don't fuss.

September 10, 1962

Dear Mom,

Once more we have survived that first day. I spent all day filling out questionnaires, buying school supplies, and marking tennis shoes. Jay was delighted that, as a first grader, he could return after lunch. He announced they played a new game and made him class president. We asked, "What does this mean?"

"Somebody gave my name and then two more names and the teacher put all three names on the board. Everybody raised hands and I got the most so I am president."

"Does this mean you have special jobs to do?"

"Oh no," he replied earnestly, "everybody but me has a job!"

My obstetrician still thinks I'm pregnant in spite of the negative blood test and wants to see me again next month. Tune in next month for the next exciting development in this soap — is she is, or is she ain't? I had begun to feel lots better after she said I wasn't, but now when she says I am, I notice more backaches.

Thanks for the grapes and the pears. Lisa and I made jelly.

SEPTEMBER 17, 1962

Dear Mom,

This was Twinkle's weekend. We didn't go to bed late until Friday night, but at 6:00 a.m. I checked on her. She had deserted her whelping bed and burrowed a hole under the woodpile where she had already delivered one puppy. We lay on the floor, talking to her and finally retrieved her and the puppy, only by that time we found two. Dann woke up Jason, the only kid who had gotten to bed at a decent hour. At 7:00 a.m. Jay woke the others. One would think after being up so late that waking them might be difficult (at least judging from school days), but they all raced downstairs in less time than it had taken Jay to walk up. They squatted quietly around Twinkle's box for hours and then we left for church. By the time we got home #11 had just checked in. Even Twinkle understands the Willett ways as she produced nine males and only two females.

As I've been feeling better again, perhaps Dr. Tomason is not infallible. This has been a busy disorganized month what with beginning school, puppies and Cub Scout reorganization and there is no time to worry about that. In fact I have no intention of even thinking about that until next month.

Jay came home from school and announced, "Our teacher tells us something once, then twice, sometimes 10 times and doesn't even get mad. Boy, do I like that teacher!" He came home Thursday broken-hearted because she had given them something to do which he hadn't been able to do. I guess the first such experience is rough. I'm sure he will have many more. Each day he keeps expecting to read tomorrow.

September 27, 1962

Dear Mom,

Thank you for the lovely matched jewelry. It sets off my new suit beautifully. Your letter broke me up. Was this to cheer me up if I am pregnant, and do I have to give it back if I'm not? I slipped coming downstairs and bounced on my tailbone. Nothing seems to be broken, but I stretch out on the couch in agony. They took x-rays and now Dr. Tomason has decided I'm not pregnant after all. I spent all week resting with the heating pad. I can't drive, can't lean over and it's agony to get up. I never realized how many things get onto the floor.

We held our first pack meeting and already have 88 boys. As soon as we sort lists into dens we can solicit new den mother volunteers. I declared this year I will be an either/or—either be chief den mother, organize and train new mothers, OR take a den. However, we still have one orphan den waiting for a mother.

I need to go trim 200 puppy toe-nails before their eyes open.

October 18, 1962

Dear Mom,

An awful weekend. On Wednesday I discovered that Lisa was taking the boys yo-yo's to school and giving them away. I called Mrs. Smith, her social worker, and asked for help. She made an appointment to come, cancelled, remade and cancelled again before she finally made it five days later. Meanwhile Lisa found out that one of her friends had returned the yo-yo to Andy, so for five days she knew that we knew, but we didn't mention it. All her problems returned immediately. It became impossible to get a civil answer and she spent all her free time rereading letters from her Mother. I thought she had a fistful of problems, but have now decided she has just one with a lot of aftermath. If we could teach her to be truthful and thus eliminate her feelings of guilt, the rest might fade away. But we're straightened out again and she's acting like the sweetest little gal imaginable.

Fourteen dens are ready to go. As we are still short den mothers I will resign from my chief den mother option and move to the OR option. Who wants to work with busy adults anyway, when kids are much more fun?

We're planning a United Nations supper. Tim is decorating with his souvenirs and I am exploring recipes in my foreign cookery book. I wanted to try them first, but Dann says people should accept this dinner invitation on a gambling basis. Hope we don't starve. Here's my menu: Borscht (Russian beet soup), goulash (Hungarian), sweet and sour pork (Chinese), French bread (this we could fill up on in case of dire necessity) English trifle (pudding with stale or leftover cake) and Italian Caffe Granita (frozen coffee with whipped cream).

Dann set up a small fence outside the kitchen window. Both kids and Twinkle can jump into it, but the puppies can't jump out—yet. Except one day when little Peanut made it by standing on her brother's head. We are asking $35 and already mentally spending that $350 (35 times 10). Maybe we need a new TV because ours doesn't work most of the time or a second canoe as we can't all fit in one anymore.

October 25, 1962

Dear Mom,

Andy's doctor postponed the surgery. Those testicles keep popping up and down.

Sunday was such a gorgeous fall day that we took the crew to the Cave of the Mounds. The four older ones are old enough to learn something, and the fifth gets in for free anyway. We climbed the observation tower, experienced car trouble and got stuck in the mud. Darkness fell before we got around to eating our picnic supper and we didn't have a flashlight.

I am now den mother for seven new boys. The new ones are the excited ones and me too, after talking to their mothers. My reputation precedes me and every mother that I called made comments about how thrilled she was to draw me as den mother for her son, accompanied with offers of help. With any luck, I should have them all trained as den mothers by next year.

My United Nations dinner was a huge success. I spent all day cooking, I typed menus, and the boys made small flags for each of the eight countries, sticking flags into the appropriate dish. The Borscht contained everything but the kitchen sink and was still delicious. The Italian frozen coffee was awful.

We are still working on the kitchen. Yesterday Dann installed new light fixtures. I have waited so long for those lights that I dared not object although who, but a man, would appear in a woman's kitchen two hours preceding a company dinner, turn out the lights (not the stove, thank goodness) and walk all over the sink counter.

We loaded the pups into the back of the station wagon and took them to the vet's for worm pills. They howled and whined the entire trip. Each morning Dann puts down ten pills—no more, no less. The little darlings spend all their time chewing, either on their rug or themselves. Twinkle has decided they shouldn't chew on each other. Whenever two start wrestling she shoves her long nose between the culprits, which keeps her busy. After watching her, I no longer complain about MY discipline problems.

Timmy suffered another severe side ache Tuesday night. The doctor thinks these are psychosomatic and suggests we should be casual about it. Difficult when Tim obviously suffers.

October 30, 1962

Dear Mom,

Andy and Timmy will come on the 5:15 bus Thursday. They plan on stuffing their pockets with Halloween loot so they won't get hungry. The rest of us will be down Sunday with a gallon of milk.

I had a delightful time with my new den yesterday explaining how to yell like mad for our Indian skit. I had to be sure they knew when to whoop and when to fall dead. Then Lisa came home and spoiled everything. She plopped into the middle of everybody, threw crayons and tripped the boys during their relay races. This sort of behavior brings retaliation from the other seven, of course. I have been dyeing old pillowcases, cutting armholes and fringing edges to make three buckskin pioneer costumes and four Indian ones.

December 11, 1962

Dear Mom,

Thanks for keeping the boys (they loved it) and for the apples.

Lisa called her father to see if he would come to her concert. He said he would, but was drunk and didn't show up. She will fly East at Christmas to visit her Mother. She is exuberant over that. I am not.

January 11, 1963

Dear Mom,

The children are back in school, thank goodness. In desperation I made myself a schedule. Every morning I work on Dann's books from 9:30-11:30. He didn't think this sounded like speedy results, but he's already surprised at what I can accomplish in two uninterrupted hours. This gives me a chance to get the house straightened and washing machine going before 9:30. After 11:30 I work on supper and miscellaneous chores. Anything that isn't done by 3:30 (when the kids get home) doesn't make it. From then on it's reading out loud to whomever, supervising homework and practicing, and advising my three Scouts on merit badges.

I always enjoy loafing at your house, even with a headache. I have had more headaches and take aspirin all day. Could this could be a sinus infection? I imagine a family our size adds considerably to the quantity of water going down the drain. If your plumbing is going to react anytime, it would be then. Sorry about that.

Andy participated in the Scouts' winter campout. His patrol won the blue banner, which they deserved after all their preparation. They received extra points for dehydrated foods, baking bread (over the campfire), pancakes, and pemmican and earned demerits for using sandwiches or sloppy dishwashing. Andy perused the list and incorporated all the high pointers (the hardest). We struggled for days making pemmican. The directions said take ½ pound of beef thinly sliced, put in oven at 160 degrees and cook until black. Pound into powder, mix with a little shortening and brown sugar and there you have it. In the first place, the butcher's machine would only slice to 1/4 inch. We said, "We'll settle for that."

"It's too difficult to slice cheaper cuts. You should use steak." We settled for that also. Planning to cook this until black caused my Scottish instincts to protest. Andy wouldn't even take bread. They used Bisquick, moistened and patted onto the end of a stick, held it over the fire until done and after removing the stick, filled the hole with honey or something. Repeating this every meal earned them two points each time.

Lisa has been a little angel. She is earning Scout merit badges and cooked oatmeal for breakfast.

January 16, 1963

Dear Mom,

This two-hour morning routine has been in place for two weeks and results are beginning to show. If I could keep it up for one more week, last year's books might get closed. It's difficult not to get distracted.

Last night's pack meeting included uniform inspection. We are trying to make the boys more conscious of their appearance. I sharpened up my boys, but still lost out to Timmy's den. That shows I make a better parent than a den mother. I told him that's the last time I help him clean his shoes. Next month is the Blue and Gold banquet. Cake competition will be tough in this household as Tim, Dann and I represent different dens.

Lisa and I are struggling again, or still. She is banned from the grocery store because she went without permission when she was supposed to be someplace else. She forfeited her new transistor for a week because she ran it in bed after hours and she and Timmy have to go to bed an hour early because they stayed up after the stated time one night when we were out. She doesn't seem to mind all this punishment.

How about going shopping together the end of January? By that time my bookkeeping will be closed or I'll be tired of trying.

February 1, 1963

Dear Mom,

You should have seen my littlest angels when they got mad at each other in the bathroom. They ended up with Epsom salts in their pants cuffs and their ears and a snowstorm on the floor.

We traded our car. We felt guilty driving it with mileage of six miles per gallon and bought a 1961 nine-passenger Dodge. The rear seat turns backwards and the back window operates only by pushbutton on the dash. That means we keep control back there.

Disaster struck on Saturday. Either Lisa is worrying about the psychiatrist visits or this is the aftermath from her Christmas visit home. It didn't matter what the issue was, I couldn't even manage small ones like shampoos. She stormed that she didn't have to do what I said. Reasoning didn't work. In desperation I sent her to her room to think about why she is here. This upset me so that I called Mrs. Smith twice even though it was her day off. She boosted my morale, told me to stick to my guns and endeared herself to me by saying she would be home all day if the need arose. When Dann put Lisa to bed, they had a long talk after which she was more receptive than ever before. He criticized her Mother for the first time. Perhaps this is the price we have to pay whenever she goes home to visit. Dann and I met with the psychiatric social worker. She scolded me saying if I was angry with Lisa why didn't I express that anger? When there is cause to get mad, I should do so, as direct feeling is not difficult for a child to understand.

We have current subscriptions to the *Post, National Geographic, Reader's Digest, Boy's Life* and *American Girl*. I'm promoting interest in current events by reading at suppertime and am presently reading the account of the Nina 2's simulated crossing of Columbus trip. Timmy sits spellbound. I have to hide the book between meals.

I have been reading Gilbreth's *Management in the Home*. I got as far as time-motion study and stopped to review our working patterns. Starting with the kids' chores, I observed and wrote down steps and operations while Tim cleared supper dishes. This involved 159 steps and 20 operations. Afterwards I made suggestions. The next night he did it enthusiastically in 51 steps, 10 operations and three delays, such as finishing up the beans and draining the last drop from the milk bottle. Gilbreth has great ideas, but we do much of this already. There is one plus that

Gilbreth didn't consider. Now everybody is volunteering to do Tim's chore to see if they can perform in less time.

February 15, 1963

Dear Mom,

Yes, we'd love to have you visit. Mike and I will meet the 2:10 bus Thursday.

The Scout banquet, in spite of numerous last minute problems, went off beautifully. The Willetts did well in the cake contest. Dann's Webelos den took first place. Timmy's den and mine tied for third. See you Thursday.

March 1, 1963

Dear Mom,

Mike found the scissors, did it again and we have a scalped five-year old. Dann gave him another haircut to even out the damage, but an x still wiggles across the top of his head.

We planned a peanut birthday party for him. Timmy managed it (with Lisa's help) earning credit towards a Cub Scout arrow point. Not only did they work together peacefully, but they did a wonderful job. Tim created invitations and name cards with glued-on peanut faces. The two of them directed peanut games. I watched and drank tea.

Lisa's social worker told her she wouldn't be going back to her Mother this summer. Lisa showed no reaction and that iron curtain came down. She neither disagreed nor argued. The rest of the day I kept her with me until she started talking.

"How come?"

"We've had so many problems that we feel that your Mother couldn't cope."

"She couldn't. I don't know what Mother is going to say though. She doesn't like anybody who doesn't agree with her."

Lisa starts Van Hise Junior High this fall and had to choose between Art and Band. She has musical capabilities which she hasn't used and could do well in Band, but I told her the choice is hers. Then I got out my clarinet and everybody tried it. Pretty sneaky. She not only decided on Band, but wants to take piano this summer and comes down early every morning and plays with my beginning piano books.

Jay brought home some phonetic homework, asking for help. The teacher had drawn pictures of words containing the vowel U. Jay was supposed to write out the word such as fuse, or mule, but we couldn't always figure out the pictures, one in particular. Jason finally decided (correctly) that it was a juke box, but it looked like two "wurms" on a rail fence to us. Jason announced scornfully, "When I need help in school the teacher helps me, but I guess the reason you're having so much trouble is because my first grade class is already doing second grade work." We sent a note to the teacher and told her that it might be a juke box to her or to Jay, but to us it would always be two wurms on a rail fence.

Yes, Lisa's custody was for one year. Mrs. Smith is applying for another year. If her mother protests, she can take it to court which would be a sticky mess and we assume she wouldn't want the publicity. There won't be any more home visits. I'm beginning to think we have an affectionate child, but we have to counteract all the years she hid her feelings.

March 21, 1963

Dear Mom,

My last den meeting could compete with the TV series MY THREE SONS. Twinkle is in heat so I have been going outside and fraternizing with all visiting dogs in order to read their license numbers. Then I call City Hall to secure owner names. This is time-consuming, but the alternative is to have them picked up by the dogcatcher. Twinkle stays in the basement during den meeting as the Cubs open that back door continually. We had one small male dog visiting yesterday and he infiltrated the house five times during den meeting. He would zoom through the kitchen under our feet looking for Twinkle and my Cubs would rush off. The more they helped, the worse it got. Can't you picture my house with one poor, confused, little dog running frantically chased by five screaming Cubs plus five Willetts? When they did manage to get the dog out, half of the boys would be out also, unable to get back in without the dog. Fortunately, I wasn't too tired to see the humor.

Grandmother Willett did wonderfully with the kids while Dann and I were gone. She sent Tim to bed for misbehaving, discovered herself to be in error, apologized and made retribution, to his great delight. She firmly squelched Lisa who kept telling her how to do things. When Jason came home from school because he didn't feel well, they talked it over together and within two hours she had him back in school. She calculated by the amount of lunch he consumed that he wasn't too sick.

March 28, 1963

Dear Mom,

We have been accepted for Philmont this summer, a Scout camp in the New Mexico Mountains. Although many troops go for backpacking experience, we will be receiving Cub Scout training, den mother for me and Cubmaster for Dann. The kids will be in activity groups by age and Mike in nursery care, but we'll sleep together in tent city and eat together at mealtime. We've been studying the atlas. Lisa announced that she can't go bowling anymore because she has to save her money. Andy and Tim are desperately thinking up new financial ventures to make them more solvent. Their present proposals are to make and sell birdhouses or to sell seeds. Could you keep Twinkle?

Enclosed is a clipping on the annual Scout Council Appreciation dinner. We have never gone before, but Dann brought it up at our Scouter committee meeting, saying we should go and adding that it's too bad if our institutional representative goes by himself.

I asked, "On choir practice night just before a concert?"

"Well, poor George deserves support."

As you can see, they awarded me the den mother trophy cup for outstanding service. This shocked me. I told the kids afterward that it was more difficult to walk up in front of 1,000 people to receive an award, than to put in all those years of work to earn it. Poor George indeed!

April 9, 1963

Dear Mom,

Our poison ivy kid improves. Andy swore that huge vine he tied his canoe to (while canoeing the Wisconsin River during the Scout campout) didn't look like the poison ivy in our backyard. The doctor gave Andy an anti-histamine shot to combat infection and tablets to dissolve for compresses. One arm swelled to the elbow making it immobile. Swelling on neck and chin prevented him from turning his head, he itched like crazy and open lesions on his arm drained constantly. He announces the coming of spring every year this way. Each time is worse.

The urologist says we have no option left for Andy except surgery. The shots move the testicles down, but they don't stay descended.

I have to figure out an under-the-sea skit before 3:00 this afternoon and have only two hours of thinking time left.

April 16, 1963

Dear Mom,

Andy is doing fine. He came back from surgery at 2:00 p.m. and tonight he's already opening cards and a package. This causes lots of pain and they tied one ankle to the bottom of the bed to prevent him from bending that knee. They operated on one testicle and found adhesions. I think that the other one might descend properly now without more surgery. Andy took along a Morse code key so he could work on his first-class requirements. He and his 11-year-old roommate happily buzz away all day. He will be hospitalized for a week.

Lisa asked to go bowling with her friend yesterday, but instead they skipped to the shopping mall with all their money, plus some of mine. Now she has lost one week's allowance, been grounded from bowling and movies, and restricted from playing with that friend. I offered to listen if she wanted to talk, but I refuse to worry about her, too, this week. If she makes herself sick, she brings it on herself.

April 21, 1963

Dear Mom,

This is a quickie because I am writing DURING den meeting. It takes an experienced den mother to manage that. The boys are outside working on an eight-foot corrugated cardboard submarine for our skit. As it will take a lot of whittling to cut through that heavy stuff, I sneaked a few moments.

Coming home from the hospital last night, I found a note in my kitchen.

"Mom, there is one treat left for Mike. How is Andy? I like him. Jason" After being at the hospital all day, I asked if he had been a good boy.

"Yep. Have you been a good mother today?" Hope I qualified, but as a pretty tired one.

April 30, 1963

Dear Mom,

Andy was thrilled with the fifty cents you sent. He's having trouble catching up with the world. He and Twinkle missed one 4-H dog obedience lesson and they frown on any absence.

Our skit worked great. We did a take-off on *Twenty Thousand Leagues under the Sea* complete with sound effects. We had constructed a ten-foot long submarine and the boys stood behind and walked it on and off the stage while one boy read excerpts from the book. We added realistic noises by dropping a box of kindling every time a ship was hit and sunk. My Cubs enthusiastically make noise.

If you're coming up this weekend could we paper the coat closet in the mud room? Dann is always busy and I'm afraid to paper by myself.

This was a good week. Tim came home from his den meeting with some official Cub Scout nail clippers which he won for getting the highest number of points for uniform inspection. I praised him for this. I commented on the Girl Scout Court of Awards because Lisa earned seven badges (Dann says I earned them, too). I mentioned how proud I was of Andy when he was elected assistant patrol leader. After all that, I found Jay curled up in the big chair waiting for me to say something, but lots of remarks about his advanced arithmetic straightened out everything.

My old college friends often talk about their frequent moves. We have created a feeling of permanency by being here so long and can be of more value in organizations if we last for more than one go-round. I love to walk the school halls where 75 percent of the children call me by name (results of Scouting). I enjoy singing in the church choir after 12 years and it thrills me to realize that our boys are fourth-generation Willetts attending Trinity Methodist Church. How fortunate that Dann is self-employed so we don't have to pull up roots and move.

P.S. We suddenly realized that Twinkle is expecting in two weeks. For the sake of her health, this is too soon. Don't tell the kids.

May 19, 1963

Dear Mom,

We've been having puppies. Lisa woke us at 6:00 a.m. when she heard crying in the garage. Twinkle birthed eleven, which Dann eliminated. We told the kids two days ago that we would need to do this for the sake of Twinkle's health. This made a vivid object lesson on why everybody must be SURE Twinkle doesn't get out when in heat. The children managed better than their mother who shed tears in private.

Last week we did a trial run campout and tested equipment for Philmont. Our tarp with new collapsible poles will work great not if, but when, the weather turns bad. With one extra blanket over every two sleeping bags and hooded sweat shirts we can withstand chilly nights in the mountains. We tried our new 35mm slide camera and we climbed the bluffs, but for three days I wished that we had quit sooner. We joined in a soup dump with the Four Lake Campers where everybody brings a can of soup and dumps into the common pot. This makes a great concoction after prolonged simmering. Best of all, when we came home, Dann backed into the garage and shifted the camping gear to the new camping shelves he has built, and unpacked in 15 minutes.

Bad news of the week: Lisa's mother is coming back this summer for a visit, we lost our social worker and have to suffer a new one, and one of my Cubs came down with mumps hours after our den meeting. Andy, my Scout den chief, has been thoroughly exposed.

May 23, 1963

Dear Mom,

Tomorrow Lisa and I leave for a Girl Scout campout at Devils' Lake. I hope Dann survives. He is working feverishly on three deals which doesn't make him a very reliable housekeeper.

Working on Dann's genealogy keeps me busy. When his grandfather immigrated to Madison, two sisters followed, but three siblings stayed behind in England and I am searching for information on that English branch.

May 31, 1963

Dear Mom,

This week has been monotonous as usual with nothing more exciting than Michael running pell mell and putting his hands through the combination storm door, a case of mumps in the middle of the Girl Scout campout, Andy blessed again with poison ivy, Andy and Twinkle getting their pictures in the newspaper during 4-H obedience class, badly sunburned faces from marching in the Memorial day parade, fervent worm business (Great Aunt Edna has set up the boys with a worm farm so she can buy worms from them when she goes fishing), Jason's birthday party on channel 15, a sick headache (me), an upset stomach (Jay) which we anticipated as mumps but wasn't, and a Homemaker picnic where we square danced in the rain. Mike shattered the glass storm door into millions of pieces and was cut across his wrist causing bleeding which was difficult to stop. I was pleased with my Boy Scout's first aid training as Andy told me exactly how to stop the bleeding. It was nice to know that he could have managed without me. Mike was lucky.

I took my Cubs on a mystery trip to the fire station and watched the firemen slide down the pole. We crossed the capitol square during peak afternoon traffic, stopping traffic effectively when I appeared on those busy streets with six small boys in uniform, one on crutches. The drivers assumed that we would never get across that street unless they stopped and waited.

My electricity is turned off. While using the dryer yesterday I lost half my power. I thought the dryer had knocked out a main fuse, but while talking to Timmy's den mother, her husband, an electrical engineer, took the phone and asked many questions. He thought considerable voltage might be jumping around in the basement so he came right over and fixed it. You remember, Dann and Pop always planned on rewiring the basement and never got around to it, but today professional electricians are finishing the job.

July 3, 1963

Dear Mom,

I have sometimes worried about this eventuality. When the kids were home alone today, they had an emergency. Dann had set up a house closing that required my signature. I thought about going down beforehand and signing blank papers, but Dann thought the closing would be short. I reminded each child to finish his chores and left Tim in charge (that title alternates between the top three). When we were delayed in the lawyer's office, I called home. The boys were building a tree fort in the woods and said everything was fine, but right after I called, Mike dropped a board with a protruding nail which penetrated deep into his big toe. I have wondered if there would be dissension among the kids if this occurred. There wasn't. They immediately deferred to Andy who took charge. He instructed everyone not to move Mike and took his temperature. Next he called the family doctor who told him to pull it out. The nail wouldn't budge so the doctor (still on the phone) told him to find a neighbor to remove it. He found one, but she was afraid to pull the nail out for fear this might start extensive bleeding, so she called the police. I inquired afterwards why they didn't take Mike to the doctor and let him remove it and learned that the board was 10 feet long. No wonder Mike dropped it. The police car, which arrived in one minute with flashing lights and siren, impressed the kids. The policeman removed the nail and Andy and the neighbor took Mike to the doctor's office. When we arrived home, the patient was resting on the couch where he had been told to stay. All were watching TV and didn't bother to tell us any of this until the commercial break. The doctor had put a Band-aid on his toe. Mike didn't even get a tetanus shot because he had one two weeks ago when he ran through the storm door. This produced guilt feelings for me because I wasn't home, but I couldn't have done any more than they did. I asked Andy if he had been worried about what to do but he said, "I learned in Boy Scouts how to treat a puncture wound, but they never said how to get the nail out of the puncture."

All five children are enrolled in Red Cross swimming lessons at the beach. They take lessons on different days so we are there by 10:00 every morning. I can't decide if this is good or bad for my work schedule. It does mean that my daily housework, the kids' chores, and a picnic lunch all have to be finished by 9:45.

Everyone does his fair share and fast. In one week Jay and Mike have advanced from being afraid of getting their faces wet to dead man floats and sitting on the bottom gathering treasures.

Aunt Edna took Timmy fishing and he caught his first fish on his new pole. I could hardly get the two of them to quit. The next time she took Andy, Timmy and their visiting cousin Peter, but when Dann went to pick them up, she frowned and muttered, "That article on fishing with children is right. Fishing with a child versus fishing with children makes a big difference." Apparently instead of watching lines these three spent most of their time climbing trees. Edna told Timmy she wants him to bring her a present from New Mexico and that it is not to cost anything, but be something God made.

June 27, 1963

Dear Mom,

More Philmont information has arrived. Sunday is family day when they send you off sightseeing supplied with a nosebag lunch. Once a week they barbecue buffalo. Horseback riding is available for those large enough to reach the stirrups, four hours at $2.00 /hour. Andy calculated that with his $12 in our safe, he could take five horseback rides or 20 hours. We'll leave on Friday giving us one extra travel day for emergencies.

We now have four kids practicing piano daily. Quiet house!!!

August 20, 1963

Dear Mom,

Thanks for keeping Twinkle. I'm sorry she gave you trouble. We didn't expect her to be homesick for us. Did it help when I sent Mike's dirty sock for her to smell? It was so late when we picked her up that we couldn't talk much, but we have many stories to tell.

We covered 7,000 miles, 15 states plus Mexico, 120 degrees to snowballs. The Philmont week, although we attended classes all morning, half the afternoon and all evening, was still a delightful rest with no meal preparation and no kids. We ate together in the cafeteria and then went separate ways. I put Mike on the small-fry ranch bus at 9:00 a.m. and met it again at 4:00. Mothers were told hands off, not to worry, not to help with projects like loading packs for a trail overnight, and especially not to turn up at the small-fry ranch as this disturbed the kids. The general idea was that if they needed us, THEY knew where WE were. The four older ones took three-hour horseback rides into the mountains. Lisa rode the first day and got altitude sickness. The boys didn't go until the last day and had no trouble as we were acclimated by then. One afternoon I dashed back to the tent for a needed raincoat and nearly collapsed. Altitude problems hadn't crossed my mind.

We lived in Tent City and were issued four tents with floors, electric lights, cots, and wardrobes. In the morning I attended classes on crafts: candle making, magic and puzzles, games, papier mache, masks, plaster of Paris molds, woodworking, song-leading, Indian dancing, goop-modeling and potato printing. Afternoons we did puppetry. Dann's class arose once at 4:30 a.m., went fishing deep in the mountains and enjoyed a fresh trout breakfast before coming back to camp. In extra moments we watched the boys make pinewood derby trucks (with no tools), square danced after evening class, visited the archaeological diggings at the base camp, and on family Sunday visited the Taos Pueblo Indians, taking a ski lift from the bottom of the Red River Valley up the mountain. One day I arrived home from class at 4:30 and announced to Dann, "My den didn't get our skit written in the 15 minutes of allotted class time, so we decided to hold a committee meeting here at my house. Would you like me to hold it in the family room of the tent or the bedroom?" He left, chuckling. We were forever finishing things in our tents that we couldn't complete in class.

After leaving Philmont, everybody wanted to fish so we found a beautiful scenic, isolated spot in the valley of Cimarron Canyon, laid our sleeping bags alongside the mountain stream and slept under the stars. It was an awesome night. Lightning spiked along the sides of the canyon, but produced no rain. I wished for a pocket edition of astrology under my pillow. What a classroom to study stars and from bed yet!

At Carlsbad, the hot weather caused us to concede to an air-conditioned motel and we stayed cool by swimming or by walking in the 56 degree cave temperature. The cave tour consists of walking four hours mostly steep downhill, but an elevator zooms you up 700 feet. They admitted all children under 12 free. When we presented only two tickets to the ranger, he looked us over and remarked, "You look more like a sponsored tour." The National Parks Service presents things in a natural state, so in the middle of the tour we sat while the ranger switched off the lights for 20 seconds of absolute silence. Complete stillness and darkness enveloped us.

We explored the Gila Cliff Dwellings in the Gila National Forest. This area is still underdeveloped and although the drive in was exciting for Dann and the kids, I must admit to cold feet. We drove 48 miles through a two-wheel track road, up and down mountains, switchbacks and along ridges through some wild scenery. The kids would shout, "Look at that. Don't you look Daddy, you drive." The man in town had remarked that the river was down. The importance of this soon became obvious as the two wheel tracks led to the creek, through and out the other side. Dann and the kids got out carefully walking through to see if the car could make it. By the time we reached the 28th ford he didn't even slow down. On the last one, Dann stopped in the middle, he and the kids jumped out, did a quick car wash and then we continued our journey.

We found a lovely isolated campsite. The entrance sign read "SUBJECT TO CLOSURE WITH ONE-HOUR NOTICE" and "DIFFICULT ACCESS WHEN WET." Soon after we bedded down in an open shelter, it commenced raining and continued all night. I lay there thinking about those dirt roads that get slippery when wet and the steep roads we had driven down, and wondered how many days food supply we carried, but in the morning the sun burst over the mountains and the roads dried immediately. One impressive thing about the Indian dwellings was the pint-size entrance doors. The ranger explained that often marauding Indians came looking for their neighbor's corn. If they had to bend over to get in the door, it was easy to hit them on the head with a big root and thus protect one's food supply.

We saw the Painted Desert and the Petrified Forest and, in ignorance, crossed the desert in the daytime, which turned out to be the hottest spot in the nation that day. We couldn't bear to stop to eat, but kept moving while munching sandwiches. It was even difficult to keep one's foot on the hot gas pedal.

Disneyland abruptly changed our life style. We arrived at 11:00 a.m. and left 12 hours later because I was cold and tired, which caused distress and yowling from the kids because the park didn't close for another hour and they hadn't seen everything yet. I thought those 75 rides, 14 hot dogs, 14 soft drinks, one pizza, tuna sandwiches, malts and popcorn filled one day to its brim and so I halted. It is an once-in-a-lifetime experience to enter Disneyland with five kids. Each of us held a coupon book for 10 rides. Don't even think that five kids might want the same 10 rides.

Turning eastward once more, we camped at Lake Mead and toured the Hoover Dam. That night we couldn't stand the heat inside our tent, stretched the sleeping bags out on the ground and tried not to think about snakes. Driving through Vegas in the cool of the morning we expected everything to be closed down because it was Sunday. Wrong!

We camped in the Grand Canyon National Park, hiking a small way down the mule trail discovering, to our surprise, that we walked faster uphill than down. We camped at the Colorado National Monument, an amazing 19 miles of rock formations and canyons, and drove through Rocky Mountain National Park going over the pass at 12,000 feet where the kids threw snowballs at their Dad. Suddenly we had seen enough and found that we could drive home in two days, a distance that had taken five days to drive out.

We are swamped trying to get five children ready for school, for this year Michael joins the ranks. Twinkle and I shall noisy up the house by ourselves every day. I am splurging with one last bit of summer fun, using my Philmont training, as we make hand sock puppets for a neighborhood show. I announced, "No puppet making until after lunch as work has to be done first."

Consequently, the universal comment, from the moment breakfast finishes is, "Gee, I'm starved. How soon can we eat lunch?"

It has been a wonderful summer.

SEPTEMBER 6, 1963

Dear Mom,

My family has deserted me. Dann took a trailer load of junk plus five kids to the dump. The boys are helping with several trips of trash because they borrowed a good saw from their Dad's workbench and left it forgotten in the woods for a month. Lisa goes along by choice. I worry about what they may bring back.

We are still making puppets. Our ghost play has seven characters which requires seven puppets. I have been conniving to get a proper puppet stage built instead of a draped ironing board, but my husband doesn't show much enthusiasm. I mentioned to Dann that he was lucky I wasn't asking him for a six-foot hole, like I once persuaded Pop to dig for a kiln. Dann graciously donated all his old window screens for the stage and then mysteriously disappeared.

Yes, we would love to come down this weekend.

SEPTEMBER 18, 1963

Dear Mom,

Lisa and I are struggling with her complicated finances. She needs to pay back what she has lifted from some of us and still be able to finance birthday presents. With a triple family, her birthday giving grows like Topsy. She commented that she didn't really care whether she was here or in some other foster home and that really rocked my boat. If I can't keep from being upset, we're all done. I need to know that she wants to be here, but in the evening she met me at the door exclaiming, "I want to stay here!" This was the result of a long talk with Dann after he had put everybody else to bed.

But the Lord obviously didn't mean for me to spend the entire weekend worrying about her and He provided other distractions. Two of Dann's brothers with their families came for supper and the 12 children chased over to the school playground. Suddenly they streamed back screaming, "Jay broke his finger." He had fallen on the blacktop which bent his little finger backwards at 90 degrees.

He told me afterwards, "I didn't cry much, Mommy, but every time I looked at it, it hurt more!" The doctor met Dann and George at the clinic. Jay had dislocated that finger, the doctor jerked it hard and it slipped back into place. Jay will wear a splint for a week to allow the tendons to recuperate.

My Sunday school class constantly challenges me. One fatherless student is basically non-English speaking and has behavior problems. I drafted him as my helper and insisted he do things my way or sit in the corner. This worked until the minister's wife sailed into class and immediately disciplined that kid. Afterwards I said, "I'm glad to know you are around where I can ask for help if I need it. But I was aware of his problem and it wasn't the right time to fuss over a minor point." If there is any one thing that I have learned with Lisa, it's that I can't change Rome in a day.

SEPTEMBER 26, 1963

Dear Mom,

Our two Junior High students enthusiastically signed up for Band. They took musical aptitude tests to determine which instruments they are best fitted for, but the bandmaster told Andy that as long as he has a cornet (Dann's) he can start on that although he would be better on something else. We got out my clarinet and Andy agreed to switch. Timmy, with great speed and enthusiasm, latched onto the cornet and moved it under his bed although he has two years to wait. When Lisa came home from school, Andy and I were sitting in the middle of the living room floor while I showed him how to blow a clarinet. Timmy was occupying a chair but with his head on the floor blowing viciously on the cornet. Jay was practicing piano and Mike, in self defense, got out the bugle and contributed from the corner. Lisa listened and then asked, "What's going on here?" Andy tried to tell the others to be quiet because he couldn't play with all that noise, but I told him to get over that. We are renting an instrument for Lisa because she also chose clarinet.

In order to get our Junior Highers to school on time we moved our alarm to 6:30 a.m. Now the younger three, who only go next door to Crestwood Elementary, eat a leisurely breakfast, do their chores and still arrive at school early. Tim rushes around after breakfast cutting out news clippings for extra credit. Woe to the person who doesn't read the daily newspaper on time. As he has to discuss his clippings, we spend breakfast discussing school riots in Alabama, etc. We made a deal. If he can raise his grades by one mark in his last year's problem classes, I will finance a movie. Now he's proudly tearing home each day with 100s in spelling and Arithmetic.

Mike does fine. I remember how faithfully I walked Andy to and from kindergarten the first week. The first day of school Tim and Jay decided it wasn't necessary for their Dad to walk with Mike. They could do it. The second day all three tore out of here so fast that I could barely remind them to walk Mike to his class door. Mike told me afterwards that first Jay and then Tim got lost amongst all the people. I inquired, "What did you do then?"

He replied nonchalantly, "I didn't need them. I just went by myself."

We have two females left behind after the school day commences. One of us is entranced with all the work that she can now accomplish in one morning. The other one spends hours lying in the driveway listening and watching the school grounds.

I have certainly been humbled this last year. Not long ago I thought I could manage any child, but there's no doubt in my mind now that if it weren't for all the helping hands around here Lisa and I would have parted long ago: her psychiatrist and his social worker, the county social worker and my two friends who listen during my down times and understand because they also have foster girls.

Lisa took more of my money and then lied. She arrived home two hours late after school because she met her friend plus three boys and they goofed around in a store. When she went over to the same friend's house, five boys showed up and they found some beer lying in the apple orchard which they drank. She smuggled stockings and lipstick to school because she knows she's not supposed to wear either at school, and has repeatedly lied when we both know she is lying. All this makes Dann furious. We are tired of having Lisa's problems monopolize the conversation every day.

October 10, 1963

Dear Mom,

There are not many places where we can visit with our large crew, but one is the farm in Shawano with Winnie, my college roommate and her husband, Don. Other college friends also came last weekend, totaling 18. The kids slept in the haymow with sleeping bags. The birth of two calves disrupted breakfast. It upset Jay that he was summoned in to eat, but he didn't miss much. He just speeded up breakfast. The rest of the kids were more concerned with eating until Jay came back and reported that the calf had half arrived. That emptied the table instantly. Don took the children up on the tractor and let them help drive. Jason is determined to be a farmer. He followed Don constantly asking questions. When he found Don relaxing, he announced that the barn was pretty dirty. So in the middle of Sunday afternoon, Jason and Don cleaned it with the automatic barn cleaner.

Lisa is making herself sick again and I don't know what's bothering her. The county is considering dropping her psychiatrist visits because they cost too much.

Dann premiers as Cubmaster tonight. I am trying to convince him that he will be a natural at this as soon as he overcomes his nervousness. With his sales pitch and my organization mania, we make a great team. We made lists like crazy—questions to bring to the committee, jobs that we need help with, etc. When I mentioned that we might have 100 parents tonight, that almost finished him. He would prefer to be one of the 100 listening rather than the one leading. My Cubs are putting on a ghost skit about fire prevention using shadow puppets.

Could you come for Thanksgiving and stay for a few days?

October 25, 1963

Dear Mom,

The pack meeting rolled without a hitch with Dann performing superbly. We have six more little boys so Dann will go calling again to find another den mother. The committee meeting also went well. After making a list of projects and responsibilities for the whole year Dann pointed out how much easier it is to discuss things in advance so someone other than the Cubmaster is primarily responsible for specific projects. Some volunteered, some got drafted and now we have a committee of three for each month to present theme ideas for den meetings and pack programming, a committeeman responsible for the Christmas party, one for the Blue and Gold banquet, one for the spring picnic, and one for registration. We're aiming for a rocking chair Cubmaster.

Last year's United Nations dinner turned out so well that we tried again. I made Russian Borscht, Kolacky (Polish rolls filled with strawberry jam), Chinese sweet and sour spareribs, Italian Ravioli, Hungarian torte and Dutch tea cakes. Dann didn't think this was representative of the United Nations as I picked almost all Communistic nations. The kids are apprehensive about new recipes, but they try everything and freely give opinions. Jason was indignant when nobody at school knew what United Nations Day was.

Dann's Aunt Nell is spending a week with us soon.

November 6, 1963

Dear Mom,

  We finally performed our neighborhood puppet show. All my kids make excellent puppeteers and hosts. We set the draped ironing board between the living and dining rooms. The boys greeted guests at the door, took coats, and afterwards served Halloween cookies they had decorated. Fifteen guests attended, NO grownups. That was accidental. I asked mothers if they would like to come, but none did. I, being backstage manager, couldn't supervise audience behavior which made me apprehensive, but they behaved like perfect ladies and gentlemen making no noise except laughing appropriately.

  Lisa celebrated her 12th birthday, her Mother phoned, her Dad took her out to supper, and we baked a birthday cake with purple (by request) frosting. She and a friend have been working on their Scout outdoor cooking badge and needed to do a cookout for 10 people before next March, or they would lose credit for what they've already done. Although it was snowing, they cooked outside for both families.

  Our littlest one leads a full social life: Monday he invited Jane over, Tuesday Terry, Wednesday he cancelled because his cough precipitated the loss of his lunch, Thursday he went to Steve's, Friday he got mixed up and invited both Creighton and Susan and had to un-invite Susan. His teacher thinks he shows potential leadership ability. This comes as a shock to me since he is the baby of the family.

  Jay popped a new question, "How does rain get in the ground?" and "Why is it clean?" We talked and then I suggested he should ask Daddy when he came home.

  Jay replied, "Oh I know the answers from school. I just wanted to see what you would say."

  Once a day Tim hassles his Dad to help him build a rabbit hutch for 4-H. He needs to hurry as he is required to raise eight litters in the next nine months, two does with four litters each. He expects this to be a moneymaking venture.

He is also working on Goodwill for Cubs, doing something for somebody else without being asked. I throw out hints which he usually picks up readily. I mentioned three times that I didn't have time to take my baked goods to school until finally he said, "Mom, I know what you're hinting, but I really don't want to do that."

Aunt Nell gets a bang out of these goodwill projects. She falls asleep in our recliner frequently, but wakes up instantly when something interesting occurs.

I walked to the neighbors the other night because she thought her twins were imminent (they weren't) and commented when I came home that that was my goodwill for the day.

"Oh that doesn't count," Aunt Nell objected. "You didn't do that without being asked."

Yes, we need mittens again.

December 5, 1963

Dear Mom,

This is the week of the COAT. It's a great idea for you to give me a fur coat for Christmas IF we can make this work. How old is that coat we found in the chest in Auntie Beth's attic? It has beautiful fur but such a funny style. Those huge ballooning sleeves, coming down to a tight wrist, must date it. That length provides enough material for restyling. We took it to four Madison furriers. One said he would have to add pelts even to make a 3/4 length, the leather is too dry and deteriorated, and putting in additional money would be throwing money away as the fur is liable to rip. Another said it would make a valuable coat, but he was too busy. He called it Minnesota muskrat, a lightweight, especially hardy and highly-recommended skin. We learned everything we ever want to know about furs. We'll try the Delavan furrier. This sounds like the real estate business where everybody tells you a different story and the customer has to figure out which salesman knows what he's talking about. Thanks again.

December 20, 1963

Dear Mom,

I took Mike to the dentist to have his infected tooth pulled. The dentist asked, "What happened?"

"Andy was picking up the living room," Mike replied reluctantly. "I charged him and I missed!"

Mike keeps a daily count on how many days until Christmas, and the number of packages under Mommy's bed. I can't clean there until after Christmas. I attended the Crestwood Christmas program as Tim sings in the boys' choir, Andy's Christmas concert at the Junior High, and Lisa's Home Economics class Christmas tea. How do mothers who work outside of the home manage this?

Mike has set the table for our traditional oyster stew tonight and his other grandmother is coming. See you soon.

January 7, 1964

Dear Mom,

It's difficult to find letter writing time when Dann needs his books closed by January 15. I cancelled everything except a trip to Lisa's psychiatrist and two den meetings, and am trying to do the impossible. After I get the books closed I am going to play the piano 30 minutes each day, no matter what. I desperately need me time.

My new, old fur coat is gorgeous. That little German furrier is one of a kind. He never hesitated to take that funny-looking coat and turn it into something beautiful, but he gave me a big lecture about the pockets I wanted. "Vat you want pockets for when you mus' not use them? It spoils ze lines of ze coat to jam hands into pockets."

Lisa is enrolled in confirmation class and in a Junior Life Saving course and she and I are working at my losing weight. I cut down on food intake and she counts the calories. I am starved. We had another long bedtime talk and for now she is doing everything possible to please us.

January 16, 1964

Dear Mom,

Notice that date! I made it and am proud. To balance my cash I ran 10 feet of tape and came out with a two-cent error. However, because of my new system I could spot immediately which month was off and found the error in two hours instead of the two weeks it would have taken last year.

Lisa's mother postponed her visit again and Lisa has been home sick for three days. I requested the department not to notify us in advance of her Mother's visits. Two hours' notice would be adequate.

The rabbit hutch construction is finally underway.

Mike has been asking how a water faucet works. Dann brought a Chicago faucet from the basement and showed everyone how it turns and blocks the pipe when the faucet is off. Mike laid it out to take to kindergarten for Show and Tell as he plans on instructing his entire class.

February 6, 1964

Dear Mom,

We hate this weather. The snow forts built to last the winter have slithered away, the toboggan slides are closed, the skating rinks are flooded, the Scout Klondike was cancelled and the ratio of indoor to outdoor mud increases daily. Basketballs have come out as three of the boys practice in the schoolyard. Unfortunately they continue to practice their dribbling in the house and this, in addition to 50 repeats of Lisa's new Singing Nuns record, and a spurt of business which caused Dann to work all weekend plus three evenings last week, makes me feel that the days are indeed getting longer. Sometimes I am so tired I just sit on my couch. All the kids' grades have slipped. I'm going to have to come up with more inspiration somehow.

Dann and I took our dens on a joint field trip to City Hall. We looked at the tear gas storage, the shooting range, sat through bicycle court, inspected the gymnasium and the physical fitness equipment, and took a trip through the jail complete with remote control door locks. Scout field trips turn out to be educational for the leaders also.

My evening supervision stretched too thin last night. I zoomed from checking Jay's school report on rabbits, to helping Andy out of a jam for patrol meeting plans, to assisting Tim make new liquid rubber molds so we can duplicate Philmont slides, to explaining 2/2 time to Lisa so she can play The American Patrol for her band test tomorrow and suddenly I wondered why Mike hadn't emerged from his bath. I went to offer assistance and found he wasn't using either soap or wash cloth. I objected but he countered, "Mom, when you stay as long as I do, it just floats off."

I need to go just sit on my new couch some more.

February 13, 1964

Dear Mom,

Today is gorgeous but like the beginning of winter over again. Everybody scurried for strayed boots and mittens that haven't been used for a month. Timmy's rain gauge filled with snow. Dann, who wasn't keeping up-to-date on badge work, came into the house last night asking indignantly, "Who left that pail and ruler cluttering up the front yard?" Things are not always what they appear to be in this house.

We have been playing the stock market on paper. Everyone had two choices so now we have part interest in US Steel, Standard Oil, DuPont, General Foods, AT&T, Rexall, Coca Cola, Northwest Air, Pepsi Cola, Ford Motor, Phillips Petroleum, Minneapolis Honeywell, General Dynamics and Chrysler. This is called diversification. I am leading the pack at losing.

The kids loved their valentines.

March 5, 1964

Dear Mom,

I sit here in the middle of the living room because this is the only place to sit. Lisa says kids make a mess, but bigger people make bigger messes. Painting Dann's study was taking a tiger by the tail, we couldn't let go. We scraped off old calcimine paint, scrubbed it three times and painted the walls sky blue. After all that, Dann decided he didn't want such a crummy ceiling and hired a carpenter to put up new dry wall. We sanded, stained, and varnished the woodwork and resealed the floor. We need to move stuff back soon. I can't find anything and wandered around for five minutes looking for something, but couldn't remember what I was looking for, much less find it. Mike helped sand the woodwork yesterday. After he got covered with sand-dust he hugged me and declared, "I sure do love you Mommy, especially when you let me help work."

Jay asks daily when he can become a Cub Scout. He walks around with the application form in hand memorizing the Bobcat qualifications. He keeps besieging his Dad to sign the application, which gives permission for the child to join and also agrees, on the part of the parent, to help if needed. His Dad gave him a hard time. "I'm already busy. I don't think I should agree to help with anything more." Jason keeps asking if I've washed his shirt yet so it is ready and he dissolved in tears this morning because I wouldn't listen to him recite the promise. As we have to hold him back for another month, I am not anxious to listen. Tim is in his father's Webelos den, busy learning the Boy Scout promise and ready to move up.

It's good you couldn't see us yesterday. The living room is still piled with the study furniture and rolled up rugs, Andy conducted his patrol meeting in the dining room, papers from Tim and Lisa's homework littered the kitchen table, and Dann dropped tools over the rest of the kitchen. The kitchen drain backed up and Dann started to fix it but got called away. Timmy asked, "Daddy, what makes that sink throw up?" Fortunately the size of our house allows me to move away from the mess.

This has been a bad week for Dann. Tuesday morning he took off work to help the carpenter put up drywall in the study, Wednesday afternoon he took off work to watch Tim's school puppet play. The teacher had taped the speaking parts in advance so that all the kids could help with scenery and acting. They used marionettes and I'm surprised that so many feet and hands worked backstage without a traffic control problem. Dann took off Thursday afternoon to unplug the kitchen sink. Again this morning he took time for massive snow removal. Those of us who don't have to shovel think the snow utterly beautiful.

I don't see any way to cut down on Andy's activities. With parents like his, how could he be different? Maybe he could organize his time better. Jay inherited two of Andy's dish wiping nights, as he is now old enough. I lectured Andy on the advantages of lists. Frequently he doesn't do first things until last. I thought he was beginning to catch up on daily activities until the school nurse called to say Andy wasn't feeling well. I was feeling lousy myself and then Dann came home and collapsed on the third and last couch.

Lately the phone occupies all my time. I am searching for a purebred Hertsford male collie for loan, two New Zealand White does for Tim, a clown outfit for the Cubmaster to wear to the Mardi Gras pack meeting next week, a slate of new officers for my Homemaker Club, transportation and menus for Dann and the 22 Webelos Scouts he's taking out Saturday to observe the Scout campout.

What would life be like without telephones!

April 23, 1964

Dear Mom,

I talked to the Van Hise guidance teacher because Lisa came home late for supper declaring she had to stay after school when she didn't. From now on, if she gets kept after school the teacher will give her a signed note. It made Lisa mad that I checked on her. The guidance counselor and I also discussed Andy. She looked up Andy's records and his grades have slipped. Granted Andy has tough competition because we placed him in a gifted class. Sometimes he produces excellent work, sometimes just enough to get by. The counselor blames lack of motivation. In elementary grades kids do well in school to please parents. Andy has grown past that, but hasn't matured enough to want to satisfy himself so he muddles around. She advised us not to allow Andy to goof like this and suggested we set a standard. If he doesn't measure up, remove a privilege. We told him, "You're capable of better grades if you'd work at it, so you have two weeks to improve your grades. Otherwise, we'll take privileges starting with your cafeteria job."

This upset him tremendously. We kept saying that in spite of being in an advanced class we knew he could do better, that we would be happy to help in any way he asked, but that it was his responsibility to make acceptable grades. After all that fuss he gave his Dad a big affectionate bear hug and said, "Gee, you're an old meanie." Last night he informed me that his social science is now a B+. These two weeks are going to be hard on me because I feel uneasy when I see him playing and know he hasn't completed his homework and I can't ride him about it now.

We found the first two tenants for Timmy's new rabbit hutch. Snow White is a six-month New Zealand White female ready for breeding, and Black Jet is a three-month, midnight black, cuddly non-pedigreed darling.

We've been trying to get our Cubs concerned about littering. One day after school the entire pack policed the school grounds. We theorize that a child who picks up litter will not throw it down.

I have a new den, Jason's. I have taken each of our sons for their first year in Cubbing, and then given those dens to others so my sons wouldn't always have Mom for den mother. My seven new boys are already working on a skit, a take-off from the Jungle Book: Mowgli, a ferocious tiger, a bear, panther, and three wolves.

May 21, 1964

Dear Mom,

Pack meeting week always produces a busy time and this ole house is bursting with activities. Our Indian pow-wow pack meeting is tonight. The tom-tom sits in my kitchen where every child coming through gravitates to it pounding out a constant boom-boom which reverberates through the house. We made the drum heads from inner tubes, lacing with soft leather thongs from scraps leftover from my Occupational Therapy days. We tightened and retightened the laces to get better resonance. My Cubs drew straws to determine who would present it formally to the pack. Jay won. We painted a thunderbird on one drum head, a Webelos arrow of light on the other and Indian sign language around the barrel. I fitted Chief Akela (Dann) in an old Indian tunic I found in my costume box, some dangly costume jewelry, splashed some textile paints on the back of the tunic, made wristlets with bells and borrowed Andy's black-braided Indian headdress. Tonight the big chief will present his third son with his first award (Bobcat) and present his second son with his last award (Webelos). A memorable occasion.

May 26, 1964

Dear Mom,

I am finally reaching a point where things don't always upset me. Today my German measles patient is entertaining my broken arm patient or vice versa. By the looks of Timmy, who is collapsed on the couch with chills, another measles case may develop by tomorrow. Dann went to get fitted for a new contact lens to replace the one which sank to the bottom of the West High pool when he took the troop swimming. Mike fell off the teeter-totter hours after Dann brought it home. Mike looked okay, but complained his wrist hurt if he moved it. Both wrist bones were fractured and his right arm is casted from fingertips to elbow.

Andy came home from school yesterday feeling sick. Today red polka dots cover his face. I suppose we have to wait weeks for the other kids to blossom.

Pack meeting was a roaring success. Our district executive called it one of the most impressive pack meetings he's seen. This may backfire as sometimes it's better to hide one's light under a bushel. Just running one pack swamps us and we certainly don't want to advance up that ladder, but we gloated over his comment anyhow.

We instructed the committeemen to come in Indian dress, at least a blanket, and I've never seen a more startling bunch of blood-curdling Indians. They removed their glasses, no self-respecting Indian wears glasses, and sat around our artificial campfire, beating the new tom-tom. When they started handing out awards to the young braves, Dann's panic-stricken eyes zeroed in on me and I realized Chief Akela was in big trouble out there in front of everybody. He held a long list of awards to present, but without glasses could not read. I quickly drafted a Cub to take the glasses undercover to the big chief. Dann has been trying to find the time for needed haircuts for the boys, so just before pack meeting, he asked Tim if he wouldn't like a Mohawk. Timmy, not knowing what that was, agreed. Dann left a two-inch strip from forehead to back of the neck, but he trimmed the rest to almost nothing. By the time Dann finished, Tim had developed reservations—too late, so Tim talked Jay into one also so he would have company. They created the sensation of the evening. The next morning Dann trimmed the strip, but it will take another week before they're presentable.

May 29, 1964

Dear Mom,

Infirmary report. I need to correct my erroneous layman's diagnosis. No German measles, but a strep throat with a rash. Dann complained of a sore throat so when he took Mike in to have his wrist checked, the doctor took a throat culture from Dann. This turned out positive strep so we took everybody in and all the boys checked positive. Only the women in this family are healthy. I took the boys back for shots and Jay is very unforgiving. He exclaimed, "You know, Mom, I've been through lots of stuff in the hospital, but I would rather you just let me march in the Memorial Day parade on Saturday. Then I'll get sick, instead of taking that shot in my seater by a girl yet!"

We're not done, yet. Andy is apparently allergic to the penicillin he was given which caused his face and hands to swell enormously. The kids don't feel too bad. Andy and Timmy set up shop every morning in the middle of the living room including pillows, blankets, books, puzzles, cards, magazines, and stamp collections. I hope we don't have unexpected company.

June 2, 1964

Dear Mom,

We are all healthy, some of us bouncing with vim and vitality after a week's rest. Andy recovered quickly when we started giving him medicine to counteract the original medicine, but he is on the never-never list for penicillin now. Mike climbs like a monkey with that stiff cast and manages better than some less handicapped persons. On the glider he wrapped his cast around to hold on so he could use his good arm for climbing. I cannot bear watching.

Every time we drive by West High we hear a chant in unison from the rear seats, "Here lays Father's contact lens, sunk to the bottom of the deeps".

We have added Peter, a Belgian hare, to our family. Peterina, I'm afraid. A Crestwood family bought him at Eastertide, he grew up, they can't keep him any longer and they discovered that Timmy was in the business. Tim went to look at him — or it — and they've been inseparable since. The family assured us that he wouldn't run away, but when we turned around he disappeared into the woods. His tricolor camouflages so well that when he doesn't move, our chances of finding him are nil. We encircled the area where we thought he was, working Twinkle back and forth until the rabbit bolted. I lay at ground level shouting directions, while five kids and Twinkle charged madly around much to the amusement of neighbors. Peter is now contained in his new pen and appears tame and cuddly.

We finally went canoeing with both canoes. I made sandwiches and we explored the back swamps of the Arboretum. Don't worry, we canoed narrow, shallow creek ways and we strapped Mike's life preserver around him, cast and all.

June 19, 1964

Dear Mom,

Darn. We've tried and tried to breed Twinkle. Now that we're willing, she's not. We counted our chickens too soon as we not only planned how to spend that Twinkle money, but we spent it on the second canoe. Right now, we can't even get our rabbits to multiply.

We dropped Andy at the dorm on campus where he will be living during the music clinic. I wanted to help him find his classrooms, but Dann picked me up by the collar and said, "So long, Andy, have fun." Each room has a telephone, but we told him not to call home except in case of emergency. He called the first day. His clarinet fell off a chair and the mouthpiece broke. Would we see if he could borrow a mouthpiece from Cousin Steve? Dann delivered. The second day Andy called again. When he ate an apple his braces locked in place and he couldn't close his mouth. Dann picked him up and delivered him to the home of our orthodontist who removed the brace temporarily. The third day he asked, "Would we bring down his poison ivy stuff as he was breaking out." The dorm nurse told him rubbing alcohol would control it, but Andy knew better. Again Dann delivered. The fourth day he said that he forgot to bring nail clippers. Would we bring him a pair because there was a cute girl on the next floor and he needed clippers? No, we wouldn't.

Two weeks ago we notified the Department of Public Assistance that we cannot continue like this with Lisa, but they asked us to reconsider. As she has been so remarkably good since we told them that, we are re-thinking. We spent our weekend mulling over pros and cons and came up with what Dann calls his counter-offer. We want four weeks separation and suggested Blackhawk Girl Scout camp, no more parent visitation or considerably less, and money for piano lessons.

Mike's arm did not stiffen up. We managed to get it clean after that cast came off and we could wash his hand. It didn't stay clean for long as he went to work with his Dad this afternoon. Dann is building a new house and sometimes he allows one boy to help. The kids refer to this house as the hole. That is an apt description right now.

July 15, 1964

Dear Mom,

The department partially granted our requests for Lisa and will send her to camp for two weeks.

This is Dane County Junior Fair week for our two 4-H kids. Tim has built carrying cages for his exhibition rabbits. Lisa made a moving picture toy to exhibit. We discovered that bedlam prevails on the day prior to opening day. Wandering cows and confused people swamp the roads as supply trucks unload, and the loudspeaker blares constantly with instructions. Tim won two second place ribbons with his rabbits. We had to be there early because of the judging and by the time I got out of bed, Tim and Mike had their chores done and breakfast made for all of us.

I have a new summer project. Every Thursday night, the four older children take turns being chef. They plan the menu, shop, cook, and clean up. They can plan anything they want with a limit of $2.00 to feed seven of us. Milk, plus anything in the freezer or garden, does not count so if they splurge on one thing they compensate with home items.

Tim produced fried chicken, peas, raspberries and marble cake. He insisted on gravy. I showed him how to mix flour and water together. When I turned around he had disappeared and was yelling into the other room, "Hey, you guys, did you know Mom puts paste in the gravy?" I wasn't too happy about his frosting either. He chose seven-minute chocolate. I insisted it had to hold a peak. To check, he pulled the beaters up looking for the peak without turning the mixer off.

We're going camping to High Cliff State Park this weekend. Lisa needs to plan menus and chore lists for everybody as part of a badge she's working on, except for Sunday dinner when Andy is cooking Boy Scout spaghetti (spaghetti made with pemmican).

This week Jay cooked: hamburgers, beans from Mike's garden, cucumbers from Jay's, raspberries from mine, and homemade vanilla ice cream cranked in our old ice cream maker.

August 15, 1964

Dear Mom,

We've always dreamed of going to the Minnesota Boundary Waters and with Lisa gone to Girl Scout camp we squeezed into two canoes plus gear and Twinkle. Collies ought to come smaller. We accomplished this by laying out the essentials next to the canoes. Next we reaffirmed the cubic footage inside the canoes and took away 25% of the stuff that wasn't as essential as we originally thought, repeating this process until we fit. Andy and I planned the dehydrated food for six people for five days and this went into Timmy's pack, plus his clothes. We originally planned to carry tarps and no tent, as our tent weighs 80 pounds. I think Dann feared we'd sink the canoes but at the last minute we changed our decision and carried a tent anyhow. We started with the wind at our backs. Not being able to find the designated campsite on our fifty-cent waterproof map, late in the afternoon we settled for a satisfactory island and set up camp. The tent putter-upper got frustrated when he discovered we had picked an island of solid rock. Besides he couldn't find a clearing in the woods level enough to pitch a tent. Not being level makes for cuddly sleeping. It comes naturally to the boys to cook, eat, and do dishes squatting on the ground. They also assume that everything cooked on an open fire comes automatically peppered with soot.

 Then the rains came. Those who had argued in favor of the tent rejoiced that they had won. For one whole day we budged out of that tent for one reason only. That is too long to coop up four bundles of energy. The next day we packed up and turned homeward, docking in pouring rain. This is the first time that we have had to use every bit of foul weather and cold weather gear, sometimes all at once. The boys loved it, rain and all.

 Lisa returned from camp. She missed us and we are temporarily one big, happy family. She loves her piano lessons and practices hard. The boys work just as hard to avoid practicing. Her Thursday night meals raise us to levels of gourmet cooking. Six of us sampled artichokes for the first time.

August 24, 1964

Dear Mom,

As soon as we returned home from your house we set up a corn assembly line, everybody working at tasks according to their ability and we froze 16 quarts in three hours. We rewarded our working crew by going swimming. Tomorrow we'll tackle the pears you gave us. We've been eating like mad, but can't eat that fast. Jason and I made dill and sweet pickles.

We've had so much trouble breeding Peterina that we consulted our rabbit expert and he tells us that all Tim's bunnies are bucks. That would do it, wouldn't it? I think they will shortly, all but one, hit the frying pan.

September 10, 1964

Dear Mom,

School has started. For the first time everyone leaves by 8:30 and doesn't come home until 3:15. This delighted me so that I promptly registered for a Bookkeeping class for three hours a week. If this proves more than I can manage, then I will have gained by however many weeks I last. I agree with you that I should cut out something. What?

Dann and Andy spent Labor Day weekend building a dog house in the corner of the garage using scrap lumber. Twinkle moved in practically with the first nail. I spent the weekend on the other side of the garage forlornly trying to decide what to throw out so that we can put cars in before winter.

The boys built four forts in our pine woods, one a tree fort. Last night Tim and his buddy slept out there.

I can think of one activity I would cheerfully like to cut back on—chasing rabbits in the woods every morning. They escape from their hutches often. I look out my bedroom window the first thing after arising and usually spot bits of white popping around in the green underbrush. As time is of an essence on school mornings, this means everybody up on the double. From experience the kids have learned how to approach this. Never chase a rabbit you want to catch. Half the posse quietly circles around deep into the woods and then starts driving back towards the hutches, hopefully into somebody's waiting arms. They use superb teamwork and surprisingly make school on time.

SEPTEMBER 18, 1964

Dear Mom,

    I have attended three bookkeeping classes and I love it. My instructor tries us on questions that are the exception rather than the rule and it's the exceptions that snarl me up. He explained the difference between assets and liabilities, and labeled accounts receivable as assets. We have some assets that are liabilities when we have to take them to court for collection.

    Twinkle thinks it's boring and monotonous around here all day, but I disagree as things are beginning to get done. It's a new experience to eat lunch by myself.

    It gets harder and harder to keep track of Lisa.

SEPTEMBER 22, 1964

Dear Mom,

    Michael can read and his excitement knows no bounds. He reads his book aloud six times, once for each of us, before his audience gives out. All this on a vocabulary of 17 words.

Jason brought homework from Sunday school, a bunch of yes or no questions. He got stuck on "does God exist in a body such as ours?" His problem was that he thought God didn't, but he didn't know. He wasn't satisfied to put "I don't know" when it asked for either yes or no, and he wasn't willing to settle for "no" without any proof.

When the Savings & Loan downtown moved into a new building they held an open house. Dann, as a realtor, got a special invitation. All the ordinary customers received invitations too, which includes the boys. Jay was surprised when he got a letter from his bank and remarked, "I don't know why they would write to me unless the bank has been robbed." Perhaps this open house gave him a wider understanding of a bank's functions.

Tim has attended his first Troop meeting. With one month before the city-wide camporee he has to pass his tenderfoot requirements if he wants to go. He was already working on those requirements last spring, so he should make it. At Andy's camporee last year it rained all weekend and half the troops went home. Our troop then walked off with all the top honors. That's getting it by default?

Everybody has agreed it's time to butcher rabbits as soon as we figure out how. The last time the rabbits got out because one was apparently looking for Mr. MacGregor's garden, they made it all the way to the schoolyard. This happened in the middle of a favorite TV show so the boys decided the rabbits' days were numbered. This morning I dragged myself out of bed, and glancing out the window beheld a fluffy, golden cat perched on top of the hutch licking her chops and carefully studying exits and entrances. I yelled for reinforcements and before that cat could say meow, Dann let the dog out who gave chase simultaneously with Tim's firing his BB gun from the second story window. I wouldn't recommend this.

We dropped Andy and a friend at the University stadium Saturday to watch the football game. They hung around the gate until they were able to pick up tickets for fifty cents apiece. We told them they'd have to get home on their own, by bus or by walking. They walked. Straight home would have been down University Avenue, but they deviated through two cemeteries, up into Hoyt Park, down the cliff, through the University Hill Farms and over all the barbed wire fences. Yes, they were tired.

Lisa has been having so much trouble with her feet that I took her to the specialist who recommended special shoes. No more tennis shoes. This angered her. All eighth graders wear tennis shoes. Gradually she has stopped fussing and goes off peacefully each morning wearing the correct shoes.

SEPTEMBER 30, 1964

Dear Mom,

Now I see why she conceded the shoes issue peacefully. I watched at the second floor bedroom window this morning as she trudged down our long driveway. Just before she reached the street, she reached under the bushes and produced the coveted tennis shoes plus a pair of nylons. Up flipped the skirt, a quick changeover took place, the hated shoes were dropped under the bush and she continued to school. I should have anticipated this. Trouble is that I don't think like a teenager.

Tim returned to school today after a week home with a bad, bad side ache. He improved temporarily and got up, but then the side ache returned forcing him back to bed. The doctor still thinks this is psychosomatic, but we question this.

Today the only patient I have to contend with is a rabbit with infectious ear mites. This requires a financial decision. Is it better to treat her, absorb the cost of the medical bills and run the risk of infecting the other ten or would it be better to destroy her now? Unfortunately she is due to kindle in one week.

My bookkeeping class continues to delight me. I begin to see the reason for doing things a certain way.

I am teaching a city training session for den mothers. This encompasses tricks and magic, genius kits, woodcraft, tin can craft and scrap projects. My assistants help me prepare demonstration samples. Jay is making me a wiener stick to show. Tim was working on toothpick creations until he felt better and went back to school. I tried a magic knot on the boys at breakfast time and afterwards overheard, "Boy, have we got a clever Mommy."

"No, she just reads a clever book." Perhaps it wasn't so clever to show them using my kitchen towel, as every time I've gone through the kitchen since, I've had to de-knot my towel.

October 21, 1964

Dear Mom,

Dann held an open house for the house he built, previously referred to as THE HOLE. A million little things still needed doing so he drafted the whole family to help and they earned Christmas money. We scrubbed stickers off windows and sinks, watered sod, buried pipes in the backyard, carried loads of trash from the basement and burned it in the backyard, scraped plaster off the basement cement floor and washed mud off the siding. Awfully dirty kids came home. The kitchen cabinet cardboard boxes intrigued them and when tired they would pop into a box to rest. Several boys could fit into each box. When Jay discovered that I was exhausted, he offered to let me sit in his box. We strung colored pennants in the front yard alongside open house signs. Lisa and I set a card table in the kitchen and laid out orange chrysanthemums, coffee and colored cookies we had made in the cookie press. Many people came so we felt satisfied.

I held my first den meeting today. Dann delayed starting the pack because we needed one more den mother. He has decided that nobody starts until there's a place for all. This puts pressure everywhere as people ask continually if we've found one yet. My den has 11. Yesterday after school three boys knocked at our door. One was from my den, but came a day early, one from my last year's den who didn't know he was re-assigned; the third hadn't heard from any den mother yet and was upset. I let them study Dann's master sheet so they could see where their friends were assigned. All went home happy.

We have weekly Tuesday visits from Lisa's social worker. Somehow Tuesdays are always pandemonium. Lisa, the new worker and I isolate ourselves in Dann's study. Today Jay and his friend were cutting out Cub Scout boomerangs in the kitchen and sailing them through the living room, Mike and two friends occupied the playroom, Timmy and friend Tom adjourned to Tim's bedroom to write speeches. Lisa and her friend have been meeting boyfriends at the shopping center after school. At age 13, we thought we had another year before addressing this problem. I am trying to set aside only Tuesdays to worry about Lisa. The other days I have to worry about other problems.

My efficiency expert objects to changing to play clothes after school. Mike solves this problem by putting on three shirts in the morning—undershirt, play shirt, and school shirt and peels as the day progresses.

November 5, 1964

Dear Mom,

Timmy has gone on a Scout hike for new boys, Andy has been building a backpack brace for his Camping merit badge, and Lisa's Girl Scouts are touring the Capitol. Jay is learning how to tie a tie. He confiscated an old one of his Dad's and ties it for me every morning and the last thing every night. I agreed to sign his book if he could still remember how to do it after one week.

Andy sold his first rabbit meat for $1.58. As his expenses for the first year came to $25, it will be awhile before he is out of the red.

Thanks for the help, that ironing would have taken me weeks.

December 1, 1964

Dear Mom,

I found a woman who does ironing which gets dropped off on my way to class and picked up the next day. She charges $1.00 per hour. My tremendous pile cost only $3.25. She is speedy, it would take me lots longer.

Alaska, Tim's prize bunny, is expecting today and the weather worries us. If it should dip to zero, that would finish off newborns, so Dann and Tim made a temporary shelter in the basement and moved her along with her familiar nest box. I hope Alaska doesn't mind.

My kitchen is a mess tonight after making popcorn balls and pouring candles for our little Christmas gift tree that stands in the hall, our Christmas tradition. As we have so much company during the holiday season, it seemed appropriate to have something to give guests. Each year we have made gifts to hang on that tree and when guests leave, they may choose a gift. As we have leftovers from the former year, each year the selection increases. The children delight in giving gifts, especially homemade ones.

I have reached an impasse where I no longer believe anything Lisa says, even when it's true. Someone stole money at her Girl Scout meeting last week. Lisa was home sick, but had she been present, nothing would have convinced me that she wasn't the guilty party. She has lied to us so often that we now presume her guilty. I cannot continue to cope with a child that I can't trust. I have tried to lessen my demands and stick to my guns about the vital issues. One constant struggle is to know her whereabouts. She lived without supervision so long that she can't accept this. Almost every night we go through a grueling session because she hasn't told me where she went after school, which usually ends up with her screaming, "I hate your guts!" I have learned to treat this with indifference outwardly, but inwardly I shrivel and don't dare let her see how much that makes me cringe.

With a summertime break from each other, our parent-daughter relationship should have improved. Not so. Lisa and I verbally abuse each other every day, making me so tired that it's hard to deal with the boys' problems. I don't know which way to turn. Lisa is special to us after three years and obviously needs us, but I cannot continue like this. I think she is desperately trying to prove that we love her no matter what she does. She'll never win that one. I can't let our family slip out of control because of the stress she causes. Every single thing she does has to be checked on now, depressing me terribly.

December 5, 1964

Dear Mom,

Parents must usually come in pairs for a reason, to bolster each other. Dann finally made the decision which has been tearing me apart. He asked the department to find a new home for Lisa. I just couldn't bring myself to make that call.

My Christmas sewing isn't started yet. I will do that under their noses as the best way to keep a secret around here is to not hide. That way nobody gets curious.

December 10, 1964

Dear Mom,

Lisa's social worker told her that she would be moving and Lisa behaved awful after that, culminating when she stuck her foot out to trip me as we passed on the stairs. Dann disciplined her and then she swamped us with hugs and kisses, making it harder. A new foster home in Stoughton has asked for a teenage girl. Lisa visits there this weekend, then flies to Massachusetts to spend the holidays with her mother and will go back directly to that new home. You will probably not see her again. We are giving her the presents from us just before she leaves. She would be delighted to get a letter from you. After all, you are the only grandmother she has known. I'm off to bed after I deliver a few words of support to Alaska, who is still expecting.

December 17, 1964

Dear Mom,

Eight Flemish Giant babies arrived just prior to my den meeting. When Tim showed off one of his month-old babies, one little boy asked, "How do you get baby rabbits anyway?"

Dann asked afterward, "What did you say?"

I replied, "The easiest way is just tell him. My simplified version takes ten seconds."

We don't have room to house that many Flemish rabbits. They get so big we can't crowd them. We expected two or three, not eight. It was fortunate she delivered in the basement as she didn't know enough to pull fur for a nest and we had to substitute with fluffed cotton.

Lisa leaves Sunday morning. We'll all see her off. She went to Stoughton for a visit and responded favorably. This week has been long for both of us. I don't think we could struggle through another weekend. She got her good-bye letter from you. Thanks.

See you on the bus Thursday.

January 6, 1965

Dear Mom,

This house has been bursting with life since Christmas. The basement resounds with jigsaws humming. Chemistry and physics experiments fill the kitchen table. Parts of an aquarium pump litter the front hall with the filters alternating between in or out of the aquarium, depending on whether the crack is leaking or holding. Stamp collections are spread on the dining table, model airplanes are in process all over, and the sled sits deserted in the garage waiting for snow. We do manage that lived-in look. My goal is to keep the boys so busy they don't have time to watch Saturday morning TV.

We are still producing offspring. When Jay's guppy gave birth, Jay fished out five babies before their cannibalistic momma got to them. Mike gave Jay a floating guppy tank for Christmas to keep him in production. We are expecting puppies again, but our AKC female crossed us up, choosing her own male. Tim hopes to raise a bumper crop of bunnies for Easter sales. His present population is 16. His first year's operation went in the red, but it should break even now. He has a few customers that buy every time he and his Dad butcher. We like rabbit meat, but I would enjoy it more if Jason wouldn't make remarks like, "Good-bye Frisky, you were better than Snow White."

January 14, 1965

Dear Mom,

I am desperately trying to close our books for the year. I keep getting interruptions. If I can get them to balance the first time, I might make the January 15th deadline (tomorrow) but if there are more than a couple errors, woe is me!

The Department of Public Welfare has verified that Lisa stayed in Massachusetts. Her mother called just before Lisa was due back and informed them she was keeping her. Lisa probably applied a little pressure and charm. We have given up our right to have opinions about her welfare any longer, but this is a bad break for her. She must be excited about staying with her mother and needs desperately to be wanted. Her mother caused so many of her problems in the first place, how is this going to be different? The Welfare Department will send someone to pack her stuff and send it east by moving van.

This is the end of an era for us. I wanted a girl and I wanted to help Lisa find a happier existence. I have always believed that God will give one strength to do what one has to do, but He didn't. Maybe I didn't ask fervently enough. I failed in so many ways and it will be a long time before my self-confidence returns, and a long time, if ever, before I stop wondering how she's coping now. We succeeded in many ways as we traveled together. I don't believe she really hated my guts but was looking for a wall that wouldn't cave in. It hurt when we had to stand firm. I hope she knows that she was special to me in many ways that the boys weren't, because she was my only girl. We opened many doors for her, didn't shove her through but showed her options. I hope she knows wherever she goes, that we do indeed love her, no matter what she does. And I think only you, Mom, realize how much we are all crying inside.

"When she was good she was very, very good, but when she was bad, she was horrid.'

5 In Sickness and In Health

JANUARY 20, 1965

Dear Mom,

No, I didn't make my income tax deadline of January 15. My teacher has been helping me set up shortcuts. We have two weeks of classes left. When my bookkeeping course is over, another class, called Plants of Wisconsin Forests and Prairies, starts. This meets only one night a week and should be easier.

We classify as the West Side Infirmary. The second batch of medicine discouraged most of my headaches. The doctor told me to get lots of rest, but didn't say how. Tim had another terrible side ache, which lasted for two days and exhausted him. Mike has had an upset stomach and Jay suffered diarrhea. Perhaps we all had flu and reacted differently. All this made an unhappy household.

Tim's annual eye checkup turned up a muscle imbalance. We need to take care of this now while it involves only two muscles. Tim sees in the distance with only one eye, either one or the other.

February 5, 1965

Dear Mom,

I taught at the den mothers' Round Table last night. Getting ready tuckers me out. I cannot teach somebody how to make something without doing it myself, so my kitchen became a workshop/art studio for the week with a Mexican theme. Andy cut out a Ferdinand the bull on the jigsaw and nailed upside-down bottle caps to make a mud scraper, Mike twisted crepe paper on the electric beater to make raffia for a basketry sample, Jay constructed a tambourine by lacing two paper plates together and attaching noisy bottle caps around the outside and also a burro piggybank of papier mache laid over a balloon. I worked on a parakeet piñata, gorgeous with ruffled tissue paper in brilliant reds, blues, and yellows, an Indian bracelet from a tongue depressor soaked and curved to fit the wrist, and a napkin ring out of a tin can done in imitation of Indian silver work by tapping a design on it. I am grateful for two things; many volunteer assistants to assist with my preparations, and inexpensive supplies.

Are you were working again at the public library?

February 11, 1965

Dear Mom,

This is designated typing day as I need to type six pages of figures for Dann's income tax and five pages of program for the Blue and Gold Banquet. I stop typing after school, as if I work with columns of figures and suffer child distractions simultaneously, things don't break even.

I consented to be rabbit project leader for 4-H this year. Only Tim and his friend, Tom, have signed up. At our first meeting we discussed the requisites of a good demonstration and kinds of breed. Between them they can show four different breeds. We have to plan around pregnant does when setting demonstration dates.

After supper we treated the boys to a sundae. I had picked out each boy's weakest subject and promised a sundae if they could move their grade up one step. All four took the bait. They were so excited about their strawberry sundaes they hardly ate supper. Dann doesn't call this bribery, just incentive.

The clutch went kaput, leaving me without a car for two weeks. The garage where we take it is on the east side of town. We drove out Sunday when the roads were less slippery and the traffic much lighter. Two boys and I followed Dann in the other car. We could tell he was having trouble. If he stopped for any reason, he would start up again very slowly. We missed a couple traffic lights and lost him, but when we got as far as the University Hospital, I spotted a traffic jam in the far lane and Andy shouted, "Hey, that's Dad." We maneuvered behind him to try a push start, but the car wouldn't restart. Finally Dann shifted the boys to his dead car and they hung out the back of it (fortunately it was a station wagon) holding a spare tire between the two cars while I pushed them the remaining ten miles through town.

The Scouts day outing at Governor Dodge State Park was warm, but they came home chilled. If it stays below freezing they do okay, but when it thaws they get wet and cold. Timmy and five other boys were in a box canyon trying to pass their stalking requirement. They came to a creek with a hole in the ice which the scoutmaster had warned them to stay off. They didn't. Three of them walked out, threw a hunk of ice down the open hole and Don fell in. The boy standing nearest quickly grabbed Don and pulled him out. He had brought the recommended extra pair of pants but was wearing both pairs. What were the boys thinking of? Perhaps they figured if they could get the outside pair off quickly enough, the inside pair might still be dry? Anyway they tried to take off his pants without removing his shoes. The wet pants froze immediately, the boys couldn't move them either up or down, and they ended up carrying him back to the campfire. This strikes me as very funny, but the three who walked on the ice didn't laugh. The Scoutmaster severely reprimanded them. Rightly so.

February 19, 1965

Dear Mom,

Yes, I remember how Dad and I used to sharpen the lawn mower by setting me on the hood of the car to steer the mower while he drove slowly down the road. I fail to see any resemblance whatsoever to that and pushing a dead car with a tire between the two cars.

We held our Blue and Gold Banquet last night. It would be a lot easier if I could stop our thinking processes when things are over. At 2:30 a.m. I was still trying to solve the world's problems and mine. The theme was famous February birthdays. We shaped our cake like a calendar, placing small objects on special birth dates: an airplane for Lindbergh, ball and bat for Babe Ruth, a little Christmas tree for Charles Dickens, a flashlight bulb for Edison, a toothpick log cabin for Abe Lincoln, a tiny tractor for McCormick, cherries for Washington, scout neckerchief slide for Lord Baden-Powell (founder of Boy Scouts), musical notes for Handel, the letter A for Gutenberg, a buffalo for Buffalo Bill, a horse and rider for Longfellow (signifying the Midnight Ride of Paul Revere). We won first place and nine excited Cubs bounced in their seats.

March 4, 1965

Dear Mom,

The boys got to watch Jay's guppy having babies. One needs to be present at that precise moment. Momma guppy was in the floating tank within the big aquarium, she birthed seven, died and then all seven died. As Jay has only one female left, we'll put that floating tank away until we figure out what went wrong.

I have been revamping my bookkeeping system. By using subsidiary ledgers and simplifying them, I can close the books each month. Last month I had this done by the second of the month following. When my instructor learned that I had been running four months behind in my posting, he complained. "What you are doing is history, not bookkeeping." No more history, I hope.

March 10, 1965

Dear Mom,

I'm not surprised that my cousin has gone back to work. I, too, often feel strong urges to do what I've trained to do. This would give me great satisfaction, but I gain greater satisfaction by getting involved in volunteer and child activities, knowing that when the boys get strep throat or have special events, my family comes first. I don't go along with the argument about needing to work to put the kids through college. We hope to encourage the kids toward further schooling and will contribute financially, but the basic responsibility lies with them. What they have to work for, they will surely value more.

We worried that Black Jet, Tim's newest rabbit, was going to produce her litter Friday night. Although roads were full of slush and snow, I drove Tim out to the farm for hay. The farmer told me to back up to the barn for loading. Neither of us realized that beneath all that slush the frost had gone out of the ground and we sank deep in mud. Tim had come without boots. I gave him mine and drove in stocking feet. No matter what we did, the car wouldn't budge. Finally the farmer pulled us out with his tractor. After all that, Jet didn't produce that night. She must not have been bred when we thought, but as we had test-mated her six days later, we are expecting again in six days.

While Tim and I groveled in the mud, Dann sold the HOLE to some people who fell in love with the house. We have had two consequent actions. One is that Dann immediately started figuring out what has to be done in our playroom which he hasn't touched for a year because we couldn't afford the materials. Jay, Mike and I spent hours picking up toys and sorting mess so that Daddy wouldn't have any impediments. We started a fire in the fireplace, thus eliminating random second thoughts about keeping junk.

The second result is that we decided on a three-week vacation in August and will stay with my brother in New Jersey so that we can attend the New York World's Fair.

Dann's mother has been feeling poorly for weeks. The doctor finally suggested she have a complete physical, which relieves me.

I am working on costumes for our next skit about a famous Mexican bandit. The skit contains much shooting. My actors are cast perfectly for this.

March 18, 1965

Dear Mom,

My Cubs performed magnificently at the Mexican pack meeting dressed in brilliant colored scarves and sashes with kerchiefs for masks. They portrayed famous battles, shot off cap guns and fell dead all over. Some of the dead bandits kept right on shooting. We dressed one boy in a wig and a gorgeous Mexican blouse and skirt making him the beautiful senorita whom the bandits abducted. Dann says he/she stole the show.

The boys have decided the animal tracks in your yard must have been rabbits. They decided the running tracks would be a doe, and the one chasing must be a buck. We'll be down Saturday night. They would be happy to shovel your gravel.

Dann's mother came home from the hospital during that storm. The physical found nothing wrong. Now perhaps she can stop worrying.

April 15, 1965

Dear Mom,

We survived spring break and things are back to normal. At the Chicago Museum of Science and Industry we tried all the hands-on exhibits, and spent a second day at the Field Museum of Natural History and the Aquarium. The closeness of buildings in south Chicago impressed the boys and they wondered where they could put their tree forts. I don't think it occurred to them that keeping 20 rabbits there might cause problems also.

Please tell cousin Fran that on her next trip she has a special invitation for a rabbit dinner. The boys have promised they won't say a word until she's done eating.

May 2, 1965

Dear Mom,

Mike has finally mastered his bike. We had promised when the last kid became mobile we would take some trips, so we did — six Willetts, six bikes, and one dog. After four miles, Twinkle got slower and slower. We rode out Old Sauk Road to a picnic area, Dann built a fire and grilled steaks, Tim made delicious biscuits, and Jay took charge of the banana boats (banana plus chocolate bar with marshmallow stuffed inside all warmed to gooey over the coals). I experimented with tin can cooking making holes in the top of a can of corn before setting it in the fire. This way is great—no pans to clean. It took all Andy's time and his Scout know-how just to keep a cooking fire going in the tremendous wind. Even a picnic table turned sidewise for a windbreak didn't help.

We spent Saturday working outside. I suggested the boys earn money for the World's Fair and listed 20 things that needed doing. They could choose what they wanted to do and keep track of their time. Andy picked the more difficult ones: taking apart old TV's, hauling rocks and chopping down small trees. Mike chose jobs proportionate to his size and skill: sweeping sidewalks and carrying leaves.

Could you come up for Mother's Day? We'd love to have you and I could show off my violent purple walls.

May 13, 1965

Dear Mom,

We had planned a wildflower hike in the woods in this beautiful weather, but suddenly we reached our limit and were so tired that Dann took us out to dinner instead. We entertain everybody when we eat out. Jason studied the menu and inquired, "What is cold straw?" (coleslaw) They seated us in a private dining room disappointing the younger contingent. They really don't care who looks at them and like being in the middle of as much noise and confusion as possible. Andy, Tim, and Dann were relieved not to go hiking after they had gotten up at 3:30 a.m. for opening day of trout fishing. The weather has been perfect for my marble-playing, bike-riding, basketball-dribbling boys and has increased the necessity of frequent baths (especially the marble playing kids) which brings dissension from the ranks.

"Why do I have to take a bath? I'm only dirty on the outside."

In Sickness and In Health

I took 12 Cubs on a field trip to the Madison School Forest. This area contains 300 acres of pristine oak woods with 12 miles of trails owned by the Madison Schools and is used primarily for an outdoor classroom. We gambled on the weather as the radio had promised thundershowers all day. However, this turned out to be my most successful field trip. Our guide was a naturalist from the Madison school system who is a mother, den mother and Girl Scout leader in her free time. The behavior, interest, and enthusiasm of my oversized den astounded her, oversize because the Cubmaster transferred two behavior problems from one den mother to another. It doesn't pay to be related to the boss. We crawled around under the leaves looking for sugar maple saplings, found fiddlehead ferns not quite open, listened to the thump, thump of the ruffed grouse mating call, and carefully inspected the giant poison ivy vines. The weather held and I hadn't heard the tornado warnings so didn't worry. We built a fire in the picnic area and cooked wieners and Some-mores. The boys climbed trees and ate their supper aloft. After three hours they piled into the cars reluctant and dirty. I have had calls since from mothers each commenting on the enthusiasm her son showed when he got home. Several want to go back with families.

Being late, I hurried to wash my dirty outside, put on a dress and rushed down to my Forest Plant lecture. This class creates a problem when Dann is out on Wednesday nights. The boys manage on their own fairly well, but this occurs too often. The professor talked so long that night that I thought bedtime would never arrive.

Mike is prepared for summer already, having gotten his tetanus shot. He fell out of a tree and wouldn't have been hurt except that he had one shoe off and cut that foot when he landed on we-don't-know-what. Trying to keep up with three older brothers makes him our accident-prone kid.

We're working frantically on the playroom. This was last

winter's project and we're close, but hate to work inside in nice weather. A couple rainy days would help our inside work.

Last week we refinished floors in an empty apartment. I had told Dann that he could pay me instead of hiring it done, and we could put it towards the World's Fair trip, providing my bookkeeping skills can figure out how to do that, of course.

May 20, 1965

Dear Mom,

I wrote a skit on Chief Black Hawk for our Wisconsin History Cub Scout theme. This centers around Black Hawk's last battle before he escaped temporarily by slipping across the Wisconsin River. A historic marker near Sauk City tells about the battle. Standing on that spot I envision the Indian fires along the far ridge and the army, under Colonel Dodge, scattered throughout the valley. History relates that a few Indian braves danced around their fires all night, giving an illusion of many braves, while the bulk of the tribe, including women and children, crossed the river under cover of darkness. In the morning Colonel Dodge found only a deserted camp with cold ashes. My skit enacted this story. Our only costumes were hats, either Cub Scout caps signifying soldiers or Indian headdresses. Each boy carried both headpieces. I did a dress rehearsal on the spot to instill proper enthusiasm in my troops. Loading them into my station wagon, we drove to the marker and pulled into the rest stop past a parked car containing a sleeping driver. All the car doors burst open simultaneously, everyone jammed on his Indian headdress and with full sound effects rolling down the valley, the skit began to roll. It took 10 seconds for the gentleman to wake. Expressions of surprise, utter confusion, shock, dismay, curiosity, and finally disgust flitted across his face before he roared away. My actors played their parts well.

We scheduled Tim's eye surgery for the end of June. This allows us only two weeks before we leave for the World's Fair. It's hard to think of things for him to do in the hospital with bandaged eyes. Perhaps we should work on his Morse Code Scout requirement.

June 10, 1965

Dear Mom,

College Week for Women was held on the University campus last week. I now know which historical sites we'd like to visit, hopefully I can identify birds we might see while there, where to apply for college scholarships and what's wrong with the furniture in my house. Leaving the house at 7:30 a.m. was a wee bit difficult and makes me appreciate not having to do it all the time.

On Memorial Day Jason got bit on his hand, probably a bee sting. By the next day his hand was swollen and streaking a brilliant red. The doctor at the clinic gave them medicine and instructed Dann to keep Jay quiet and out of school so Dann picked up a library book, took Jay with him to his office and settled him at an empty desk. Dann's only comment at supper, "Boy, does that kid ask questions!"

I'm going shopping with Dann's mother. We're looking for new hats.

June 24, 1965

Dear Mom,

Timmy and I worked frantically on his and Tom's demonstration that they're doing for 4-H competition. Miss Parsons, our pseudo-grandmother next door has been a wonderful ally. She drummed into the boys that a good demo has three parts: first, you say what you're going to say, then you say it, and lastly, you say what you've said. We added to that—hang on to your rabbit. We've practiced over and over. Their demonstration lasted 13 minutes using colored posters and charts, flannel board, and of course, live exhibits. I waited tensely for the unexpected incident that we had warned them always occurs. As Tim turned his Flemish Giant, she kicked out the little scatter rug. Rabbits are hard to hold on a slippery tabletop and a small rug underneath the rabbit corrects this problem but as she kicked, the rug scooted across the table and plopped on the floor. Tim hesitated only a moment then tightened his grip and nonchalantly continued. Afterwards the judge commended him for this, saying it would have been distracting if he had tried to retrieve the rug. He thought that the boys had accumulated a mass of information and knew their subject well. Two blue ribbons (first place) will be awarded in their class and those two will repeat their demonstrations at the fair. We won't know for a week. This has been a huge job. It would have been easier to do it myself. Thanks for the weekend.

July 1, 1965

Dear Mom,

Timmy and I laughed over your comment to keep him quiet in preparation for his operation. We failed.

Monday, armed with cupcakes and birthday candles, I called on Aunt Edna leaving Timmy in charge at home. They related later that Jay spun his marble on our non-level floors and it rolled into Andy's partially rebuilt radio. Sparks flew, which burned the floor, the rug, and Jay's hand when he tried to retrieve the marble. Tim called the clinic and the doctor told him to apply ice. Although the burn was deep, the first aid seemed adequate and for once we didn't have to take him in.

When canoeing with the Scouts on the Wisconsin River, Andy didn't recognize the gigantic tree-hanging variety of poison ivy. The doctor gave us more pills to dissolve in the bathtub. I feel like Dr. Wilton is almost one of the family. Maybe he feels that way too.

July 18, 1965

Dear Mom,

You probably think no letters means I have broken both wrists, but we are all healthy for a change. Tim returned for his check-up and after a quick look, Dr. Jeff swung his chair around and exclaimed, "His eyes turned out exactly as they should." He acted as proud as a new poppa. Often this operation doesn't have good results.

We squeezed in one week's vacation at the family cottage up north and then with only a few days prepared for the Dane County Junior Fair. Loading up seven of Tim's rabbits, three of Tom's, Andy's four woodworking exhibits, four boys plus Tom and his mother, two sleeping bags, two suitcases, 20 rabbit dishes and a bag of feed, we departed for the fairgrounds. Jason took one look at the loaded car and remarked sarcastically, "Mom, we forgot the trailer."

We signed Tim and Tom in for bunks for one night, signed in the rabbits to their proper quarters and arrived home to find that Dann's brother Bruce and family had stopped for overnight. Cousin Sarah slept in Mike's bed, because Mike was sleeping in Jay's top bunk, because Jay was sleeping in Tim's, who was gone. Sarah was up before breakfast with the rabbit-feeding crew. They let her help and then she climbed Andy's tree fort. What goes up does not always come down, but Andy rescued her. I drove to the fair three times that day: to check on things in the morning, to bring the boys home in the afternoon and to see the winning demonstrations in the evening. Tim's three black meat rabbits won a blue ribbon. The next day we went again for Children's Day on the midway. I had promised everybody they could take a friend. As the 4-H sticker on our car gets us in free, and that day rides were half-price, this seemed a good way to entertain. Dann threatened to buy me a chauffeur's hat.

July 10, 1965

Dear Mom,

We can't possibly be ready to leave on schedule for vacation. We now plan on leaving Friday, the 13th. Good thing we are not superstitious. We'll stop overnight with Dann's cousin in Corning and at my brother's in N.J. the following night. We allowed five days there, three at the World's Fair and two at the nation's capital and Shenandoah Valley. We have been studying our National Geographics for anything we can find on Washington D.C. and the Appalachians.

We operate like a revolving door as we picked up Tim at Scout camp Saturday and dropped off Andy at church camp the next day.

Mike does Andy's table setting chore while he's gone. He questioned, "Why don't we just put everything, like silverware, in the middle of the table and let people take what they want?" This stems from his inability to remember what goes where.

This dry weather hurts my garden. Yesterday I questioned the mess of branches and sticks strewn on my front lawn, and was told, "That's for our rain dance." I wish them luck, but I'm afraid mean Mommy is going to make them pick up their props whether it rains or not.

Last night I overheard Jay ask to be included in a game and was promptly told, "You can't play because you don't know how."

"Of course I know how," he replied vehemently. "I made up those rules."

August 4, 1965

Dear Mom,

Sorry I forgot to send Tim's sock size and didn't remember until the day of his birthday. Thanks for the breakfast invitation, but we won't get on the road that early. We could use some lunch sandwiches to eat on your lawn.

We really need this vacation because Dann has been working so hard. Thanks for the offers.

August 16, 1965

Dear Mom,

We have encountered trouble and don't know what the problem is. We hospitalized Tim here in New Jersey. Thank goodness we have family to stay with, but let me back up.

We drove all day after leaving you, spent the night with cousins in Corning, tenting at the Girl Scout camp, as our cousins there were in the process of closing it for the season. Some tents were still up and we spread our sleeping bags on the tent floors. We had gotten so hot traveling that after getting the kids asleep, we four adults went for a midnight swim. Swimming in the cool water in the pitch black was heavenly. That constituted our first day of vacation and our last.

As soon as we hit the road the next day, Tim became sick and threw up all the way across New York state. Towards the end of that long day Mike, too, acted ill. He might have had a touch of the flu, gotten overtired or perhaps just sympathetic to Tim's distress.

Charles and Jean's welcome smiles faded when we started removing sick kids from the car and carrying them directly to bed.

It became obvious in the morning that Tim suffered from his same side ache problem, more severe than ever before with pain so excruciating that he couldn't stand straight. We took him to a doctor who asked over and over, "This child has a congenital curvature of the spine. Why haven't you ever noticed it before?"

"Because he's normally not like this."

"Haven't you ever bought him a coat? Surely you noticed then that he doesn't stand straight?"

"He did stand straight." Round and round we went. We admitted him to the children's ward of St. James and find we don't like that hospital any better than the doctor. Tim was filthy from traveling and camping. It took Dann 30 minutes to persuade the staff to find something we could use for a washcloth. They finally produced a child's terrycloth bootie. What kind of a hospital doesn't have washcloths? Tim was too sick to eat, but several hours after lunch Dann realized that none of the children in the ward had been given lunch trays. He went storming off and the staff finally admitted they had forgotten that room. Tim doesn't care about anything.

The doctors keep remarking, "Isn't this strange?"

I don't like it here. I want to go home and I can't and I'm frightened. Will keep in touch.

August 17, 1965

Dear Mom,

Today was no better. Doctors streamed through Tim's room shaking their heads. They took x-rays of his right side and diagnosed a possible kidney problem, probably a tumor. Nobody says malignancy, but we're all thinking it. Dann and I spent our day walking the corridors or sitting with Tim. In the hall I hear everybody talking about that interesting case in Room 110. Not very interesting to some of us. I am cursing myself for listening, over the years, to doctors telling me Tim's problem was probably psychosomatic and to downplay it. Meanwhile, back at the ranch, Uncle Charles and Aunt Jean have their hands full coping with six kids. Mike did have flu and shared with two of his cousins.

The doctors finally decided to operate. They don't know what for, but feel they have to anyway. We've asked for alternatives and requested that they call our urologist in Madison. They finally agreed to do that and we're coming home. Tim and I will fly and hand carry Tim's X-rays which Dr. Spanicek insisted the hospital send with us. Charles has arranged a non-stop flight out of Kennedy Airport in New York, requesting a wheelchair. Dann's brother will meet us when we land in Madison and take us directly to the hospital. Unfortunately Dann refuses to leave here until he knows that Tim and I are aloft, so he may be two days behind us in arriving home. It will be another day before the hospital here clears us for discharge. Charles will call you as soon as we are en route.

August 18, 1965

Dear Mom,

In spite of anguish over Tim, we have been troubled by another issue, the World's Fair. The boys worked so hard to earn money for this and have talked about nothing else all summer. What a shame for all of them to miss out. So we decided to go for it. We are taking the two that are still walking and Jean will tell the hospital she's Tim's Mother so that she can visit Tim while we're gone. We stopped at the hospital on our way out of town. Incredibly Tim was sitting up, eating and smiling with no pain. His first words were, "Now

I can go to the Fair with you, can't I?" The stream of doctors past Tim's bed doubled as they can't believe this change. They really don't want us to go, I think they are totally puzzled and want to solve this problem themselves. This now fits the pattern that Tim has exhibited over the last six years – side aches for a couple days and then suddenly nothing. But it changes the picture, for if Tim is temporarily okay, we can drive home together.

Andy and Jason loved the Fair. We had passes which put us at the front of the waiting lines so we did quite a few things even with a one day limitation. Dann and I didn't enjoy much. As Tim was still fine when we arrived home that night, we have asked for a discharge and the X-rays. We'll all get a good night's sleep tonight and leave early in the morning. By the time you get this, we'll probably be home. I will call as soon as we admit Tim into the Madison hospital.

I don't know if I ever want to come back to New Jersey again.

August 22, 1965

Dear Mom,

It was good to talk to you yesterday from home. I never appreciated home quite so much as when I couldn't go there. We took Tim to see Dr. Spanicek early this morning. He asked, "Vere de hell you been? Vat took you so long?" We explained that when Tim's attack suddenly ceased, we drove instead of flying and we handed over the X-ray of the right kidney.

"Vere is the udder vun?"

I explained, "The pain occurred on the right side so they took X-rays of that side."

He streamed unintelligible German by us, "Do you mean they were going to remove his right kidney without checking his left one?"

He explains this simply. Tim was born with a duplicate blood vessel to his right kidney. This second one would occasionally move across the bottom of the kidney and block it from functioning causing the liquids in the kidney to back up, which created a side ache. This blockage deteriorates the kidney tissue. Whenever Tim got a side ache, he would lie down which shifted the organs and within 48 hours, would release the blockage. Dr. Spanicek scheduled Tim's kidney surgery for the day after tomorrow.

August 28, 1965

Dear Mom,

It helps me to talk to you every night. Dr. Spanicek was able to leave one-third of Tim's right kidney. It will be three months before we will know if the vital connections are still viable, keeping this an operating kidney. It makes me sick to think of all the years (and kidney tissue) that we wasted. Never again will I let anyone suggest that my kids' problems might be psychological.

Tim's only comment for days has been, "I didn't know anyone could feel so terrible."

September 6, 1965

Dear Mom,

Tim has had intravenous feeding for days, which for some reason they had to keep re-inserting. With his small veins, this became agonizing for both Tim and the nurse. I couldn't watch. When he progressed to food they offered lots of plain Jell-o. On the seventh day he received another blood transfusion. The doctor explained that after surgery they had replaced what Tim had lost. Normally bleeding stops when it comes in contact with other tissue. However, each day after surgery Tim's hemoglobin had been dropping, which meant that he was bleeding internally. They stalled as long as they could, but when the count reached a certain point, they had to give him another transfusion. We had two offers of blood donors for replacement, but this comes gratis from the Red Cross. The hospital is so crowded that they put a fifth bed in Tim's room. Another 12-year-old was in the next bed until they diagnosed him with encephalitis and quickly transferred him to isolation. Fortunately, Tim has had many shots of antibiotics.

His many callers and piles of mail pleased him. Mike offered me a quarter to take to his brother. That was almost two weeks allowance but I couldn't turn down a gift, so we compromised on lifesavers.

On Tim's first day up we walked the hall to the phone and he talked to all his brothers. This improved morale on both sides. Poor Timmy. He was good about being stuck, but he hated it. Andy kept track of Tim's shots. Everyday I would report the daily total, until the day they tried to put the intravenous back in and couldn't find the vein and Tim said, "Just tell Andy 200."

He was very patient and seemed to have an adult understanding and acceptance through all the misery. We are thankful this is behind us.

SEPTEMBER 20, 1965

Dear Mom,

After almost three weeks, Tim returned home. No king ever had such doting subjects and messengers as gathered around his couch. The quantities of games, gifts, cards and money that he spread out flabbergasted his brothers. Tim admits, however, that it is the hardest money he ever worked for. He got to the point last week where he realized one could accept the inevitable bad parts and still enjoy the fringe benefits. He will start back to school one hour at a time. Dann took him over for math class this a.m., then he comes home to rest. This afternoon I will take him back for geography. Fortunately we have a second car and don't live far from school. No gym for a semester, in fact no physical activity because he hemorrhaged so long. He still runs a low-grade infection somewhere.

It has been a long, hot summer, but things are moving back to normal. Dann and I started teaching 7th grade Sunday school and boys appear daily at our door to inquire when Cub Scouts will begin. That means fall has arrived. Thanks again for everything.

September 24, 1965

Dear Mom,

Here we go again. I went for my annual checkup and discovered I have a fibroid tumor. No surgery until it's the size of a three month pregnancy. I go back in six weeks. No one seems to think this is causing my backache. Dann thought I went in to see about my headaches, but now nobody is the least bit concerned about that end of me. I'm glad we can wait as I'm too busy right now.

Thanks for the birthday pillowcases. We gave Andy a 30-pound bow for his birthday and Dann is taking him out opening day. Hope it doesn't rain.

P.S. It looks like we're trying to pay for the whole darned hospital.

October 19, 1965

Dear Mom,

I love Fridays when I finish all the things that didn't get done on Thursday. We held our organizational pack meeting last night. This month's theme was a barn dance and we hung apples on strings and directed folk dances including 86 participants—adults, scouts, and little ones. Dann's voice gave up by 8:00 o'clock. Planning a pack meeting is like planning a birthday party only 10 times larger.

The Scouts leave tomorrow for a canoe and hiking campout. Those who can't pass the canoe requirements will hike ending at the same campsite. Andy goes and also Tim as his Dad will be there to watch him. Tim cannot hike or backpack, but will sit in his Dad's canoe. He attends school full days now and anxiously wants to go with the Scouts. We didn't have the heart to say no as he has missed out on so much.

I feel good. My backache almost disappeared, but I get tired. I don't usually put off unpleasant things, but am relieved that this surgery is delayed. There are so many things that I need to do right now, such as driving Tim to and from school twice a day. But this maybe business isn't so hot either because I can't commit to things. People could easier understand a concrete reason instead of a feeble, "I can't do that now." If I make any reference to health, they assume I am pregnant. Only my Cubmaster husband understands why I didn't take a den. Thanks for your offer to come and stay. Do you realize I might be gone ten days?

We have poison ivy again. Tim and Jay a bit, but Mike appears to be following in his big brother's footsteps. Andy remarked, "I don't know where those guys have been, but I hope that I didn't go too!"

October 8, 1965

Dear Mom,

Andy has been in bed for three days with poison ivy. Tim managed fine on the canoe trip. Andy did not. We know the

Wisconsin River is lined with poison ivy. Andy saw and avoided it. I believe some vines must have gotten on the campfire. Even Andy doesn't usually break out that fast. When he came home he looked like he had a sunburned cheek, but I knew better and put him into the tub immediately with a Dome pill. On Monday he looked like a chipmunk with cheeks stuffed full of nuts. I gave up immediately and took him to the doctor for a steroid injection. The scoutmaster asked at troop meeting how many boys contacted poison ivy and half raised their hands. Since then, my phone rings for advice constantly. I seem to be the authority on effective treatment.

Without warning, Andy is growing up. His voice growls in a low range, his shoe size zoomed from seven-and-a-half to ten over the summer, and he has discovered the other sex, at least one of them. I didn't realize until he said he wanted to ask Doltons over for his birthday cake. I thought we have been seeing them quite a bit, but Andy pointed out that it has been a whole week. He dressed up. When they arrived he took Jeanne off in the corner to talk. She spent the entire evening happily listening to him.

OCTOBER 20, 1965

Dear Mom,

Tim is struggling to catch up on Scout work. First class cooking badge requires him to make supper over a fire. This includes fresh meat and vegetable, bread, drink, and dessert — no small task when it rains on your campfire. Using stew meat, he added potatoes and carrots, made biscuits in the frying pan, instant cocoa, and a banana, marshmallow and chocolate concoction warmed over the fire for dessert.

Dann and I agreed to be a Sunday school teaching team. We tried to stimulate the kids into asking questions. Now we are having trouble with answers. I thought 7th graders were silly and giggling, but we get questions such as: "Where did God come from? How long is eternity? Why isn't it all right to drink when the Bible tells of Jesus doing it? What does it feel like to die? In the beginning how did God make something out of nothing? Why do we have unanswered questions?" I wondered who is learning the most in this class? See you Saturday.

November 10, 1965

Dear Mom,

Thank you for the package. Jay hadn't missed his yellow toothbrush yet. After five days he should have. Also thanks for the new shirt, but that's not fair. In the first place the burn hole is small and on the collar, so that he can still wear the shirt. In the second place you originally gave that shirt to Andy and now it belongs to Mike so it has exceeded a normal life expectancy. In the third place the minimum wage you receive for ironing doesn't cover the price of a new shirt. After much thought I decided to return the cost of the shirt by taking you out to lunch at the Simon House.

Our experimental weekend at the cottage over Teachers Convention turned out great. Weather stayed good although the boys were disappointed that we narrowly missed a snowstorm. We lit a fire in the woodstove and once things warmed up, they stayed toasty. November weaves a special spell as the woods appear deserted and quiet. Andy and Tim fished madly with no luck. Dann walked, stalked, and hunted madly with no luck. We ought to do this every fall.

NOVEMBER 19, 1965

Dear Mom,

I still feel fine. Michael's part of your letter pleased him and he planned on writing you an answer right away, but it snowed. You lost out to the weather.

Using a theme of Achievement Parade at our monthly pack meeting last night, we established a series of 12 stations representing the 12 requirements for Wolf rank. Each boy escorted his parents through the course doing both fun and funny things. We set up and filled 150 chairs. I consider this a small miracle when Dann keeps 150 people moving about having a good time for more than an hour.

We purchased another dilapidated old building behind Dann's office. It's an eight-room house which originally housed a family of 11 kids and an awful mess. We plan on renovating it into two four-room units and work on it two days each week. We enjoy remodeling.

Have a good Thanksgiving at Frank's. We'll miss you.

DECEMBER 9, 1965

Dear Mom,

My tumor remains the same. This looks like a long wait.

We took everybody to a brass choir concert at the University. The boys asked endless questions, much to the amusement of the man in front of us who turned around and asked if they were enjoying the concert. Mike smiled sweetly at him and said, "No." I think he fibbed. The antiphonal choirs in three balconies, also the harps and kettle drums kept them entranced. Mike and Tim pantomimed the trombones and the conductor. Fortunately their smart father had insisted on seats in the last row of the balcony.

We have started Christmas preparations. I promised to take Michael Christmas shopping and to the dismay of the other kids, left them home, but this didn't squelch their feverish Christmas spirit. Coming home, we found them happily at work. They had taken out my Christmas Ideas books. If it is hard for an adult to browse those fascinating pages and choose, it is obviously harder for a child. They each began at least two projects spreading out on the kitchen table, dining room table, and living room and office floors. They started match stick villages, crowns for wise men, ornaments from egg cartons, a fireplace and stocking scene, popcorn balls for the gift tree and more. Dann laughed when Jay came to kiss me goodnight and inquired if I had any more ideas and I replied, "I wouldn't tell you if I did." I talked to them at breakfast about what a big house we own, but we have to live in it too. I can't get too upset with them for doing more than one thing at a time when I have started three projects myself.

In between the Christmas preparations, we are still having the same problems of daily survival. Jason stuck an ice pick in his hand when he was making candles, which necessitated a tetanus shot. Andy broke another mouthpiece when he laid his clarinet on a chair and it fell off. Michael is thrilled to have real homework and is studying about world worms (do I need to translate to earthworms or are you on his level?) Tim is making a terrarium for Nature merit badge and must keep it growing for one month. He planted anything he could find. In five days the lima beans and popcorn were hitting the top. Why do we always do these projects in the winter when there isn't any choice of seeds?

December 15, 1965

Dear Mom,

Do you have any seeds you could save for Tim? We are desperate. Something ate his lima bean leaves and the popcorn developed a white fungus. This makes it more interesting than if things went right. No, that tetanus shot didn't bother Jay, but now he has strep throat so that means another shot.

Michael was entranced by your letter and said he wished HE could catch a mouse by the tail. See you soon.

January 7, 1966

Dear Mom,

Andy had a date with Chris, a 9th grade girl who also works in the school cafeteria. He didn't want to go alone but couldn't get his friend, Dean, to ask a girl so it ended up as a threesome plus his Father as chauffeur. Andy looked pretty sharp in his new sweater and white pants. Although I tried to divert it, Tim, Jay, and Mike pondered publicly for the two days prior about this strange event. They were not teasing, they simply could not understand why anybody would pay money to go someplace with a girl. Andy took it nicely and kept telling them what they didn't seem to realize was that they were going to grow up someday. A good squelch. As far as we can figure, although this was a dance, Andy didn't. He did say she was just fun to be with.

The tumor remains unchanged. I don't go back until spring.

New Year's Eve was special with oyster stew and individual choice sundaes and we played games with the boys until midnight.

January 11, 1966

Dear Mom,

We can't come this weekend because Dann has a board meeting. We invested $1,000 in Green River Ranch stock. It is "a castle in the sky" but we cherish great hopes. The ranch consists of 837 acres along the Wisconsin River, hills and valleys with a stream running through and a possibility of caves underneath. The dream is to build a convention center with ski hills, campground, and to dam the stream for a marina. The problem is to sell enough stock to get working capital. The promoter toured us around the grounds in his four-wheel drive Jeep, zipping up and down the potential ski hills and across the flattop hill where he proposes to put the heliport. I don't know how this happened, but Dann was appointed a director.

It looks like we have taken up a new sport. Andy and Tim are working on skiing merit badge and this involves a common problem called transportation. If Dann and I are stuck with driving, we might as well enjoy so we've all been taking beginning lessons. I have mastered the downhill part fairly well. It's the stopping that worries me. I can't.

Andy went skiing with the senior Scouts. He was excited all week as this was his first chance to use his new skis on a real ski hill. The men secured all skis on the cartop rack for the drive to the ski area. At 60 mph, the ties must have loosened, Andy's skis fell off and smashed to smithereens. Andy was following in the second car and saw the whole thing. It hurts to remember the three months he propped those skis in the corner while he earned the money for them. The men rented skis for Andy. They felt so bad they each offered to pay for one third of new skis.

We have a new tenant who attends Alcoholics Anonymous. At supper Dann said, "We have a problem. Our new tenant has fallen off the wagon."

"Is she suing us?" Jay asked. Our kids absorb more of our conversation than we realize.

Last night he insisted I help with his spelling, phonetics which he could guess at as well as I, but he insisted. Eventually we figured it out. He immediately remarked, "See Mommy, I knew you could help me if I showed you how," and, "What's the matter with Daddy?" I answered that Daddy must have read a funny story, and privately thought Dann was about to bust. Next time I'll let him figure out those darn phonics.

Our car transmission locked in reverse. As it is in the garage backwards we can't pull it out. Frustrated, Dann had to call a heavy duty wrecker.

January 27, 1966

Dear Mom,

I am already working on my second ski hat and am just using up yarn following no design. The knitting stays by the phone and lots gets done this way.

Would you like to know how to get a car (a non-automatic, of course) out of a garage frontwards when it won't shift out of reverse? It took Dann and the wrecker man a long time to figure this out. Dann simply shoved in the clutch!!

I keep squirrels out of my bird feeder by feeding them on the ground. Flippy turns up every noon to eat lunch with me. He operates by the clock and appears on the wire when I start to fix lunch. I throw out a stale bun and he tears down the trunk stopping halfway to flip his tail vehemently, picks up the bun and retreats to the first branch on the oak tree, watching me while I eat and likewise. Yesterday he brought a friend, who ate three buns. My class lecturer says we can forecast the weather by watching squirrels. When bad weather is on the way, they eat extra so they don't have to go out in a storm. As it is ten degrees below zero, I wonder if Flippy will come.

Michael has finally become a Cub Scout and this puts me back in the harness again, as no one knows how long this tumor will take. This den has too many den mothers' sons who know all the answers and think they don't have to listen.

P.S. Flippy came. He obviously thinks my bread line too good to miss.

February 4, 1966

Dear Mom,

  Dann and I left town for a funeral, leaving the boys to fend for themselves. I put Tim in charge leaving a spaghetti casserole in the refrigerator, leftover peas and carrots, and homemade raised donuts to be warmed in the bun warmer. He followed my time schedule, but left the kitchen in between. The peas and carrots went dry so the dog got them. The doughnuts also went dry and got crusty, but they ate enough spaghetti for eight boys. Andy cleaned up and remarked next time he'd cook. He didn't mind eating what burned, but he sure didn't like scrubbing burned pans.

February 24, 1966

Dear Mom,

  Mike loves his sweater. He is fine, bouncing all over. I don't know where the measles came from. We had no advance warning.
  I came down to breakfast Saturday but promptly went back to bed for two days. My head hurt something fierce. My stomach promptly rejected the aspirin and my head hurt too much to even move. Finally Dann got a prescription to settle my stomach, so I could take aspirin to settle my head. My co-den mother had to take over. Four of my ten Cubs are absent with the measles. Mike spread them generously. His teacher stopped with letters from his classmates and a valentine chocolate bar. With our infirmary in full swing, Andy and Timmy automatically took over. Andy made poker buns for lunch and a casserole for supper while Tim baked a cake. I don't know how I've managed to teach them this.

February 24, 1966

Dear Mom,

Dann's mother is not well. Again we delayed our plans to take her and the kids to the Sound of Music. We had planned it for the day after report cards and her birthday, but Mike got the measles, tried it again one week later, but I was sick.

We are having Mike's birthday party early while his brothers are off for Teachers Convention and can help. We decorated the cake with a circus tent canopy with dancing circus figures under the big top, invited guests for supper and took them to the Shrine Circus. We have $18.00 worth of free tickets which limited Mike's party to nine boys, plus three brothers each get to take a friend.

We spent last Sunday at the Green River Ranch. The president of the board grilled rib-eye steaks all afternoon while the Jeep truck (with all our kids in the back) drove prospective investors up and down those hills. We hiked to a sink-hole which might be the top of a cave. A kid from the neighboring ranch asked if he could catch rattlesnakes on our cliffs. That impressed my sons.

March 3, 1966

Dear Mom,

I am desperately working on my fourth ski cap as spring approaches rapidly. Timmy waits patiently, but if I don't make it this weekend he won't need it until next winter. The first two caps each took a week, Andy's took a month.

Dann's mother is still sick.

Mike's party was a howling success and lasted for five hours. The boys liked the trained collie act and the dancing bears. We made up 15 bags of popcorn and peanuts that we passed out at an appropriate time.

March 10, 1966

Dear Mom,

Your tour of Fairhaven Retirement Home sounds great. If they have a long waiting list, why not put your name on even if you're not sure? Remember there is always a room with private bath available for you here. Dann says you are his favorite mother-in-law.

His Mother has gall bladder surgery tomorrow. We finally did take her, plus all of us, to see the Sound of Music.

I still get tired and my back bothers at the end of every day. I take iron pills and plan lazy things for the latter part of each day.

I finished Tim's ski hat this morning while everybody else ate breakfast and he clapped it on immediately.

March 18, 1966

Dear Mom,

Dann's mother has been in intensive care for three days. They removed gallstones and an infected gall bladder.

This month's pack meeting theme was Knights of the Round Table. We held a parade with 63 Cubs decked out in helmets, swords, shields, etc. They marched round and round the gym entertaining themselves with miscellaneous sword play as they went.

P.S. Jay and Mike are going to sell seeds together.

March 31, 1966

Dear Mom,

Can you come for Timmy's confirmation?

I have never seen so many sick people. The school has 50% absent. I moved the boy's bedtime up half an hour (much to their horror) and increased their vitamin C in an effort to stay healthy.

Dann's mother convalesces slowly. She knows she must eat but nothing appeals, so yesterday I brought her lunch.

Jay and Mike's seeds have arrived. In one day they sold out the flower ones. Nobody around here, except us, grows vegetable gardens.

We attended a white elephant auction where bidding started at five cents. Jason sat next to Dann. Dann would nudge him at appropriate times intrigueing Jay, who would sound out loud and clear with a bid. Apparently Mike thought this looked like fun, but couldn't see the nudging. Guess what happened? Brother bidding against brother. We quickly explained the principles of auctions to our youngest.

Last night I presented a program on historic Dane County for my Extension Homemakers and listed 54 scenic or historical spots, drew them on the map and talked about all. This should take care of 54 Sunday outings for us.

April 21, 1966

Dear Mom,

I will do with your advice like Andy does with mine—listen to all and take some, but I am grateful that he listens. Our communication lines have re-opened. Sometimes he seeks me out to talk. He apparently needs to get Dann or me alone, which proves difficult.

I did take your advice: this week I turned down soliciting for the cancer drive, doing decorations for the Mother-Daughter banquet, and decided against doing a cookout for the Scout leaders and wives. However, I did make arrangements to visit our seven-year-old friend Karl for an hour each week and lay out an Occupational Therapy program for him. His X-rays show the beginning of hip disease which means he stays flat in bed for six weeks and then a cast.

I am writing an excerpt from Rudyard Kipling's Jungle Tales for Dann to use in his award ceremony. He would also like a wolf mask (which I have) and a tail (which I have not) so I must go and do something about this tale.

MAY, FRIDAY THE 13TH, 1966

Dear Mom,

We started off wrong. Timmy's alpha doe, Black Jet, was due to have a litter today, which Tim planned to use for a fair exhibit. When he went out to check her, he found her dead and this upset him so much that he didn't tell us for a long time. This kid can raise, butcher, and eat rabbits without a qualm, but to lose his favorite is a different story. I hope he has a busy day at school.

Tim knows how to get things done. In going through pants pockets before loading the washer, I found a paper which said, "Mom, please mend all the holes in these pants." signed "Timmy". I mended the holes and left a different note in that pocket.

MAY 18, 1966

Dear Mom,

Saturday was opening day of trout season. Dann, Andy and Tim arose at 4:30 a.m. Dann caught his limit early. Andy got several. Tim came home skunked, so they talked their Dad into going out again on Sunday in the rain and taking the whole family. By this time most of the fish were caught, but nothing dampens these young fishermen.

What a busy family I have. Jason's den planned a picnic supper. When he came home, I was in the bathtub so we conversed through the door. He had fallen in a puddle and didn't want me to look at him, although he had stripped and his den mother had supplied him with a new set of clothes. He said his shirt looked like the measles and he couldn't see his shoes for the mud. Andy is working fervently on a report on the War on Poverty, due Friday. Much to his delight I have excused him from house chores for two weeks because of this report. Tim is busy mapping for his Scout requirement.

May 25, 1966

Dear Mom,

We just came home from a great work weekend at the cottage. Three families came and everybody worked except Norma and me. We just cooked. The crews painted the entire exterior, replaced the canvas screens on the sleeping porch, brought the sailboat across the lake from where they purchased it, did soil erosion work to protect the roots of the big pine, some guys went fishing, some of us tramped into the swamp looking for wildflowers, some even went swimming.

We are trying a diet of high protein with no carbohydrates. Grapefruit juice at every meal and all the meat you can eat. The boys have studied the sheet and want to join us. They offered to give up desserts and potatoes in exchange for all the meat they can eat.

June 3, 1966

Dear Mom,

We decided on a home work weekend. I listed two pages of jobs. The boys could choose anything on the list. The most popular jobs were varnishing the picnic table, fixing bikes, chopping down trees and sawing wood.

Andy chose to make easels for Headstart for his Eagle service project, Tim is still struggling with his compass in the park, Jay has mounted piles of pressed wildflowers, which Miss Parsons gave him for his 4-H demonstration.

We have both lost five pounds on this crazy diet. Jay announced he hopes it doesn't take on Daddy because he likes to bounce up and down on Dad's stomach.

Flippy, the squirrel, has gotten so smart that he climbs the ladder to get his treat.

June 10, 1966

Dear Mom,

I attended College Week for Women on the campus for three days, leaving home at 7:30 and not returning until 5:30. This is not taking on something extra, it's getting somebody else to take over my work. My junior leader did the 4-H conservation meeting as she needed the practice. Instead of going to school to observe Jay's practice demonstration to his class, I sent an evaluation sheet to his teacher and she did a better job critiquing than I could have. My co-den mother took charge of the Cubs schoolyard clean-up, and when Mike came home from school sick, Dann worked from home. I chose practical classes, Teens and their Parents and Better Meetings.

June 22, 1966

Dear Mom,

I have just returned from the fairgrounds with three rabbits, four boys, charts and pictures by the score, rabbit nest boxes, feed dishes and everybody's props for demonstration day. Jay gave a demo this year entitled Getting Acquainted with Wild Flowers. He rattled off all the Latin names, which impressed his judge. She thought he did wonderfully for his age. He replied in tones that carried all the way to the audience where his mentor, Miss Parsons, was sitting, "That's because I have a good leader".

July 2, 1966

Dear Mom,

Dann's mother had exploratory surgery today and they found inoperable cancer of the pancreas and gave her possibly six months. We have had lots of company as all five of Dann's brothers have been here. One evening we collected all the kids at our house—delegated Tim and a cousin to baby sit, took out the canoes and the adults paddled under a full moon at Vilas Park. The moon shimmered across the black water as we dipped paddles noiselessly. We all needed that beautiful peace and quiet. Dann's Mom has always worried about cancer. She was right.

July 7, 1966

Dear Mom,

Dann's mother feels better, but the reports are terrible. Although no trace of cancer showed three months ago it has now spread to the stomach lining, lungs and liver. We have many questions about what is to come.

Jay and Mike are attending city park day-camps. I pick them up at 4:30 when the bus drops them a mile away. They come in on separate buses as they attend different parks. Yesterday Mike came, but Jay's bus was late and when it arrived Jason was not on it. I checked all the other stops thinking Jay might have absent-mindedly gotten off, went back and checked his stop three times and finally in desperation went all the way to Olin Park and found him sitting forlornly in the grass. He hadn't listened in the morning and thought I was going to pick him up at the park. As the hour progressed and I got hotter and hotter, and tired and tireder, it became difficult to remain calm. Today worked fine. As he had an overnight under the stars, he didn't come home.

See you next week.

July 26, 1966

Dear Mom and Jay and Mike,

I know Tim told you about the trouble we encountered yesterday driving to the fairgrounds to pick up exhibits. I slowed for a traffic light, but the guy behind us mistakenly stepped on the gas instead of the brake. He crashed into us pushing us into the car in front, which jammed into the next one. This wrecked our wagon. It buckled the roof, broke the middle seat where Timmy was sitting, sprung the frame and severely damaged both ends. Dad couldn't believe the car could be damaged that badly and we could walk away unhurt. Our game of charging a nickel to anyone who left our driveway without fastening his seat belt has paid off. I was so grateful for that game that I dropped a quarter in that penalty pot just for thanks. It felt like somebody picked up the car and shook it. I asked a bystander to call the police, sent Andy to call his Dad, while Tim and I hunted for our glasses. We finally found them unbroken in the back of the station wagon. I don't even remember mine flying off. By the time the tow truck arrived, the traffic jam extended half-a-mile. Andy and I have stiff necks today, otherwise we're okay.

However the day's tragedies continued. Dann gave us his car so that we could continue to the fairgrounds to pick up rabbits and we found that Tim's purple ribbon Grand Champion Flemish Giant had been stolen. Tim had already sold her and the boy was waiting, but in vain. This so upset Dann that he wrote a letter for the editorial page of the Journal.

"Where is the moral fiber of this day and age? What's wrong with parents whose child brings home something of value and the parents don't bother to question where it came from or where the money came from to buy it? Is it possible to add a rabbit to a household and the parents not know it? Is it not your duty as a parent to know not only where your youth are, but how they finance their activities? On the other hand, if an adult took it so that their child can achieve next year, heaven help the youth of tomorrow whose successes depend upon stealing from the youth of today. Looking at this fair from the eyes of a 12-year-old — is his three years of work to achieve a goal a success or a failure?"

Next year we will put padlocks on each cage and never again will Tim display a blue or purple ribbon on his rabbit cages.

Tim and Tom placed third out of 80 junior demonstrators. We're missing a grand champion rabbit and one car, but all of us are okay. We miss both of you kids, know that you've had a great visit with your grandparents and we're anxious to have you return tomorrow.

P.S. Grandma- We couldn't have had a better time for Jay and Mike to visit you. Thank goodness they were not in the car.

July 30, 1966

Dear Mom,

Tim requested a lemon birthday cake and we're taking lunch plus some of his birthday cake to Grandma Willett. She has been discharged from the hospital. I set up a program with the Visiting Homemaker Service so that someone comes every morning, does necessary housework and prepares food. Dann's mother wants desperately to stay at home as long as possible.

I met Jay and Mike at the Greyhound bus station and we came home on the city bus as we're still short a car. The bus drove past the salvage yard where they had towed our car, which brought forth a lot of questions. I'm still suffering a persistent stiff neck. I'll put Andy on the 5:15 bus Thursday and we'll be down Sunday to collect him. He won't wear you out like those other two. If he gets bored point him toward a book and you won't know he's around. Thanks loads.

August 20, 1966

Dear Mom,

A camping excursion to the Apostle Islands provided the highlight for our Lake Nebagamon week this year. Dann's cousin, John Paul and wife, came visiting and they own a small piece of Basswood Island just off Bayfield. We loaded eight of us, one huge collie, and all the gear into three canoes and paddled across to Basswood. I had objected to canoeing on Lake Superior so Dann and John Paul made arrangements for us to be ferried across from the mainland. However, when we arrived there that morning the lake surface mirrored the clouds in the sky and the ferry boatman was re-roofing his house and didn't want to stop, so we paddled. For my peace of mind they arranged that he would pick us up in two days if the weather worsened. Shortly after beaching our canoes, an ocean liner steamed through the bay where we had paddled across. This classifies as wilderness camping—no tables, no camp lights, no stove or icebox, not even tent stakes as we needed to travel light. The boys hacked out a clearing for the tents. Andy lashed a work table between two trees and Dann and John Paul made what we called our frustrated bear trap to hoist up supplies overnight. We canoed around the island, stopping to check on a huge glacial boulder that created its own island. John Paul climbed up the side of the rock with the agility of a monkey and Mike followed but, without monkey capabilities, he slid back and sank into that frigid water. Unfortunately, Mike doesn't swim. We all watched as he sank to the bottom through that crystal clear water and pushed off with his feet. The minute his head broke the surface, his father grasped the back of his shirt and hoisted him back into the canoe. He may not swim, but neither does he panic.

September 1, 1966

Dear Mom,

Arriving home we found that Dann's mother had fallen, was unable to stay alone any longer and had been re-admitted to the hospital, which she hated. I talked with her doctor about moving her here. I would have to give her shots, but he encouraged me by saying that nothing I could do to her now would hurt her. My back bothers me lots, from that tumor I suppose. We're going to move her here. May the Lord give me strength.

September 6, 1966

Dear Mom,

We took Mom for a trial weekend and then kept her. A visiting nurse comes for her daily bath and shots. Any excitement makes her nauseated and she suffers a lot of pain. Her liver involvement will speed things up. She is alert and interested in everything around her and making a tremendous effort not to be a burden.

The boys run to answer her bell and often sit in her bedroom making visits of five-minute duration. Sunday morning I sent Jay to ask if she would like scrambled eggs on her tray and he came back and ordered one tablespoon that he got to deliver. I derive great satisfaction in seeing the "what's the use" attitude she had in the hospital now disappear. She is appreciative of everything and gets obvious enjoyment from little things like a fire in the fireplace, a grandson's goodnight kiss or the sound of crickets tuning up outside. She loves it when I read to her and worries so that I am overloaded that she gets all steamed up if I don't rest. It's easier to rest than to object. Either Dann or I get up every night for her medication.

Today is that momentous opening day of school. I remember the saying "school days are the best years of your life providing your kids are old enough to go to school." I don't put myself in that category. I'm glad to see school start, but I get equally excited to see it cease in June as we do such fun things in the summer. I am happy to have them gone this year though because they've been so good about waiting on their Grandma and being quiet, but they need to get out part of the day.

Thanks for the pears. Jay spread them in the basement. The minute one ripens it's eaten. We feel badly about the broken branch and should have realized that your heavy harvest of pears plus Tim on that branch would be too much.

Mom Willett asked me to empty her refrigerator and to order Christmas presents for all Dann's brothers. She talks to me a lot, often in the middle of the night. I should put a pad and paper by her bed and take notes as I'll never remember all the things she wants done.

September 13, 1966

Dear Mom,

Mom Willett doesn't eat anymore. As she now needs shots in the middle of the night, the visiting nurse taught me to do this. We practiced on an orange much to the boys' horror. I suggested practicing on them and they immediately vanished. I seem to have two problems. One is keeping this household operating on a non-exciting level, the other is operating day by day with no advance plans. Yesterday a friend sat with her until school was out so that I could help Dann paint an apartment that we're remodeling. My back now bothers all the time. Mom W constantly wants to be turned and I can no longer do this. Often she has to wait until school is out so that the boys can turn her. My four noisy wildcats have been wonderful. She needs hypos as often as allowed, which means every four hours all night.

The pears are ripening fast. I am torn between canning pears or sitting with Mom and losing many of the over-ripe ones.

September 20, 1966

Dear Mom,

It is late but I need to write to you. Today was Dann's birthday. Don came to sit with his Mother and told Dann and me to do whatever we wanted to celebrate his birthday. We chose to walk on Picnic Point. And we talked. I have a doctor appointment for tomorrow because my back pains have increased so much. I faced the fact, with tears, that caring for Mom Willett is more than I can manage. This causes me more distress than my back because we didn't want her to have to go back to the hospital. I think we have to concentrate on what we have been able to do for her, and not feel that we fell short. Today has been awful.

September 21, 1966

Dear Mom,

Again, it's late at night. Even though Dann called you this morning I need to write. Mom Willett got so much worse last night that I hardly slept at all. We sent the boys off to school a trifle early to get them out of the house and called an ambulance. Dann held her hand as she was having trouble breathing, but we didn't tell her that she was going back to the hospital. The ambulance men rushed into the bedroom. One leaned over Mom, straightened up and announced, "She's gone. Why didn't you tell us it was an emergency?" I felt relief that her problems were over.

"It wasn't an emergency," I said. "There was no hurry." I shall miss her very much as I saw her oftener than I realized. I kept my doctor appointment and after the funeral, I will have a hysterectomy.

October 10, 1966

Dear Mom,

I am fine. My doctor says I can do as much as I feel like doing. Two weeks of your time was a rare gift. With me in the hospital for a week, it would have been pandemonium without you holding the fort. The week you stayed after I came home was pure luxury.

I have thought a lot about Mom Willett. For 16 years I lived only blocks away from her and didn't realize how much she influenced my early married life. She was quiet and patient and never seemed to worry. I am none of the above. She lived with us for three weeks. At the end she taught us a much-needed lesson that a million blessings surround us each day, but in the stress and turmoil of daily living we don't stand still long enough to see, hear and appreciate. I am doubly blessed to have had both a mother and a mother-in-law that I couldn't have done without.

6 The Family That Plays Together

NOVEMBER 3, 1966

Dear Mom,

I hope now we can plan for more family fun. We visited Dann's Aunt Belle in Cataract and took along the hand-embroidered white dresses I found in a barrel when we closed my other Mom's house. I hoped Belle might recognize something. She told us that a dressmaker lived-in and sewed dresses and petticoats for all four girls for Belle's high school graduation in 1907 doing this for a total of $27.

We plan to have the big Willett Thanksgiving dinner again. We can do it if we don't redecorate the whole house in anticipation. If it weren't for helping Dann in our apartments, closing his Mom's house, and training den mothers, I could manage real well.

Try doing your windows with newspaper. It works better than paper toweling.

I measured the boys again. The other measurements got lost. The instep measurement is from crotch to hemline. Where I listed two measurements, the smaller one would be okay if you were buying now; if buying ahead, use the bigger one.

The boys and I made a feeding station under the spruce tree for sundry animals and filled it with peanut butter, nuts, oatmeal and cabbage. Now we watch squirrels.

NOVEMBER 25, 1966

Dear Mom,

Thanksgiving dinner, with 25 Willetts, came and went without a hitch. My sister-in-law came Wednesday and we spent all afternoon setting tables. I used Grandmother's individual salt dishes, nut cups hand-turned in eight different woods, individual miniature butter plates with knives and decorated the table in fall foliage. Housecleaning commenced the Saturday before. Andy and I doused everything with either furniture polish or floor wax. Andy wanted me to take him to buy ski equipment. Complaining that I didn't have time with Thanksgiving looming, he offered this exchange. Starting that far ahead, things might not stay clean but they did. Tim used my punch bowl and your recipe and froze lemonade in a cornucopia mold for a bowl floater. I taught the boys a Thanksgiving hymn as a surprise for their Dad. Jay and Mike carried soprano, Andy bass, Tim and I alto. Jason sings with a bell-tone soprano. Mike never listens and sings off key unless I sing in his ear. Andy sang tenor, but suddenly turned bass. The next day the family brought me breakfast in bed as compensation for getting up at 5:30 a.m. on Thanksgiving.

DECEMBER 1, 1966

Dear Mom,

We managed Thanksgiving without getting sick, but not by much. Before Thanksgiving Dann patched a spot on the living room wall and mixed some light brown paint to cover the patch, but once on the wall it metamorphosed into delicate lavender. Furniture rearrangement solved the immediate problem. After Thanksgiving, Dann moved the furniture into the middle of the room and applied a first coat which didn't cover, so we applied a second coat. Still not enough. Monday morning I managed to get to the breakfast table long enough to say I didn't want any and climbed over the furniture to a couch where I stayed all day. Jay came home from school at noon and occupied another couch. By Tuesday morning we kept Mike home. Dann saw the handwriting on the wall and painted furiously, finishing the third coat by Tuesday night. Wednesday morning he didn't make it out of bed. Even though we'd completed the painting, the furniture stayed piled.

When Mike came down this morning he asked, "Isn't anybody sick today?" Isn't it nice that we waited until after Thanksgiving?

Andy made the swim team. Dann attended the meet with Tim and Jay. The kid officiating at the door looked at the boys and said, "You guys get in for nothing, but he (Dann) has to pay half-a-rock." The boys were ecstatic with this expression and are planning on supplying their Dad with half a rock for the next event. They sat on folding chairs along the pool edge because the machine that moves the bleachers from one gym to another wasn't operating. Some of the relays get pretty exciting and Dann worried that, if Jay continued bouncing up and down on his chair, there might be another participant in the water.

We are learning how to live with dead batteries. Somehow we acquired multiple transistor radios, flashlights, and race track cars, all of which run by batteries providing the batteries aren't dead, which they usually are. Mike announced that his friend's father fixes old batteries by freezing them. Mike collected all the dead or half-dead ones intending to fill my freezer. I don't look kindly on this and suggested they limit their experimenting to one dead battery. The next day Mike turned up with another friend who had a recharger so he gathered all the batteries again and gave them to Doug for overnight. I need to know — is there any basis to this?

I took the boys window shopping but they grow impatient with money in their pockets. Timmy announced he didn't need to go window shopping because he didn't want any windows for Christmas.

I made an apple pie, got distracted listening to the boys and didn't notice until half-a-teaspoon too late that I used pepper instead of cinnamon. I washed off each individual apple slice. Will this help?

December 13, 1966

Dear Mom,

The apple pie tasted delicious. I didn't confess until it was gone.

Tim is thrilled to be elected patrol leader. The troop went camping when the temperature was 25 degrees. They do well because they're prepared. I worry at the wrong times and fretted all weekend. They got along fine even though it snowed, but Tim came home, went sledding down the driveway and crashed into a rock. The gash on his leg required both internal and external stitches.

We've been trying deviously to find out if Michael believes in Santa Claus. He doesn't commit himself. I think he isn't about to spoil a good racket.

December 21, 1966

Dear Mom,

We arrived home from your house with the livestock intact. Nobody guessed that two live rabbits were hidden under the luggage. We were pleased to find two purebred Californians for Tim's breeding stock and housed them in the basement in a temporary pen of storm windows which Timmy made last year. The basement is not off limits but old salt bags hang haphazardly around the sides of the pen.

We had company for supper last night and it's tough when they arrive 30 minutes early with the kitchen drain plugged. Dann fixed the drain this morning with Jason at his elbow asking questions. Jay finally rushed out the door two minutes before school, only to come back because he forgot his white shirt for the concert.

January 3, 1967

Dear Mom,

Long live Christmas, but how do I get candle wax out of my carpet? We missed you. Hope your cold is better.

Just before Christmas I took Tim for his one year kidney checkup. That afternoon the rabbits got loose in the basement. Andy went down for something and a white streak zoomed past him. He thought it was a white rat, but he and the rabbits finally made friends behind the water heater. We put the rabbits under the tree in a cardboard box at the last minute. When Tim discovered them, he stopped opening packages and just played with them. The boys couldn't believe those rabbits had traveled in the car with us.

Tim's X-rays were okay, but the dye they injected caused an allergic reaction and Tim started to itch and turned bright red.

We partied for a week: caroling parties, oyster stew parties, tobogganing parties, a piñata-breaking party and an open house for our Scout co-workers. The kids helped prepare and we loaded the dining table with fancy food. At the last minute I got cold feet. We sent invitations to 64 people. What if they all came? The kids scampered upstairs and watched TV, coming down between shows to sample the food.

Cleaning up afterwards, I sent Jay out to burn the trash. He loves to do this, hastily grabbed the matches and rushed out the door. I muttered, "But he forgot to take the wastebasket."

His brothers watched at the window, "He's going up the driveway. He's gotten to the incinerator. He's lit the match."

January 12, 1967

Dear Mom,

Christmas is still with us. Dann has twice exchanged the cotton pants I gave him, I returned Andy's swim trunks for a better size, Andy and Mike have taken down the outdoor lights, and I shopped at six stores before I found the size 10 boots that Andy needed. In the meantime he wore his Dad's and can't fill his Dad's shoes. Pete the canary, guaranteed to sing, uses his voice only when this typewriter is going. Adam and Eve, the Californian rabbits, are turning snow white again. After running around the basement, their smudged coats resembled storm clouds scooting across the horizon. Jay checks his new aquarium thermometer constantly. When he went to the pet store to buy new fish, the man wouldn't sell him any because Jay had just put fresh water in his tank. The clerk said to wait two weeks but then he discovered Jay had no thermometer. "That water temperature has to be 72 degrees or tropical fish will die."

I contributed, "Obviously our tank is at 72 degrees now. Those fish have lived there for a year." Stony stares shot in my direction from both Jay and the salesman and Jay promptly bought a thermometer. It registered 72 degrees in his tank, but the morning after when the house thermostat had been turned down, his thermometer registered 66 degrees. He figured out why and we are about to have the irresistible object meet the immovable force when he approaches his Father on the subject of night-time thermostat settings.

Mike has been madly recharging batteries using his new recharger and is frantically looking for friends with dead batteries. What do you suppose happened when they put a new one in by mistake? Now nothing we do recharges it.

I need a chauffeur's license.

January 18, 1967

Dear Mom,

I'm almost too tired to write tonight. I have been painting in our Franklin Street apartment every day as the new tenants arrive February 1st. I worked out a routine, working here for an hour after breakfast, packing a lunch for Dann and me and painting until 3:00 p.m. I dash home before school dismisses and the hours between 4:00 and 6:00 vanish. After supper I soak in the tub to get rid of aches and pains and snuggle in bed by 9:00 p.m. with a book.

We took Mike shopping for shoes. The salesman was fascinated to discover Mike wearing two left boots. Dann erupted with laughter when Mike kept trying to put his left shoe on his right foot so that his right foot would fit that left boot.

Banks are not infallible. We deposited a tenant's check, but he had two accounts and his bank charged it to his other account. This balance was too small so the check bounced to us, but they cleared it through our business account, reducing the balance there so our checks bounced. This challenges my bookkeeping. Indian wampum would be easier.

FEBRUARY 6, 1967

Dear Mom,

Thank you for the rye bread, the honey and the relaxing weekend. Who, but Jay, could forget to take pajamas and then bring home the pajamas that he didn't take in the first place? I hope you haven't had any more guests who need pajamas. We are all looking forward to seeing you on Wednesday. Mike cleaned Pete's cage so he'd look nice for you. His timing was off, but his intentions were good.

FEBRUARY 16, 1967

Dear Mom,

Tonight is our annual Blue and Gold Cub Scout banquet. Excitement has accelerated all week. Jay walks around with my hair spray, working on his cowlick in preparation for uniform inspection. For the first time, our entire family will attend. Mike takes his Dad, Andy substitutes as father for Jay, Tim goes as den chief for his den, and I as den mother.

Andy talked me into slimming down the pants of his uniform. He wants them skin tight. After that I had to type Dann's history sketch that we researched for a closing ceremony.

Jay is practicing as he is one of 12 boys I selected (some from each den) to sing four songs. Tim is delighted because we cancelled his cornet lesson for this banquet and Mike raves about their den cake. They added 57 candles: 54 for the anniversary of Scouting, one each for Washington, Lincoln, and Mike—all February birthdays.

March 6, 1967

Dear Mom,

We had a backwards birthday party for Michael. This is the first party we've ever had when the guests didn't arrive early. Our boys decided that's because it takes more time to get dressed backwards. Guests came with shirts and pants turned around, mismatched shoes and on the wrong feet. We played musical chairs walking backwards, drop the clothespins in a bottle watching in the mirror, and drew pictures blindfolded. Small prizes went to the losers of each game. You should have seen the look on little Doug's face as he had won almost every time and didn't receive any prizes. We started giving birthday parties for boy #1 at age three so this must be #32! Enough!

We bought two two-man lightweight mountain tents for backpacking or canoe camping but need three before we can do anything. This is like having half a horse.

We are considering camping in the Ozarks during spring vacation. Wish Easter wasn't so early.

March 9, 1967

Dear Mom,

Dann issued pinewood derby kits to all the Cubs and everyone has been inseparable from their model cars as they frantically prepare for the big race. Jay and Mike finished the final coat of paint and left them drying overnight on the basement floor when catastrophe struck. In the morning screams of horror floated upstairs. We were devastated and they had to do a lot of work over when time was short. I wrote them a poem. Its truths are self-evident. Prelims are next Saturday and I plan on presenting this to them just before the race.

Dear Mom

Oh, once there was a Cub Scout race
Made up of Pinewood cars
All sawed and whittled and weighted
   down
And painted bright like Mars

For hours and hours, the jack knives
   flew
The sawdust piled high
The days flew by, the cars not done
And race day drawing nigh.

But then the tools were put away
And paint cans opened up
The cars left on the basement floor
While the makers went off to sup.

But woe is me, in this same place
Two friendly rabbits lived.
Born in the fall, and yet too small
To have the outside habit.

And so while waiting for the spring
A temporary duplex they did share
In the warm basement all tucked away
Were these rabbits, a playful pair.

But friendly rabbits that they were
Liked it not to be apart
So they wiggled, squirmed and pushed
And out they went, quick as a dart.

The Family That Plays Together

Off they went in this basement warm
To see what they could do
A new home to find, some food to eat,
Perhaps something to chew-

You guessed it friend, as they looked around
The first thing they did see
Was a beautiful piece of forest green
And they wondered what that could be?

So those big buck teeth tried a piece off the nose
And a hunk from behind the cockpit
He sharpened his nails down the fuselage
And in the gas tank left a slit.

And she went on to a farther place
Attracted by the shiny red,
Chewed around on the sharp points all
Until she felt well fed.

The night passed through, and the screams that rose
With the coming of the dawn
What a shock to find this horrible mess
All hopes of winning gone.

The anguish and tears are lessened
Now what are we do?
For time is short and damage too great
To make these cars like new.

Dear Mom

Off with their heads, we're mad enough
And into the frying pan?
Or secure the hutch?—or feed them more
And love them all we can?

Blame someone else, 'tis not our fault
For all things that go wrong?
Or can we turn a tragic mishap
Into success for which we long?

Quick, out with the sandpaper, plane, and knife,
Out with the plastic wood
Sand those corners, streamline those cars
Like soft pine can and should.

More tender loving care that adds
The lines so slim and sleek
What first seemed tragic circumstance
May add to what we seek.

With an eye on the clock as the hours tick by,
Will that touch-up paint be dry?
And when not working on the cars
We've learned to put them up high!

And so the big day finally arrives
The day of the pinewood race
Will they win?—the forest green and the shiny red
Or failure do they face?

The cars streak by, professionals all
The Cubs are yelling too
Brother versus brother, friend against friend
Who is winning? Who?

As our flashy models are placed on high
We already know their fate
For win or lose, these boys have won–
They've learned at this late date

To make the most of what one has
Not pass the blame along
To take one's mishaps as they come
And use them is not wrong.

It matters not what tools we use
But that we use them well
Our Cubs learn to do their best
And this is the story we tell.

March 16, 1967

Dear Mom,

    The derby race prelims stretched interminably. It took Cubmaster Dann five hours just to get through the roster once. Competition was by dens with each first and second place winner going on to finals next week. Mike was ahead, but at the last minute placed third. Jay's nerve-wracking race was the last one of the day. His den reduced from 11 cars to three, but the judges couldn't rate the three because they raced close and inconsistently. To win a heat a car has to win twice in two different lanes and every time these cars switched lanes they placed differently. Dann excused himself from judging. The committee decided to run six more times using points for placement—i.e. three points for first place, two for second, one for third with high scorer winning. Jay won three times, but placed second to  his friend. Jay's wheel kept coming off. He and his Dad would quickly apply first aid by jamming a piece of toothpick into the axle that would hold for about two trips down. It has now had major repairs and waits safely on the living room mantelpiece for the finals.

We are having second thoughts about going to the Ozarks since they got a four-inch snowfall yesterday.

March 23, 1967

Dear Mom,

We decided against the Ozarks because of the weather and concerns about business. So would you like to come for Easter or could we bring dinner down?

I took my nine-year-old Michael character to the grocery store yesterday. As he checked out, the checker asked if he would like a bag. "Oh, no," he replied as he snatched off his ski cap, stuffed in the candy and plopped it back on. Very efficient cap I knitted.

He has been talking about his new swim class teacher and

commented, "It has funny hair and I don't know if it is a he or a she."

"Didn't you notice the swim suit?"

He grinned from ear to ear, "Okay, I know now."

April 4, 1967

Dear Mom,

Happy belated Birthday. Between vacuuming mud and cooking for this hungry mob, I don't seem to get letters out on time.

Our Cubs are holding a light bulb sale. Because of the prize involved everybody started simultaneously, so at 9:00 Monday morning eight cars lined up in our driveway to pick up their allotments. By 11:00 people were coming back for more bulbs. Since then Cubs and den mothers have appeared constantly at my door. Managing this accountability challenges us. At night we pull the drapes, dump the day's haul on the office floor and sort. Timmy checks quarters for his quarter collection, Jay checks dimes, Dann does nickels, Mike checks pennies, Andy rolls and totals on the adding machine and Dann locks it away in the safe. We ordered 3,000 bulbs and have reordered three times. Jay turned in $75 and ranked top salesman until yesterday when his friend Steve zoomed ahead, making Jay frantic. He plans to sit at the polls tonight. I hope this isn't illegal. Mike is running third and I hope never to see another light bulb. The two brothers work as a team one working each side of the street and have divided up friends and relatives. They extend further each day. The first day I worried, deciding that if they weren't home in three hours I would search with the car. I broke down after two hours and 45 minutes and drove through that area. No boys. When I came home I found them sitting on the front steps wondering where I was. I think they have memorized every street within two miles.

Dear Mom

We survived spring vacation with only three unpleasant events. Mike stepped on a nail which required a tetanus shot. Harder to cope with was the dead canary we found one morning. Andy unobtrusively performed last rites while Dann talked to Mike. And Tim's new California doe produced her litter, but all died. She pulled fur for a nest and hadn't gotten them into it. Perhaps she was too young to know what to do.

Mike and I are growing plants. Now, in addition to Dann's study being a clearing house for light bulbs, we are raising tomatoes, peppers, marigolds, asters, petunias, strawflowers, begonias, thyme, dill and marjoram. Poor Dann.

He took us to the Sweden House Smorgasbord. It hurts his Scottish blood to see Mike fill his plate with baked beans, but at least he is admitted for a child's price. Jay told us repeatedly that he ate five pork chops.

My 4-H class had a meeting at the Fairgrounds. I drove and could have cheerfully hung them all before we got home. The boys needled the girls. Jay found a box of Spic and Span and threw it over the girls who screamed and threw it back. With his priceless sense of humor, Timmy remarked, "The car is certainly Spic and Span!"

Early the next morning I got two boys out of bed and insisted they vacuum the interior of the car. They did a superb job, I thought, until we put the vacuum away and water ran out of the hose. Timmy had wondered if the vacuum would pick up that water on the garage floor so he had checked it out. We laid all the sweeper parts out to dry for the rest of the day.

Sunday we hitched up the trailer, loaded six bikes, drove to Aztalan State Park and rode around on country roads. It would have been more fun if it hadn't poured.

April 10, 1967

Dear Mom,

    We run a crazy household. Mike and I called on friends (selling light bulbs on the side) and got home late. Before I could start supper one den came to pick up more light bulbs. The next thing I knew a line of protesters filed through my kitchen bearing a sign which read, "We want our supper." They wouldn't let Mike march with them. He was setting the table and they decided he was doing more good where he was. I told them that struck me so funny that I could hardly continue to cook.

    A tin man sits propped up in our yard. I took my Cubs along the roadside picking up old rusty cans which Andy nailed onto boards making a five-foot man. The sign alongside says, "Keep America Beautiful. This is your trash picked up by us. Cubs of Den 3." The boys named him Norman and Norman startles me every time I look out the kitchen window.

    Only one more week of selling bulbs. Jay again holds #1 position with sales of $140. Mike ranks third. Every time any Cub comes to the house for more bulbs, Jay and Mike grab their bags and start peddling again. Is this an unfair advantage?

    I'm helping Dann in one apartment. The tenant died after living there 30 years and it looks like the apartment hasn't been cleaned for at least 20 years. My solution of ammonia, vinegar and baking soda works wonders. I am cheap labor. I send my ironing out in exchange for working, a neat exchange.

    Yes of course, I would be executrix.

May 11, 1967

Dear Mom,

Jay wants to know why I write to Grandma every week when nothing interesting ever happens around here to write about.

Norman, our tin man, now resides on the roadside next to the mailbox, which causes a bottleneck in early morning rush traffic. Last Friday's rainstorm knocked him down and broke his arm. That being trash day, the boys lugged him up to the house. They were afraid he would be collected. They administered first aid and put him back after the trash trucks departed.

June 1, 1967

Dear Mom,

We camped at Devil's Lake last weekend. The boys canoed or fished every available minute. The first campout of the season is notorious for forgetting something as things get moved during the winter. We forgot the cook-kit and learned in a hurry that we can cook out of tin cans and eat off tinfoil. It tastes even better.

We left Twinkle chained in the campsite when we went hiking. Either she was looking for the boys or the mosquitoes pestered her so much that she tried to get away. The chain and her paws

ripped the front of one pup tent, and also tore a hole in the netting of the second one large enough for her to crawl through. We were using our three backpack tents for the first time. At least she didn't touch the third tent. We've worked hard for that one as we couldn't use two until we had three. I pinched and saved but came up short $10. The boys remedied this by shaking out $3 in pennies from the piggy bank that we all pay into when we forget to fasten seat belts, by gathering empty pop bottles, and by convincing their Dad to contribute from his sail fund. Lastly Mike went through my desk hunting for change. All this totaled $10.05.

The Scouts planned a canoe trip for next weekend and requested Dann and our canoes. The Explorer Post planned a canoe trip and also requested Dann and our canoes. Dann will divide the canoes. I don't know how he will divide himself.

June 16, 1967

Dear Mom,

Everybody arrived home safely Sunday night and clustered around the kitchen table spieling separate tales. It isn't often that we all travel in different directions. The Scouts managed to get out short one tent so Dann and another Scouter slept under a tarp the first night when it poured. A torrent caught them on the river and some canoes took in three to four inches of rainwater which their gear sloshed around in. Willett canoes carry sponges so our canoes bailed out, but the rest of the boats carried excess water all the way to the Mississippi.

Andy is receiving his Eagle Scout award and I planned a surprise open house for the boys of his Post. His cousin, Valerie, was visiting and helped me prepare fancy sandwiches, cookies and a huge cake decorated like a spread eagle. Hiding things was difficult. Val worried as Andy kept popping through the kitchen. I finally reprimanded her, "I can come up with reasonable explanations for everything if you would stop looking guilty."

Andy was surprised. So was I. Four kids in the same house were in on the secret plus 14 Explorer Scouts and none gave it away.

July 13, 1967

Dear Mom,

This morning we found 100 deer tracks crossing my garden. Thanks to the dog, that doesn't happen often. The boys picked elderberries in our woods and I made 17 jars of jelly which Mike figured cost six cents per jar. I bake eight loaves of bread every Monday, which lasts the week and it fills up starving boys cheaply.

July 19, 1967

Dear Mom,

Dane County Junior Fair is here and we are ready. Tim and Jay finished their naturariums yesterday. These are scrapbooks with specific collection requirements. One or the other asked me a question every 15 minutes all day long.

Jay and Mike became so enamored with the elderberry jelly experiment that they climbed the mulberry tree, brought me a bucket of mulberries and are waiting to see what I can make out of that. Red berry elderberries are supposed to be poisonous but we ate the jelly before I discovered this. In retrospect, I wonder if anybody developed tummy aches.

July 25, 1967

Dear Mom,

Junior Fair is over. Three boys invited friends. I refused to subsidize the midway with seven hungry kids and packed a picnic lunch. At noon they filtered back and we ate in the shade of the rabbit tent. On the last night the Spotlight on Youth program announced its winners. The M.C. called the blue ribbon demonstrators onto the stage, announced third place, and then second and finally called up Tim and his friend, Tom, announcing them as top demonstrators in the county for their rabbit demo. We all cheered wildly.

Tim, Dann, and Jason arose at 6:00 a.m. Monday, picked up rabbits and exhibits and were home by 7:00 a.m. They didn't take any chances of somebody coveting our prize winning rabbits this time. They had taken all the blue ribbons off in advance and wired the cages shut.

We settled the rabbits back in their home hutches and Dann and I left to finish the apartment which we have rented for tomorrow.

I can picture what must have happened. Dann has been cleaning eaves troughs and left the big extension ladder leaning against the house. Tim must have decided to see how far he could go, and Jay and Mike followed. At the end of the ladder they continued up our steep roof to the ridgepole and slithered down the other side to the dormer windows. Two of them entered the attic and then refused admittance to Mike, forcing him to backtrack. All this with only thongs on their feet. We were speechless. Dann wouldn't attempt that steep incline himself. This must be the first time they have misbehaved and not been punished as Dann and I were in deep shock for the rest of the day.

I found a neat mulberry-rhubarb jam recipe which disposes of those mulberries.

August 20, 1967

Dear Mom,

We got rained out on the Gunflint Trail. We thought we were better campers than that. The boys' new tents were not waterproof and rain pounded the roofs. Dann had attached a tarp for Twinkle to one end of Andy and Tim's tent, but when she laid on the ropes during the night the tarp collapsed. A swift current running across their tent floor filled Tim's shoes.

Dann put up another tarp in the morning and we tried to dry out over a fire. Rain would pour for 20 minutes, then the sun would re-appear for an hour and this kept repeating. Four of us each took corners of a stretched taut, soppy sleeping bag and stood around the fire. As soon as we laid everything out to dry, it would pour and we would scoop and retreat under the tarp.

I put a two-gallon canvas bucket under one corner of the tarp and remarked, "If that gathers enough fresh water, I'll make lemonade." Much easier than boiling one's drinking water and better-tasting.

Two hours later Mike looked dubiously at the overflowing bucket and muttered, "I can't drink all that lemonade, Mom." When it became obvious that we weren't going to be even half dry by nightfall, we packed up in a brief spell of sunshine, and paddled back to where we had parked the car. We had locked the keys inside so broke a window to get in and spent the night in a cabin on the shores of Lake Superior. We turned up the heat, spread drippy sleeping bags over the floor and wearily climbed into warm, dry beds.

After drying out, we explored Port Arthur. The boys were thrilled to trade seven American dollars for $7.50 Canadian. They used to be excited to pick up Canadian change. No more. I tried to give Andy a Canadian quarter in his allowance but that quarter got quietly passed down three times and then returned to Dann.

Rabbit business flourishes. The boys worked all day cleaning and moving rabbits so that we could pick up a pair of New Zealand Reds and start Jay in this business. That gives us three breeds as Tim raises both Flemish Giants and Californians. Present population 24, I think.

August 31, 1967

Dear Mom,

With 11 tenants moving out today, I'm stuck with phone duty. Tomorrow 11 new ones move in. This takes coordination. Dann is hastily finishing last minute repairs. Jay, Mike and Tim are tearing down an old garage and loading it onto our trailer. This is commonly referred to as barter. Dann gets the garage down. They keep the lumber for hutch-building. They do have fun and they do get filthy.

We have two retired Home Economics professors living next door. With a great interest in our boys' activities, they make wonderful pseudo-grandmothers. One of them asked me to manage her garden while she's traveling in Switzerland. Her purple beans and cherry tomatoes produce daily, but she was disappointed when her eggplant didn't mature before she left. The boys have gone over with blown-out eggs and wire and created a new kind of egg plant for her.

Trying to relieve the tedium of daily chores, I added a special to everybody's list. A special is something that gets done for someone else. They were slow to grasp this concept, but now eagerly jump at anything. I have gotten corn husked, half a wild rabbit reburied, cucumbers picked, my bed made, tents erected and watered nightly, (we wrote to the company and they suggested this should shrink the weave and make them waterproof), hutches scrubbed for one's brother, and the basement cleaned. Andy spent all afternoon straightening his father's work bench.

The boys built a tree fort last spring. It lay abandoned for six months, but suddenly they're out every available minute and have constructed a second story where they sleep at night.

October 5, 1967

Dear Mom,

The family decided if Uncle Frank is so expert at rummaging in attics with TV antennas, we need him. A repairman adjusted our set several times, but the picture still jumps. My junior repairmen have figured out a foolproof way to hold the picture. Mike lies in front of the set and places his feet underneath. This works. I would like somebody to explain the scientific principle.

I quit baking bread because nobody comes home for lunch anymore. I had one last package of yeast in the refrigerator and made one last batch of bread. Timmy asked, "How much does yeast cost?"

"Nine cents," I replied. Now I can hear him and Mike in the dining room plotting how to sneak more yeast into the refrigerator.

When Twinkle barked, Dann strolled out into the yard and eight invaders popped out the roof trapdoor of the boys' tree fort and streaked for the schoolyard. Timmy found considerable breakage, plus the remains of somebody's lunch. Our boys spent hours last night booby-trapping it. The next guy to go through that trap door gets a pail of water on his head.

October 13, 1967

Dear Mom,

What a mess! Cub Scout books litter my dining room table. Clothes and junk for the school resale cover the guest room bed. We decided that any money we made from the resale would be saved for a canoe sail. Mike was upset to hear us talking about a canoe sail; until I reassured him that we will add a sail, not subtract a canoe. Yesterday a contractor retaped the study ceiling plus two bedrooms and we piled furniture in the living room. The only place one could sit was on the toilet. Please, no unexpected company.

Jay and Tim convinced the Scoutmaster they shouldn't be in the same patrol. When I was snatching beans from the impending frost, the similarity of the triple compound bean leaf to poison ivy caught my attention. Wrapping the stem I took it into the house. Jay called it poison ivy.

Tim muttered, "Watch it, Jay. Mom's been reading those nature books, again." Dann took my offering to troop meeting and fooled everybody.

This isn't a quiet place, some times less quiet than others. Andy has started saxophone lessons and follows me around as he plays. Simultaneously last night Andy played sax in the kitchen, Dann listened to Indian dance records for the next Pack meeting in the living room, Timmy held his patrol meeting of eight Scouts in his bedroom and Jason practiced piano. It's nice to have a big house. Last night it wasn't big enough.

Fair premiums will be handed out tonight. The checks range from 25 cents to $11 and yes, Tim gets the $11.

Norma, my geographically closest sister-in-law, and I have attended three holiday cooking classes and consider ourselves experts on turkey rolls, squash with pecans, Waldorf salad, wild rice and mushrooms, pumpkin ice cream pie and turkey leftovers using sour cream, curry, and poppy seed noodles. Hope my men will eat this stuff.

NOVEMBER 3, 1967

Dear Mom,

Dann took Andy to work with him yesterday. Andy wants to take a scuba diving class at the Y but doesn't have any money, so we are proposing 50-50 on the expense and Andy earn his share. Dann is enclosing the furnace in one of the apartment buildings and Andy's carpenter skills have improved rapidly. With the advent of his driver's license, he cheerfully runs errands.

The kids are working on Scout requirements. . . "But we don't have a 30″ fence. I would only need to vault the couch once in order to qualify" or "I don't have to go look at old houses in Madison, we can count ours."

NOVEMBER 12, 1967

Dear Mom,

What an awful weekend! Today we attended the funeral of one of our Cubs. Bobby's Mother had gone camping with the Girl

Scouts and Bobby's father took Bobby and his brother along when he went to work at his Enco station. The boys climbed up 10 feet on the tire rack and Bobby fell off onto the concrete. The State Patrol located his mother on the highway and sent her home. The hospital did immediate brain surgery, but the surgeon never held out any hope, and Bobby lived only 24 hours. He was a new Cub, due to get his Bobcat award. His parents have worked with our Scouts for years. Dann ordered a spray of blue and yellow flowers in the name of the pack. Many turned in cash donations so we planted a maple tree on the school grounds in Bobby's name and gave the rest to Big Brothers. Some of the den mothers went with me to the house during the funeral where we vacuumed and washed dishes, all of us remembering episodes when our own kids have climbed more than 10 feet. This sobered the Cubs. It sobered the parents more. I think about nothing else.

Our garage sale sold scads of penny-ante things, but we're still stuck with the big stuff. The boys climbed the rafters and watched for shoplifters. We put out the little white desk from Lisa's old room. When we pulled the drawer all the way out, we found an upside down note written on the back. "I love the Willetts." Lisa hid that pretty deep.

December 8, 1967

Dear Mom,

I am hopelessly behind in everything: bookkeeping, Christmas shopping and housework. Mike and I are making Christmas candles, earrings and a cookie train. I have been helping Tim with his Latin, which strains mine, but he scored a 100 on his last vocabulary test, which we displayed prominently on the kitchen bulletin board.

The boys never received their last rabbit-sitting check. I suggested Jay write Wendy and inquire as we have noticed rifling of mail in our rural box. And so he did. "We wondered if you sent our check as we have been having trouble with people in our mailbox, signed your rabbit sitters, Tim and Jay."

I decided on a picture of the boys in Scout uniforms for Dann's Christmas present. There was only one day when all four were available. Unfortunately Dann made a 3:00 appointment for that day and decided he would take the rest of the afternoon off. While I drove to the high school to pick up Andy and Tim, the other two were supposed to get dressed but on no account should they let Dad see them in their uniforms. When we came back, Dann was already home. To make matters worse Jay came tearing out of the house in full uniform. I learned afterwards they had both gotten dressed, but Jay had answered the phone and right then Dann arrived. Mike raced upstairs and took off his gear, but Jason was stuck on the phone. Although he tried to hide in the study around the corner Dann came looking for him, "What are you doing?"

Jay answered, "I'm on my way to den meeting." and then, of course, he had to leave. We picked him up on the street corner and reversed the process coming home. It's a good thing fathers don't think about details because Thursday is never den meeting day.

We are expecting three litters of rabbits, a first for Jason. We're not positive that all three does got bred. This darned stray rabbit, whom we call Harvey, is using our housing system which is strained at best. Most of the time he sits under the hutches and eats the food which falls through the wire. He has lived with us for a week and we can't find anyone missing a rabbit. I took Harvey to the school lost and found, but had to bring him home again.

DECEMBER 15, 1967

Dear Mom,

Thought I'd never get to letter writing today. First, the mother of one of our graduating Cubs stopped with a pan of homemade fudge and stayed for coffee. Next, the social worker stopped to pick up the 70 cans of food we collected at pack meeting. Each Cub earned the money for the can that he brought. Mike earned his can of blueberry pie filling by spending two hours cleaning my thread basket. This goes to a family with 14 children along with a tree complete with 60 fantastic homemade ornaments. One hundred and sixty attended our December pack meeting and all this detail-planning exhausts me. One parent commented that this was the best pack meeting she had ever attended. I realize what a challenge this is for Dann, who has always avoided public speaking, to stand in front of that many people and keep them interested and under control for 90 minutes. He actually enjoyed himself—laughing, scolding, instructing and congratulating.

We have 10-14 baby rabbits. Tim's does produced. Jay's did not. His buck is a dumb bunny. However Jay has time to try again and still have entries for next summer's fair.

I'm sewing a liner for Jay's sleeping bag. The Scouts leave for winter camping tomorrow so Jay gets the liner early and then gives it back until Christmas.

JANUARY 11, 1968

Dear Mom,

At 1:00 a.m. our bedside phone shrilly broke the stillness as the Fire Department notified us of a fire in Sherman Hall, the apartment building that Dann manages. By the time Dann arrived, TV cameras and Red Cross were there. The fire department evacuated all 26 apartments and the Red Cross placed many pajama-clad people in motels. Dann called a heating man and an electrician who worked most of the night closing down the systems. Then he hired off-duty policemen round the clock as security guards to avoid vandalism, boarded windows and met with fire marshals and safety inspectors all day. My phone rings continuously. The tenants don't know what to do. Dann called me with a partial list of apartments which can be re-occupied if they can live with smoke damage and no water. The apartment, over the point of origin, fell through into the basement minutes after a young couple helped their older neighbors from the premises. Water rose to a foot deep in many apartments. Smoke filtering through the laundry chutes encompassed the entire building. People are asking if we carried insurance on their personal belongings. We don't, of course.

All week we've struggled with the flu, car trouble and the cold. Finally Dann struggled out of bed and installed a new battery but the generator light turned red. When it stayed red he insisted we couldn't take the car out of the garage. So on Saturday night when Andy went to work, he took the other car. That night the temperature went down to minus sixteen degrees. I suggested he warm the car during his supper hour, but he couldn't. At 2:00 a.m. he woke us to say goodnight, without the car. Only one of the help managed to get her car started and she took everyone else home.

Harvey is still with us. A little girl asked if we had found an owner. If not, could she have him? I asked, "Is this okay with your mother?"

She answered yes so we happily gave her Harvey in a shoebox. Minutes later the phone rang. "Is this the Willetts with rabbits? Have you lost one? My daughter just came home with a white rabbit she found in a shoebox at the bus stop."

As we finished supper, the doorbell rang. Mike answered and said, "Mom, its Harvey." Dann thought we would have to dispose of him but during a 4-H meeting here, Tim brought Harvey in.

Somebody volunteered, "I think Camerons lost a white rabbit." Just then Mrs. Cameron walked in and confirmed this. We produced the shoebox and this time he's been gone 48 hours. We have great hopes.

The new litters have to stay in the basement because of bitter cold weather. Those darned rabbits figured out how to escape from their pen and our darling black and white babies are now gray all over. The boys spend their spare time trying to catch them.

Although we bought a second-hand organ last month I never find time to play it so I have signed up for group organ instruction. The theory is that if one pays for instruction, one practices.

At one of our committee meetings they talked about the Scout skiing trips (all my chairpersons are Scout mothers). In the five minutes that I allowed wandering off the agenda, they decided that if our husbands and sons ski, we ought to learn too. Four of us went to Mt. Horeb on Ladies Day when it's not crowded and found a great package deal: rented equipment, T-bar tow tickets, one-and-a-half hours of instruction and lunch all for $6. We skied until we were exhausted and barely made it home before the kids came from school. Our involvement delighted all the husbands.

Andy's Explorer Post is working on the Skiing Merit Badge. They need drivers so we've succumbed and if we're going to drive, we might as well ski too. The first day my ankles hurt from the top edge of the ski boots. I go pretty well. It's the stopping I can't handle.

January 19, 1968

Dear Mom,

The state fire marshal spent days raking through the ashes and determined the fire started in an empty storage locker. Police picked up three boys, who admitted that they had entered that empty locker using a cigarette lighter and lit a corrugated box to see better. When the fire raced out of control they ran. Our boys were impressed with the 24-hour security guard costing us $100 per day. The night Dann took that guard off somebody broke in through the boarded-up front entrance.

Dann muttered, "It's too bad he didn't fall through the hole in the floor. I wouldn't walk across there for anything with those supports gone." Only seven tenants are moving back, the other 19 found other quarters. A Red Cross poster "Need Help?" listed the location of their disaster headquarters. The smoke smell permeates everything and Dann smells like a Boy Scout.

My turn for another Cub Scout skit. Adhering to the communication theme we created a time machine. I found a gargantuan packing box, attached various odd shapes, wired in lights and spray painted it. This time machine takes us back to caveman days.

January 25, 1968

Dear Mom,

Yes, we carried fire insurance on Sherman Hall with 50% coverage on furniture. The judge decreed, unless the police could prove intent, the boys could not be charged with arson, only petty thievery. This frustrates the police.

I've formed a bottle choir, including Mike, to perform at the Blue and Gold Banquet. I practice with Mike alone and when he gets mad, he does well. He must be thinking about something else the rest of the time. The February theme is Freedom so we are decorating our competition cake as a replica of the Liberty Bell.

The Family That Plays Together

February 16, 1968

Dear Mom,

Dann and I survived another marvelous banquet last night. My Liberty Bell cake had an authentic crack and stood six layers high (three cake mixes) decorated with a metallic gray frosting. We placed second, losing to Uncle Sam. Nobody, but me, realized that the back side of the bell was slipping, opening the crevasse on the front wider and wider. Three cake mixes creates a lot of weight on slippery layers of frosting.

My bottle boys sounded terrible in practice. In performance they sounded great. The bell-like harmony tinkling out of those bottles kept the audience spellbound. My assistant den mother and I delivered lectures about not spilling a drop of water because that would alter the pitch, but just as we started to eat dinner, she knocked over a bottle with her foot. We both lunged for it but ALL the water ran out. At the last possible moment, amid the accumulated noise of 130 men and boys, I re-tuned. I had anxious moments over Dann who had gone with the directors to the Green River Ranch. He told them he had to be back by 5:30, but riding with others makes this difficult. The banquet started at 6:00 with uniform and cake judging and dinner scheduled for 6:30. Everything was delegated so all events proceeded and nobody realized Dann was missing. I knew by 6:30 I would have to notify the committee that we had a problem, but at 6:28 Dann walked in and took over.

Yesterday, Tim looked out the window and announced, "Harvey is back." Having traveled a mile through the woods and across two roads he was contentedly cleaning up the spillage under the hutches. We called Camerons, but it took them two days to pick him up and the following morning Harvey reappeared. Obviously he likes it here. Tim gives him water, but Harvey scrounges for his food, spending most of his time under the hutch where we housed him last month but which now has another tenant.

March 1, 1968

Dear Mom,

Jay came home from his campout in the middle of Sunday afternoon. I saved his noon meal as I hadn't known when to expect him. He had already eaten, but happily announced that he would eat anything I had anyway. The boys woke up on the campout with snow covering their sleeping bags. Tim has advanced to Life rank, but can hardly wait to drop out. He is fed up with all those little guys and wants to join Andy's Explorer Post.

We have a new gadget for the office called a code-a-phone, actually two tape recorders in a little box with electronic equipment. Now Dann can receive messages 24 hours a day without going to the office. The first day he picked up a dozen messages that read . . . "Hi Dad, this is Jay."

March 14, 1968

Dear Mom,

The code-a-phone works great but it still says a lot of "Goodnight Dad, it's 9:00 and I'm going to bed," or "how is choir practice?" with various squeaks and beeps as some guys are trying to make an imitation code the machine will accept. Each morning we run through garbage to get the real messages. Hope the novelty wears off soon.

Jay's doe has finally given birth. He went out to feed her and came rushing back saying she had pulled fur for a nest and had already delivered one baby. He got so excited that four hours passed before he remembered he hadn't fed her.

March 21, 1968

Dear Mom,

Our week has gone its usual "boring and monotonous" way. Monday morning neither Tim nor Andy made it to school. Dann took Tim to the eye doctor; I took Andy to the clinic. Timmy was lucky as the lenses just popped out of his glasses and the frames broke at the hinge. Our three younger boys had been flying kites on the school playground while two brothers were playing ball. The ball rolled past Jay into the woods and he tried to stop it with his foot, but missed. They thought Jay had kicked it further and demanded that he retrieve it. He refused. Their father, a professional fighter, has taught them a lot. One tripped Jay. The other kicked him when he was down. Tim came rushing over, told them to lay off, and a free-for-all commenced. Since then Dann has been giving pointers to all four boys on the art of self-defense. Andy felt left out when he discovered what he had missed. Our boys may fight among themselves, but they present a unified front to the rest of the world.

Andy's problem was a bite. He felt a sting and yanked off his boot but never found what bit him. His foot swelled immediately. We elevated his foot but by Monday it was swollen and bright red. The doctor gave him pills but the swelling remained for days. Andy wanted crutches—or at least a car for school, but no luck. I have just been stuck with extra chauffeuring. How do one-parent families stretch themselves? We barely make it with two.

Working mornings in Dann's office makes me an unhappy working mother. If I could teach my family to pick up or cut out extras it might help. All last evening Jay and I constructed a costume for social science class. He insists that we match the picture he has of an old English peasant. Using an old green Robin Hood costume from the attic, a sunshine yellow yoke over the shoulders, and belted in with a pillow it made a perfect replica of his picture. Duplicating the hat created the problem. Timmy came to my rescue carefully explaining, "You have a neat costume and a pointed hat doesn't matter even if the picture shows it rounded."

Could you come for a few days? Hope our bathrooms are fixed by then. Dann keeps running into difficulties. Sometimes an old house is not easy to maintain.

Jay bought a chemistry set and all the boys participate enthusiastically on my kitchen table, leaving the table for me only during school hours. The rest of the time it is piled with experiments.

Another Cub turned up this week, which makes nine in my den. My little salesmen should quit promoting. Enough is enough.

March 27, 1968

Dear Mom,

Would you be interested in dog boarding this summer? We applied for a seven day float trip down the Middle Fork of the Salmon River in Idaho. We wanted to do something memorable with the money from Mom Willett's estate. This year is ideal as, with our present age ranges, two boys qualify for half-price and two for three-quarter.

We're going to the Buffalo River State Park in the Ozarks for Easter vacation. Dann's brother, wife, and daughter are also going. Dann has been working weekends to eliminate his guilt about leaving. Sometimes being your own boss backfires. He purchased a Coleman heater for warming the tent if the weather gets cold or rainy. Course it won't do that!

The Family That Plays Together

April 7, 1968

Dear Mom,

I proclaimed our trip outstanding because we didn't need the heater. Redbud trees and dogwood heavily laden with red and white blossoms swayed in the breeze. Purple violets, pink wild geraniums and snowy trilliums and poison ivy carpeted the woods. I went prepared and was Johnny-on-the-spot for the first itch. Gradually all the boys suffered from poison ivy, but we beat this round as we didn't call a doctor.

Our two challenging 12-mile canoe trips were each supposed to take four hours, but the river was running high and we traveled fast without hard paddling. We set up a shuttle depositing a car at each end, a necessity if you want to paddle only downriver. On the first trip we experienced bad roads getting to the put-in point, one spot so bad that Dann asked everyone to throw rocks and sticks into the roadway to solidify the mud. When we arrived at the river, we unloaded the canoes and Norma and I settled down with all five kids to wait, while Dann and Don shuttled one car to the other end. Driving out, the first car mired down in the sticky Arkansas red mud. In the process of jacking the car to get out of the mud, Don locked his ignition keys inside the trunk and had to walk back to us to get a duplicate set. By the time we launched it was 3:00 p.m. which is NO time to be starting a 12-mile canoe trip. But you can't change your mind in the middle as the only way out is downriver. Dann designated me, with our oldest and youngest in the lead canoe, Don in the safest or middle spot as Norma doesn't swim, and Dann plus the two middle boys, took the troubleshooting sweep. The troubleshooter has to be last because it's hard to back up on a river. Andy found the lead challenging. Many times willow trees, downed because of the high water, gave us only seconds to decide which way to scoot around. We traversed the 12 miles in two hours, but distant thunder boomed as we approached our campground.

A rope, hanging from the huge swamp oak on the other side of the river, was a favorite swimming hole and the kids begged to stop. Two canoes with all the other adults continued. Andy and I waited with the third canoe, planning to let the kids swim alongside when we were ready to cross back to camp. Mistake, as the distant thunder suddenly turned into a torrent. We couldn't even see the other side and Andy and I were afraid to let them swim. Instead we laced on life preservers, piled all four into the midsection of the canoe, which sunk our gunwales almost to water level. With a stern command from Andy to not so much as wiggle, he and I dug in our paddles and stroked blindly across. An appropriate finish to a day of difficulties.

Easter Sunday, driving over ridges and through creeks, often stopping to move boulders out of the two-wheel track, we located a Church of Christ congregation back in the hills. The little church was packed and we felt conspicuous with nine of us in the front row, especially when the lay leader started calling on members of the congregation for Biblical answers. The hymn singing proceeded without the assistance of piano or organ or even a pitch. The leader simply began. It took a measure or two with all those exuberant voices until blended four-part harmony emerged. We stayed for a full two hour service complete with communion, altar call, and Bible study. They invited us to stay for dinner, for an Easter egg hunt, for services that night (which last longer) and to their homes. Church is obviously something which comes first with these mountain people—not just something fitted around a busy schedule.

April 20, 1968

Dear Mom,

I now leave the office for an hour on Tuesday mornings and scoot over to Madison Area Technical College for my organ lesson. Last week nobody came but me, so I played for the entire hour. We did my lesson quickly and then, with the teacher on the baby grand and me sight-reading on the organ, we sailed through duets. This compares to my feelings on the intermediate ski hill. I go faster and faster and know that I can't stop. When playing duets, I neither stop nor break the rhythm no matter what.

Jay has been giving his Sunday school teacher a bad time. Whenever she's not watching, he entertains the rest of the class until they are in hysterics. I told her that at the first indication of giggling she has to move him out to the office. The second giggle is too late as the kids can't stop laughing once he's got them started. Then we informed him that every time she did this, he would lose his Sunday night TV. She says she cannot believe the change in his behavior. This worked so nicely with Jason that I tried a modified version with Tim who procrastinates everlastingly. When he kept putting off his chores, I sputtered, "Unless you have that done by Sunday night you lose your TV."

On Sunday morning I checked to make sure he understood and he replied, "Sure, I'm just not going to do that chore, because I have a lot of homework I should work on and this way I won't be tempted to watch TV." I couldn't get mad at that shrewd philosophy.

May 3, 1968

Dear Mom,

We are experiencing a frenzy of hutch-building. Timmy and Jay started counting what's in the hopper and Tim immediately gave Jay a 30-day notice to move out of the hutch he has let him use. Both disappeared into the basement and started building. We have three new litters and three more due.

Tim asked me to type his history paper. This is my favor to the teacher as Tim's penmanship is lousy, but it's unfair for me to correct his spelling. I circled the misspellings and returned the paper to him before typing. He had started with "at the beginning of the war" misspelling beginning. He simply changed to "at the start of the war."

Jason and I are studying edible wild plants for his first-class requirement. Last night we sampled day lily tubers for supper, not bad! Elderberry pancakes come next.

June 12, 1968

Dear Mom,

The Battle of the Poison Ivy rages again. I noticed it alongside the path when we climbed to the Chapel on the Hill Park last weekend. Andy was careful. Twinkle was not. However the jewelweed in our yard flourishes and its stems are full of a watery substance which controls the itching if we rub it on quick enough.

Andy is making a coffee table in Industrial Arts. He did the top over because somebody stole the first one. By the time he redid that, the wood grain Formica was gone and only colored Formica remained which I don't want. We talked Dann into purchasing some from the lumberyard, bad news because the school pays $.30/foot and we pay $.70. When Andy glued it, the Formica broke. It was difficult to talk Dann into purchasing it the first time and 10 times harder the second time. Poor Andy was afraid to even work on it by then. But now when the morning light streams through the living room bay windows, light beams shimmer and slide across the wood grain of my new coffee table.

July 11, 1968

Dear Mom,

We camped at Pine Lake over the Fourth of July weekend. Andy, who had to work, brought his friend and diving gear and came on Sunday. He was eager to try his new scuba gear. They arrived after lunch but walked in, because the car had gotten stuck in the sand. Andy had gunned the engine in a futile attempt to drive out and the clutch went kaput. One of the men, a Ford mechanic, picked up his tools and all the men walked back with him to our car. The mechanic crawled under, turned some nuts and fixed it. We strolled down to the lake and watched the boys dive until they used up their air. I feel better about their diving now after watching them.

We're working hard on fair exhibits, especially Jay. As the Dane County Junior Fair conflicts with Scout camp, he has to complete his exhibits ahead of time and has a tough decision. He can give up one day at camp to show his own rabbits at the fair or he can stay at camp the whole week and Tim and Mike will handle his rabbits. If he elects to stay the week he won't get home until 1:00 p.m. Saturday and at 3:00 he and Mike, as blue ribbon winners, are scheduled to repeat their demonstrations, a tight schedule.

I am attending a 4-H leader's conservation camp next week. The family thinks they can manage and are busy figuring who will clean house and who will iron. I hope somebody worries about who will cook. Clearly coordination will be the biggest chore. If you wanted to come for a day they would be delighted, but they can manage if they have to.

August 15, 1968

Dear Mom,

    We will always remember our adventuresome float trip on the middle fork of the Salmon River in Idaho—a trip equally challenging for all ages and a great family sharing experience. We traveled 100 miles downriver on rubber rafts and most of the time, in true Willett style, it rained. We would have enjoyed a wee bit less rain but have had lots of rain experience so we survived better than most. Many areas in this great country are still unspoiled by man. We traveled through a primitive wilderness area accessible only by raft, airplane landings on the fire-fighting landing strips, or occasionally, by horseback.

    They limited us to 40 pounds apiece which included tents, air mattresses and clothes. All this had to be stuffed into two waterproof bags. We each laid out what we had to have and packed our two bags, then unpacked and eliminated, repacked, unpacked again and revised our thinking about what is essential. The boys do this better than I. Their scout training showed as they immediately eliminated pajamas, towels and extra clean clothes. The loaded rafts could not be started at the customary point of origin because of low water, so the boatmen brought the rafts down partway empty. They flew us in over the mountains and we rendezvoused with the rafts farther down. Our small four-seater plane took off from and landed at a Forest Service landing strip, maintained for bombers coming in for fire fighting. As none of the boys had flown and I not much, flying down the valleys and skimming over the mountaintops was scary. They told us that a swim suit and T-shirt was proper river gear, but when we arrived at the strip at 6:00 a.m., our breaths came out in frosty puffs. Not many crazy people fly over the Rockies in swimming gear at 42 degrees Fahrenheit. Dann and I flew on the last shuttle and I was thankful to be reunited with my family.

Our group consisted of six rafts, each carrying three passengers and one boatman plus gear. The head boatman was a teacher, the others were college kids working summer jobs. Boatmen received spring training on the Stanislaus River in California and picked up cooking experience from the head boatman as summer progressed. In addition to the excellent maneuvering on the river, they produced superb meals. All we had to do was lay out our sleeping gear at night and pack it in the morning. The brochure stated we could help with supper and fires if we wished, if we didn't feel like it we shouldn't. With the best intentions every morning, by the time we made camp, those best intentions had vanished. We carried fresh meat and produce for half the week and picked up fresh supplies air-dropped on another Forest Service air strip. Unfortunately, the plane dropped the supplies on the wrong end of the strip and this caused much anxiety until we located them. Every night the crew produced hot biscuits (for strawberry shortcake with whipped cream), brownies, birthday cake, or blackberry cobbler using their Dutch oven. Fresh salads appeared daily, plus T-bone steaks, pork chops, beef stroganoff with sour cream and almonds, or spaghetti with mushrooms. Breakfasts started with hot oatmeal followed by canned fruit, bacon or ham and eggs, French toast, coffee and hot chocolate, hot blueberry muffins or cinnamon rolls and fresh trout. Although we carried out everything we brought in, this does not solve the problem of careless humans. All summer long two young rangers on a Forest Service raft floated downriver picking up litter. They even dove for trash strewn across the river bottom.

The crew gave safety lectures as the rafts sometimes flip. Everyone wears life preservers and if we go overboard, they taught us to roll onto our backs with feet downstream to protect our heads from rocks. Just drifting, and paddling a little will gradually float you into shore for a boat pick-up. Instead of staying with the boat as we have taught the boys, in white-water you must move away as the current alongside might pull you under the raft.

The river is narrow, often lined with steep canyon walls. The excellent condition of the wilderness impressed us when we realized 700 boats rafted down last season. The drop here, greater than the Grand Canyon, makes rough water. We plowed through waves four to six feet high and scooted around huge boulders. The first half day we hung on. After that we slid through the huge waves without bothering to take our feet down off the sides. Water coming over the front of the raft by the bucketful reconciled us to being soaked. We bailed often and frantically with #10 cans. One day we had to cross a four-foot falls. All boats stopped to reconnoiter and only one went at a time as rafts often flip at this point. Dann asked for the last raft so that he could snap action pictures if one overturned. All went through upright although they did fold into a V as they flew over. It was Mike and Dann on the last raft that hung up on a submerged boulder just below the falls, much to the delight of the shore watchers who waited for them to tip. Water from upriver poured over them as they bailed frantically on the downriver side. The river will flip the raft if they can't get loose quickly. They jumped up and down. They shifted weight. Finally in desperation, the boatman stepped out on the rock and pushed and at the last moment took a flying leap back into the boat. I was glad that each raft carried a licensed boatman and equally glad that licensed boatman made it back into his raft.

Many pictures are imprinted in my head. . .watching that overloaded plane roll down the strip with parts of my family aboard and wondering if it would lift in time. . .the two elderly ladies that had never camped and finally mastered their brand new tube tent with the help of our young-uns. . .the boatman reaching through the tent flap to serve us hot coffee in bed each morning. . .the tears, plus rain, streaming down Mike's face the first morning when he saw only oatmeal and thought that was breakfast. . . dunking your feet in the river every time you boarded the raft so your shoes wouldn't bring sand aboard. . .the steep canyon walls we passed between on that section called River of No Return . . either completely fearless or dumb chukkers that stood and stared at us. . .endless rain . . .the numbness seeping through me when the cold water soaked us repeatedly as we tilted and rolled. . .trying to keep my feet dry by placing them into a bucket but not noticing the difference when the bucket filled with ice cold water. . .only three of us holding four corners of a soppy sleeping bag over the fire trying to keep that extra corner from dipping into the flames as we dried the bag. . .the horrible worry when Tim vomited all day long. . . fresh grilled cutthroat trout each morning. . .finally getting warm after I sat in the hot springs for so long that my bottom turned crimson. . . the rattlesnake that appeared from nowhere when our boatman and Dann were searching for firewood. . .the beautiful, sparkling, never quiescent river. Dann's inheritance from his Mother was a gift that will remain with us forever.

September 5, 1968

Dear Mom,

    We didn't stay long at the cottage, merely stopping enroute on our way to Idaho, but did I tell you that some of us swam across the lake this year? Dann told the boys he swam it the year he turned 12. Jay, being 12, wouldn't rest after that. So Andy, Tim, and Jay swam across with their Dad alongside in the canoe and Mike and I riding guard also in the rowboat. Reaching the far shore, Andy climbed aboard the boat and Mike and I joined the swimmers and swam back. Mike swam half-way which is what we had predicted, but he was so anxious to try that we let him.

It's hard to revert to school schedules and strange to have three kids at the new middle and high school and only Mike going to school next door. Thank you for sending the jacket, we hadn't missed it yet.

My tramps did get their beards shaved off. Mike came home yesterday and said the kids at school asked if we had our electricity back on yet. I inquired, "What for?"

"So Dad could shave his beard." Dann kept it until after the first Scout meeting and I heard whoops when the Cubs spotted it.

Tim has been a stinker—unreasonable, argumentative and dissatisfied with everything. I keep asking if he's tired, which annoys him. He has always been so sweet and diplomatic that I assumed he was bypassing this stage. Anything I suggest is wrong. He butchered his first rabbit all by himself, but says he needs to watch his Dad again as that rabbit had no heart. Andy, on the other hand, has gotten pleasant to have around and only yells at us occasionally.

Secrets are flying fast and furiously. Our last pack meeting comes up soon and we'd like to make it special so Dann asked to do the closing. We have planned a ceremony using all of us in uniform saluting the flag with a roving spotlight, all top secret. The den mothers had so much fun dressing for their clown skit last year that they've asked for a skit again using this pirate theme. Weekly we connive over coffee. I have been admonished not to breathe a whisper to Dann. Last year's lion outfit is now a monkey suit. These crazy den mothers are all so busy, plus working with their own dens, but without hesitation they took this on, too. I guess the fun balances the work.

The Family That Plays Together

September 12, 1968

Dear Mom,

I thought preschoolers kept a mother busy. Wrong. That was nothing compared to the interests, demands, and expectations of four school age kids.

Jason, now at Jefferson Middle School, has changed the most. He has to learn everything the hard way and I have to learn to ignore this as there is no use both of us suffering. We tried to move him out of here in the mornings, but he enjoyed talking to us so much at breakfast that it didn't bother him when one brother and then another departed. The first day he came back twice to tell his Dad that his pack was strapped incorrectly on his bike. When he noticed the time, he wanted Dann to take him, only Dann wouldn't and Jay departed in tears because he was going to be late. It would have been easier to take him. He arrived three minutes tardy, but his gym teacher was in the locker room and never knew it. Every morning thereafter when the first boy left the breakfast table, Jason promptly stopped eating and departed.

Yesterday he put on clean pants, leaving his lunch ticket in the old pants so he went without lunch. He was sick to his stomach the first day and had a tremendous headache. He asked permission to go to the bathroom, vomited, and returned to the classroom. Tim asked indignantly why he didn't go home. "The teacher didn't say to go home," he replied.

"If you'd told her that you'd been sick," Tim replied, "she'd have been glad to get rid of you."

We cogitated all summer on how to tie a trombone onto Jay's bike. After listening to a talk on all the instruments, Jason switched to baritone. This pleased Dann because that was his instrument, but now we can't figure out how to tie a baritone onto a bike. Jay followed me around blatting on it and when

Dann went out to the garage, Jay shifted and followed his Dad. Dann finally took the baritone from him and triple-tongued the Carnival of Venice.

I have had to tell Dann about the special oncoming PTA recognition night. His reaction was, "Nuts, I hate those things." My monkey suit for our den mother skit is completed. We have two monkeys, two hula dancers and 10 pirates but that's still secret.

September 17, 1968

Dear Mom,

Mike took Tim's black crossbreed baby rabbits to school to show this week. After school he came home with three potential buyers. He also offered Cottontail, one of Tim's does that we don't breed any more. Tim can't bring himself to butcher her, so is offering her for free. Mike told his friends they would have to come back with their mothers or a note. After supper Terry appeared with his little sisters and the money. He said we could call his mother if we wanted to check but we didn't. They took the Cottontail giveaway and two black babies. Within 15 minutes they returned Cottontail. The other friend showed up and he also took the Cottontail giveaway and two black babies, but forgot the note from his mother so I'm expecting them back. Mike and Kevin, another friend, work on a hutch every afternoon. His mother said he could buy a rabbit if he could fix up a hutch. Then she called me commenting that she wished the Willetts would stick to selling houses and canoes. I told her to come for coffee and I would console her.

Night before last was the PTA meeting publicized as Dann Willett night. The planning that our friends put into this shook us. They listed things we've done over the last nine years, gave speeches and showered us with gifts. As Jay said this morning, "Gee, it wasn't even your birthdays." They presented me with a snow white orchid, an electric can opener, a lightweight canoe paddle, and gave Dann a tape recorder. The table, decorated in blue and gold, displayed a cake delineating our names on the icing. All our current Cub staff attended and many of the earlier ones. We were speechless.

The next night was our grand finale Cub pack meeting. Den mothers paraded in pirate, native girl and monkey costumes. I strutted past my entire family and they didn't recognize me. Dann said he kept waiting for one more to come out from the rest room, but finally figured out which was me by elimination. I had used my old red flannel one-piece p.j.'s, cut off the feet, pinned up the drop seat and dyed it dark brown, added a sofa pillow in front and back to straighten out some curves, attached a tail, and used an old nylon to make a beanie cap which covered my hair. I cut two floppy ears from leather scraps and painted a monkey face using brown makeup with white circles for eyes and mouth and carried bananas. I had decided that if one is going to do this sort of thing, the more anominity the better and was delighted when Jay said, "I never did figure out which one was you."

But asking my Cubs afterward if they knew, one said, "Sure, I recognized your shoes!"

I held up a Silence sign when Dann told jokes and Nancy, the other monkey, kept chasing me off. I repeatedly snapped my tail in her face until it caught in the back of a chair, much to the delight of the audience. Frantically pulling at one end, she tugged at the other and I was left with only half a tail.

At Bobcat ceremonies, Dann pins the boy's pin on upside down. When the boy does a good deed he may turn it over. However for the last two months, Dann has simply picked the boy up and turned him over so that his mother could put the pin on right-side up while the boy was upside down. Naturally, when the den mothers' skit got around to Dann, they stood him on his head while they pinned on a grand champion jokester pin.

The evening finished with our Willett closing. Dann and I alternately read the script we had labored on for hours. "As we come to the end of our last pack meeting we wish to show personal thanks to the scouting program. After nine years as den mother and nine as Cubmaster and committeeman we have seen many fine boys learn through Cubbing.

"Step 1 is the Cub program. (Here the spotlight shone on Mike in uniform.) All about us are boys, the makers of history, the builders of tomorrow. We hope we have had some part in guiding them up the trail of Scouting onto the high road of noble character and constructive citizenship. A hundred years from now it will not matter what our bank account was or the sort of house we lived in or the kind of car we drove, but the world may be different because we were important in the life of a boy.

"Step 2 is Boy Scouting. (Here the spotlight played on Jason in his Boy Scout khakis.) A boy looking up to a man and wishing that he could be more like that man. As a scout he will store up memories of campfires, rain drumming on the tent, the flight of a bird, making fires without matches, burnt pancakes, backpacking, poison ivy, swimming and canoeing. As boys living through boyhood adventures they are not conscious of how important these years are, for they are busy rebelling against teachers, holding authority at arm's length, enjoying new found freedoms and discovering the world of adolescence. But the adage holds true 'as the twig is bent, so grows the tree' and these are the bending years.

"Step 3 is Exploring. (Spotlight now on Tim in his Explorer uniform.) These are the years when a young man makes the decisions that will serve as guideposts for a lifetime. If we instill in as many boys as we can, abiding notions of decency, trustworthiness, loyalty, and responsibility plus the ability to stand on their own feet and be willing and able to help others, then we will have done as much as we can.

"Step 4 is the Eagle. (Here the spot zoomed in on Andy complete with Eagle rank sewn on his shirt.) The road for the scout is rough with pitfalls along the way. One in one hundred makes Eagle rank. Scouting has been good for us and we are proud to have had a part in it. However, in any movement there is a time when the pioneers disappear and others must carry on. Invariably things are done differently as time brings changes; but, if the original idea was a great idea, it will persist despite changes. We'd like to pass on to each of you this great gift which has been ours to hold for a few years—the privilege and thrill of working with boys—all kinds, sizes, and color. It becomes evident as we reflect back over these years that whatever we may have contributed to Scouts is dwarfed by what Scouting has done for all six of us. Will you stop and think tonight what Scouting could do for you? Scouting has a language understood by all—a love of nature, a fellowship for man and a respect for God who created both.

"And now may the great Akela of all Cub Scouts bless us and guide us until we meet again."

The conclusion was Tim playing Taps on his bugle while the spot picked up the other three boys standing together saluting the flag.

The nice thing about always being the clown is that when you want to be serious, it creates an impression. The faces of the den mothers glistened with rolling tears. Me, too. I suspect that we are only seeing the tip of the iceberg when we look at the benefits we derived from being a Scouting family. Our family togetherness will go on long after our Scouting activities are past.

7 This Land Is Our Land

November 14, 1968

Dear Mom,

    What a nasty day. I didn't feel like working in the office, so didn't. One of my 4-H boys stopped after school by my request. We lost a basketball at the last club meeting and my grapevine informed me that this kid took it and intended to keep it. I approached this from all angles but he wouldn't admit taking the ball. Finally he said he had seen it in somebody's house and would get it for me. I had debated whether to tackle him, his mother, or the lady who loaned us the ball, so asked my Scouter husband who has been attending Boy Behavior training sessions. His advice was to approach the boy. We'll see if this works.

    I'm glad if you've decided on Fairhaven Retirement Home. The facilities impressed me and it provides many in-house activities so you won't have to drive. You can retreat turtle fashion to your small apartment when the togetherness proves too much. If you reach the top of the waiting list before you are ready, just bypass and stay on top.

    I've enclosed excerpts from Jay's Christmas list "wallet just like Tim's, racing car (Andy makes good choices), racing track pieces, some for Mike too, money (lots, thank you), 104 instamatic or better camera, top quality New Zealand Red rabbit (pedigreed, please get from Mr. Lyndall), bike fender—not plastic and preferably green, new bike handle grip, sodium silicate, sodium iodine, baritone, NO candy or maybe a little, radio and/or record player, scuba diving equipment" and at the bottom "THANK YOU FOR CONSIDERING THIS". His imagination knows no bounds.

November 22, 1968

Dear Mom,

We are counting down to Thanksgiving. I have painted, washed curtains and cleaned closets until I cannot move. Our living room rug has a worn spot in front of the couch and if we turned it, this could extend its life expectancy. Last night, while Dann attended a Scout committee meeting, Andy and Tim helped me. They moved all the living room and hall furniture. I warned that the hardest part was spreading the rug out straight again, but they didn't believe me. One boy took each side and they raced rolling up the rug. In the process it got screwgee and the mat hung out two inches on one long side. They snapped it, pulled, pushed and re-rolled. By the time Dann, Jay, and Mike came home, the rug lay in perfect alignment and the furniture back, walls were washed, the floor edge waxed, and Andy and Tim were watching TV enjoying a cold pop. As the show they wanted to watch started at 8:00, they went through this whole scenario in one hour and fifteen minutes. Dann didn't have to do that lifting and now the boys are wiser about rolling rugs. They learned that Mother thinks crooked is crooked even if its one inch.

My doctor told me to lose thirty pounds. This will spoil my entire winter. I could not do it without the gleeful assistance of my family. They watch the weekly wall chart like hawks. When the line goes up or stays constant they make saucy remarks. It takes all the fun out of cooking. The weight comes off slowly, but perhaps it is more lasting that way. If Mike comes through the house and finds me eating between meals, he screams. Every time Andy goes by the wall chart he makes snide remarks about plateaus and Tim shakes his head worrying over what will happen over Thanksgiving and Christmas.

We enjoy *Newsweek,* but it's not fair for this to be Dann's gift as he gets it last. Jay grabs it first. I have often done without Jay's chores because he found *Newsweek* in the mail and disappeared into the big chair. The week of the elections intrigued him when they showed five different covers depending on how the election went. We do the weekly news quiz in our paper. The boys read *Newsweek* first so they score better on the quiz. If they beat Mother they get a check off their dishwashing list. Thanks, from all of us.

Our Green River ranch dream is in a dilemma and operating without sufficient capital. The promoter has taken what capital there was, calling this his original investment. Easy, because he is treasurer. Dann finally got the books, but he couldn't figure out many of the entries. It looks like the investors will lose everything, many of whom are people that Dann sold to and this hurts. Dann took another buyer to the ranch today. We are desperate to sell. (The board meeting this week will probably declare bankruptcy.) We are being sued by the former owner trying to repossess the land. He asked that we insure the property for $48,000, although he had insured it for only $12,000. Our insurance company would not insure for that much. We are waiting for a decision from the State Supreme Court. We may all get sued personally. I don't have any extra time to worry about this.

December 12, 1968

Dear Mom,

We certainly demolished your scrumptious Sunday dinner. We enjoy your cooking, even those of us dieting. One more pound hit the dust this week. Often I just break even.

Your Santa's helper was pleased to be asked, and willing, but incapacitated. He jumped off the trampoline in gym class and twisted some ligaments in his ankle. He didn't tell me until later that he worried because he couldn't get his tight pants down past the swollen ankle. He wears elastic bandages and tries to keep off it.

Dann came rushing home during Scout meeting to warm up the station wagon while spreading a mat in the back. The senior patrol leader had broken his arm during a game of Battleball. Ironically, the leaders had thought that game too rough for the boys to play, but the senior patrol leader argued and prevailed. The leaders had taught first aid earlier in the evening so a practical demonstration followed by immobilizing the arm with Scout kerchiefs. They treated for shock when the senior patrol leader started to turn green. Dann drove him to the hospital emergency room.

December 19, 1968

Dear Mom,

The boys trooped to the school hill yesterday laden with skis and sleds. My kitchen has been clustered with wet coats and boots since. At supper I offered a check off the list to the guy who could guess the number of black marks, made from their ski boots, on my kitchen floor. Mike won with 62. Dann sat chuckling, but now all are conscious of the problem.

January 6, 1969

Dear Mom,

Thanks for sending the coat back and the new mittens are great.

Saturday we got up at 5:00 a.m. for a skiing trip to Rib Mountain. I was driving, everyone else sleeping, when an oncoming car pulling a U-haul hit ice on the bridge. His trailer jackknifed back and forth and Dann woke to see the U-Haul approaching us sideways. My problem was whether to brake to give the other driver time, or to accelerate and try to pass before the swing got worse. Choosing to instantly accelerate, we scooted through. On the next swing the other car turned completely around, slithered into the ditch and tipped. The driver was unhurt so we took him into town to get a tow truck. I shook all morning. It started our day off all wrong.

It ended wrong too. The skiing was good, but cold. We used the warming room often, but at least this kept the crowds off the slopes. After lunch four of us climbed on the rope tow. Mike and I unloaded halfway up and skied down the easy slope while Dann and Jay chose the steeper run. Mike and I reached the bottom first, and then Jay, but Dann didn't appear. Finally Jay and Tim went back up and found Dann on the ground. When he fell, the safety release on his bindings didn't kick off and he sprained his ankle. He managed to take his skis off and limped downhill to the first aid room where the ski patrol applied an Ace bandage. At home, we iced it and he kept off his feet for several days. When he walks, that ankle swells again and he can't drive so all the chauffeuring on this terrible ice has fallen to me.

After arriving home, the boys went out to water their rabbits and came back with Jay in tears. Something (perhaps a weasel) had chewed its way through the screening and killed the rabbits. Jason lost all of his. Tim has three left. We went to bed last night with Dann's gun next to the window and floodlights set on the hutches that we could snap on instantly if we heard any disturbance, but all remained quiet.

Better news is that we rewarded all our adult Scouters with a party. We divided 30 guests into four teams and each team competitively decorated a cake. One made rockets orbiting around the moon. I fretted about managing everything, so Dann hired a caterer (Tim) at $1.00 per hour. Wonderful. Tim replenished supplies, made punch, and ran the electric knife on the sandwich loaf. We had ham in buns, shrimp sandwich loaf, chicken and cheese, and four different gorgeous, delicious cakes a la mode. Goofs did pop up; the decorated pineapple top that Mike and I worked so hard over wouldn't float and sunk to the bottom of the punch bowl, the ice cream balls that I scooped in advance to save time all melted into one big glob, and I found the strawberry Jell-o in the refrigerator afterwards. A friend called today saying that she noticed I had good hired help in the kitchen, but did I have to hire a watchdog? Apparently she went out with intent to snitch and got her hands slapped, much to her amusement. We will be eating decorated cakes for a long time as each team had a double cake and they ate very little. Dann and I cleaned the kitchen until 2:00 a.m.

The income tax progresses slowly. If I could spend a couple evenings doing nothing but going to bed, the next day's work might progress faster.

January 16, 1969

Dear Mom,

Dann couldn't squeeze his shoe on for a week and whenever he stopped wrapping the ankle, the leg would swell again.

Jay has been sick and unable go on the Scout winter campout, but he did go on Saturday night to receive his Life award at the Court of Honor. The temperature dropped to 22 degrees below. The troop performed the ceremony using torches and candles set in the snow. Deep snow and darkness made walking difficult as we struggled the half-a-mile through the woods to their campsite. If you stayed on the invisible path you were okay. If you stepped off the path you sank in over your knees. "Ole Limpy" had trouble. He walked in on snowshoes, but coming out the boys grabbed the snowshoes and zoomed ahead.

Every night someone asks, "Which cake are we having tonight?" Fortunately we have four different flavors.

Dann and I are PTA program chairmen. The PTA president frustrates me. She always puts us last on the agenda and lets the meeting drift. We're lucky to get five minutes to present our long range plans. The speaker for our last program was Dr. Jim Zimmerman talking about the Madison School Forest and the school's outdoor education program. Madison owns 300 acres of oak forest 13 miles south of town where teachers take their classes for nature study. This intrigues me. I'd like to learn more.

FEBRUARY 6, 1969

Dear Mom,

I am working in the office again, but promised Mike I would quit by noon so that he could come home for lunch and we can eat together.

I am organizing a PTA social for Valentine's Day and have set up ten committees totaling 40 people. This should mean that somebody else does all the work, shouldn't it? Dann says that means we should have at least 40 people present. I'm betting on 300.

Timberline Ski Area desperately needs ski patrol members and hired ten of the experienced skiers from our Explorer Post 10.

Andy is thrilled although he feels he isn't good enough. Each boy works every other weekend receiving basic First Aid and skiing with toboggans and then spends the day systematically skiing the slopes. It pays only in prestige, and they can ski anytime without charge. Andy will be out all day tomorrow and if he isn't good enough now, he should be shortly.

Sarah Lynn has joined our rabbit family. She is four months old, timid and snowy white with black ears. Mr. Lindall, who bred her, says there is no competition around that could knock Jay off the table with her. Mr. Lindall sells cheaply to the kids as he wants them started with good stock. I worry about Sarah Lynn as I think she would taste better to the predator in the woods than any of the others, so Jay and I prevailed on Father to allow temporary housing in the basement after Jay made all sorts of rash promises about housekeeping.

Mike has been working frantically on his Webelos and we will soon graduate our last Willett Cub Scout. He also has joined 4-H. I wish his electrician Grandfather could see his circuit board which decorates my front hall. IF you turn the switches the right way, little lights go on all over.

February 14, 1969

Dear Mom,

Today is our PTA-sponsored Community Barn Dance. Don't know whether to expect 60 people tonight or 600.

Are you reading about us in the news? I come home from the office each day at 11:30 to eat lunch with Mike. Yesterday it took an hour to get through the campus as police cars and National Guard buses blocked University Avenue. Protesting students closed the street. Police used tear gas to break them up while the National Guard stood by with bayonets.

Jason is raising shrimp in our front hall (next to Mike's circuit board). He has set up a pan with filter which nobody is supposed to touch for 24 hours. Sarah Lynn has gotten so tame that she runs all around my kitchen.

MARCH 12, 1969

Dear Mom,

Andy has received housing acceptance for somewhere on campus. This will give him at least one year away from home.

Yesterday Dann drove to the Green River ranch on business and I tagged along and tried to explain to the boys when we came home, about corn base land that we put in the soil bank. Jay can't understand how we can divert 25 acres of corn base and receive $1000 from the government. The boys were incredulous that the Soil Bank office offered us an advance, which we refused on the advice of our lawyer, as the ranch is currently in receivership. If we took payment now, we might lose it.

Supper talk varies daily. Last night Dann reported on a sizable supply of narcotics he found stashed in a jacket sleeve under a trapdoor in the basement of one of our apartment buildings. He called the police and while the tenants were out, Dann and the policeman entered the basement. The policeman identified and removed the drugs. The police think that the tenants will fight among themselves when they discover the loss, so we expect to find them suddenly moved without notice. Dann brought the jacket home. We inquired if he wasn't going to take it back. "Certainly not," he stated emphatically. "Nobody would claim it." We don't discuss this outside the family. If nobody knows Dann's part in this, we'd like to keep it that way.

We're being sued for $80 by a former tenant. He had not moved out by the first of the month and the new tenants were moving in at noon, so the boys and I cleaned and stored the old tenant's stuff in boxes. He claims the boys put dirty clothes next to clean ones which got them all dirty and that they lost his coin collection. We're not very popular this month.

March 20, 1969

Dear Mom,

Our young male tenants, who are under police surveillance, have acquired two puppies that are doing things to our carpeting. Dann promptly gave three-day notice to get rid of the dogs or move. Unfortunately, they got rid of the dogs so we still have the drug problem.

Sarah Lynn discovered how easy it is to jump out of the pen, so we instigated a basement patrol that operates every morning to chase her out from under the woodpile. We desperately need spring vacation as Jason is not planning on repairing his outside hutches until then.

April 16, 1969

Dear Mom,

We've developed an appalling problem with our back land. The 15-foot easement, which stretches across the back of our orchard, belongs to the man owning the adjoining four acres of woods. He sold to a builder who apparently plans to tear up fences, trees, etc. and take heavy equipment through on the 15-foot strip, so we hired a lawyer. He worries about the vague wording on our abstract. As it doesn't specify what kind of usage on the easement, we interpret this to allow a walk through and nothing else. The Pest, as the boys privately refer to him, insists that this is his land

and he can do whatever he wants, so we served papers to bring it into court for a legal decision. In the meantime he has driven through and chopped down trees. We worry about what he might do during the three months while we wait for a court date. Our lawyer assures us this is indeed our land and we can do whatever we wish, providing it is always possible for the pest to walk through.

I am taking a bird study field class that I love even though I have to get up at 4:30 a.m. in total darkness. As I've been making remarks for years about crazy fishermen who roll out at 4:00 a.m., my chickens are coming home to roost. I roll out fast and throw on my clothes before I have to listen to too many sleepy, saucy remarks.

May 1, 1969

Dear Mom,

Dann and I have become vice-presidents of the PTA which means co-presidents next year. We're encouraging environmental projects so we, the PTA, sponsored a unique litterbug contest. We had 20 entries from Girl Scouts, Brownies, Cubs, Boy Scouts, Explorer Post, 4-H, and family units. Each unit gathered litter for several months and built something. Last Saturday we awarded cash prizes for originality,

beauty, and size. Dann solicited cash from businesses and everyone received a coupon from MacDonalds for a hamburger, malt and French fries. One hundred and ninety individuals worked on this and that required three city collection trucks the following day to pick up the exhibits. Once started the kids were unstoppable. Picking up trash is like eating peanuts—as long as there's another in the dish (or in the ditch), one can't stop. I took Mike's patrol out in the country and they filled boxes and cans recklessly until I told them if they didn't stop filling my station wagon, they would have to walk home. They found a double-compartmented kitchen sink that they turned on its side and, using a two-engine motor, built an entire airplane around that. The Explorer Post found an old Volkswagen frame and Andy spent one month repairing our trailer so they could haul it home. Then they drove all over the countryside picking up abandoned car parts. They found a stick shift, steering wheel, white wall tires

and created a back seat bar of whisky bottles, bucket seats (real buckets) a "200 can" engine and so on. The Post won the grand prize of $25. All exhibited unlimited ingenuity: a dinosaur, steam shovel, tin man, litter eater, demonstrators, electric chair, litter bug, pig, and even a horse made from barbed wire complete with feed bucket created by the 4-H horse class. The kids could not believe the amount of litter that gets thrown. Best of all, I believe that any child who has picked up litter will never throw it down.

May 10, 1969

Dear Mom,

Would you settle for just me this weekend? Thirty Scouts, including Jay and Mike, six men including Dann, and 12 canoes are leaving Friday night for a weekend on the Kickapoo River. Dann built a rack for our trailer to carry four canoes. At 6:30 a.m. Saturday the Explorer Post, including Andy and Tim, are leaving for a weekend fishing trip. This provides me with lots of uninterrupted time.

I need a rest after last Thursday. Arising at 4:30 for my last bird class, I rushed home to breakfast with my family and left again for a day's outing to Mineral Point that I had planned for my Homemakers. We visited Harry Nohr's workshop and watched him working on his famous wooden bowls. We toured Pendarvis House, a Wisconsin Historical Society restoration of Cornish miner's homes. We owe our nickname of Badger state to those miners because, in order to survive the first winter, they dug holes and lived in the ground until houses could be built. We toured several studios, did a guided auto tour past all the historic buildings and old mining sites, and visited the bakery, picking up our order of 49 pasties. I returned home barely in time for an Explorer Post family picnic supper and rushed from that to a going-away party for our choir director. I anticipated an overloaded day and prepared by carrying aspirin in my pocket, and informed my lenient boss in advance that I wouldn't be recovered enough to work the following day.

We drove to the Green River Ranch to take pictures for the insurance company and fell in love with the place all over again. Under the circumstances, it might be better if we don't go there.

May 20, 1969

Dear Mom,

   We have traveled to Michigan and back. Tuesday night Dann announced that he had talked to the Pere Marquette factory in Ludington, Michigan and our four canoes are ready. Would we like to pick them up the next day? We took only Tim and Mike as these are the two who didn't get to the World's Fair. Arising at 4:15 (my normal bird-watching hour), we boarded the ferry in Milwaukee by 7 a.m. Back home Andy set his alarm for 7:00 to get himself and Jay up for school and friend Leta called them at 7:15 to see if the alarm had gone off properly. She also invited them for supper. The ferry trip takes six hours each way. We snoozed in the deck chairs, played cards and ate our sack lunches on deck, so we all have wind burned faces. Within thirty minutes after boarding, the boys had inspected the boat from bow to stern. We arrived at Ludington at 1:00 p.m., went through the factory and learned how to make fiberglass canoes. We secured four canoes two-deep on top of the station wagon, stopped for a cold root beer, got distracted in a used car lot and were back on board two-and-a-half hours later. Discovering a leak in the radiator, we didn't dare take time to fix it if we wanted to make our boarding time. Then we discovered after boarding that, because of a non-functioning fire pump on the boat, the Coast Guard wouldn't give clearance to sail, so we sat in the harbor until 5:30. During that wait Dann secured permission to go below to the auto deck to work on our troublesome car and he had a delightful time wandering around in the hold visiting with the crew. After finally sailing, we splurged on supper in the dining room, slept some more, watched TV and for the last two hours stood in the prow and watched the approaching harbor lights of Milwaukee. Observing at night from the deck of a boat under a full moon was dazzling, but we didn't get home until 2:00 a.m. We stopped to add water to the radiator three times. Each time this necessitated untying the front ropes on the cargo in order to wedge the hood up enough to open the radiator.

June 10, 1969

Dear Mom,

Our first-born loved having you here for his high school graduation. I'm sorry we worked you so hard. I never intend this.

Dann and the two younger boys left with the Scouts for a week-long canoe trip in upper Michigan. The other half of us went north to Rice Lake for a Willett wedding, passing the Scout caravan on the highway. We spotted them easily because they have canoes on top and the inside of the car is crammed with paddles.

Andy often asks, "Why do we always have to be late for everything?" but we arrived at this wedding 90 minutes early and curled up in the car for naps. After the ceremony, Andy, Tim and their cousin Steve put a smoke bomb under the hood of the groom's car and declared the wedding satisfactory. Andy drove the entire four hours going home. I offered, but he just wanted to see if he could do it. He is going to be an excellent driver, like his Dad.

June 15, 1969

Dear Mom,

It was supposed to be a quiet week with Dann gone, but it wasn't. I coped with problems for seven days, but the eighth was too much. People complained so much about Dann being gone that I delegated Tim to answer the phone and say I was out. He asked nonchalantly, "Okay, but are you coming home again?"

Our big story of the week is our easement sitters. We drove Andy and Tim to Pine Lake church camp, leaving Jay and Mike home. They heard the pest enter with his car and they investigated. Jay said to him, "Please show me your court papers." The pest was shook up when such a small child made such a serious request. He pulled out a map showing the easement and announced that this was his land and he was going to use it. The boys sat down and Jay responded, "I'm sorry, but my brother and I are using it. You will have to come some other time." The guy whacked down some bushes so Jay sent Mike inside for his camera and snapped a picture. When we drove in, they jumped up from the orchard where they had been sitting all afternoon, greatly relieved to see us. The man had been gone for half-an-hour, but they were afraid to go inside as they thought he might come back.

I was proud of them and asked, "Jason, how close did his car come to you?"

"Three feet, and I hoped he wouldn't come any closer as I am not cut out for this hippie stuff." When asked if he was frightened, he sighed. "Oh sure, but it helped to have Mike sitting behind me because then I had to act bigger."

When I asked Mike if he was afraid, he grinned. "Oh no. I just sat behind Jason." I think our two elderly neighbor ladies were worried too as they kept sweeping the deck over their garage the entire time that the jeep was edging so close to the boys. The way of justice grinds slowly. I wonder how long we're going to have to keep this up. If the courts decide in October that we are right and all our trees are already cut down, what good will that do us?

June 20, 1969

Dear Mom,

Tim has enrolled in the Madison Schools four week summer Work-Learn program. He came home acting a foot taller the first day. Using chain saws in the School Forest, they cut down 12 large trees that will go through the saw mill next week. He proudly wears a yellow hard hat.

That tornado, which came so close Monday night, woke us when the wind started. I stood in the kitchen and wondered how trees could take that buffeting. While I watched the apple tree crashed across the driveway. The new martin house stood. Air raid sirens sounded and the radio warned over and over to take cover. We listened to the radio until midnight, but did not go to the basement and didn't discover until morning that Jay's new rabbit hutch had been flipped. The four rabbits were unhurt but were the wettest rabbits I have ever seen as they had no roof. Worse still the roof, now their floor, is solid so the rainwater couldn't run out and they sat in water all night. We brought them into the kitchen and gave them rubdowns with old bath towels. Do rabbits catch cold?

After one day working in the School Forest, Tim is suddenly crazy to use his father's chain saw and is cutting some of our dead trees.

June 27, 1969

Dear Mom,

Tim's last two weeks of the Work Learn program buses them to creeks to work on bank soil erosion problems caused by cows. They take a fish count by sending an electric shock through the stream. Yesterday was 4-H demonstration day competition. Jay and Mike practiced on anybody they could find. Mike gave an eight-minute demonstration on rocks. He depended on his notes and I feared it might destroy his self-confidence if we removed them. He did leave out one section and I wondered if he would come apart when he realized what he had done. Suddenly he looked up startled, I winked at him, and he smiled and blithely continued.

Jay presented a polished performance on rabbits. He ad libs and doesn't need to look at his mother anymore, but talks directly to the judge. Afterwards, the judge announced that Jay displayed the clearest, most visible set of charts he had observed all morning and Jay bounced all the way home. Now comes the hard part, waiting for the results.

July 1, 1969

Dear Mom,

Mike and I arrived home safely and found our Scouts already here, sunburned, mosquito-bitten and tired. A good trip except for one bad incident. Dann with three Scouts joined the canoers one day late. As they waited at the designated pick-up point, one of the boys yelled,

"Hey, that's camping gear floating down the river."

Dann and his senior patrol leader shoved off a canoe. Paddling furiously upriver they didn't stop for gear lazily floating downstream. One bag came so close that they grabbed it without breaking rhythm. They began to pass canoes that had pulled over to the bank, but two canoes were unaccounted for and one was Jason's. As they zoomed around a bend, the disaster scene spread before them. Scoutmaster Hoover had turned to check on Jay. At that precise moment the Scoutmaster's canoe had hit a partly submerged log throwing them off balance and tipping the canoe. One boy had climbed onto a stump in the middle of the river. Jay's canoe had picked up the second kid who had swum to shore and Hoover had propelled his submerged canoe to the opposite shore. Although Dann had lectured the kids the week before on always tying gear to the boat, they hadn't. The Scoutmaster bemoaned his $200 camera, but that turned up in the one bag Dann had retrieved. One boy lost a new sleeping bag and Hoover existed without shoes for two days. That night around the campfire the boys sang "Down Went the Titanic" but in place of "women and children lost at sea" they substituted "Flaherty and Shomberg and Hoover's pants". The next morning Dann lectured again on his stringent canoe safety rules. They embarked as 21 boys. They came back as one troop.

We invited a neighbor couple out to eat last night. I explained to Tim that this man was responsible for giving Dad a listing which subsequently sold and we wanted to say thank you. Tim asked, "How much was the check?" I emphasized that family business was not to be repeated outside the family and then added that it was around a thousand dollars but couldn't remember exactly. I hadn't noticed Mike's presence until he announced, "$1,118.00." Sometimes I feel that nobody listens around here. Not true.

Our pest came again and only Andy and I were home. I agree with Jay that it is easier to handle problems with somebody standing behind you. I told Mr. Dufson that, as we question his right to come in with a vehicle, I could not allow him to do so until the courts decreed his legal rights. I rushed to call our lawyer after Mr. Dufson left and asked why the papers we've served don't prevent this sort of the thing. The lawyer replied, "The only way we can stop him for now is exactly what you're doing." Last night all four boys and their father, with great glee, took turns digging a deep trench across the easement. They plan on filling it with water and raising frogs. They placed a plank across to allow for walkers. The next day our pest filled it in. The day was sweltering and he worked long and hard. Fifteen minutes after he left the boys dug it out again. Every day they hose water into it, which produces goopy mud.

Jay says when he finds a girl he likes he's going to ask three questions: does she like swimming, camping, and liver? With the first "no" she's all through. See you Saturday.

July 8, 1969

Dear Mom,

It's hard to cover home base all the time. This time Tim was home alone and he complained this took three hours of prime TV time. While the pest shoveled dirt into the hole on his side, Tim wet it down with the hose from the other side. Unfortunately our pest managed to cut down half of our cherry tree and called the police in an effort to scare Tim into being more cooperative. The policeman said to the pest,

"I can't interfere in a legal argument, only in the event of a disturbance and I suggest you remove yourself before there is a disturbance." By this time many curious neighbors had gathered.

The guy came again the next day. Mike and I were on duty this time. When he parked his jeep off the easement and on our land, I announced that I was calling the police and went into the house to do so but he left.

Mike invited his friend Kevin for overnight. They pitched their tent in the orchard, took Twinkle for support and spent the night out there. We have a hearing scheduled for next week. This will not restrain him, but it might discourage him temporarily.

Dann, Mike and I cleaned an apartment where we had evicted the tenant. Mike found lots of curious objects—burned spoons, needles, and so forth that he brought to me with questions, so again we called the Narcotics Division. The detective who came confiscated all the equipment, powders and pills and talked about what and how different drugs are administered. Mike absorbed this like a sponge. I'm afraid he's now an authority. I wouldn't have taken him if I'd known, but perhaps it doesn't hurt for him to hear this stuff. He worked industriously cleaning for four hours.

July 14, 1969

Dear Mom,

We rested all week at the cottage except when we were swimming, sunbathing, sleeping or picking blueberries in the swamp. We ate blueberry pie daily and sailed—or tried to sail the canoes. Dann had thought with two identical canoes we could race, but first we need to learn how to sail. When the rudiments of sailing come so naturally to Dann, he can't understand why we don't pick up these elementary truths in one telling. Like, for instance, DON'T turn with the wind. When that sail starts to fill out or the boat starts to tilt, or another boat is coming head on, or it's four times more distance if you go the right way—then in the five seconds I get to decide, I cannot remember which way NOT to turn. Besides when I concentrated on which way was into the wind and then turned, I still did it wrong because the wind had turned. Fishing was so good that every two hours somebody traipsed through the cottage with drippy fish to show off the latest catch.

We've had a week without our easement caller. When he did come, for the first time Dann was here. I listened and was impressed how politely he talks to Dann as compared with the blustering he uses on the rest of us. Dann either cows him or else he figures women and children don't count.

I have quit working for Dann for two weeks because piles of material have accumulated waiting to be made into summer clothes. Besides, Timmy says I've been fired from the position of head painter. While painting last week, I tipped the paint tray off the ladder and splattered the entire carpeted room. We sweated through three hours of cleaning up.

In three days the Dane County Junior Fair opens and we're working frantically. Tim takes pictures all day and develops at night. Mike is still trying to make his electric buzzer work.

August 15, 1969

Dear Mom,

We took our second week of vacation wilderness camping in the Sylvania National Recreation Area in upper Michigan. Not a restful week. With Don's family along, we filled three canoes. Norma and I spent hours eliminating weight from the food and gear lists, and thought we had done well until we loaded the canoes. Tentage and supplies for three days for eight people for a campsite two lakes back over a mile of portages meant many trips back and forth. Jason figured that everyone walked eight miles with heavy gear. We were alone in our beautiful campsite, except for wildlife: the unseen raccoon that swiped the warm brownies off the picnic table (we found the pan by the lake in the morning), the unknown creature that chewed around the edge of Mike's new canoe paddle the night we forgot to tie it to the clothesline, and whoever adopted our privy door for a woodworking project noisily chewing on the panels every night. In the morning we always found new wood splinters and droppings inside. None of us used that facility at night! A chorus of loons entertained us during the day and owls at night sounded off constantly.

August 28, 1969

Dear Mom,

Yes, Jay is home, speechless and not eating, but otherwise not missing his tonsils. We drove to Chippewa for another family wedding. Dann's father used to be pastor there. Although Dann left at age 18, he still knows many people. We called on his 83-year-old friend. All Danny's young men charmed her; she looked them over thoroughly and told them they were cute, much to their delight. We stayed with friends in the country who allowed the boys to drive the riding mower and little tractor. After the wedding, the boys, prepared with cans, rice and notes for the gas tank and accompanied by cousins and sisters of the bride and groom, disappeared for hours and finally found the car hidden in a nearby garage.

Summer is almost over, but we managed one more outing and canoed the Wolf River with the Sierra Club. We weren't carrying gear, so when we portaged we only carried canoes. Tim loves whitewater canoeing, especially when his Dad lets him take a canoe alone through the fast water. On one rapids Tim and I waited third in line when the second canoe tipped in front of us. We grabbed the closest boulder and hung up against it while the leaders swam across and righted the upset canoe. At a number four rapids a kayak expert offered to help anyone through and, of course, Dann volunteered rather than to portage. It was not reassuring to see the trip leaders with coiled ropes space themselves out in the river. Jay paced the bank, sure that Daddy was going to break the canoe in half. We came home pooped, but within 24 hours the crew was ready to go again. It took us old folks a week to recuperate.

September 4, 1969

Dear Mom,

The only way we're going to get our garage back is to have another garage sale. The theory is that when the sale is over, the half that didn't sell moves directly to Goodwill. Sometimes that works in reverse. Dann asked our neighbor, Bill, if he had anything to sell and Bill brought a unicycle, offering it for half his cost. Jay quickly announced that he had always wanted a unicycle and bought it. Have you ever seen people ride one of those crazy things? It requires difficult balancing as the seat rests on top of one wheel. With no handle bars to hang on to, one sits on top of nothing, but not for long. Presently you are sitting on the driveway. Bill told Jay to wrap the pedal ends with adhesive during the learning process so that the cycle won't get banged up. He didn't say how to prevent people from getting banged up. Jay persuaded his Dad to park the car in the middle of the blacktop and then goes round and round it putting hands on the car for balance.

We invited friends for a picnic supper Sunday. This made ten kids for the evening. Their ingenious entertainment ideas kept them so occupied that we adults visited uninterrupted all evening. The kids started with caroms, switched to touch football on the school grounds and finally disappeared to the basement where they have been holding salamander races several times a day. Did they show you their tiger salamander? Not long ago they found one on the dirt floor of the fruit room, ideal habitat for salamanders. They tried to convince me that if I forced them to take the salamander outside, it would die because the weather has been so dry. I caved in, provided it stayed in the fruit room. They named him Charlie, but the next day when they went down to converse with Charlie his spots were different! They started looking around and soon discovered Hank! Now they have also found Tom, Dick, and Harry. It worries me that Charlie might be Charlotte. I certainly do mind where I step in the fruit room these days as I hate those slimy things. Excitement soars to a high crescendo when they are holding a race downstairs. I don't participate. I just listen. They each pick a salamander, placing him or her on one end of the plank. They allow prodding with a matchstick to encourage the creature to speed to the far end of the plank. No doubt frantic screaming when your entry sits down helps. After the salamanders finished their jogging that night, all 10 kids moved outside where they invented their version of volleyball over the garage roof. And lastly they settled down to unicycle attempts. No one even thought of watching TV. We've worked hard to promote creative recreation instead of TV.

A man called yesterday saying he understood we kept rabbits. He had found this tame, brown rabbit wandering on campus and couldn't keep it in his apartment. It lives now in a box in his store and wouldn't we like it? The boys agreed and named him George. He turned out to be Lady George and a tame rabbit she wasn't. If the boys let her out of the hutch, she ran. She adored sitting on laps and being petted, but if they stopped, she would dig frantically with her paws. We kept her for two days and then Andy donated her to a guy at work who raises meat rabbits and needed more does.

Jason now has a paper route which he has wanted for a long time. About every four months he has called all the newspapers to re-sign up. This small Milwaukee Journal route delivers afternoons and Sunday morning. Earning $5.00 per week makes it possible for him to afford that unicycle.

My mending stack has grown a great deal since everybody wants his pants tapered to skin-tight. This loused up my hand-me-down system. Nobody will wear their old bell bottom trousers any more unless I alter them.

SEPTEMBER 11, 1969

Dear Mom,

With great misgivings I have undertaken an upholstery class at Vocational School and hope the teacher exhibits tolerance toward dumb students. We're assembling a footstool. As I didn't bargain for woodworking thrown in too, I move slowly.

Dann and I graduated (?) to co-presidents of the PTA. He set up what he called a short committee meeting to plan our fund-raising carnival. He shouldn't have said short. The last person left at 11:30 p.m. The late committee meetings aren't so bad. It's lying awake until 1:00 a.m. sorting out problems and then waking at 6:00 a.m. and doing it again. We picked a really live committee, giving me the feeling that instead of us leading the PTA, we're going to have to slow things down. No lack of interest and everybody volunteers for chairmanships.

September 19, 1969

Dear Mom,

Upholstery class fascinates me but I am all thumbs. Dann contributed a beat-up rocking chair so I will do a footstool with matching rocker for his office. I have been listening to the gals in class tell about this auction or that sale where they picked up a chair for 25 or 50 cents. The teacher is delighted with my chair because of its terrible condition. I have been pounding my thumbs and tying down springs until my fingers ache.

Tim and Jay will be participating in the Walk for Development. Each of them signed up 20 sponsors. Tim said that his price per mile has risen so high that he'll have to finish the entire route even if somebody carries him. See you next week.

October 10, 1969

Dear Mom,

Is your foot better?

We have just acquired a female Brittany Spaniel puppy named Cinnamon. She is either a devil on wheels, or asleep. I now have chewed house plants, smudge marks all over the full length mirror where she's been trying to grab that other dog, and a large collection of bones, old shoes, and miscellaneous hidden in the bottom of the coat closet. No more using the boys worn-out underwear for sink rags in the bathroom. It's too embarrassing when friends drop in and a pair of under shorts dashes by. She loves to climb on our laps and has discovered I sit down when I talk on the telephone. Now whenever the phone rings she plops there waiting for me to answer it.

The boys have cleaned and winterized the hutches. Jay set up the rabbit scales and was weighing Sara Lynn when Cinnamon zoomed by. Sara Lynn took off like a shot, with Cinnamon a scant two feet behind. This is not why we chose a hunting breed. The two raced round and round and just once ran close enough that Jay could reach out and grab at Sara Lynn. She has perfected avoidance instincts, she swerved and Jay caught Cinnamon instead, who didn't swerve. He brought her inside and called out the reserves, because Sara Lynn had taken off in haste for the woods.

Mike's face has been covered with poison ivy all week. He looked like measles. We worked so hard to get his face under control that we neglected his fingers and they are so swollen that he can't hold a pencil. He must have been exposed on the Scout campout.

As Jay is working on his hiking merit badge, he backpacked ten miles with full gear into that campout on Saturday and back out on Sunday in pouring rain.

October 17, 1969

Dear Mom,

When I tore my chair apart in Upholstery class I found half an Indian, tinker toys, bobby pins, an old comb, a sucker stick, car key and a brand new Cub Scout badge. No wonder we lose things.

Cinn acts like sin. She runs off, looks at us if we call and runs the other way. The boys have discovered the best way is to call Twinkle and Cinnamon will come immediately. Jay has been teaching her to speak. He lay down and crawled around the kitchen floor for hours trying to get her to bark. She just looked mystified. Eventually he discovered that if she barked for any reason he could say, "speak" and reward her with food. Consequently she has decided that barking is synonymous with food. She sits patiently at my feet in the kitchen and expectantly says "Woof" every fifteen seconds. She has learned that I not only sit at the telephone, but at one other place quite often. Every time I disappear into the bathroom, she lands on my lap with a great whoosh and a flying leap. When the boys came home from school, they discovered my red fuzzy slipper in the coat closet. They raced upstairs to check and down again complaining that Mike's room was full of chewed up paper. Tim requested a shovel. Since then he carefully shuts his bedroom door when he leaves for school in the morning. And Mother was in the doghouse for not diligently watching. Cinnamon moves with the speed of lightning, and silently. She repents after misbehaving, coming to sit in front of me after I've spanked her, but with her back turned.

Our friend, James, has been arrested for a $3,000 supermarket robbery. The robber wore sunglasses and baseball cap and two employees in the store identified James as the robber. Another eyewitness saw the man leaving the store and swore it was not James. We have known him for years: in church, as a neighbor and as an active Scouter in the troop. Dann testified as a character witness. The University chancellor, who is a neighbor, a vice-president of the University who worked with James in our troop, the school principal, the Scoutmaster's wife, and an Episcopalian priest all testified as character witnesses. After three months of agonized waiting and irreparable damage to his reputation, four days of trial, and lawyer and court expenses of $5,500 he was acquitted. This incensed the entire neighborhood and we put on a community potluck supper to show both moral and financial support and collected $1,000 in contributions. It gives me the shudders and we've all been thinking, that could have been us!

October 24, 1969

Dear Mom,

You won't need to close your bedroom door when you come this time. Cinnamon was hit by a car. She will be okay, but is in the hospital. She wandered off, had been gone ten minutes and Mike and I were searching for her. I have taught her to come to my whistle and was whistling. A friend of mine, driving down Old Middleton Road, said that Cinnamon responded to my whistle and shot across the road so fast that the dog never saw the car. Laurie tried to turn, but the puppy hit the car and rolled underneath. We haven't name tags on her yet, but school kids coming down the hill knew she was ours. Laurie came trudging up the hill gingerly carrying the dog. I took her to the vet immediately. As soon as he diagnosed internal hemorrhaging, he administered a shot to clot the blood and wrapped her in rugs and hot water bottles. The next day the vet became concerned about a possible back injury, as she would stand, but not walk. I stretched out my arms; she studied me carefully and walked slowly to me. It looked agonizing, but the vet said, "She couldn't do that if anything was broken." She won't be sneaking upstairs for a while.

Eight thousand children participated in the Walk for Development. Dann and I worked at checkpoint seven on mile 20. It inspired us to see so many put in so much effort. We stamped their cards verifying mile 20 and offered drinks. I saw a man walking with a baby on his back, a boy in a wheelchair being pushed, a girl in a walking cast, kids barefoot with their shoes under their arm, and one little boy whom we pulled out when he told us he had thrown up twice already. Jay and Mike walked 17 miles. Many walked to mile 17 because MacDonalds served free lunch there. Tim walked from 8 a.m. to 9 p.m. and finished all 32 miles. The three of them made us proud. They had signed up 20-30 sponsors pledging from two to fifty cents per mile. Tim turned in $100, the younger boys $60 each. They'll collect from you when we see you.

I think the boys from Andy's dorm are in the yard practicing for their dorm football team every minute they aren't studying. The combination of that and the tight pants of today's society brings Andy home regularly asking, "Mom, would you please sew up another pair of pants that split?" He usually brings friends, and they depart with large quantities of homemade cookies. He is learning fast how expensive the little needs of life can be. One Sunday afternoon he trudged up the drive with a duffel bag slung over his back, and sheepishly admitted that he didn't have enough money to buy soap for the washing machines. So we washed clothes and gave him Sunday night supper.

Our carnival turned into a smashing success with 700 attendees. We offered free babysitting, served supper, and provided live bandstand entertainment all afternoon. Different organizations manned booths: a spook house, puppet show, costume contest, darts, car racing and car smashing, photographers, a white elephant shop, homemade ice cream, homemade root beer, homemade bread and cheese, baked goods, cotton candy and fudge. We were so pleased with all the hours of work that our committee heads had committed, that we invited them here for chili and pumpkin pie afterwards. I prepared so much chili that I feared we'd be eating it for days, but most of the workers hadn't eaten all day and they devoured everything. Then those wonderful gals set me down and they cleaned up my kitchen.

The paper yesterday reported on a Liberated Women's Convention that met here. They expressed annoyance at men who are suppressing women and more annoyance at satisfied women who don't realize they are being suppressed. That's me! Their platform stated that women were good for more than having babies, knitting, and cooking. I would like to have them sit-in around here for a day if they think that's all we do!

P.S. Dann's Batman outfit for the carnival created a sensation.

October 30, 1969

Dear Mom,

Our day in court arrived and we lost. Our lawyer prepared us by forewarning that we had little chance of winning, but we're sad to think of losing any of our big trees. We took Mike out of school so he could observe. Both Dann and I took the witness stand. This was my first time and I don't care for it one bit. I was afraid I would say something that I didn't mean. A couple times when the other lawyer cross-examined me, he got annoyed and yelled. The judge came to my rescue and said I didn't have to answer. We will have to allow Mr. Dufson to put a driveway across. Our only consolation is that we also can use the driveway, but don't have to maintain or plow it. We informed him that our beautiful big crabapple tree is on the easement line, so he is entitled to take only half of it. And he did.

This is the end of an era of struggling against something. We wasted money, lots of time, and created tremendous stress for all of us. Conversely all six of us learned to work together for a common goal, forcing us to do things that made us uncomfortable. It increased our appreciation of any land. The boys learned that even when we expect to fail, we should try anyway.

This land is still our land. We pay the taxes on that strip, but can no longer control its use.

P.S. I didn't plan on fighting easements when I said a housewife's job might be "boring and monotonous!"

8 Bugs and More Bugs

January 16, 1970

Dear Mom,

    After the courts declared it legal for our pest to use the easement, the city notified us that zoning ordinances require 30 feet on the street for newly platted areas. As the easement is 15 feet, this will not be allowed as the only access. The builder platted a street through his own land which allows the necessary 30 feet for this lot, but he still plans a roadway out the back of this lot across our easement. Perhaps when he builds he may change his mind, as we have fenced in our yard to allow Cinnamon freedom, because Brittany Spaniels need to run. If anyone activates the easement, we will place gates at the entrance and the exit from our land to allow the required access. When using that for a driveway, they will have to open and close two gates every time they enter or leave. Maybe that's better than a legal deterrent.

    Lisa's stepmother gave me Lisa's address. When Lisa graduated from the Catholic high school, her Mother told her never to darken her door again. She started college in Massachusetts, dropped out and worked in an ice cream parlor. She decided she didn't want to do that all her life and wrote her father asking for money to go back to college. He sent a big check made out to the school but she returned it with the request that he make it out to her and he did. She is presently living with a guy she hopes to marry. She does ask for trouble, doesn't she?

Jay and Mike, with the Scout troop, left for a weekend at Powderhorn Ski Area in Upper Michigan. As they would be skiing for two days, Jay informed me that if he broke his leg he would try to do it the last day.

Andy and Tim left for a winter retreat at Pine Lake Church Camp. I sent extra blankets to wrap around the car as it would have to stand outside. That left Dann and me alone. I cooked Dann's favorites which the boys don't like. We fed and watered rabbits, exercised dogs, and delivered Jay's early morning paper route. After we finished the kids' work, we took one dog and snowshoed in the hills and valleys around Mt. Horeb. Cinnamon sank in up to her neck. She could have followed in our tracks, but wouldn't. She was so tired that we carried her to her bed in the garage.

Andy is preparing for a Hoofer ski trip to Switzerland. We told him to apply for insurance to cover air fare home. If he should be unable to leave on the chartered flight we couldn't afford to fly him home at the regular price. He laughed and said, "Nobody is going to break a leg."

January 23, 1970

Dear Mom,

Madison is clearly a land of opportunity and learning. I have signed up again for Upholstery, dropped my organ class and succumbed to a Crafts class that includes rosemaling, leatherwork, stenciling and block printing. I am teaching a 4-H class in leatherwork and need to keep ahead of the kids. Dann and I are taking the Reading your Landscape course I attended years ago. Jay too. He plans to use this towards his Nature Merit Badge. Many people take this class over and over as you can't absorb it all the first time.

Jay insisted he was going to use his bike on his paper route all winter. Yesterday he came home late and disgusted after carrying his bike through shortcuts.

January 30, 1970

Dear Mom,

Cinnamon is such a pain. She ran away to the school grounds, didn't come when called, so we had to chain her. She chewed Mike's comb and got slapped across the nose for that. She happily went down in the basement with Dann, who was working on Tim's darkroom, scratched on the temporary rabbit hutch, which is occupied, and got kicked upstairs. She nudged me with my slipper that she had hopefully retrieved from under my bed. As I hadn't commanded her to fetch, I made her take it back. She reminds me of the Fuller Brush man. Once you order, he keeps coming back when you don't want any. I have taught her to bring my slippers and she loves to tear upstairs when we ask, also many times between commands hoping that we wanted slippers but forgot to ask. She is lying here by me with her "I forgive you for all this nonsense" look. Fortunately Twinkle is well-behaved and Cinnamon picks up habits from her. Twinkle also benefits. When she thinks we are not around, she will play with the pup, which keeps her active.

Jay and Mike have tried to breed rabbits in order to display juniors for the fair, but some didn't take and those that did delivered on a minus 20 degree night. Jay lost 13 babies in one night.

I never want to hear any more jokes about rabbits multiplying. People may be having trouble with the population explosion, but Mother Nature, in our hutches, has her balance of nature under control.

Andy has not returned from Switzerland in time for second semester registration. He and his Dad anticipated this and Dann, using Andy's ID, stood in lines for him. He is changing his computer courses to Oceanography.

I have gained a disgusting seven pounds. Mike and I made a deal with Dann. If we can lose a combined 20 pounds by spring vacation (seven weeks) Dann will buy us a strawberry sundae, a delectable, inappropriate reward.

February 5, 1970

Dear Mom,

Andy arrived home late Sunday night. The charter left Zurich on a 9:00 a.m. flight, stopped in Amsterdam and then landed in Milwaukee, where they were held in the plane for two hours while officials checked their papers. After deplaning, they still had to pass through customs. When I asked if he'd had supper he looked puzzled and replied, "I don't really know." Crossing time zones all day, he had just kept eating breakfast.

Of course I asked, "Did anyone get hurt?"

"Some faculty traveled with us," he grinned, "and upon arrival one of the women slipped while stepping off the bus and broke her leg."

Non-English speaking waitresses caused them trouble. When they ordered cokes, they got coffee. When they asked for the bill, the waitress brought beer. Each morning they walked 30 minutes to the edge of town and took the cable car up the mountain. Ski runs were five miles long, which means 30 minutes of skiing. This translates to five runs per day. I looked at the pictures of the cable cars and remembered that this was the kid who panicked every year halfway up the steps of the fire tower.

I worry about those striking TAs on campus. Andy crosses picket lines when he goes to class, but so far things have remained peaceful.

FEBRUARY 19, 1970

Dear Mom,

Darn, darn, darn. I let Cinnamon out and lost her. She raced through the orchard behind a German shepherd, gave me a "so long" look and departed. I called and I whistled, put on coat and boots and took off on a run for school. It was noon recess and kids all over were yelling "Here Cinnamon". They showed me which way she had gone so I came home for the car. Driving slowly up Old Sauk Road, I noticed boys in the woods beyond the school where they're not supposed to be. They had captured the dog and were waiting for me. That grapevine is good, but it doesn't speak well for the puppy's wandering that all the school kids know her. We started dog obedience class. Seventy-five dogs registered, most of whom misbehave continually. Last night the German shorthair next to Cin barked so abruptly that it startled her into a somersault.

MARCH 30, 1970

Dear Mom,

We're home safe, sound and weary from a trip that I'd not care to repeat. The good things are: we arrived home with nobody sick and with both canoes intact. The bad things are: we had car trouble and stalled three times on the Northwest Tollway in a blinding snowstorm at night, delaying us 18 hours in the Chicago area and Dann, Mike and I tipped our canoe in the Red River. When we woke Sunday morning, four inches of new snow covered everything. The next time this family goes for a vacation in the sunny south, we are taking boots and mittens. A bad distributor cap caused the car to malfunction. The first time Dann re-started the car. The second time we sat until a patrol car pulled up. Dann walked back to the police car while I tried once more and it started. Jay complained, "This is embarrassing when the police are already here."

I countered, "Embarrassing, but cheaper." We turned off the tollway and the engine quit for the third time at a service station. Everybody, but me, pushed it into the garage just as they closed for the night and they drove us to the nearest motel. I only had time to snatch one pair of p.j.'s and five toothbrushes. In the morning Dann left us in bed watching TV, wrapped plastic bags around his feet, used a bath towel for a scarf and hiked back to pick up the car which had been fixed. A family conference voted to keep going. We went around Chicago on the expressway inch by inch, passing stalled and abandoned cars everywhere and stuck semis that blocked the ramp exits and entrances. I counted eight cars buried on one exit. Helicopters hovered overhead. After reaching Gary, Indiana, we turned south only to be stopped by squad cars with bellowing bull horns. "All roads south are impassable. Please go home." We did not take their advice, but returned to the toll road and tried the next road south and the next and the next, until finally we went north instead.

Arriving at Daniel Boone State Park 18 hours late, we missed the first day's easy canoeing. Whoever told us that Kentucky weather was a month ahead of Wisconsin goofed. The water temperature was 42 degrees and icicles hung along the riverbank. We canoed 12 miles that day, through grade two and grade three rapids. Grade five classifies as a waterfall. We hit a rock within the first hour and leaning upriver instead of down, we were immediately flipped into the frigid water. With all the clothes I had on it's surprising I didn't sink, but the heavy clothes insulated me from the initial shock. We carried dry clothes in waterproof bags, but the leaders suggested we not change as we were approaching a long stretch of rapids. We stayed wet for hours and have decided we are not grade three canoeists. Grade three is fast and requires much maneuvering. We left colored paint on many rocks and the hard paddling required to steer through rapids exhausted us. One of the aluminum canoes jammed between rocks and constant water pressure pounded on it. The men walked into the river, tied ropes and pulled, pushed and levered, but two hours elapsed before we could move on. Only constant bailing kept that damaged canoe afloat. Andy and Jay hung their canoe up between a rock and a tree. It's a terrible feeling to swish by one of our own canoes hung up and empty, wonder where the kids are and realize that we are not competent enough to stop and help. However, there were lots of experts and they got the boys' canoe loose before the river damaged it. This embarrassed Jay until one of the leaders swung around that curve and hung up the same way.

Darkness had fallen by the time we shuttled back to camp. I heated cans of hash and we gratefully burrowed into warm, dry sleeping bags. In the morning Dann cracked open the tent flap and stared at the feathery winter wonderland. Four inches of new snow, covered every twig and branch, burying all our gear. Without warning the weight of that snow collapsed our tent. We decided that we had done enough exciting canoeing and that we hadn't come for winter camping as we can do that in Wisconsin. We dug out, gave away our dry firewood, packed up and left. The boys thought it a great vacation.

April 16, 1970

Dear Mom,

This appears to be our outdoor education year. Tim has been accepted for the DNR Conservation Camp in northern Wisconsin. They pay $20 per week plus board and room for six weeks. I have been accepted for a two-week Audubon camp session also in northern Wisconsin, receiving a partial scholarship on the basis of my conservation work with Scouts and 4-H. The more nature I am exposed to, the more I want to learn.

We are again conducting a litterbug contest. Jay's patrol has spread their trash over the south end of the orchard and Mike's patrol covers all the rest. Three hundred fifty participants registered, twice the enrollment that we had the first time. We are drawing from farther away as we even have an entry from a second-grade class in Oregon. Dann has been soliciting cash prizes.

I finished upholstering the chair and am tackling a couch. I never have enough class time, so Mike and I are tearing down the couch and repairing the springs at home before I take it to class.

May 29, 1970

Dear Mom,

This class hopelessly bogs me down, but if the sun is shining I have a great compulsion to work outside. Only if it's raining does my half-finished couch, plunked in Dann's study, take precedence. I attended the last class yesterday but have consistently gone early and stayed late, so hope that now I can finish by myself. When the instructor discovered that I have small bouncing boys, she insisted I take off the bottom covering and double the reinforcement.

Last weekend the Scouts canoed the upper Dells. The Wisconsin River grows poison ivy so exuberantly that I made them all take baths immediately upon their return. Jay pitched his tent in the middle of a dense patch and was annoyed with his Scoutmaster father for insisting that he move it. Jay contended he didn't get poison ivy like everybody else, but there is justice after all. Both his hands and feet broke out.

The teacher sent Mike home from school with a badly swollen hand. A desk had fallen on him but the x-rays showed nothing broken. The doctor teased, "You don't have to study that energetically."

Andy's dorm has been in the middle of the campus trouble. Last week he called home every evening to let us know that he was okay and in for the night. He and his roommate went to the evening rallies to watch until the night they ran into mace and tear gas when trying to get back home. He never went after that and I'm thankful for small blessings. About fifty National Guard trucks, loaded with soldiers, roll past Dann's office every morning. It's pretty depressing.

June 4, 1970

Dear Mom,

This must be the monsoon season. I had planned on putting everybody to work outside Saturday, but the rainy day option was to paint the kitchen. Five of us worked for hours, the boys earning extra money. Tim scrubbed the ceiling and filled cracks; Jay and Mike soaked and scraped off wallpaper. We finally started painting, but Jay slipped off the top of the refrigerator. This made a big gash inside his ear, which he survived, and then the boys took a break and raced up to school to play ball during a lull in the downpour. However, Mike got hit in the eye with the ball, so they decided it was safer to come home and paint.

Afterwards we took a picnic supper to Governor Dodge State Park because the blue gills were biting. We sat in our canoes in the rain for three hours, which none of my crazy family minded, ate soggy sandwiches and fished. We threw lines out and counted to three. When we pulled them back, we had one on every time and threw all back to wait for next year. So nobody had to clean fish and none of my crazy family minded that either.

On Sunday I needed to do something different so I made strawberry-rhubarb jam and homemade bread. We asked the preacher for supper and I made raised donuts. The boys have been complaining that I haven't made any since I went on my diet, so I promised to make them if they'd do the frying. A great way to spend a rainy Sunday afternoon. Considering the terrible weather we enjoyed a relaxing weekend and got something done for a change. We leave early Friday for the cottage — six of us, two dogs, and two canoes. Hope the monsoon season is over.

June 9, 1970

Dear Mom,

This was work weekend, but we arrived at the family cottage a half-day ahead of the uncles and cousins. Dann and Cinnamon swam in the frigid water and we turned pink from lying in the sun. Everyone fished for non-cooperative fish.

Cinnamon constantly provides a barrel of laughs. She rode in the back of the station wagon to begin with. After everybody fell asleep, I saw her wiggle across the sleeping bags, slide over Andy's head and plop on his stomach. When Andy woke up she moved over, tromped on Mike and settled on Dann, licking his face thoroughly. Upon arrival the boys and Cinnamon raced to the lake. She never slowed down when she reached the water and swam at least ten times a day, then shook all over anyone near, and now is snowy white and feels soft as crushed velvet. We don't tie her up. She wouldn't dream of running off. There is too much going on.

Dann and I walked in the swamp early Sunday morning and found a pink lady slipper, encouraging us to keep going until we counted 14. We paid for this with wet feet.

On the way home we dropped Tim at Conservation camp. When we left, they were showing him how to make his bed with military corners. This impressed Andy so that he wondered if he could counsel there another year.

June 16, 1970

Dear Mom,

Mike and I set out 80 tomato, broccoli, and cabbage plants that I raised in my little greenhouse. He muttered, "Gee Mom, no wonder you have back trouble!" I think exercise helps. What makes it worse is to sit and do nothing. I don't do much of that.

We have already received a letter from Tim. When the counselors heard the boys talking after taps, they got them up, made them run around the muddy baseball field three times carrying foot lockers, then do pushups for ten minutes. One of the ringleaders was sent home. I commented, "I had hoped Tim would have some fun there."

Andy responded, "Don't worry Mom, why do you think he had to run around the field?"

June 23, 1970

Dear Mom,

   Tim writes every week. The staff requires a letter every Wednesday before the kids are allowed to enter the dining hall. He has enjoyed working on the trout streams, but they haven't been allowed to go to town since the weekend one of the boys stole some things in Spooner. They denied everyone weekend passes until the stuff was returned.

   Thank you for volunteering to come while I'm gone. I will leave you a note here someplace. Jay and Mike are taking alternate nights as chef. Whenever you arrive, they'll just push the schedule back. I am making a list with headings—main dish, salad, dessert, and lunches with many choices under each. The chef will have options, but he has to decide in the morning so he can thaw it. Don't work too hard while you're here. Let the boys wait on you.

July 13, 1970

Dear Mom,

   I've never been away from my kids and husband for two weeks. The first week Dann wrote from Castle Rock Scout Camp where he had taken the troop, including Jay and Mike. They voted him the most unpopular Scoutmaster in the camp because, when his troop all got diarrhea, he instigated boiling water over the campfire to scald every utensil. The weather had turned miserably hot. Standing for long periods over a hot fire did not make happy campers, but it solved their health problem. Thanks for your help the second week of my absence. They must have had plenty of food as things were stacked in the freezer that they didn't use. Mike said cooking was fun, but cleaning up was awful. I enjoyed every bit of Audubon Camp. We attended outdoor classes in geology, birds, botany, and insects. We went canoeing on the Namekagen, where it rained so hard I couldn't see my bow paddler, climbed the rocks at St. Croix Interstate Park, wandered one whole day in the Crex meadows sinking to our knees in the cranberry bog, and spent an afternoon up the creek (walking upstream in an ice-cold stream) sinking to our ankles into the goopy bottom, while seining for water life. I could shoot that man who innocently inquired, "Isn't that a snake there in the water?" We observed 67 bird species on our pre-breakfast hike. When looking up produced stiff necks, we looked down for agates or blueberries. Between classes we cooled off in that crystalline lake and floated at length while discussing the sex life of a spider or similar topics, much to the delight of the lifeguard hovering nearby in a rowboat. Forty-four campers came from all over the U.S. It was not an easy session. By the end of the two weeks, we had sent to the hospital one heart attack, one gall bladder attack and one emotionally disturbed. Most of the women in my dorm were teachers and one asked my friend Nancy if we were teachers. "No," Nancy replied.

    The teacher tried again. "What do you do for a living?"

    After a moment of silence Nancy replied, "Jean and I each live with a man and he provides the means."

    After days of class from 5:00 a.m. until 10:00 p.m., I didn't think I cared to hear the word nature again. Ever. That was short-lived. The outdoor world of living creatures fascinates me. I wish I could retain everything they tried to teach me.

August 7, 1970

Dear Mom,

    Tim experienced six memorable weeks at Conservation camp. He sent us a letter every Friday. They worked five days a week plus one-half day of education. Every morning trucks drove them to location, where they grubbed out gooseberry bushes that are host to the insect causing pine rust. They worked under rangers in state parks and fish hatcheries. Tim especially enjoyed the fish management when they laid brush in streams to provide breeding grounds. After-hours they swam or fished. On weekends trucks took them into nearby towns wherever things were occurring. The camp cooks prepared fish the boys caught or baked pies if the boys picked the blueberries. I liked it that they made them cut their hair and shave their beards.

Many of Andy's college friends went without jobs this summer, but Andy worked for his Dad on apartment maintenance. This slowed Dann as he kept moving Andy to different jobs and had to keep showing him how, but it provided invaluable training for Andy. He did plumbing, roofing, painting, carpentry and learned how to pacify old ladies with leaky faucets and jammed doors. Even so, he'll have a tough time making his checkbook stretch this year.

We were fortunate to have both older boys working at something this summer. They earned a little and learned a lot.

August 19, 1970

Dear Mom,

After a week of swimming, sailing and blueberry-picking at the cottage, Mike and I departed for 4-H camp, he as camper and I as resource counselor. This is my payback after that Audubon scholarship. It's tough to go to camp with your Mother on the staff, so Mike and I didn't talk to each other. I even refrained from commenting on his dirty face. We took 60 girls on the overnight and traveled without tents, just laid sleeping bags under the towering pines on Blackhawk Island. The night watch challenged all of us.

Each unit counselor made an eight-hour schedule and the girls laid down sleeping bags in that order. The watch started at 10 p.m. with one girl from each unit sitting cross-legged at the fire on the sandbar, recording on her clipboard everything she heard or saw for one hour. At 11:00 p.m. those girls rousted out the next in line. It is no easy job to wake and get up in the dark in the woods after only an hour of sleep. I found one girl sleepwalking in her sleeping bag.

Rosemary, the county naturalist, and I sat at the fire visiting and decided we were both odd because we were wide awake, whereas if we had been out socially at those awful hours, we would have had trouble staying awake. She does guide training for the Dane County schools outdoor education program and is trying to recruit me as a naturalist guide for the Madison School Forest. She thinks my experience with kids and my outdoor education interests would make me a natural. This intrigues me. If I want to go back to work, I should look for a position in my professional field of Occupational Therapy. But working as naturalist would have great advantages as I could be home when the boys were home, I could fit it around my working in Dann's office, and I enjoy teaching children. I wonder if I could handle two part-time jobs plus four boys. Sitting around a campfire all night provoked lots of speculation. At 5:00 a.m., we woke the entire camp. The girls cooked breakfast and the camp barge picked us up at 8:00.

At staff table over lunch, Rosemary asked if I had used the canoes. She wanted to take out a canoe to gather poster specimens and would I come along? "I'd be delighted," I replied, "except I'm on dishwashing duty and have promised to lie down in C cabin during quiet time so that unit counselor can help plan the waterfront festival." Rosemary simply convinced the waterfront director to hold the planning session on the porch of C cabin and volunteered one of the college boys for my dishwasher duty.

Off we went as she declared, "It's just too bad when you are in charge of the canoes and never get to use one." She knew we couldn't just take off so had figured out a legitimate excuse to carry me off. We brought home specimens and I received an hour of tutoring, questioning her extensively as we paddled upriver and drifted down. Mike's unit chopped down an aspen tree to feed the beaver and went out at night to beaver-watch. Half of them saw the beaver, half fell asleep. Our water project became the favorite activity. We tied the boys to a rope, strapped them in life jackets and using compass and knotted rope lengths they charted the river bottom. One boy was delighted that he went in over his head twice.

I was assigned many responsibilities: canoeing supervisor and instructor, dishwashing machine operator (a hot steamy job), nature resource counselor (directing any nature activity which a unit counselor chose), and cabin inspector. Susan and I inspected all cabins every morning. We listed every particle of dirt we could find, everything that wasn't lined up straight and threw in lots of humor, giving our report at suppertime. Once we read 15 grievances against a cabin: so many humps in one bed we thought it was somebody sleeping, the next Kleenex was coming out of the box crooked, what was the broom doing in the top bunk, crooked pictures on the wall, shoes on the floor sitting skigee, clothes on the line not lined up, and always dust on the floor. The kids roared with laughter. The kids from that cabin roared with another emotion. You'd be surprised what nice cabins we found after that. Walking out of the dining room behind two small boys I overheard their grumbling, "Who needs a mother like that!" But we won the popularity contest on the last day when we entered a staff cabin and proclaimed it worst of all.

We're getting ready to leave again. I don't put my suitcase away, just take out the dirty clothes, wash and put them back. We leave tomorrow at 6:30 a.m. for the north with ten Scouts, the

Scoutmaster, Dann and I, Mike and his friend Kevin. The Scouts will start their bike trip from Duluth and after we've dropped them off, Dann and I hope to do some quiet camping in the Chequemagon National Forest—just the four of us. We devised an emergency system and will make a person-to-person call to the Scoutmaster's home every night at 6:00 p.m. Unless a problem has surfaced, his wife will refuse the calls.

It's hard to keep track of us, isn't it? It's been a fun summer.

August 28, 1970

Dear Mom,

Our trip didn't go according to plan. We stopped at our cottage for two nights. When I needed something to be done, I notified the senior patrol leader and a volunteer would turn up. Dann took the boys out in the big sailboat and let them use the sailing canoe. They swam often and floated down the Brule in inner tubes. We dropped them on the Skyline Drive in Duluth on Saturday and I was looking forward to that promised time with just the four of us, but returning to the cottage we found two of Dann's brothers had dropped in. My Scout family of 15 changed to a Willett family of 13. They stayed overnight and we sailed and swam. In the morning we closed the cottage and drove leisurely toward a campsite we had picked out. Suddenly Jay appeared at the side of the road yelling wildly. Two bikers had collided. One of the riders had disentangled himself from the mangled bikes, but promptly fainted into the ditch. The other boy had broken his arm. The Scouts scrolled their road maps, splinted the arm and Bob, the Scoutmaster, flagged down a car to take them to the nearest hospital. He delegated Jay, with another Scout, to stay with the slightly damaged bicycles. The rest of the troop had continued under the direction of the senior patrol leader, as they needed to find a store to buy supper provisions. Jay had assumed that he might be sleeping in that field all night with no supper and our happening along was a pleasant surprise. We were driving two vehicles (ours and the Scoutmaster's), plus pulling a trailer. Dann piled the extra bikes into the empty trailer, picked up Jay and John and continued along the route looking for the Scouts. I, with Mike and Kevin, drove back to Hayward looking for the hospital. At 5:55 p.m. I walked into the lobby and saw Bob in the phone booth, frantically trying to call home. I walked up behind asking nonchalantly, "Were you looking for me?"

After the doctor casted the broken arm, we followed the prearranged route and eventually found where Dann had stopped the troop for the night in a Ranger's yard. Dann approached me hesitantly, "I know how anxiously you're waiting for that time with just the four of us, but would you mind—much?" and so we, too, pitched our tent in the Ranger's yard. In the morning, we took the wounded boy and the wounded bike and spent our last night in that quiet secluded campsite that we had pre-selected days before.

Jason arrived home one day early. They rode 425 miles with no more difficulties, often riding in the cool of the evening and swimming during the heat of the day. He says he's not tired, but he's not moving around much.

This is one of the few times this summer that all six of us are home. I can tell this in a hurry when I'm grocery shopping or cooking.

September 3, 1970

Dear Mom,

School has started for all but Andy, and confusion reigns. Mike's new school isn't finished. Although it's raining, he refused to take a coat because the lockers aren't done. Their schedules are calculated by computer. Much to Jay's embarrassment, I threatened to write a letter arguing that I understand the value of using computers for many things, but would somebody please explain to that darned machine about humans and lunch. Jay is scheduled straight through three days each week. No lunch! I thought this was an error, but many have the same problem and the school suggested that they: (1) drop a subject,(2) talk to teachers and make arrangements for leaving class early or arriving late or(3) skip lunch! For two of those days, Jay leaves class ten minutes early. The third day he goes without.

Tim and his Dad have kicked tires for weeks and now Tim has a '61 Plymouth. I sigh with relief as it could have been a motorcycle. Tim enrolled in Auto Mechanics at school and spends hours with his head under the hood or his whole self under the car. Last night one son took apart an engine in the driveway, one turned the gears on the malfunctioning mini-bike that he's been trying to fix for weeks, one made a bicycle from parts he's picked off curb trash collections and he rode it to school today.

If you can come on Tuesday, give me a call. If you can't come, do nothing.

September 8, 1970

Dear Mom,

To make matters worse with Jay's no-lunch schedule, he signed up for football and practices daily after school until 6:00. So no snacking, either. Yes, it was Mike who created the bike. I think he is still missing parts, but he rides it anyway. Lisa had a baby girl yesterday. The baby's father called to tell us.

October 9, 1970

Dear Mom,

I don't know how out every night happens. Monday I attended a Board of Ministries at church and Jay appeared before them for a review of his God and Country award. Tuesday we manned a booth in the Kroger parking lot for their weekly flea market, planning on getting rid of some junk, but it didn't work that way. We took in $3.00 but spent $9.50. Jay sold his old fishing rods and Mike sold the bike that he built out of trash for $5.00. Wednesday we attended middle school PTA. I am objecting because they want to drop their national affiliation and I find that every time one opens one's mouth with opinions, one ends up spending more time somehow. Thursday we went to choir practice. Tonight is 4-H registration. I have been plugging for more parent participation. Tonight, I plan on delivering an ultimatum. "Please help, or take your marbles and go home."

I'll bring a gallon of milk on Sunday.

October 15, 1970

Dear Mom,

We've been miserable. Cinnamon wandered off and we looked everywhere. Dann thought she might be stolen as this is hunting season. He checked the pound every day. We advertised over the radio, in the newspaper and in the vet's office offering a reward. Every kid in the area was looking. Finally a lady called, asked the dog's name, repeated it after me obviously speaking to the dog and then said, "I guess there isn't any doubt that she is yours." Cinnamon had wandered into their yard Saturday afternoon. They had kept her confined, gotten attached and were hoping that we didn't turn up. After five days I had given up. Cinnamon was delighted to see Twinkle again and her old shoe from which she was inseparable the rest of the day.

We've had another Walk for Development. All three boys completed the 32 miles although it took Mike 12 hours. About 9,500 kids walked and our little competitor competed in fine style, ran part of the mileage and checked in at the last checkpoint as the 21st one finished. And yes, he is going out for cross country. I worked at mile 28 checking cards, handing out food and Band-Aids. Dann and Jay stopped to check on me and then Mike and Kevin came through and announced they were quitting. Jay immediately told them they would be sorry after they got home, because that's what he did last year, and why quit when they were so close? I gave them sandwiches and lemonade and they continued. Tim walked with his girl and when she quit, he stopped, took her home, and came back, took up where he had quit and finished the course.

October 28, 1970

Dear Mom,

I gathered dried weeds and grasses along the bank while canoeing on the Wisconsin River and asked Mike if he recognized any of my collection. "Sure, I recognize the bug." He was right. We had found hundreds of red and black ladybug beetles that had covered the dusty green milkweed pods and one still patrolled up and down the stalk.

Cinnamon ran away again. Whatever she got into, I couldn't stand, so gave her a bath and sprayed her with perfume to the horror of the boys.

Four little rabbits and I visited second grade yesterday where my friend Alice teaches. We sat on the floor and discussed rabbits. The droppings intrigued the kids. I placed one on my open palm asking them to study the shape so that they could be observant in the woods. The Dann Willetts held a family conference, conferred with the Don Willetts and subsequently decided to have Thanksgiving again. It becomes obvious to us that to our boys Thanksgiving and cousins are synonymous. If three families or less come, the Don Willetts will host it, if four or more, it's all ours. Hope you can come.

November 4, 1970

Dear Mom,

Last weekend Dann, Mike and I backpacked into the Porcupine Mts. in upper Michigan, hiking three hours to a lake cabin we had reserved: eight bunks, cupboards with cooking and eating utensils, wooden picnic-type eating table, a heating stove and a cooking wood stove. This stove proved difficult even when boiling water. When I finally mastered the fire-stoking, I burned everything. A kerosene lantern provided light equivalent to one candle. The most expedient thing to do after dark seemed to be to retire, so we slept a lot. Unfortunately darkness fell by 7:00 p.m. After that, star reflections twinkled over the still lake surface. I had new hiking boots and a heavy pack. Those too-big boots allowed my feet to slip back and forth as we climbed up or slithered down. By the time we arrived at the cabin, silver dollar blisters covered my heels. Before hiking out, Dann bandaged my feet and padded the boots so my feet wouldn't slide. Since then I've had trouble wearing shoes and one ankle swells daily. The doctor diagnosed a deep infection caused by the broken blister, complicated by venal incompetency and advised surgery to strip my varicose veins.

I know what a job it will be for you to sort things. If you decide to move, I will help.

November 13, 1970

Dear Mom,

It seems like all I do is wash greasy pants. Tim has put in a car transmission three times. Twice he and his father went back to the junkyard and swapped transmissions, as they didn't have the right size. He comes home with black pants. I don't like finding black fingermarks on my newly painted stairwell either.

The Scouts worked at the University auction fund-raiser selling food. Dann, Jay and Mike were scheduled to work until 4:00 p.m. I finally managed to snatch Mike away at 7:00 p.m., Jason by 9:00, but Dann didn't come home until 1:30 a.m. He bought a huge kettle for the cottage, (for making spaghetti during work weekends), some long bread pans, (hint, I think) and 100 heavy metal trays, all for 75 cents. The boys plan on using the trays to slide down Battlefield Hill. They must be planning on a new tray for each trip down.

Tim is considering the University of Wisconsin-Stevens Point so we're going to visit the campus.

November 19, 1970

Dear Mom,

Twinkle has inoperable tumors.

We desperately hung onto Cinnamon when she was in heat, but we have now bred her and expect Brittany purebreds in January.

I froze all weekend thinking about Jay and Mike on their Scout winter campout. As part of Pioneering Merit Badge, they cut and lashed saplings to make patrol sleeping shelters. They constructed monkey bridges (you must have the agility of a monkey to cross), which they strung over the ravines. They crawled across, usually falling through, and worked so hard they never got cold.

Tim has put his car back together again. They managed to get it running at Drop-In Center, but something is still leaking.

December 9, 1970

Dear Mom,

A week of little problems makes everybody a lot ornery. Looking back, I guess Tim had reason and he agitated the whole crew. A bookkeeping test that he didn't understand dropped his A standing, and then a guy ran into him as he turned into the gas station and banged up the rear of Tim's car. The other driver said he didn't see Tim and gave him $30, which pleased Tim although the crash shook him. A friend called asking for Tim's help, but while working on his friend's car he spilled battery acid on his new flared jeans. Tim had put them on lay-a-way, but it had taken him a month to save the $8. He avoided telling me he ruined his pants, but his little brothers did it for him.

Things improved when Dann's cousin called from western New York, asking us to come out after Christmas to ski. Dann's brother from Connecticut will come also. The boys asked for time off from their jobs and Mike has found a rabbit sitter.

I don't think skiing hurts my legs. The worst times are after standing.

December 17, 1970

Dear Mom,

It's difficult to shed responsibilities when one goes on a trip. Mike needed a paper route substitute. The price goes up as weather worsens. Mike expected this and prepared to bargain. He offered Ronnie $3.00 (50 cents above the going rate). Ronnie said no. Mike asked what he thought it was worth. Ronnie said $5. Now Ronnie has been hired for $4.01 and Mike's matchbox car, and everybody is happy.

All I can say about that snowstorm is WOW! We shoveled and shoveled and didn't get cars up our driveway until 10:30 p.m. Tim and Dann arose at 6:00 a.m. and went downtown to shovel out the apartments. They shoveled some and started home to get Tim to school on time, but when the car radio announced school closures, they turned around and went back to finish. We shoveled off and on all day. Dann used three tanks of gas before the snowblower broke down. Jay had so many shoveling jobs for neighbor ladies that he talked most of them into having it plowed.

December 31, 1970

Dear Mom,

We drove for 16 hours encountering a snowstorm that slowed us down, as the passing lane wasn't passable. When we exited the freeway into western New York State blowing snow blocked the road signs, making navigation nigh impossible. We enjoyed the beauty of the winter wonderland anyway.

Sixteen of us stayed with John Paul and Toby. For three days we visited at night and skied all day. John Paul, who has been skiing for 55 years, took Andy, our expert, to the top and Toby took Mike, our beginner, on the bunny slope. I graduated from the bunny slope and rode the lift to the top, discovering that the slopes on the top are not all expert ones. We chose the green dotted ones which denotes easiest. I love skiing because it takes me outdoors. Trails, the width of a driveway and lined with snow laden pines, crisscrossed the slopes and we could see for miles from the top of those runs. It takes a special hostess who can go with her guests each day and still keep the cafeteria operating, but

Toby did. She and J.P. have a big old house and she put placards on bedroom doors so we could find our accommodations. Three pairs of adults got bedrooms; the newlyweds had a bed in the attic equipped with electric blanket, although Dann unknowingly, kept turning off their electricity. One big bedroom was labeled boys dorm and the one lone girl inhabited the living room couch. Toby had prepared food in advance and each night she offered all the leftovers from the day before, plus new additions making a great smorgasbord. I learned about crowd control. She made it seem effortless. Happy New Year.

January 8, 1971

Dear Mom,

We have been enjoying all our Christmas presents. The Corning ovenware makes delectable casseroles, the afghan is constantly draped over somebody, and we are taking turns with Newsweek. Tim still hasn't spent your clothes money. He was swamped with a history report on campus violence and hasn't even taken time out for his car that still doesn't go. It lives in the garage while mine sits outside. Jay wears his new blue sweater often. I don't dare tell him, but he looks keen with it over a bright blue shirt and blue striped pants.

The dogs did fine in our absence. Twinkle came back skinnier and Cinnamon fatter. She bulged so much that Dann immediately set up the whelping bed and we moved the dogs in from the garage at night to accustom Cinnamon to it.

The weather blasted us again. Andy went skiing and we were glad to see him home safely, as the highway was bad. Tim took the other car with the snowblower to work on the apartments. We were glad to see him back in the driveway too. We asked how many times he got stuck. "Only twice!" he replied. Snow piles have built high along the lilac hedge as we strive to keep the driveway clear. Jay says with the next storm we'll have to go out of business, because he can't throw it any higher. Mike has been shoveling the garage roof before the drifts of wet snow there put too much weight on the roof. Schools didn't close this time, much to the boy's disappointment.

January 14, 1971

Dear Mom,

    I anticipate three major achievements this weekend: the income tax (deadline is tomorrow), Tim's Christmas sweater (didn't make it in December) and a litter of puppies. The income tax comes first. I am tired of working on the dumb thing and have skipped lots of evening events because I am too tired when I bookkeep all day. Dann went to choir practice without me so I can knit tonight. I promised Tim his sweater by the next ski trip and am 2/3 of the way up the last sleeve. It would go faster with a shorter boy.

    Cinnamon looks so uncomfortable and doesn't tear around acting like sin anymore. All she wants is to lie by our feet. She can't keep food down and the boys figured there isn't room for anything more down there. I spent Saturday morning wiping up after her, until finally Dann took her to the vet. He said she just has big puppies. We make quite a canine feeding station. I cut everything into small pieces for Twinkle who can't chew anymore, take the meat scraps that Andy brings home from the restaurant kitchen, cut out the fat and warm it for Cinnamon. My friend told me about a Brittany spaniel litter of 11 where the mother developed mastitis. They hand fed 11 pups every two hours for two weeks. I don't need friends with stories like that.

    I have signed up for nature classes at the Arboretum. The call of the wild is getting to me. Perhaps it's time to start a third career.

February 3, 1971

Dear Mom,

We loved having you here. Thanks for demolishing the ironing, again. My new drip-dry clothes help lessen the ironing stack. The pups have opened their eyes and we moved their bed to the kitchen. Now that we can tell them apart, we have Star (the only female), Charlie, Wino, and John Claude.

Yes, Lisa is here visiting her father and I will give her the baby mittens you sent. She will be thrilled as she has always considered you her grandmother. They have been here three weeks. Their station wagon is in her father's garage, the engine spread out on the floor. I inquired if they weren't getting short on cash. Her stepmother said they were down to $12, but her father keeps giving them whatever they need, with a statement that this is the last time. Miriam says they are polite, helpful and pleasant to have around; she likes Lewis and adores the baby, but would like to see some direction towards moving. Something Lisa said gave me the impression they had neither time schedule nor any special place to be. I have to work harder on my philosophy that one doesn't worry about things one can do nothing about.

What's with the weather this winter? I don't know if you knew, and hope you didn't, that the Scouts were scheduled to leave Friday to ski up north. Dann was one of three drivers leaving here dubiously at 6:00 p.m. Friday as that is a long way to travel in questionable weather. They came home at 9:00 p.m. Mike said, "Hi, we're home."

"What took you so long?" I asked. "I've been expecting you." That's because I knew the roads were closing. Dann said the wind, besides being terribly cold, was so strong they couldn't see. Roads drifted. Snow blowing in through the radiator wet the distributor cap and kept killing the engine. I thought if they made it as far as

Wausau, Dann could have called his brother and spread 32 sleeping bags on his floor. They'll try again this weekend.

The doctor commented at my last appointment that my legs are like a hole in a sock. They will never get any better, eventually get worse and I should take care of it.

Arboretum classes will provide guide training for the Madison School Forest. I am much too busy for the good of the family and hesitant about committing to this, but working with kids in the outdoors appeals to me. Actually I would work six weeks in the spring, again in the fall and only as many hours per week as I request.

FEBRUARY 9, 1971

Dear Mom,

Yep, they called off the ski trip again. It gets hectic around here when this happens, as nobody else can make plans. Tim is patiently waiting for a Sunday when he can have the car so the Youth Fellowship can go skiing. They can't go if Tim can't drive, and Tim can't drive if the Scouts are gone with the wagon. They try again each week. They didn't make the decision for NO GO until 4:00 p.m. Friday, a little late when blastoff was set for 4:30. By that time lunches are made, bags packed (most of them are staying packed from weekend to weekend) ski equipment for eight people clutters my front hall, and worst of all, the kids hopes have risen again.

Andy and his friend, Woody, took the car to Rib Mountain for two days skiing. They stayed with Andy's Uncle Bruce, with the understanding I needed the car back by Friday night so that I wouldn't be stranded for more than a couple hours without transportation. When the Scouts cancelled, I called immediately to tell Andy that, as I no longer needed that car, I didn't want him on the highway either. They paged him at the ski hill, but he had been so concerned about the worsening weather that they had stopped skiing early, so they could drive home in daylight. They had a wonderful time skiing in the blizzard.

In desperation, the Scouts decided to take a nearby one-day trip and invited families. As they get a rate reduction, I opted to go. It wasn't too cold if you kept moving and Dann and I had fun skiing together. "Shouldn't you be with your Scouts?" I asked.

"No," he answered, "I don't ski their kind of hills." We could watch them schussing down every time we went up the lift. The tows close at 4:30.p.m. but shortly after 4:00, Dann suddenly stopped. "The boys need me. They're upset."

We skied down and found that Bob, the Scoutmaster, had broken his leg. He must have been overtired for that last run. The ski patrol splinted his leg, loaded him on the toboggan, and gently skied down the rest of the hill. Dann put down the back of our station wagon and spread a sleeping bag. I gave Bob a couple aspirin and the ski patrol lifted him directly into our wagon. Someone called Madison General Emergency Room saying we'd be there in 90 minutes and to notify Bob's orthopedist. He has broken his leg so many times that we felt he needed his specialist. Jay and Mike rode with me, Dann shifted our other passengers to another car and Dann drove Bob's van. Wasn't it convenient they had me for extra driver? Bob groaned in agony. When his other leg cramped Jay massaged that and rubbed Bob's hands, but Bob got so cold that all three of us removed our jackets to wrap around him. I knew he was going into shock, but I had a first-aid kid in the rear, and we needed a full-time driver maneuvering on the snow-packed roads, so I just drove. Mike and I looked in vain for a police car.

This is tragic. Jay calls it family togetherness. Both their twins broke legs skiing before Christmas, so three members of that family are wearing casts. Bob broke this leg skiing last March. He broke his finger on a Scout canoe trip and it was one of his twins that broke his arm on that bike trip. This adds up to six broken bones within 12 months.

The Scouts have scheduled three more ski trips, plus some canoe trips in May, plus a Philmont trip in July. I fear where this puts my assistant-Scoutmaster husband. Bob's wife quit skiing. She says somebody has to walk.

Some Scouter wives went out again on ladies day. We took morning lessons and practiced all afternoon, as the more instruction we get, the safer we are. Also we realize a tired skier is a dangerous skier and adjust accordingly. Try not to worry. We are not foolhardy on the hill. I love to ski. I also love being outdoors.

Lisa is still at her father's and was thrilled with your mittens. She thought they might get their car back together last week so they could leave, but they didn't.

I finished Tim's ski sweater again. It turned out shorter than he wants, but we think it will lengthen with wearing.

February 20, 1971

Dear Mom,

I've given up accomplishing anything until these puppies find other homes. We are either playing with them or people are here visiting them. They reduce my kitchen efficiency as they ride around on my feet when I'm trying to cook, especially if I'm wearing slippers. A training paper by the back door man-

ages to catch about two-thirds of what should be outside. Card tables block the kitchen doors or if we holler NO loudly twice they will brake at the threshold. After the confusion of school departures this morning, I was short one dog. Crawling around on hands and knees I found her lying in the sun behind the stereo happily chewing the cord.

The Scouts are trying again. This time I think they'll make it. There are 34 Scouts and men, three station wagons, two vans and Andy and Woody as emergency help, all ready to blast off. They have whipped their food out of the freezers and piled my front hall with skis and boots once more. I have accomplished nothing except baking cookies for them, answering phone and chasing puppies. Blastoff time is 4:00 p.m., but Dann is sending cars off in pairs. The first pair ready will leave at 3:00 to catch some daylight driving. I am tired of this getting-ready-to-go bit.

Our Scouter wives went skiing again. I just can't do it like the instructor says. I learned to turn around on the hill, but the next time I took the wrong trail and ended up on the expert slope. Traversing crosswise gradually gets me lower on the slope. The trick is to turn on each side without facing downhill or that is where you will go. I feel better now that I know I can stop.

March 20, 1971

Dear Mom,

I couldn't have managed without you. Although surgery lasted four hours while he repaired those veins, he told me that he sent me home in two days because you were here. My surgeon calls the hospital an expensive motel. Keeping me on the couch for two weeks was only possible because my legs hurt too much every time I got up. Even worse was walking in the kitchen amongst jumping puppies. My legs look awful with 14 incisions, but they work dandy. They'll fade and I squeezed this between skiing season and canoeing.

April 20, 1971

Dear Mom,

Tim arrived home safely, after visiting in Indiana. He announced proudly that his Valiant made it, although one headlight fell out and the floorboards kept moving around. The house where he visited was the home of a Church of Christ pastor. When they discovered Tim playing cards, which they don't allow, they tried to straighten him out. He came home loaded with literature about the dirty deck and how this is increasing immorality and murder in the U.S. Tim has been quoting dramatically ever since. I encouraged him to take this stuff to Sunday school class.

The Scouts are holding a gigantic sale in the Willett's garage. We've worked a week on the garage trying to clear it out. I invited some Scout mothers over and we made Sesame St. puppets. Fourteen sit on pop bottles marching down my buffet. Actually only 13, because we sold the cookie monster to our weekend houseguests. We expect to have the garage plus the entire circle-drive full of treasures (junk) and have scheduled shifts of boys, plus one adult, changing the guard every two hours.

April 27, 1971

Dear Mom,

We have survived the garage sale. Weather turned out great, the puppets sold fabulously, the boys worked their tails off as per schedule. I got to sit down frequently to rest my legs. We even sold kittens and a purebred Golden Retriever puppy and cleared $400.

Tim's car broke down again. He was coming home when the gas pedal fell off. I'm surprised he made it home. He simply turned the acceleration up so it idled high and at each stop sign, he killed the engine.

I start guiding in the School Forest next week so this week I observe. This must be like lake swimming early in the year—that first frigid minute comes as a brutal shock, but after you get accustomed to it, it's fun. I hope.

May 10, 1971

Dear Mom,

I've been guiding about four tours a week, sometimes morning and afternoon the same day, which means three to four hours walking up and down hills. I discovered after the first week that I can tire the kids out and not vice versa. With a rowdy class, I increase the pace and the distance and this squelches discipline problems. One guide starts at the school and rides the bus. Using the microphone, we teach the children geology and glacial background as we pass points of interest. The rest of the guides meet the bus at the forest and we each get approximately 20 children for a two-hour hike. All winter we've been learning identification. Now we have to remember not to do that. Identify, if asked, but teach concepts like the balance of nature, plant succession, the importance of the food chain, how man disrupts it, and habitats. The kids get pretty excited crawling around on the forest floor looking for animal tracks, turning over leaf litter looking for bugs, and pulling apart decaying wood to see why. My training instructor emphasized the priorities for a guide. "When the day arrives that you have discipline problems or inattention," she said, "your first priority is to make this an enjoyable experience for the kids, second priority is to teach if possible. If you can only accomplish the first objective of enjoyment in the outdoors, you have still opened the door for the next naturalist." Her other favorite theme was, "Be sure to spend time with the teacher, especially if she or he is a novice. Otherwise the children's outdoor education will stop at the end of your tour." I worried about that first priority, but kept telling myself to think of them as lively Cub Scouts. Walking back to the bus on my second tour, one little boy muttered, "What a neat trip!"

Getting lost on those 12 miles of trails can be a problem. Although I observed for five tours before I took one, I still get confused when trails cross, so I announced to my class that we were taking a poorly-marked trail, but if they stayed behind me, we'd all be lost together. They were disappointed to get back safely.

Jay is working on recycling for a Scout Life project. After our Litterbug contest, he organized the Scouts and they tore apart the exhibits separating glass and cans, which he took to the Recycling Center. He collects from ten families on our street, stores this in our basement for six weeks and that creates enough to warrant a trip to the Center. You should see our basement the fifth week.

May 28, 1971

Dear Mom,

On this last week of school tours I had a class of 9th graders. Worrying that I couldn't hold the attention of teenagers, I just talked about the sex life of insects and that captivated their attention.

See you Wednesday for Tim's graduation.

June 10, 1971

Dear Mom,

I am weary with decision making, all that petty stuff that needs checking before the summer trips. We spent two days shopping for extra thin socks and extra heavy socks to go over the thin ones, also film, suntan lotion, soap dishes to hold a tiny bar of soap, fire starters, foot powder in small cans, etc.

Summer plans are as follows: Tim is going to California for five weeks of Whitewater School. Their California office offered Tim a $375 scholarship. We have, with difficulty, dissuaded him from leaving this week via hitchhiking. Instead he will fly student standby Madison to San Francisco for $75. He almost pays for his ticket by working that extra week before he leaves. He is tremendously excited.

Next Monday, Dann and Mike leave for a 65 mile backpack trip on Isle Royale in Lake Superior. The same Monday Jay starts the four-week Work-Learn program in the School Forest. Tuesday, Andy leaves for six weeks in Alaska on a geology field trip. Saturday, I put Tim on the plane and Jay and the older Scouts bike to Devil's Lake for the American Wheelman's Convention. Would you like company Saturday and Sunday? Cinnamon and I would be delighted to help with your moving.

I did a tour for our Vacation Bible School, giving them a double-barreled lecture on man's effect on the environment and how we are upsetting the balance of nature. The kids loved it, the teachers were enthralled and one of the kids commented, "I didn't see why we needed a guide to walk in the forest, but I do now." I came home waving the $10 bill under the boys' noses. "That's $3.33 1/3 per hour," Mike said, but it was nice to get paid at all for doing what is fun anyway.

June 20, 1971

Dear Mom,

Many reports have trickled in from many Willetts. Tim flew to San Francisco, and then a fellow picked him up at the airport and took him home to make a sign. He found another hitchhiker and they hitchhiked together to Sacramento. Today he starts on the American River, and then will switch to the Tuba River to learn kayaking.

Andy was scheduled to start class yesterday on mile 375 of the Alcan Highway and they have probably been driving frantically all week. Tim covered his mileage easier by air.

Jay's mileage was the toughest, as they encountered strong headwinds on their 50 mile bike trip, which brought him home exhausted.

One of the men came home early from Isle Royale giving me news of Dann and Mike. This Scouter hadn't done the conditioning hikes and after three days, his knees gave out. He walked to the ranger station and came out on the ferry. He reported rain, flies, and much uphill hiking. They couldn't get the Scoutmaster to slow down. He takes off like the Army. Dann likes to see things while he's walking so they switched Dann to lead and the Scoutmaster to sweep, which slowed things. I am having all the Scouter wives for lunch so none of us will get lonesome.

June 27, 1971

Dear Mom,

A letter has arrived from Dann. Jay rushed out for the mail. "Boy, is this an old letter!" he remarked. "This stationary looks like birchbark! Hey, it IS birchbark." One day the Scouts unexpectedly spotted the mail boat, but they weren't equipped for letter writing.

Dann quickly did the best he could with the materials available. He folded the birchbark neatly and wired it together with twisties.

A friendly moose hung around their camp. They must have camped in its meadow. A strong wind arose one night and snapped Dann's tarp with such a bang that the moose took off like a house afire across Mike's tent ropes, uprooting everything and collapsing their tarp on top of the boys. Dann didn't realize what happened, but could hear Mike and Kevin asking, "Why can't I see? Where is our tent?"

Tim, coming back from the Oregon Whitewater School, was the next one home. He walked in at 2:00 a.m., accompanied by two teenagers in a Volkswagen van who had picked him up as he hitchhiked around Chicago. These kids were headed for California with limited funds. In the morning I fed them breakfast and they departed, only to have their van break down in two miles. They were towed back and stayed with us several days. Although I can't condone what they are doing or their way of thinking, we liked them immensely as we got better acquainted. She helped with the gardening. When Dann asked him if he wanted to earn money cutting brush, he worked until he almost dropped of exhaustion. The garage gave an estimate of $35 to take the van apart just to see what was wrong, but Dann prevailed upon some people he knew to do it for nothing. They diagnosed an engine replacement cost of $300. The kids reluctantly abandoned the van and departed using their thumbs. Dann paid them $25 for the van. Their parting comment, "You aren't like most people," was meant to be a compliment, I think. They came from Grosse Point, Michigan, from upper crust families. Perhaps we underestimate the younger generation. Many are great if we just talk their language, but they underestimate our generation when they assume all we're interested in is money. No, they weren't married. This precipitated much family discussion.

Tim had a great time at Whitewater School. He rafted or kayaked on two rivers in northern California, on the Rogue River in Oregon, the Salmon in Idaho, and the Green in Colorado and Utah. He learned to navigate the rafts, the students did all the menu planning and cooked in Dutch ovens or over wood fires, had instruction in ecology, conservation and human relations. The first question I asked was whether he tipped over. "Oh sure," he replied. "Once the waves rose so high the raft rode up them and just flipped."

A couple days later, Jason and the Scout troop arrived home from Philmont Scout ranch in New Mexico. They traveled by train, spending ten days on the mountain. The Scoutmaster didn't break his leg this time.

We waited and waited for Andy to come in from Alaska. He finally called from Seattle saying he had a ride to Minneapolis. From there he hitchhiked home. He got an A for the course in spite of, or maybe because, the professor had dumped their field notes and exam papers out of his canoe and had to grade on memory. On the trip home, one of the girls carried marijuana across the U.S./Canadian border. Andy woke at night to see a pair of high leather boots standing at the tent door. One kid was shaking him. "Wake up, Andy. This Canadian trooper wants to search you." They wouldn't even let him go to the bathroom by himself, but the courteous conduct of the troopers impressed the kids.

August 30, 1971

Dear Mom,

We have turned into a used-car lot. One night Dann announced at supper that he had bought a Volkswagen bug for $35.00 which didn't run. If Tim would provide the labor, Dann would provide the money for parts to fix it for resale, profits to be split fifty/fifty. Now, whenever people are home, feet stick out from under a car. Buying another Volks bug with a bad body and good engine, they removed the bad engine from the good Volks, added Mike to their crew, removed the good engine from the bad Volks, and now have the good engine in the good Volks. Tim, Mike and friends worked all day transferring that engine and found numerous other things that weren't right, but about 10:00 p.m. a great roar erupted from the garage. By Saturday noon they lowered it off the winch, charged its batteries, readjusted its brakes, backed it out and drove it up and down the driveway. Now Tim has $70 in his pocket, Dann has $70, Mike has $25 and I have greasy fingermarks all over my walls. Yes, it's worth the trouble. Tim had been wanting to go out every night, so anything that keeps him home is a plus.

We delivered Tim to the Stevens Point campus yesterday. Now I can worry about somebody else.

When I got to the part in your letter about professional movers, the boys booed. They will come with a U-Haul. Are you aware that, (although Dann and my brother worked so hard making four piles of things removed from the garage — one pile for Frank, one for Dann, one for the auction, and one for trash), Jay and Mike scrounged through the trash pile and took out many treasures? When I look at our house and what we've added since you decided to move, I don't think we can ever move from here.

Thanks for the berries and rhubarb.

October 1, 1971

Dear Mom,

The more I learn about guiding, the more I want to know. Michael chuckles over the antics of his Mom. Like when I was raising woolly bear caterpillars, one got lost on Dann's desk and turned up a day later crossing the rug when a woman from church came to visit. Or the day I chased a long-horned grasshopper around a cornstalk in the garden. They will move to where you aren't, so I finally slid a stick around to the side where I wasn't. Or the day I crawled under a bush trying to locate the chirping temperature cricket so I could see him rub his wings together. Or the day the meter man changed the meter and called from the basement, "Hey lady, there's something down here."

Realizing he had found the tiger salamanders, I hollered back, "Be careful where you step. There are six more." Dead silence. Then whoosh, the man zoomed out the back door.

I need to collect 200 insects for class. I'll never make 100. The boys know I don't like to kill, so they keep bringing home butterfly road kills. It isn't safe for even a fly in this house anymore.

October 7, 1971

Dear Mom,

I attend Arboretum classes on Tuesday afternoons, plus this week I guide for four field trips, although I requested less. Yesterday everything that could went wrong. Two buses totaling 110 second graders came in late. The kids brought lunches, which means they stayed after the tour was over, and I was the only guide with a car. I had brought my lunch as I was scheduled to work again that afternoon. But I had to drive the other guides back to town, went home to have lunch with Dann, who wasn't there, and started back to the forest with just enough time to catch my afternoon tour, when I ran out of gas. I called Leta, "I'm looking for a friend that can help me quick." She came tearing over with a gas can she kept for her mower. I was only ten minutes late. A stroll in the woods on such a gorgeous day cured my headache. As I prepared to leave, the afternoon campers got a phone call, saying that the car bringing their supper had stalled. I thought cheerily, "That's their problem, not mine", and left.

October 14, 1971

Dear Mom,

I like to do same things on the same day so I don't have to keep changing clothes. This does not work. After getting soaked in the School Forest this morning, I have to go to church soon and my hair looks like a drowned rat. It rained when we got up, poured as we ate breakfast and I stared at the phone willing it to ring with a cancellation for my second grade tour, but it didn't. This is not a fair weather game we play.

Tim struggles with indecision. He wants to transfer out of Wildlife Management, but doesn't know what he wants and is disenchanted with college.

Jay sleeps, eats, and breathes cross country, practicing until after 6:00 every night, and runs in meets every Saturday.

Dann is building another house as this slack real estate season allows him time to work. He and Mike moved the house-plans around the lot many times, trying to save another tree.

A friend called, saying he had heard we tinkered with Volkswagen bugs. His needed work and he would sell cheap. Andy has been waiting for the Volkswagen van to be repaired, but now he wants the new bug. Inoperable cars fill our circle driveway.

November 4, 1971

Dear Mom,

Dann is trying to enclose that new house before winter and comes home tired and frustrated because of all the rain. As it has become crucial not to pull Dann away from the house, Jay and Mike are doing Dann's chores: digging beets and carrots, cleaning eavestroughs, changing combination windows and cleaning heat registers before heating season.

Our Scouts did a first-aid demonstration at the Scoutarama this week. They acted hurt after using the chain saw or the power mower. The victim, painted with a blood-like substance, would rush into the aisle, fall down screaming, and the Scouts would administer first aid. But once a doctor was in the crowd and he pushed the Scouts aside. He wouldn't listen to their explanation and when he finally realized it was a demonstration, lost his temper. About then Dann showed up and lost his temper also. "If you've got a gripe, take it up with me. These boys are doing what they've been told."

The boys went home jubilantly. "You should have heard Mr. Willett tell that guy off!"

November 11, 1971

Dear Mom,

Our weekend matched the comic strips. We square danced until midnight, Andy woke us at 1:00 a.m. to say goodnight, Tim woke us at 3:30 a.m. to say he was home for the weekend with three buddies, and at 5:30 a.m. Dann and Mike got up to go hunting. We've always required the boys to wake us and say good night. I thought it a good idea until last night. Delayed reactions kicked in and I collapsed two days later.

Tim plans on visiting you and I warned him he must let you know in advance.

The new house construction needs two more weeks of warm weather. Thirty-six trusses arrived this week with a crane that lifted each one, dropping it easily into place.

Could you come for Thanksgiving? Mike says you can have his room and he promised to pick up his five cardtables of track.

November 18, 1971

Dear Mom,

Thank you, but we can't decide how to spend your birthday check. I placed a bowl on the supper table and we dropped in ideas. I want a new front door.

Don't worry about Tim turning up in the middle of the night. Hitchhiking is lousy then.

Andy enjoys his new Bug, but got frustrated when it didn't start the second day. He doesn't have Tim's attitude on car ownership. Andy expects cars to go. Tim expects them not to.

Your ability to throw things out before your move inspires me to try, but this is a terrible house when it comes to cupboards and closets. There are too many and we've filled them all.

I am not anxious to go to insect class this afternoon, as I fall short of the 100 bugs we're supposed to bring. I'd be even shorter if it weren't for the cooperation around here. Jay cleaned his overhead light bringing me 30 bugs. Unfortunately 29 were the same kind.

January 5, 1972

Dear Mom,

Tim dropped out of school. He says that he hated it and it's wasting his money until he knows what he wants. I always assumed our kids would go to college, but see now that's a narrow view and it's time we explored Tim's natural aptitudes further. He is working for his Dad and between job sites they stopped at used car lots. It's hard to tell which guy enjoys this most. Tim bought a snazzy red and black sports model Falcon. The body is in such great shape that we figure the engine must be awful. Thank you for the Outward Bound flyer. Tim sent for more information.

January 14, 1972

Dear Mom,

Tim is still looking for a job. His car sits in the driveway with no insurance and no license plates. He spends all his free time cleaning it and working under the hood, but can't afford to insure it until he has a job. He needs to work on its problems while he has time, but can't find the problems when he can't take it out on the road. If he finds a job he needs the car immediately.

Your patch on Tim's pants turned out to be temporary, so he decided if I set up the sewing machine he could sew another. I call it a three-dimensional patch, as it curves around the seat and crosses the inseam onto the other leg. He has NEVER used my machine and that is not a beginner's exercise, but he was determined. I let him flounder several times and then offered to start it. He finished by reinforcing with cross stitching. I showed him how to reverse and he exclaimed, "This is just like driving a truck."

January 19, 1972

Dear Mom,

Our chill factor dropped to minus 61 degrees. We got four heating trouble calls while we were still in bed and when Dann swung his feet onto the floor at 7:00 a.m., he knew our system was down also. Our temperature dropped below what the thermostat will read, and it took seven hours to raise it to 72 degrees.

Tim still doesn't have a job. He and his Dad finally decided to insure his car so he can drive. The pressure gets worse daily. Tim got contact lenses, put them in and immediately lost one. Tim, Jay, and I spent hours crawling around the kitchen floor looking for one invisible lost lens. When Dann came home he found it immediately, right where we'd been looking. Dann is experienced at this game.

The Scouts are traveling to upper Michigan for a skiing weekend. That means Dann, Jay, and Mike. I don't relish having them gone as that's always when the emergencies occur, so Dann showed Tim how to juggle the heating systems in all our old buildings.

January 25, 1972

Dear Mom,

The Scouts arrived home exhausted. One of the younger Scouts fell when night skiing and broke his leg. They left him in the hospital to be collected later by his parents. The second night when the kids took their skis off the car top, they neglected to relock the carrier. When Dann discovered this two hours later, his skis had been stolen. So he didn't ski the second day. I asked why he didn't rent skis, but he said his heart just wasn't in it.

Andy went skiing after work and his car quit halfway home. Blowing wind and dropping temperature caused impossible conditions. He parked in Sauk City and everyone piled into the remaining car. Both Andy and Tim's cars succumbed to frozen batteries during that cold spell. Now each night I have two batteries sitting on my kitchen counters.

Andy will be moving into an apartment on campus. Tim still checks with the Youth Employment Bureau twice a day and with his leftover time he works for his Dad. What a depressing winter.

I have learned not to worry about things I can do nothing about and there is a lot of that kind. Only our bug collections keep us enthusiastic. We have nine cars in the yard now, giving me high hopes that the intense interest in this hobby may lead to something—somewhere—sometime.

I have gone back to guide winter training sessions once a week. This, too, pushed me beyond my original bug collection as we study anything pertaining to environment. I enjoy kids. I enjoy the outdoors. I take one day at a time and always hope tomorrow will be better.

9 The North Woods

JANUARY 18, 1972

Dear Mom,

Our crazy family is taking off for a winter weekend at our summer cottage. The three younger boys go with us. Try not to worry. We have lots of muscle power to chop firewood or to shovel or push and the boys plan to ice fish and snowshoe. Dann's brother and family will join us late Friday. By then we should have a warm cottage and a shoveled path.

We have joined the Y Squares square dancing club. I was exhausted until we started dancing, when my exhaustion suddenly disappeared. Your floor length centennial dress creates a delightful swish and swing when I dance.

FEBRUARY 4, 1972

Dear Mom,

Andy moved into his apartment Sunday night after raiding his Dad's storage for furniture. The next afternoon when I was debating about taking a nap, he returned. He had $.77 to last until payday so I gave him back the cans he brought home from Alaska, plus packaged spaghetti dinner, baked beans, homemade cookies, bacon grease and a dozen eggs. The next day, when I was again thinking wistfully about a nap, he called because he needed my signature on his lease. As we finished supper, he and his roommate and the puppy walked in. When I inquired if they would like some ice cream Andy said, "We'd eat a hot dog too if there's any left." We had just cleaned the table, but I fixed more hot dogs with fried potatoes, cooked a package of frozen vegetables and mixed more fruit salad and they devoured all of it. I had thought Andy's living in an apartment would mean less work for me. Well, maybe.

The minute he moved out, Tim tore apart Andy's room. He wanted Andy's double bed, so we've shifted all the furniture. Andy invited his Dad and me to his new apartment for supper. Wow! I don't know when I taught him to cook like that. He produced mouth-watering shish-kabobs with beef, onions, mushrooms, peppers, mushroom sauce, potatoes and gravy, lima beans, tossed salad with four choices of dressing and blueberry turnovers. That should have shot his wad until payday again.

Dann and Tim appeared in court to appeal Tim's traffic ticket. The judge looked at Tim's record, "As this is not a serious offense, it seems severe to lose your license for an illegal U turn. I'll send you to traffic school instead." This requires 12 hours and wipes out the ticket, no points lost, no $27 fine. Still no job and he lost his contact lens again, but found it when he stepped back and scrunched it.

I sounded off at him for staying out so late one week night but apologized later. "I really do agree that it is your decision to make, but I just can't help telling you what I think."

He smiled charmingly, "If you'd only known, Mom, how hard I tried to come home earlier and how tired I was." He had ridden with a buddy and must have been upset to have me land on him so vehemently, but he always keeps his emotions under cover.

Mike pointed out that if Jay quits track, I can put Jay back on the table setting chore, but Jay is running again. He limps all the time, uses the heating pad and takes soaky baths.

February 15, 1972

Dear Mom,

Our cottage weekend turned out great. We enjoyed perfect weather, although some of us hoped it would snow so we couldn't get out on Sunday. We carried extra dried food along for that contingency. Deep powder snow

prevented us from walking without sinking to our hips. Tim and I used snowshoes to walk from the car to the back door. We boosted Jay onto the roof where he sunk into knee-deep snow as he struggled to reach the ridgepole and remove the chimney cover so I could light the wood stove. It took two hours of shoveling to make driveway space for two cars (the second one for brother Don's family), plus a narrow path to the cottage door. Then my shovelers quit and announced every place else we wanted to go, we had to snowshoe: to the outhouse, to the woodpile or down to the lake. After hours of a blazing wood fire, we could still see our breath. Ice crystals covering the floor sounded like sandpaper as you walked or skidded. The salt in the shakers was frozen, the sink detergent was solid and the trap beneath the sink was frozen shut. Once the corners warmed up, the room stayed warm. The boys snowshoed across the lake. They dug fishing holes in the ice and encircled them with windbreaks, but had no cooperation from below. Tim, Dann and I snowshoed back into the swamp and spotted a huge, white, snowshoe rabbit, also tracks of fox, skunk, deer, shrew, deer mice and squirrel. The shrew tracks ended in the middle of an open space. Large wing marks imprinted nearby showed where a hawk or owl picked it off for lunch. Cinnamon plunged into the snow without hesitation, sank up to her neck and dog-paddled. By the end of the weekend she learned to follow the snowshoes instead of breaking trail. Was she wiser or tireder?

Our lovely weekend was marred when Tim lost his contact AGAIN. He lost it in the morning when he pulled on his sweater and we crawled around on the frigid floor until we found it. He lost it in the afternoon during a snowball fight when snowballs plastered Tim in the face, moving both lenses. One slipped out of place in his eye. The other was gone forever. We volunteered to pay for half of it this time and suggested that considering his activities, perhaps he should become a two-glasses guy and switch to regular glasses before going on the river, in the woods, or doing athletics. Continually buying lenses destroys his finances, so Dann told him we have an entire apartment that needs repainting. Tim arose early the next morning, picked up paint and directions and drove off enthusiastically. At noon he came home for lunch downcast, because he had parked in the driveway partially over the sidewalk and received a $10 parking ticket. He may have dropped out of school, but he is still acquiring an education the hard way. Thank goodness, we can provide him with paying work.

One of the Hoover twins broke his leg again. This makes eight broken bones in that family in three years. I sent over lasagna and fresh raised donuts. Mike moaned that by the time Mom sent donuts to Hoovers, fixed a bag for Andy and sent some to Tim's buddies, our supply lasted only one day. Tim's buddies rated because they said such nice things last week as I took hot cinnamon rolls out of the oven. Jay and Mike really got their share only they ate all theirs in one afternoon.

March 1, 1972

Dear Mom,

Dann has sent Tim on all the plumbing trouble calls. It helps Tim's finances and besides Dann doesn't like to be called away from the house construction. Last week Mrs. Jones called, saying that she just couldn't tolerate her toilet anymore. It never shut off. She was sick with flu and couldn't get up all the time to jiggle it. Dann told Tim what to do. Twenty-four hours later she called back. Unbeknownst to her, Tim picked up the upstairs extension as I picked up downstairs, "There's something funny about that toilet and I thought you ought to know." I groaned. I didn't know how much more bad luck Tim could stomach. "I don't know what the hell he did to it, but the damn thing works better than it has in all the years I've lived here. I want you to know that I think that kid is a genius." This from one of our little old ladies.

Tim streaked downstairs, shaking with laughter, "Mom, Dad told me what to do, but I couldn't reach where I needed to in that cramped space, so I just put it back together."

Dann found him a temporary job at a lumberyard. This yard supplied all the lumber for our current construction job, so Dann has frequent contact with the top boss. On Monday he told Dann to send Tim out to work the next day. Dann had mentioned that Tim wears his hair long, but the man replied that didn't matter to him. This job involves heavy lifting, which Tim doesn't mind because he is working outside.

I keep having problems, too and every day something upsets me. I am tired of working constantly and keep putting things off because I am tired. Then I feel tired because the work is not done. See you next week. You cheer me up more than anyone.

March 21, 1972

Dear Mom,

We purchased new carpeting for the living room, which necessitated cleaning the entire room, starting with throwing things out from bookcases and files. Progress stopped when I found a 200-year-old book of advice on how to cure everything from indolent young men who can't find employment, to baldness, how to make wine and so on. Next I found Dann's old telegram collection. At the dinner table we passed around the telegrams, dating back to 1904, while everybody tried to put the stops in the right places. The choice one says, "Please send my black bloomers. They are in the back closet."

The boys looked at me blankly. "Explain please, what are bloomers?"

Mike announced that we now own eight cars, five which run, two which run occasionally, one not at all. Tim spent last week looking at motorcycles. Fortunately, Dann found another Volkswagen Bug, which has diverted Tim's attention. Tim's red convertible always has to be jump-started, so now he's advertising to sell two of his cars.

March 28, 1972

Dear Mom,

Our choir rehearsed Saturday morning. Dann wanted to check on the state car auction at the Coliseum first, so we drove separately. When he didn't show up at choir practice, my heart sank. Either he ran out of gas or he succumbed at the auction. I prayed for him to be out of gas, but he wasn't. This one is a maroon station wagon and will be mine. I can't believe nine cars and told Jay, "Your father has done it again." He didn't believe it either.

We're already back to eight because Jay and Dann sold Tim's convertible while Tim was gone camping. Jay took some of the calls and looked to me for help. "Is it a six or an eight?"

"Heavens, I wouldn't know."

He responded to the caller, "Why don't you come out and see what it is." When the man came, he informed Jay that it was a six. Jay said that he looked over the man's shoulder and couldn't see six of anything. He can now, because his father heard that remark.

Now Jay can tell you about every car in our yard. When Dann bought the last two, he registered them in my name to avoid getting a dealer's license. Individuals are allowed to sell four cars per year, but Dann had reached his limit. Perhaps now that Governor Lucey has signed the bill defining eighteen-year-olds as adults, the boys can buy their own cars. We're delighted you can come for your birthday. See you next week.

April 12, 1972

Dear Mom,

What fun to surprise you on your 80th birthday. I knew that if I told you just before church time that I was getting a headache, you wouldn't question it, but go with Dann and Mike to church. As soon as you drove away, the other three boys popped out of bed. We scurried to set up tables, took flower arrangements out of hiding and  picked up the 15-inch triple cake decorated with apple blossoms and roses, which my friend Marion had made. Did you realize 48 people from five states came to tell you Happy Birthday? You may not have been exhausted afterwards, but I was. Mike came home from school and asked, "What's going on around here? Every day when I come home, you're asleep on the couch!"

Dann has been trying to figure out what happened to Saturday. We ran two car ads in the paper plus three apartment-for-rent ads. Dann and Mike cleaned up the Ford wagon between calls. Most of the calls came for Tim, who was still in bed. He has decided that one of the nicer fringe benefits of living at home is a mother who refuses to wake boys except for meals.

I phoned Andy to tell him his muffler had arrived in the mail and woke Tim for lunch, but then Andy called back to say that something had happened to his clutch on the way over. He was stalled on the Beltline and couldn't shift. Mike and Dann, with Tim who was barely dressed, raced off and towed Andy home. With those ads in the paper and my mechanics now all unavailable this put me in deep trouble, so I took the offensive by tying up the phone. Andy's original engine was being overhauled and he had already put 5,000 miles on the loaner engine in his car. They towed him to Stoughton where they had just finished his original engine and switched engines back. I can figure out where Dann's Saturday went.

Tim's foreman told Tim last week that if he did cut his hair and beard he would be more eligible for promotion to driving truck where he meets the public. Tim thought the foreman presented this nicely and I think he is going to do it.

May 4, 1972

Dear Mom,

Your surprise party was such a success that I tried again and gave a party for our retiring Scoutmaster. We invited 125 people and decorated two cakes (each requiring four cake mixes). Every crumb vanished. In one corner of the flat cake we sculptured the mountains of Philmont covered with trees and tiny plastic buffalo, bear and deer. A skier sprawled in the second corner, his poles standing nearby crossed in a distress signal. The miniature signal tower, constructed from twigs, was tied with authentic

Scout lashings and topped with semaphore flags. A lake filled the third corner with swimmers and canoes and racked canoes along the shore. Bikers rode through the center. The top tier of the layered cake displayed a Pinewood Derby race track made from Popsicle sticks with miniature race cars stuck on the track with icing. Pendants flew from the second tier denoting awards Bob has earned. The bottom tier portrayed a campsite surrounded by cows (a reminder from the time they camped in a pasture), plus a pine tree plantation signifying their Christmas tree sales and a miniature sugar mold plaque with the Scout oath. I got carried away, but was having so much fun I couldn't stop.

The lady, who made your cake, helped with this and we had such a good time that she agreed to take six of us as a class. Every Tuesday morning we each appear at her house with a cake and we each come home at noon with a decorated cake, much to my family's delight. Lousy for people on diets. One of my classmates commented, "We're fighting a losing battle just licking our fingers!"

Guide season has begun and I've already done four tours this week, including special education kids and some high-school students. One brought along a snake in his pocket. Fortunately one of the other kids warned me. I carefully avoided telling the bus driver as we had cross Mary driving that day.

Saturday morning I baked my special coffeecake. Dann walked through as I took it out and questioned, "Why such a large batch?"

"Just crack open the boys' bedroom doors please, so the smell carries. They have lots of chores, but Saturday is their sleep-in morning and it isn't cricket for me to wake them just for chores." He raised a questioning eyebrow, but did it.

As we finished breakfast, Mike came barreling down to the kitchen. "You know, Mom, this is really a dirty trick." Dann's mouth dropped in amazement. He thought I had been kidding.

Five minutes later Jay arrived in the kitchen muttering, "Yeah, that's what I thought." Both of them did a lot of work for me that morning.

I'll enclose my *Saturday Morning Special*. Pop might enjoy it.

Batter

1 ½ cup flour
¼ cup oleomargarine
2 ½ teaspoon baking powder
1 egg
Dash of salt
½ cup milk
¾ cup sugar

Sift flour, baking powder, salt and sugar. With pastry blender or spoon cut in shortening. Beat egg and combine with milk. Make a well in the flour mixture, pour in milk and egg. Stir until just mixed. Turn into greased pan.

Topping

3 Tablespoons flour
½ teaspoon cinnamon
¼ cup sugar
2 Tablespoons oleo (cut in)

Sprinkle batter with topping. Bake at 315 degrees for 15–20 minutes.

All the extra cars are finally gone. Mike worked all week stripping the old Volkswagen frame. It's not every 14-year-old that has the opportunity to take a car apart. He and Tim attached the remains to our station wagon and towed it to the sand pit. We were delighted to see the junky thing leave the driveway, but not so delighted when it returned in two hours. They drove to four different places only to find them locked as it was Sunday. A police car tail had picked them up, so they came home. At the same time some guys came to look at Tim's other junker and when they finally got it going, Tim sold it for $10 and a shotgun. Mike and Tim found a place to junk the old Volks frame, but first jacked it up and removed all the tires. This is called squeezing to the last drop. Our garage rafters are loaded with spare Volks parts.

This was an awful week. How do women work full time? Part time throws me into a tizzy. I worked seven tours, spent two half-days in Dann's office, and we flew to Colorado and back one day—my first flight in a big plane. We traveled to Pueblo West, a planned city just opening up. The type of construction and the land sales interested Dann, the government reclamation project where a series of tunnels, four reservoirs and a huge dam divert water from the other side of the continental divide for this semi-arid land, interested me. Our salesman carried a pair of powerful field glasses in the jeep, so I viewed cliff swallow nests, a falcon, magpies, ground chickens and prairie dogs. He drove over the future lake bed, up and down steep inclines which the jeep took easily. Coming home I sat with nose glued to the window while drinking champagne and watched the lightning spiking below us. No, of course we're not interested in buying. Leave Wisconsin?

May 24, 1972

Dear Mom,

I guess I deserved your scolding, in fact I expected that letter. I'm doing better this week. I can't cut down on my school forest guiding, Mom. I love it and it's good for my family to have to help at home. This only lasts a month or two every spring and fall. Besides, how awful it would be if I spent all my time worrying about the boys. I will give up something else.

We've been having trouble on tours because of this heat. The kids wilt. Leaves aren't out yet to provide any shade in the woods.

I had a 5th grade class with a teacher who has been here often. She barely stepped on the bus before she started telling me what a wonderful class she had — and she was right. How could they be anything but, with a teacher who thinks they're wonderful? I accomplished more with that class than I've ever managed before. When the tour was over she was just as emphatic about what a great tour I had given.

I am struggling with my conscience concerning your offer of help. This is the last week for tours but days will be frantic with Andy moving home in the middle of the week and Jay getting ready to move.

June 5, 1972

Dear Mom,

Everybody thought it wonderful having you here, although you worked too hard. We enjoyed your cookies for days. I took lots with us to the cottage, gave Jay a box to take to camp, gave Tim some for his weekend campout and left a few at home for Andy.

Dear Mom

Our weekend at the cottage proved too short. Having a summer residence presents more work and maintenance problems, but owning this with Dann's five brothers, theoretically we share the problems. Memorial Day weekend is work weekend, when everybody who can comes to help. This sounds like a mess with six co-owners but it works. We issue priorities for summer use. Everyone places a summer request by May 15th. If someone with a lower priority bumps you, you pick another and gradually you work up to first choice. This cottage is special to all Dann's brothers because the Methodist conference moved pastors often from parish to parish, but this was home base. The boys and their Mom spent summers there, with their Dad joining them during the week.

We arrived late Friday night. Shortly after snuggling into sleeping bags, we discovered that during unloading we must have let in hordes of mosquitoes. All of us suffered with an all-night buzzer. Jay figured they must have a system. "Charlie, you take that kid over there, George you cover this one, oops, send in a replacement for Charlie—he just got wiped." I explained that those names should be Charlotte and Georgianna.

The outdoor crew raked leaves away from the house, painted half the dock and installed it in the lake, floated the raft, painted

cottage trim and took down dead trees. The inside crew scrubbed floors, washed windows and removed cobwebs and mice nests. We still found time to drive to Superior to see the 25-mile-long ice jam on Lake Superior, and stopped at Bridgman's for triple treat sundaes. The rest of the time (there was some) we lay in the sun and dropped Jay off at DNR Youth Conservation camp on our way home.

    I led 30 school tours this spring and swiped Dann's pedometer which showed I walked a few seven mile ones. I often taught the Mammal special. We have acquired an extensive collection of bones and teeth and some road kills, which we injected with formaldehyde and use them for teaching identification. I also taught predator-prey relationships, food chain, camouflage and adaptations. On mammal specials we did hikes, looking for footprints, homes and deer browse. I took squeamish kids into the meadow, hunting for fox droppings, which I pulled apart to see what the fox had been eating and we found rabbit fur, dried apple skins and wild grape seeds. We studied owl pellets, which is what an owl regurgitates as indigestible. Taking these apart we found tiny field mice bones. It takes me barely five minutes to turn squeamish kids into eager little beavers, yelling for me to look at what they've found under the pines. I have a neat mini-lecture on how most people walk in the outdoors and don't see what is there.

June 14, 1972

Dear Mom,

    Last weekend Dann and I went camping without any family. We've never gone alone before. It's easier to cook and wash dishes. We were with school forest guides and husbands and canoed the Kickapoo River on the section that will be destroyed by the proposed dam. How sad to think of losing this rare arctic primrose that clings to the cliff walls.

The campground rests on the top of Kickapoo Mountain and during the night a howling wind arose. By 6:00 a.m. campers were foregoing the last day of canoeing and folding camp. The couple who had borrowed our second canoe placed it on our cartop rack without tying it on. As I walked past minutes later, the wind picked up that 80 pound canoe, sailed it over my head and dropped it on the ground on my other side. We had used our new outside frame tent. Dann packed and loaded all the gear from inside the tent, but when he went back in to sweep out the tent, a gust of wind picked it up like tumbleweed, rolling it down the field end over end with Dann inside. I sprinted after it, catching one corner, laughing so hard that all I could do was hang on until friends rushed up and tipped it so we could open the hatch and let Dann escape.

We arrived home a half-day early to find the kitchen piled with dirty dishes. "But we would have had it clean by tonight," the boys protested. "You mean you quit and came home early just because of a little rain. You never do that." They were right. We don't quit for rain. Wind is another matter.

We have heard twice from Jay asking for mosquito dope, soap, and a towel—immediately, please. As any boy at camp who requests soap ought to have it forthwith, I dispatched a package with those items, plus the sports pages, funnies, and election primary returns. I foresee a busy summer. In his next communication he claimed the camp record for picking 80 wood ticks off himself in one day. They are working in Douglas County taking down jack pines to allow the Norway pines a better chance. He wrote, "This camp is okay," (a supreme compliment) "but they sure are picky about keeping cabins clean."

We leave next week for five days of backpacking in the Porcupines with Mike and friend Kevin, plus Andy and his friend.

Following that, Mike and Kev will bike home. We practiced hiking up and down the steepest trails in the School Forest, with each of us carrying 26 pounds of Encyclopedia Britannicas. Menu planning consists of listing each meal on a scrap of paper that I place on the dining room table, and then accumulating piles of food by each paper. Each item measures the right amount for one meal. Everything goes into small sandwich bags and each complete meal goes into one large plastic bag, so when we delve into somebody's pack, we can find Day 4 breakfast or whatever. Sorta like a jigsaw puzzle.

June 29, 1972

Dear Mom,

We survived the backpacking with only minor problems. Andy's friend changed plans at the last minute but Andy decided that didn't matter, so we dropped him off alone on the north side of the wilderness. He wished to do his own cooking, wanted to do extra hiking and needed some time to think. We entered on the south end. Andy knew our route and expected to catch up in two days. We hiked six miles to our first cabin, exhausting ourselves. Warm weather brought the bugs out en masse, making us miserable. Imagine our surprise when Andy walked in at 8:00 p.m., after hiking 14 miles, which exhausted him also. He walked along, stopped and fixed lunch, walked some more and stopped to fix supper, while the bugs feasted on him. He calculated that he must be only five miles away from us, recollected we had an empty bunk, and besides he kept seeing lots of bear droppings. He had his thinking all done, so he just kept walking. Mike called the mosquitoes Cutters Battalions as they seemed immune to our massive applications of Cutters. Within minutes we perspired so much the darned Cutter's just floated off.

Dear Mom

The first day we woke to a steady soaking rain that persisted all day and night. Our luck was better than average that this happened on a cabin layover day, so we were neither on the trail nor camping. We did have to move out the next day on damp, slippery ground, making the going tough, but having Andy helped. We had traversed a steep, slippery river trail when our lead hikers informed us the trail now crossed the river, and no bridge. The natural crossing was gone because 24 hours of rain had raised the river and submerged the rocks, which normally made stepping stones, so we gingerly picked our way across on a downed tree. Everybody walked upright with backpacks except me. Mike came back for my pack, Andy carried Cinnamon, and I crossed on the seat of my pants. Later Cinnamon exhibited the agility of a mountain goat and the balance of a tightrope walker on those downed trees. Reloading, we soon caught up to our lead, who announced with great glee that the trail crossed the river again, but no tree. We tied boots around our necks, rolled up pants and unfastened hip straps. These hip belts strap around below your waist designed to shift weight from your shoulders onto your hips. However, if you lose your balance and fall with a hip strap on, you resemble a helpless turtle on its back. We needed tennis shoes to protect against the sharp, slippery riverbed stones. The icy water and erratic current pushed at our precarious balance. By day's end we had survived four river crossings. If not for that 24 hours of rain, we probably could have crossed on stones. After climbing out the steep bank on the last crossing, we shed our packs and sat down to put boots on. Standing up, Dann bumped my pack. It slid down the bank into the current and floated peacefully away. Dann jumped in to grab it, but not before it took in a lot of water in the top compartment where I carried food in plastic bags. We dumped out the water, but didn't remember until too late about the ax handle hole in the floor of that compartment, and that soaked all my clothes in the compartment below the hole. Camping on the trail that night, we dried my clothes around the campfire. We crossed the last time ten feet above a waterfall on a deadfall tree inclined uphill, I again on the seat of my pants.

Our next cabin faced the shores of Lake Superior. Hilarious stories of people's mishaps filled the pages of the cabin logbook. Some hiked in carrying suitcases, some carried 70 pounds (I thought 25 was too much), some rigged a pulley after a crossing to pull their packs up the slippery, steep bank on the far side. Many questioned the water reservoir in the wood cook stove, "Why the devil is there water in the stove?"

Speaker cabin perched on the mouth of Speaker creek, and millions of 20 inch suckers fought their way upstream to spawn, puzzling Cinnamon. She would stand in the creek while many big fish swam by. Apparently she could neither see nor smell them, but when they flipped tails above water for momentum, the water splashed around her. She whirled round in circles and eventually would stick her head under and come up with a big fish that she took to the bank and dropped. She caught ten. We swam in the icy waters of Lake Superior. Racing out of the lake, Mike stepped on a rusty nail causing his foot to swell so that he couldn't walk. Lucky timing again as we had planned another layover day. I soaked his foot in salt water and eventually a small piece of decomposed wood floated out of the wound.

Emerging from the park, Mike and Kevin repacked and, as a trial run, biked across the northern part of the state to our cottage. We drove, waited there for them and they turned up in a day-and-a half. Their first supper, cooking on a small Sterno stove, had consisted of ten wieners, a whole cantaloupe, a bottle of Welch's grape juice, and a quart of chocolate milk. No refrigeration and no leftovers. Camping in a field, they had spent the rest of the day picking wild strawberries, which they consumed for breakfast on scrambled pancakes. When Mike experienced brake trouble, he took his brakes apart putting in their spare universal cable, which means they're traveling without a spare until they find a repair shop.

They left the cottage, headed for Trego planning to spend the night with friends, but ran into a terrible storm. They phoned ahead and their friends drove out in their truck and carried the boys home to dry out. We had cautioned that if they saw a storm coming, they should stop immediately and put up cover, but they had replied they would just run for the nearest gas station. They learned early that there aren't many gas stations in the North Country.

This year Dann and I are on the 4-H camp counselor training staff and are teaching survival. I cover food and water in the wilderness, Dann teaches warmth, fire building and shelter.

July 8, 1972

Dear Mom,

Mike and Kevin arrived home, after traveling 540 miles. They became separated their last night out. Mike thought Kev was in front so he speeded up. Actually Kevin was behind. Deluged with a downpour and approaching darkness, Mike put up his tarp at a wayside. Kevin, with no tarp, slept in a barn. Kevin called home to see if we knew where Mike was. Two calls or none would have been infinitely less worrisome. The next morning Mike reversed direction and found Kevin seven miles away.

Tim has been accepted for an Outward Bound program. He will participate in three weeks of survival training in the mountains, a program designed to build self-confidence.

Have I told you about Fred? He rented a desk in our office in return for answering our phones when we are out. This is not working well. We learned that he is serving a six-month jail sentence for forging checks. He claims he can get released on the Huber law and still supervise our office.

July 26, 1972

Dear Mom,

Working near Fred provides better entertainment than a "soap". He left for Chicago to attend his grandmother's funeral the weekend before he was supposed to be incarcerated. Tuesday came and went, but no Fred. Dann visited the Dane County jail, hoping to sever contact with Fred and his contact with our office before we left on vacation. No Fred there either, but they welcomed Dann and ushered him into the District Attorney's office. Dann learned lots in a hurry. Fred had told us that he would have six months in jail, which would reduce to six weeks for good behavior, but actually his sentence ran nine months. He had asked for 16 hours out per day instead of the customary eight because he told them he was in partnership with us—Madison Realty. The D.A. allowed Dann to look at Fred's record. This is his third sentence. The first was 15 years for burglary, the second stretch for narcotics. I can't understand how we got mixed up with this. Fred appears personable and tells convincing stories, but actually he is a smooth, shrewd con man who doesn't miss an angle. He received permission from the University to audit a course. On the strength of that he applied for an ID card, applied to the University credit union, borrowed $2,500 and lived in Witte Hall free. Burglary, narcotics and prostitution police personnel were all checking on him. We had wondered why he turned on a red light in our office window every night. The D.A. told Dann that two days earlier they had observed him leave our office with a woman (me) in a blue Chevy (he had asked for a ride to the square.) They ran a license check which came back with an identification for a '63 red Ford Falcon convertible (Dann had shifted plates when he sold the last car). I'm surprised I didn't get arrested for a stolen vehicle. The police, with our permission, searched our office twice. Fred hired a secretary, who was supposed to answer our phone when we were out, in return for rent. After two weeks she approached me hesitantly. "Fred hasn't paid me. When I asked, he said I could take my salary out in company stock."

She asked what she should do and I replied, "Quit. Immediately."

Two days later when I was cleaning house, Mike announced that Fred was on the phone. "Where have you been?" I asked. He gave me all that baloney about having to take care of his Grandmother's affairs. "I thought you were supposed to be back on Tuesday to start your jail term."

"Oh yeah," he sighed, "I just sent them a telegram telling them I was going to be late."

"Where are you now?"

"Working at my desk here in the office."

I signaled to get Andy's attention, and wrote a note asking him to go next door, call the D.A.'s office, ask for Bill and tell him Fred was in our office. Meanwhile I encouraged Fred to keep talking. "Please Mrs. Willett, you gotta give me another chance. I guarantee that everything will be all fixed up. "

"Sorry, your only choices are what Dann offered last week. Either we take you to court and press for compensation for services you haven't performed OR if you move out right now we will forget all that." Big bluff. We didn't want to go to court any more than he did.

When Andy returned, I told Fred good-bye and hung up.

Fifteen minutes later Dann called. I asked where he was.

"In the office."

"Alone?"

"I am now, but the strangest thing just happened. I came in and found Fred loading his typewriters and stuff into a taxi. Two policemen walked in behind me. They stood on each side of Fred and remarked,

'Well, well, imagine finding you walking around here.' They switched Fred's stuff from the taxi to the squad car and departed." We haven't seen him since. Dann changed the lock immediately. Now we can leave for vacation.

July 31, 1972

Dear Mom,

Our sailing canoes enlivened our cottage week. Dann purchased sails for both canoes thinking the boys could race. The first time out a stiff wind blew out of the northwest and they couldn't get off the beach until Mike pushed Jay clear of the dock. By the time I steadied Mike's boat so he could grab his lines and clear the dock, Jay had sailed halfway across the lake. Mike heeled his sailing canoe in an effort to catch up but suddenly Mike's sail disappeared. Using binoculars, I could see a small brown head bobbing in the middle of the lake. Two sailboats stayed by him until a speedboat arrived and circled. It took us a while to rescue him with our rowboat going against that headwind and Mike was far out. When we arrived, he had secured everything ready for a tow. We headed for the nearest point of land pulling the canoe full of water with Mike sitting in it to keep it upright. When we were almost there, a small motorboat zoomed up, the fellow leaned over to Mike and said, "Hi, I'm Eric, the waterfront director from the boy's camp. Drop your tow and I'll pull you in. I've just fished your brother out and he's drying off at the Camp."

Jay told us later that he was almost to the far shore going too fast and he tried to turn the way his Dad had told him. It wouldn't go, so he turned downwind the way Dad had said never to do and over he went. The waterfront director came out and towed him in, much to Jay's embarrassment, until a sailboat sailed by and a guy hollered, "Hey, there's a rig just tipped over in the middle of the lake that looks just like yours. Hey, the guy looks just like you."

"Thanks," Jay replied. " That makes me feel a lot better." Both boys obviously felt sheepish and won't sail anywhere near the Boys' Camp anymore. Jay says if they're going to continue sailing, we need a motor for the rowboat for rescue purposes.

More on Fred—he got Huber privileges but on the first day out he didn't return. They found him and added another six months to his term. A furniture company called yesterday and wanted to pick up their furniture.

Dann asked, "What furniture? Fred told us he paid for that." Apparently he talked their salesman into letting him take an orange upholstered chair for display purposes, signed a sales slip and helped himself to more pieces as he left. I turned over one of the end tables and found a label which read "Property of University of Wisconsin Residence Halls."

August 1, 1972

Dear Mom,

We have rented our front office to a rental housing outfit and we're moving into the back office. What a mess! Jay and Mike work for us afternoons. They packed Fred's remnants away and finished the painting which Fred had left half done and are eliminating the bright red wall Fred painted in the front office. Jay is a good careful painter but Dann has hired him in body only. His mind is fascinated with the mechanics of starting a new office: like how do you hire three secretaries if you don't have any business yet, or the alternative, how do you handle business that comes in if you don't have any secretaries? They have a phone but no desks yet and Jay says it sounds like an office even if it's empty. His paintbrush keeps going steadily, but he doesn't miss a thing.

August 13, 1972

Dear Mom,

Tim is not coming home from Colorado. He found a temporary job working in a new ski area and is staying with one of his Outward Bound instructors. Actually Tim gets the shed attached to their house trailer. He went mountain climbing one rainy day and when he was lead hiker he slipped, falling 15 feet to a ledge. They were roped and Tim was wearing a hard hat he had just purchased for $2.50. As he wasn't hurt, he thought that the hat paid for itself, but says he won't do that again.

Mike periodically tries to start Tim's car. Sometimes it starts, sometimes not.

I am doing fall housecleaning. I informed Mike at supper that I would be doing his closet today. Jay immediately piped up, "Watch out for Mom. She goes in your closet and makes an awful mess. Then she says YOU put it back so you know where everything is."

September 14, 1972

Dear Mom,

School Forest tours have begun. The first one set me up for the whole season when the teacher remarked that her kids learned more from me in one afternoon than from all their science classes. One guide stepped in a yellow jacket hole, which immediately sent hornets buzzing in all directions and up her pants. Her kids panicked and ran screaming helter-skelter through the woods.

One girl lost her glasses. One boy's leg started to swell. A class was coming through from the opposite direction and that guide collected all the kids and loaded everybody back on the bus. When the boy mentioned that he was allergic to bees, the guide called base on the bus radio, asking them to call the school and notify the parents. The boy really wasn't allergic as 30 minutes elapsed before they arrived back at school and that would have been much too long.

Dann and Mike went bow and arrow hunting. Mike walked into the house and said, "Mom, I was sitting in the bushes when that deer came and stood less than seven feet away from me. All I could think was what is he doing here?" Mike sighed and said, "Finally the deer turned and I couldn't shoot him when he was looking at me." Dann reassured him that this happens to everybody once and is commonly known as buck fever. Mike is in a frenzy to go again, back to the same place to look for the same deer.

October 5, 1972

Dear Mom,

Mike scrounged in my school forest shoulder bag last night and finding a pill jar with a giant dead grasshopper, he muttered, "Mom, I can't understand you. You stuff dead grasshoppers in jars, take droppings apart looking for mouse bones, and then you almost get sick when Cinnamon catches a squirrel."

Mike doesn't understand. I feed the squirrels.

Many Willetts biked on the Sparta/Elroy Bike trail last week; three of Dann's brothers plus wives, with one wife driving the "sag wagon" that followed, loaded with gear. We rode 37 miles in two days. I expected to be weary but was pleasantly surprised when we arrived at the hostel to find that I was the only female who still had enough get-up-and-go to make supper. To arrive at the youth hostel we had to leave the bike trail and bike five miles uphill.

We counted 24 beds in six different bunkrooms all unoccupied, and chose the bunkroom with black wallpaper and dancing pink ladies. We observed a hole in our ceiling and found somebody above had apparently stepped through the floor and then placed a captain's chair over that spot. A little sign hung on the bathroom wall. "This is a country toilet which plugs easily so watch all that paper you put down."

This bike trail is an old railroad right-of-way and that makes level riding. Even going upgrade it rose so gradually that we didn't notice until we coasted down. We rode through a mile-long tunnel lined with water-filled ditches that needed to be avoided at all costs. Bikers passed constantly. We couldn't see them in the darkness, but knew they were there and then we started singing. What great acoustics in those tunnels! Passing bikers joined in until gradually the singing faded away.

November 15, 1972

Dear Mom,

I have lost Mike for all practical purposes. He's out working on OUR car. That means his and his Dad's — Dad's money, Mike's labor. Boy, can that kid get dirty!

Tim is home. He just walked up the driveway last Friday with his puppy under one arm. He secured a ride from Denver to Chicago for $10 and hitched the last 150 miles. His five-weeks-old pup is part Siberian husky and part I know-not-what. Cinnamon is training the pup as fast as she can.

Tim will stay until after Thanksgiving as he came home between jobs to pick up his car and skis. He bought a bus which has been converted to insulated camper for his winter housing.

November 26, 1972

Dear Mom,

Jason has been giving me so many arguments about church attendance that I finally wrote him a letter. Enclosed find copy.

"Dear Jason,

I am going to put together some jumbled thoughts I've had about you and church. I think you resist for the following reasons:

(1) You want to sleep Sunday morning—nuts to that, unless you had a hectic Saturday.

(2) You question parts of the Bible and the existence of a Master Planner. You must realize all of us do this to some lesser degree. I find some things hard to accept so I don't, but I don't throw out all of Christianity. A person's values and beliefs change constantly as life changes and your belief in the church may get even weaker, but I do not worry about this, Jay, as I feel all of you have a strong religious upbringing and when you need it you will find it.

(3) I think you object to the sermons on the basis you can't get much out of them—valid complaint. Ministers have different strong and weak points. However, there is still gain being there. Perhaps this is the only hour each week which you have without interruption to think about where you are going and why. In the next ten years you have important decisions to make and sometimes we move so rapidly from one problem to the next that we never stop to think what life is about. As long as you're living at home, I don't want you to lose contact with your church. Let's try once a month plus special occasions. Try to pick one thought from the sermon which you agree or disagree with, just to think about and forget about reviewing the sermon with me unless you wish to argue.

"I wish you kids could stop thinking of church as one hour Sunday morning. Christianity is a way of living, of being concerned and doing something to help that other guy, not being wrapped up in oneself. 'One cannot walk on this earth and not pay rent.' I feel this philosophy every day in many ways. It is the only way I can live a happy and fulfilling life. Sorry to be so serious this morning.P.S. Please pay your church dues."

End of quoted letter. Mom, did I give you this much trouble?

November 30, 1972

Dear Mom,

Thanksgiving also means redecorating. We replaced the dining room ceiling, Dann installed paneling halfway up the sidewalls, I papered the rest in an old tavern print and we bought new carpeting. Family Thanksgivings are my goal for all the things I want done anyway. Thirty-six came for dinner. So many guests coming days ahead worried me, but this works great. The boys doubled up and we filled all the bedrooms. With three extra women in the kitchen everything was ready ahead of schedule. Some of the guests were shirt-tail relations. We invited Pete whose grandmother was sister to our kids' great-grandfather. This confused everyone until I laid out my genealogy notes and Mark drew a huge wall chart. Everyone was so enthused that Jay and I have been working non-stop researching the gaps.

December 18, 1972

Dear Mom,

Tim has left for Colorado again, taking car and skis after being home four weeks. He needed to do car repairs, and to work to pay for those repairs, but was worried about getting back through the mountains to his camper bus before the heavy snows. His car blew a valve enroute. He limped as far as Denver, stayed with friends and got a construction job while he waited for it to be fixed. He finally arrived home, but is still having expensive car troubles and gets long distance advice from his father and brothers about fixing it or dumping it. He and his puppy live alone in his bus with a gorgeous view of the mountains on one side and a gurgling mountain stream out the other.

Jay and I are creating recycled Christmas cards. We made envelopes, purchased a stamp which says "this has been recycled", picked the gorgeous old cards you can't stand to throw away, put decorative tape over the old signatures and added our signatures.

Dann and Mike bought another $50 Volkswagen!!

January 7, 1973

Dear Mom,

Our skiing luck ran out. Andy called last night from the Aspen Hospital. He had taken a week off work and he and two friends left here on New Year's Day driving Andy's Volkswagen. He stopped momentarily in Denver to check up on Tim. Only a brother could wake a guy at 5:00 a.m., say hi, and visit for 15 minutes and leave. They arrived in Aspen at noon. These eager skiers couldn't waste that beautiful day and purchased half-day tow tickets. Within two hours Andy fell, breaking his leg. The next skier stopped at the hill phone and called for help. The ski patrol, equipped with walkie-talkie and toboggan, arrived immediately and called for a snowmobile. They took Andy to the clinic at the bottom of the mountain where they x-rayed. Although they set bones there, they send the worst ones, like Andy, to the hospital. He now has a plate, four screws and a rod inside his fibula and will be hospitalized for a week. It took him four days to reach us because we had gone up north skiing. As soon as they release him he'll fly home on standby. Meanwhile his friends will drive his car home. I thought this calamity should have waited until the end of the week so that he could do some skiing but he replied, "No, Mom, if I'd skied I couldn't afford to fly home."

January 15, 1973

Dear Mom,

Andy is home. We expected him Monday but he called to say he was stuck in Aspen. Only three flights leave Aspen daily and all the skiers, who had reservations, were flying home. He picked up a reservation for the next day as far as Denver. His buddies took him back to their apartment and put him to bed. I was glad to know that he had a place to lie down, but he said it was so crowded that night that he couldn't keep his crutches with him so he couldn't get up. I lay awake and worried about how he was going to sit on the plane. As I remember, there isn't much foot space, but Aspen Airways must encounter this problem frequently. The stewardess gave up her seat and settled him crosswise on two seats. From Denver on, he sat on the right side and used the aisle for his cast. The distance from the plane into the Denver terminal stretched out like a ten mile walk, but he spotted the Travelers' Aid and knew he needed some. They drove him around the airport in an electronic cart, took him to be searched (the screws and plates set off the security) and booked him on the next flight to Milwaukee. In Milwaukee he barely had time to call home before beating us to the Madison airport. He talked that night, but then we got no more stories for three days. He was so tired and miserable he just wanted to be left alone. Along the way he had picked up a bad cough and a temperature which really bothered when he was lying down, which was all the time. He is already planning new skis for next season.

Mike has been busy with all the junker Volkswagens. He and his friend, Kevin, stopped for lunch one day and Kevin asked Mike to show him something which was in Mike's bedroom. Mike looked Kevin over and said, "Nope, we can't leave the kitchen. We're too dirty." And you'd better believe it, they were. On Sundays I ask him to sit on his hands during church because I know cleaning nails is hopeless. We call Kevin our fifth son because his hand is in the cookie jar as often as the other four. Although it will be a year before Mike can drive, he has already taken a whole car apart AND put it back together. The suspense around here gets greater than a soap opera as the question of the day always is "will it run after he puts in the new whatchamicallit?"

January 15, 1972

Dear Mom,

We took Andy to his apartment for a visit, but he wants to stay. Mike helped me cut Andy's pants off and I installed a zipper up the outside seam so he can dress himself. No way can he drive, not even an automatic. He talked to his boss and they will hold his job, but he has dropped out of school for second semester as he can't manage the campus hills. He expects to wear a cast for six months.

Guess who walked into the office last week? Fred. He served only six months and the first thing he did was hightail it to our office to pick up the rest of his stuff. He needed to borrow a truck so Dann told him to come back at 4:00 but he never showed. That was four days ago so perhaps he's already back in jail somewhere.

January 31, 1973

Dear Mom,

Andy has been reading, constructing model ships, watching TV and baking bread from scratch. He progressed from his long cast to a short below-the-knee cast. Now he can sit properly and can drive as I traded with him, my automatic for his manual shift Volkswagen. I actually enjoy running around town in that fluorescent yellow thing. He took me out so I could get used to the floor gears and when we stopped to see my friend he said offhandedly, "Oh, she's doing all right." After the comments he has made about his roommates ruining the gears, I judged that to be a compliment.

We're relieved to have heard from Tim because he had to relocate his bus and we didn't know where he was. He is now parked in a lady's field and in exchange, splits firewood for her. No electricity. Perhaps he just goes to bed at sundown. His ski resort job is over, but he works part time splitting wood.

February 8, 1973

Dear Mom,

Andy announced with great glee that he can now sit in the bathroom. His leg swelled after they changed his cast and this sent him back to bed for two days. One of the problems of a cast is that your bare toes stick out. The Aspen Ski Corp gave him a hand knit toe sock with a skier design. I do believe that every cloud must have some silver lining, but it took me awhile to find anything good after this ski accident. We have seen a lot more of Andy as he comes to supper once a week. When he carried a full class load plus 20 work hours we felt favored if we got a phone call.

He called to say he wished he had a garbage bag as he needed to take a shower. I dropped one off and called later to see how he did. All the guys helped him. Andy commented, "It worked fine except I'm not going to do that again for a long time. It took me an hour to undress and redress." How would you like Andy and me for lunch some day, weather permitting? I won't admit this to him, but am cautious about driving in bad weather with him along and as I don't consider him an asset at the present time.

Jay is taking scuba diving lessons. The class sits on the bottom of the pool and does somersaults. He has been invited to an engineer's banquet at the University, including a tour of the University facilities and the nuclear reactor. Quite an honor for a high school junior. At present he would like to be a space scientist and has written to the Russian ambassador asking for information on their space program.

February 15, 1973

Dear Mom,

Tim replied that he has a lantern so doesn't need electricity.
No word from the Russian ambassador yet.
Mike got a call from Minneapolis. An automotive distributor company thought they were going to sell him a Volkswagen body. Dann had a hard time discouraging them until he mentioned that Mike is 14. That did it.

February 22, 1973

Dear Mom,

Would you like to knit an un-birthday present for your one-legged grandson? He came over last night because he wanted me to wash his toes. He cannot reach even though he tried with a washcloth between two pencils. He also needed me to mend his knitted toe sock as he had worn a bare spot on the bottom. This won't work for long. He has worn this one two months and we have four months to go. I figured out how to do it and am enclosing written directions. At his request I also have started a toe sock made out of scrap leather. When he works in the restaurant kitchen he needs protection from hot liquids which frequently drop on his feet. I set it up and then showed him how to do the advanced double-cross lacing stitch and he picked it up in seconds. Wish I could snag his interest in leather work as he is so bored. Jay has gotten on somebody's mailing list. Today he received a letter offering to explain their get-rich-quick scheme for only $20 and then he received another for $10. I called the Chamber of Commerce and they gave them a bad report, but Jay complained, "But they guarantee results or you get your money back."

The Russian ambassador finally came through. Jay received three big packages containing eight magazines entitled Soviet Life (in English), each one containing an article on space. Hope this doesn't put him on the CIA list.

Tim called Sunday to say his car blew up. Everybody but me understands what this means, not that the car actually blew up. Something bad is wrong with the engine and it will be out of commission for several weeks and so he can't work. He has been inundated with problems this winter.

March 13, 1973

Dear Mom,

I am drinking tomato juice to compensate for the fudge bottom pie we demolished last night. Several years ago Dann told me that when I got down to 145 he would take me to the Union for their notorious pie. I almost made it two years ago, but at the last minute, zoomed back up. Yesterday the scales registered 145 for the third consecutive week and that did it. I lost 22 pounds and need to lose another ten to earn another piece of pie. I am tired of dieting. Every once in a while I get frustrated or mad at the kids and devour at least 12 cookies.

Andy's knee is doing fine, we haven't heard anything from Tim, Jay has an appointment with an astrophysicist on campus and vacillates with college choices and Mike struggles to get his last Volks acquisition to start. I am tired of perpetual meetings: Scouts, church, Homemaker, P.T.A., School Forest, etc. I need you to visit and help me say no. In two hours I made myself a beautiful, bright red, flannel nightgown. Now I'm desperately bleaching my bed sheets to get the red out.

March 14, 1973

Dear Mom,

Fifty years ago the Willetts built their summer cottage and this calls for a big family summer reunion. We are considering exciting ideas like canoe racing, inner tubing on the Brule and homemade ice cream.

Someone threw a rock through the big glass window in our office last night. Dann fears it might be the tenants we evicted and it depresses him to think that somebody might be that angry at us.

Dann and I have separately spent hours counseling a couple who are considering divorce. Neither seems willing to compromise and he's probably moving out. This sharpens my appreciation for what we share. No matter what you do, life is full of problems, depressions, drudgery, and boredom, but when you know somebody is counting on you, it becomes worthwhile. And no, I still haven't found the "boring and monotonous" part. If Dann should leave me it would destroy the purpose of my life. These friends have been married 20 years. It really upsets us.

March 25, 1973

Dear Mom,

I have reached my saturation point. I am tired of doing so much for the good of the community or the school or the church and am going to say no firmly to everything. At least for a while. I have been cutting out pillow dolls for our scouting women to sew for our Scout garage sale.

At choir practice our director got upset because people are frequently absent. Finally Dann's brother got angry, sounded off, left and the director cried. I know she just wants to do a super job and feels we have our priorities wrong and don't put God first. I wish she could understand that it isn't that we don't put God first, but we can't always put choir first.

Tuesday was awful. I ran out of black felt for the pillow dolls and went out to buy some, but stopped at the post office first and, without thinking, spent all my money so couldn't get the felt. I took Mike to his tuba lesson, but he forgot his mouthpiece and his valves stuck. The teacher advised him to work them loose and return after supper. On the way home we stopped at Treasure Island for the felt and to show Andy, who is working there now, some pictures of Tim, but I forgot to take the pictures along, Andy wasn't working that day anyway and they were out of black felt. By that time we were laughing. We couldn't get the valves loose, so cancelled the lesson, probably a good thing as I might have smashed up the car or something worse.

April 5, 1973

Dear Mom,

Happy Birthday. Jay would like to share his birthday cake with you providing you don't want lemon. Can we pick a date?

This house copes with anything. Last night my Homemaker Club met here in the living room, but when I turned around I saw Kevin scooting up the stairs. He made a peace sign and vanished. Six more little Scouts scampered quietly up, and then I realized with dismay that we were about to have a patrol meeting over our heads. Not every house can accommodate a ladies meeting AND a Scout meeting simultaneously. My meeting went on endlessly. People got restless. Finally Cinnamon took care of everything when she sat down in front of the speaker and gave a huge yawn.

April 10, 1973

Dear Mom,

The suddenness and intensity of this storm so late in the season caught us unexpectedly. Three-foot drifts sealed off the garage and piled up along the driveway. The snow is too wet and heavy for shoveling, but expanses of bare lawn show where the wind swooped and blew the snow away. Fortunately, we still had snow tires on one car.

Dann and I were working in the office Monday morning. At noon the boys called to say schools had dismissed and they were home. They walked and Mike was cold and wet as he and Kevin stopped to push every stalled car they passed. Nobody was making it up the avenue in front of the office so we closed the office and went home by way of Madison General. Kevin's Mom had just had major stomach surgery and we knew we couldn't get back. Upon leaving the hospital we'd left our car lights on. We sat and ate our brown bag lunch to see if the battery would recoup, but no go. Andy lived three blocks away. I called him and could barely restrain him from jumping into his Volks. By this time the car in front of us was stuck so Dann took his shovel and helped him while I took off for Andy's apartment, walking down the middle of the road. Wind made near zero visibility. Andy loaned us jumper cables, heavy mittens and a pair of dry pants for Dann. By the time I returned they had dug out the other car and lined it up next to ours waiting for a jump. This worked, but we had to dig both cars out again. We aimed for University Avenue and, stopping at the first bus stop we filled the car with guys going west. At any intersection that we stopped, the car would get stuck and all would get out and push. We managed to get to the foot of our drive when Dann declared, "Far enough." Neither he nor our boys had any intention of shoveling those huge drifts this late in the year. The city called in their buses by 2:30 p.m. All county roads, the Interstate and city Beltline closed. We were asked to limit phone calls. Some kids spent the night at the High School. I can't imagine two snow days with one storm, but the wind still created many problems the next day and everything remained closed.

May 4, 1973

Dear Mom,

Rain caused the cancellation of half of my school forest tours. The rest should have been. The paths filled with rushing torrents of water. I had a bunch of little hellion sixth grade campers. They had already been told they were being sent home at 4:00 p.m. for misbehavior so they saw no future in behaving. I decided to do anything that worked. We walked to the pine meadow looking for mammal signs. One of the boys found a fresh cardinal kill and I had their complete attention from then on as we studied the remains of the dead bird. All of the guides had disciplinary problems. On days like this my Scout experience helps more than my conservation classes.

May 17, 1973

Dear Mom,

This time Dann bought a new car, a pumpkin orange '72 Fiat. He needed a low mileage car for city driving. This should get 20 miles per gallon and brings our count back to nine once more.

Andy moved back home when his lease expired. The surgeon removed his cast and Andy immediately indulged in a bath. He still has to be careful.

Cinnamon's pups are chewing each others' ears, growling and charging all over. I scrub my kitchen floor every night.

Of course we'll help you move to your new apartment. When?

Dann and Mike went canoeing with the Scouts. Dann planned stew for Saturday, taking fresh meat, frozen vegetables and packaged gravy from here. Commandeering some boys, they gathered dandelion greens, plantain leaves, violet leaves and day lilies and threw all that in too. One father, who hadn't camped with them before, stood around the fire eating stew and said, "This is delicious. You wouldn't have the recipe, would you?"

June 10, 1973

Dear Mom,

I thought we had reached the point when all our kids would disperse during the summer. Just the reverse. Tim has not left because the Scouts' canoe expedition is short one man and Tim is delighted to fill in. Andy is still home. The cooking and dirty clothes have doubled. My family numbers six humans, seven dogs.

But things quieted down while three of my men canoed in northern Minnesota. I had to cope with one excitable mother who decided, after they left, that she needed to pick up her Scout son one day early to register for Music Clinic. She wanted to fly him home from Superior and made a flight reservation for 3:00 p.m. Saturday. That left her with the problem of locating the Scouters to tell them. She called the ranger at Tofte and was put out when he wouldn't go look for them and said, "Heck lady, I don't ever expect to see those men and boys again."

She finally found a sheriff who consented to leave a message on their car windshield. When the first contingent of canoes landed at 2:00 p.m. Saturday, that Scouter drove 20 miles to a phone and was disgusted when he found out the nature of her emergency. He told her there was no way he could get John on a plane by 3:00 p.m. as John's section was still out on the lake. John canoed with Dann's group, which came in last. When Dann finally beached, he called her and said he didn't know if John could even go to music clinic, as his eyes were partially swollen shut from an allergic reaction to his new down sleeping bag. Then she wanted John put on the 7 a.m. flight but made a mistake when she added," If it's not too inconvenient." Dann told her they had been paddling for five straight hours in high wind, were exhausted and that he wouldn't ask any of the men to drive an extra 80 miles the next day to backtrack to the airport. He added that they weren't carrying alarm clocks and he didn't think any of them were still capable of waking at 5:00 a.m. We discovered later that early flight was fogged in. They started one car homeward early Sunday morning and assigned John to that car. Unfortunately that driver got sleepy, pulled over for a nap and that first car was the last one in.

The Scouts had perfect weather until the last night and on the last day had difficulty moving through heavy fog and high winds.

If it hadn't been the last day, they wouldn't have tried. Fortunately they didn't have far to go, but it took them five hours to do it. Dann said all the landmarks disappeared and the waves rolled high, drenching the bow paddlers.

In the middle of the lake a paddler in the stern stood and bopped the bow paddler over the head with his paddle because he thought the fellow wasn't paddling hard enough. Dann quickly separated them.

JULY 7, 1973

Dear Mom,

Although I don't usually work in the School Forest during the summer, this year I did work at an experimental day camp. We had third, fourth and seventh graders, two weeks for each grade. My week consisted of 60 fourth graders with a staff of four naturalists, four teachers, and four high school students. Mornings we did nature programs, afternoons the teachers did cultural arts relating to the morning excursions. I had fifteen kids each morning plus my assigned teacher and a high school boy. We broke into small groups with a ratio of five to one and had the same kids all week.

Using an acclimatization approach, we avoided teaching identification, which frequently turns the kids off, and instead made ourselves part of the environment by using our senses. We did blindfold hikes after we trained our feet, crawled around on the forest floor, laid down like spokes of a wheel so we could observe at a snake's eye level, and we felt, smelled and tasted when blindfolded. We taped the students' thumbs to their first digit to remove the opposition that man has and other mammals don't and crawled through a culvert under the road. We sat up all night recording night sounds. Midway on our morning hikes, we stopped and read a chapter-a-day from *My Side of the Mountain*, a story about a boy who ran away and lived in the wilderness, making his home in a hollow tree. Once we did our story by the grandfather hollow tree so that half the class could sit inside while I read. I taught the children "Seton sitting". This comes from Ernest Thompson Seton who felt people blast through the environment when they should meld. Sitting silently and motionless for a set time period (longer each day) we changed ourselves into dead logs. Silence is easy. Motionless is not, when we live in a world full of mosquitoes, spiders, and wood ticks, all of whom appear immediately when you stand still. I watched a mosquito bite me for three minutes.

July 15, 1973

Dear Mom,

Some time ago Tim and Mike bought a truck at auction and fixed it to sell. Their newspaper ad produced lots of calls and to increase visibility they parked the truck at the end of our long downhill driveway. Nobody had been near it for hours when suddenly it started to roll, smashed into a tree across the road and appears to be demolished. There goes not only potential profit, but original investment. Fortunately it didn't hit anything but the tree. Tim was just driving up our hill. Fifteen seconds later it would have hit him and demolished his car, also.

I'm updating our genealogy before our cottage reunion, an endless job with a family the size of ours. You were right about dropping the females out of a true genealogy, but when I discussed this with my all-male family they didn't care for that idea. They want to know all their relatives.

Dear Mom

August 15, 1973

Dear Mom,

   After months of planning, our Willett reunion is suddenly over. The cottage birthday cake used four cake mixes and my big pan. I had sketched a view of the cottage last July and duplicated this across the top of the cake, wrote Lake Nebagamon and 50. I did each tree in its characteristic shape, and colored different species various shades of green, put blueberry bushes in the yard, but left out the skunk. The weather was beastly hot so we left home at 6:00 p.m., looking for a cooler time for a frosted cake to travel. I packed the frozen cake gently into a cardboard box and laid Grandma Willett's old dress, which 12-year-old Sarah was going to model, across the top. After hours of ironing that dress I didn't want it crushed. What sun came into the car was diluted by the dress and as the cake thawed, the cool air stayed within the box. Dann drove carefully, especially over railroad tracks, and whenever he abandoned caution, all the non-drivers instantly reminded him, "Remember the cake". Nevertheless, some quivering parts just slithered down but I had taken along replacement frosting for repairs.

   We arrived at midnight and tried to figure out by the welcoming dogs who was there, as all the people were in bed. Our vacation week was one week before the reunion so we had left Mike there alone for three days. He had our tents up and we crawled wearily in. Brother George and family came up even earlier to set up in the improvised campground across the road and they caught Mike unprepared. Mike's aunt said he was a perfect host, first apologizing for the dirty cottage as he explained that Mom had said to clean it on Thursday, and then offered them hot cocoa. His cousin Dean moved into the cottage with Mike as he didn't want to put up his tent in the dark and he and Mike finished off the last of Mike's food. Mike said three days were too short. He and Cinnamon walked four hours one morning checking out a dirt road. He didn't have time to go to town, caught some fish, but didn't know how to clean them. I can't understand how that happened. He kept them alive in water and when his Uncle George came, persuaded him to do it.

Dann's brother Art and family put their tent up in the new campground also. Mike had erected our three tents on the old beach road and brother Don's family and two of Mike's other cousins tented there. One family took the wee house and our old family friends parked their 5th wheeler just off the road. We teased them that this wasn't a primitive site because they were under a street light.

In addition to people, a lot of vessels were constantly in use. We had four sailing canoes, a sail on the new aluminum boat, old Chuck our resident sailboat, and two other canoes. A west wind blew every day and the fleet sailed out regularly. When the boats were in, the beach was full. Swimming was great. There were sturdy souls who swam every morning before breakfast and groups of cousins swimming off and on all day while they waited for a sailboat to come in, and then those who never quit, but went for a cold dip before bedtime.

Jay, in training for cross-country, ran every night just before bed, traversing the new road up and back twice. The first night he got his Uncle Don to go along. The next night all his cousins decided to accompany him, even the younger ones, and I inquired if they didn't have trouble keeping up. Jay replied, "It works fine, they just spread out in layers." Joel and Jay ran up front and Nancy kept tabs in the rear.

After that they'd all plop in the lake. We worried that Jan, the youngest, was not a good enough swimmer and hollered, "Can you see Janice?'

The answer would drift back, "its okay. We can hear her."

We had no rigid scheduling but special events were promoted. Pushing 30 people around was no easy task. Jay and I and his Uncle Art put up a bulletin board of current events on the big jack pine by the beach where the traffic was heaviest. The first notice was the departure hour for the inner-tube float down the Brule. The kids took our station wagon to town and blew up tubes filling all the air space in the car. Next we tried to count, and come out with the same number of participants as floatable tubes. Twenty-two, I think. Transporting 22 blown-up tubes to the Brule River is a grand scale operation. Dale disconnected his fifth wheeler and we squeezed the tubes into the back of his pickup. He asked for volunteer kids to ride back there and got eight offers. Three cars lined up on the road and trying to fill them with people, who kept jumping in and out, was worse than Boy Scouts taking off on a trip. We finally transported everything and shuttled the cars. When Dann shouted, "Go!" 22 people simultaneously sat in the frigid water. The sound effects of that moment of impact should have been recorded. We floated downriver for two hours. Jay and Mike, experienced tubers, led and Dann rode sweep, trailing a small tube which carried a plastic bag containing a bicycle pump. Picture the frustration of canoeists going through this whitewater stretch trying desperately to maneuver between boulders and 21 other inner tubes. The river was alternately sunny and warm or cloudy and ice cold, placid and quiet or whitewater rapids, deep or so shallow that we bumped along the stony bottom, but beautiful, wild and unspoiled. We stopped periodically to pump up my leaky tube and discovered that big Chris couldn't hold his head up for long because of long ago neck surgery. We rigged an extra tube under his head and he floated downriver lying flat. Phyl floated over to the edge to get out of the main thoroughfare and the overhanging brush tipped her backwards. When she didn't come up again, Dann rushed to rescue, tripped and fell on top of her, which brought them both up sputtering. Bill lost his tube at the top of little Joe Rapids and he and it went down separately. Dann traversed Little Joe silently, which worried his audience who knew that he always went through rapids vocally. He acquired a sore rump as a result of a big rock he didn't miss. The bigger cousins took care of the littler ones because all the heavyweight adults had their hands full worrying about their behinds. We anticipated Little Joe Rapids and knew when we heard cheering in the distance that we were close. The kids arrived there ahead of the adults, went through three times and then made up a cheering section as their elders floated and tumbled down. We stumbled out gladly after two hours, cold, battered and laughing.

We posted a notice for the ice cream social on the bulletin board and cranked four batches of homemade ice cream to go with my giant birthday cake. Nancy and I helped Sarah dress in the 65 year-old, white ruffled dress of Grandma Willett's, which Sarah wore while she cut that cake. As we slipped the dress over her head, we realized that she was wearing a red, white, and blue swim suit which, for practical reasons, we couldn't remove but hoped the tiny tucking would cover it.

Thirty-two people were present. I know because I had a tough time finding 32 spoons and finally broke up the kids' game of Spoons because I needed their props. My cake took a beating waiting two days for the party. People kept removing it from the refrigerator to take pictures causing it to tilt, but the linden tree I had frosted by the corner of the house, and the pine and birch trees were still identifiable.

People were dubious about our proposed soup dump. We tripoded my big kettle over a beach fire. Everyone brought cans of soup and two of us dumped. Some contributed leftovers, and these gave it a homemade taste. Dale and I tired of perpetual questions about what was in the pot, so we set the empty cans in a row on the big log and announced that was the recipe. It simmered and simmered and simmered. All were allowed to smell and stir and when everyone was starved, we ladled out bowls until the kettle was dry.

Sitting around the campfire, we drank homemade root beer brewed in the same bottles that the Willetts had used many years ago. It has a flavor all its own. By firelight the elders swapped stories about early cottage days. Into every life some rain must fall and it did the last night. We retired to the gentle pitter-patter on the tent roof. At 2:00 a.m. we woke to a stereophonic performance and shuddered, thinking of the big trees over our heads. At 4:00 a.m. we woke to a clammy feeling from beneath us and realized we were taking in water through the tent floor. Dann mopped, using the big canoe sponge, but dampness continued to seep, and by 7:00 a.m. we each had only a one-foot dry strip on the outside of our bags. The rain had poured down the hill and onto the old lake road where we had pitched our tents.

Dogs swelled our numbers. Each dog seemed to know which tree to call home except for Skipper who roamed all over and stirred up the skunks every night. One day Skipper and Peter fought. Lynn tried to separate them, Dean dumped a pail of water over them and all the other dogs rushed up and ringed the fight just sitting and watching.

Monday morning, wet, tired and sunburned, we reluctantly packed for home. Like Mike, we didn't accomplish everything. The wind was too strong for a mass swim across the lake, we didn't get a chance to try the Brule using canoes, we didn't browse all the way through the old picture albums, and we didn't get our visiting done. And we missed all the Willetts who weren't there so we're planning to try again for the 60th.

I have always been impressed with the closeness of the six Willett boys and their families, and the tremendous enjoyment of the cousins for each other. Our traditional Willett Thanksgivings have encouraged this, but the strongest factor in holding this family together has been the cottage. Owning it jointly has worked. We've solved problems together and celebrated many happy occasions. It has provided the many descendants of Hazel and A.D. with a bursting memory bank.

10 New Horizons

AUGUST 20, 1973

Dear Mom,

 I am sorry if you think I neglected my family this summer. If you asked whoever said he missed me, you would probably discover he was just tired of doing housework. Whenever I asked for help they complained it was somebody else's turn, so it seemed like a great idea to leave for four days and let somebody else cook. I had a wonderful time, but came home to find that Jay and Dann weren't speaking because of an argument over a car, Andy was upset with Tim and couldn't wait to move out and Dann was annoyed with a friend who wanted Dann to appraise his house up north while we would be on vacation.

 Tim has been admitted to Rocky Mountain College as an in-state student and has been working frantically to finish his car. He and Mike placed a newspaper ad for Volkswagen parts and people streamed in all day. The boys made $46. The value of that car when it was whole was only $25. One man was looking for a coil. The boys inspected his coil, said he didn't need one and sold him something he did need. We have raised a couple super-salesmen.

Dann called home Monday to say one of our new tenants wanted to earn extra money housecleaning and when would I like her? I protested, "We haven't got money for that!"

"I know that. When would you like her?"

Both Jay and Dann suffer with dust allergies so I worked alongside her and we did a thorough housecleaning. My house shines and even smells clean. She was intrigued with everything around her, such as the discussion when I accidentally stepped on a salamander in the basement and thought I killed it, until it walked off. She liked Mike's pumpkin-colored room and black lights. Mike's expertise impressed her when he showed her how to take care of her five-speed bike and she commented as she left, that our house was more exciting than cleaning at the Convalescent Home. She has just graduated with a degree in Psychology. An interesting summer. With a little luck I might make it to the end.

August 28, 1973

Dear Mom,

Tim spent yesterday packing. He was reconciled to leaving his Volkswagen for his brother and Dad to sell, but when he drove it yesterday the engine blew. His friend Tom towed it back here. They pulled the engine out and worked on it until 3:00 a.m. Nobody knows what to do at this point as Tim has $400 tied up in that car and perhaps the engine is unrepairable. We must persuade him to leave now or he won't make Colorado in time for school, but he feels he shouldn't leave his problems for somebody else.

I found another Volkswagen in the yard when I came home today. When the boys were selling parts last week, they sold some to a man who fixes cars. He was impressed with Tim and Mike and today brought them a Volkswagen that looks beautiful, but doesn't run. He offered Mike 50% of the profit if he can fix it.

I would like to come for lunch, but can't. I will worry until Tim leaves and then worry until he's landed. That kid goes from one crisis to another.

Andy has moved into his apartment on campus.

SEPTEMBER 11, 1973

Dear Mom,

We finally heard from Tim. He has an apartment and a roommate and we're relieved that he won't be living in his bus this winter. He hopes to sell the bus to pay for school expenses. He dropped his Mountaineering course when it interfered with his Carpentry course.

Mike rented a hydraulic floor jack. He and Tom, Tim's friend, put the engine back in Tim's Volkswagen Fastback. While he had the jack, Mike put engines into two of his own junkers.

Our Russian friends invited us to dinner. They are living in our neighborhood while the homeowners study abroad and we are house-watching. He is retired, after 40 years as Moscow UPI correspondent, and moved here with his Russian wife, daughter and granddaughter. I fidgeted all day puzzling over what to wear. Dann laughed and asked if I was afraid we'd get vodka and borscht, and we did. It was a large dinner party and all the guests were Journalism or Russian professors and everyone, except us, knew everyone else. We drank vodka and discussed Russian history. I mostly listened, if I opened my mouth I would display my ignorance. The vodka and grapefruit juice tasted just like grapefruit juice, until I stopped drinking it. Our hosts entertained us with stories of Lenin and personal accounts of Stalin. We viewed his large art collection and icons dating back to the 1600's. An icon is a religious painting portraying different events telling a story without words, as centuries ago many Russians could not read.

Summer borscht followed the vodka. There are 36 kinds of borscht and this one was a cold variety containing pickles, strange things I couldn't recognize and sour cream. It was okay, in small quantities. I didn't dare look at Dann.

My tours this week kept skirting the rain. Dann says I am due.

October 10, 1973

Dear Mom,

We didn't drink that much vodka, Mom. I can walk around with half-a-glass for quite a while.

Tim's Fastback Volks still causes trouble. Mike finished it and placed an ad for $895. Expenses now total $700 and Mike hopes to sell for $800. The first guy offered $825. Mike asked, "How about $850?" but settled for $825 and a '62 Volks that quit one night and never ran again. The man paid Mike with a check and Mike gave him the title. Dann and I went square dancing but shortly after we left, the buyer called back very angry because he hadn't made it home. The car wouldn't steer so he assumed the front axle was broken. Mike wanted to check the car so the buyer drove him to where the car had collapsed, but it was dark and Mike couldn't see. He waited up for us. He and his Father worried about the car being on the street all night, but couldn't arrange a tow at that hour. Early Sunday they left to inspect it and came back beaming. Apparently Tim hadn't tightened the wheel bolts sufficiently when he worked on the brake assembly, as Dann had found a bolt lying on the ground which caused the wheel to slip. They drove to the man's house, but he was no longer interested. The car is fine, but unsold. This really hurts to have the money in hand and have to return it. The man gave them the defunct Volkswagen anyway so Dann and Mike towed that home for Mike's collection.

Dann, Mike, and I had a lovely weekend at the cottage, leaving here late Thursday night and arriving at 1:30 a.m. The night was warm with high winds and a sky filled with dark storm clouds that scudded rapidly across a full moon. Strong winds rattled the cottage all weekend. Thank goodness, we were under a roof instead of a tent. Mike and Dann hunted at dawn and dusk. In between we drove fire lanes and across ridges looking for new places. When they hunted in the early morning I stayed in bed. When they hunted at dusk I put my feet up on the old wood stove and read.

Early one morning they spotted smoke through the trees and found a burning cabin. Mike wrapped his arm and smashed it through a glass window while Dann pounded on the door until they were sure no one was inside. They went for help but high winds had taken out the phones. Eventually someone drove to town. The fire department let it burn to the ground, a reminder of how careful we must be in the North Woods.

October 16, 1973

Dear Mom,

I have just finished my Dane County Parks tour, and am exhausted. I did this tour in conjunction with my job as Education chairman for Community Life for Dane County Extension Homemakers. I love that title. Mike says judging by the title it must be a well paying job. We swung through the county in a chartered bus for six-and-one-half hours as I lectured by microphone. This was a gas conservation effort to acquaint people with the excellent resources within our own county so that they could plan recreational trips closer to home. It was a windy day with eruptions of fall color everywhere. We visited six parks. I discussed others, taught geology as we rode and explained the Dane County Land Use Plan.

United Nations Day

Dear Mom,

We drove to Terry Andrae State Park for the hawk migration. It takes a northwest wind for them to fill the flyway along the shore of Lake Michigan. No northwest wind—no hawks. We settled on the sand dunes and using field glasses, Dann watched other interesting things strolling on the beach. At the hawk-banding station we peered out the observation slits watching a bunch of live pigeons. Six-foot poles in the field and strings (painted green to be invisible) lie on the ground. They tie the pigeons, who wear a leather corset containing shoe horns so the hawk can't squash them, to the pole. When the hawks dive on the pigeon, people pull the strings, which drop the pigeon to the ground. As the hawk hits the ground a net snaps over him. This station sometimes bands 60 per day.

Continuing up the shore, we visited Dann's brother at Manitowoc and went sailing on Lake Michigan. They berth their boat on the river and motor out, under three drawbridges, to reach the lake. The cabin sleeps four, a tiny sterno stove mounted on the wall has a hinge that swings to stay level, the bathroom is so small you can't shut the door and there is a small hatch cover up front. I crawled halfway through the hatch cover that provided a beautiful observation post and kept me half-dry. We tilted up and down going out, but wallowed sideways coming in. My stomach protested vigorously.

Every time we touch Tim's fastback, we get hurt. We parked it on the street with a For Sale sign posted prominently and bricks jammed in front of the wheels. Dann tried to bring it up the driveway because we've had a run on bullet holes through car windshields left on the street at night. He could hardly get it up the drive and the next morning Mike couldn't keep it running. We had placed an ad in the paper and Mike had to tell all those callers that the car wouldn't run. Suddenly Dann rushed out of the house, drove off and came back in beaming, "The car runs fine now that I put gas in it."

November 8, 1973

Dear Mom,

Dann and I spent all week painting a house which he has listed for sale. The owners are in the midst of a divorce so the house has stood empty for six months and needs decorating. Dann wrote to the wife saying it would be profitable for them to spend some money and if she would authorize him with a limit, he would do as much as possible. She responded, "Okay to $300."

Dann then said, "Let's you and I do it for Christmas money." We cleaned the whole huge house, painted four rooms and a hall in 22 team hours, eight hours short of our spending limit.

That darned Fastback! A guy named Bruce bought it for $662.50 plus his car, changed the plates and departed, but he came right back because he couldn't restart it. He and Mike pushed it into our garage and worked until midnight. He asked permission to take it to McCann's Garage and they told him it needed $500 worth of work. We gave him back his check and don't know what to do next.

Mike has an impressive report card as he is working hard to get reduced insurance rates. He talked his geometry teacher into changing a B to an A. I hate to think of him ramming around in his own car when he turns 16, but won't be able to say no if he keeps up this dedication. Last Sunday he talked me out of church for both himself and his Dad so they could attend a car auction.

November 26, 1973

Dear Mom,

Dann took the Fastback to a friend in a Middleton service station who claimed it only needed a $60 sensor which he replaced. Now Dann has been shopping at area dealers looking for a trade on anything. Dann says a Fastback is a car that comes back fast every time you sell it!

We missed Andy and Tim for Thanksgiving but still had 35 people. When Mike's friend, Kevin, complained that his family wasn't going to eat until evening Mike offered, "Why don't you come here? Nobody will notice the difference."

I enjoyed getting up before dawn to start the turkey, took my coffee, walked around and admired the house: the absolute silence, the way the house sparkles and smells clean (result of four days constant scrubbing, waxing, and polishing), the tables set with Thanksgiving motif tablecloths and the shellacked bread centerpieces tied with gingham ribbons and dried flowers (this is called stone bread which it is after eight hours of slow baking). Mike was disgusted as he watched me ruin that good bread. I sniffed the 18 blossoms nestling on the Thanksgiving cactus

and smelled the pumpkin man on the porch, aged enough that his head was wrinkled. The ping pong table was uncharacteristically devoid of junk and the dollhouse had been moved from the attic to a bedroom, waiting for small housekeepers. I love the 5:00 a.m. part of Thanksgiving, but didn't feel the same at 5:00 p.m. when I was still working non-stop in the kitchen. I am ready to change this tradition of Thanksgiving always at our house. It frustrated me when one called after the tables were set to say he was bringing a friend, when I couldn't get into my own kitchen because everybody arrived via the back door and stopped to visit, when dinner guests arrived an hour late, and when people came to say thank you as they left and I realized that was the first time I had seen them all day.

One stove element was obviously burning out. I used that one constantly, hoping it would expire before Thanksgiving, but when Dann and George were carving the turkey and nobody was available to help with anything, it sent up a fireworks display and died.

We had invited our Russian friends and Jay was our designated driver to pick them up but he raced back into the house to say that the battery wouldn't kick over. I walked out with him and then he noticed that the hood wasn't latched. Opening it he exclaimed, "That's funny. There's no battery here!" The funny part is that the thieves stole a seven-year-old battery.

I had coached Mike to watch over our little Russian Alexandra who doesn't speak English. Mike quickly learned how to say, "Nyet." I planned on moving Mike to the adult table this year, but he insisted, "Mom, there's no way you can leave all those kids alone in the kitchen."

Now we're like the English when they say "The King is dead, long Live the Queen." Thanksgiving is over, what's for Christmas?

December 20, 1973

Dear Mom,

We'll meet your bus on Monday. Tim is coming home for Christmas and bringing a girl. I am trying to knit, bake and entertain and not succeeding in any. We held an open house for School Forest guides and spouses, another the next day for scouting friends. Our Scoutmaster has just had a kidney removed so I coordinated suppers for them for nine nights.

Dann and Mike sold Tim's Fastback and took a big Lincoln on trade. Now they have sold the Lincoln and taken in a Toyota.

January 6, 1974

Dear Mom,

Christmas was great, but I am ready for peace and quiet, boredom, and a smaller family. Mike and Dann sold the Volkswagen convertible which Mike has been working on for a year. He had to take the engine out twice. The original cost was $75, cost of parts $250, and sold it for $540. They used Dann's money and Mike's labor.

Tim called last night. They drove to Denver without weather problems, but there the reports were so bad that they stayed overnight with friends, preferring to do the last 100 miles of mountain driving in the daylight. His carpentry instructor has been hospitalized with back problems and the substitute teacher is not as good, so Tim has dropped out of school. No, we did not get Tim's pup, Zaccarius, house trained. We seemed to be working in reverse. By the last day, he wet every time we petted him so we never petted him unless he was sitting down. I was glad to see the darling little squirt leave.

Jay is taking an astronomy course at the University under a special student status. He goes to the campus every morning and after his hour lecture takes the bus back to high school. He came home excited the first day, "Mom, when classes changed I watched out the window and you wouldn't believe all the people out there!" He looked at us questioningly, "Well, maybe you would."

Dann is trying to hold the Scout troop together because the Scoutmaster is so ill. He decided not to cancel the winter campout, but will take George's place. Hope they have a warm weekend.

January 18, 1974

Dear Mom,

I have worked hard to get the office books closed and income tax done by the fourth quarter estimate deadline of January 15. This spoils January but I made it, mailing the forms at 6:00 p.m. and then we celebrated by taking Jay and Mike to the Ponderosa. Jay asked if we had so much money left over from taxes that we needed to throw it away.

Andy met a girl at a party who was here the night we tried to sell the Fastback. I remember that bitter cold that night. She came in by the fire and visited for two hours while the guys worked in the garage. Andy said she told him that I said enthusiastic things about my boys and that she wished she had a mother like that. Andy told her, "You probably do and don't know it, because I didn't know it either!"

I finished Dann's ski sweater. It looks gorgeous, the color coordination is perfect, and it fits. When everybody at choir practice admired it, Dann entertained them telling how I kept trying to get his chest measurement by coming up behind and hugging him, and then asking the boys to measure my arms. That didn't work so, in desperation, I tried hugging with a tape measure in my hands but he caught me. Mike's sweater comes next.

Jay likes his Astronomy course but says putting forth a lot of effort is not enough, that he has to think, too. What worked easily in high school doesn't work easily on campus.

I announced that it was time to either get a part-time job as our bills are so high, or get busy writing my book. The family thought if we really need the money, writing a book is not the answer, so I started reading want ads. Dann never said he didn't want me to do this; he just produced so many things to do that I can't find time to look for a job.

FEBRUARY 6, 1974

Dear Mom,

We skied at Cascade Mountain. We wanted lessons for Jay and Mike as they need to polish corners. We found a young female instructor who would take them both for an hour for the price of one, an excellent skier, but an inexperienced instructor. When the hour was up, Jay skied over and said, "Mom, that was a waste of your money, but when are we going to waste it again?" He had asked her age and discovered she was only 16. She had a set order of things a skier should do and although the boys already do advanced things, she discovered an elementary step they had missed.

We've talked to Tim the last three nights. He wants to buy a woodcutting business: saws, trucks for hauling, and a federal permit to cut in the National Forest. He hopes to cut madly in the summer and deliver during winters while he's going to school.

Our Scoutmaster's malignancy continues to spread and he is scheduled for lung surgery. Dann has taken charge of the troop again.

We had homework in our Reading the Landscape class to keep track of when and where we hear a cardinal. I put a note on the kitchen door. "I'd like to know whenever anyone hears a cardinal sing," but somebody erased the final "g."

I knit all the time, but Mike's sweater goes on endlessly. With two boys now conquering their worlds elsewhere, maybe it's time for some of that "boring and monotonous."

11 Dear Tim

FEBRUARY 24, 1974

Dear Tim,

Your Grandmother fell yesterday. She had gone uptown to get groceries, walked home, collapsed outside her apartment door and lay outdoors for two hours before someone found her. It looks like a stroke. She did manage a few yesses and noes at first, but now lies unconscious. She was cold when they found her so they gave her oxygen, IV and packed her in old-fashioned hot water bottles. I am staying in her apartment for now.

MARCH 4, 1974

Dear Tim,

For 15 years I've recorded family happenings in my Dear Mom letters but not now, because I'm with her. The family voted unanimously that the Dear Grandma letters should continue as Dear Tim.

Grandma remained unconscious for four days. The doctor gave us no hope, but Sunday after church I breezed in with a, "Good

Morning," and she responded. Since then she has slowly come back. Her speech is often confused and irrational. She can do nothing for herself. Uncle Charles flew out from New Jersey. A blizzard struck the day he was to fly home. Dad was at her apartment that night also, planning on driving back to Madison early in the morning for a Scout weekend ski trip but nobody went anywhere. For hours we had neither light nor heat. I bundled up and trudged out to the car to pick up a weather report on the car radio and to bring in Dad's boots. Never leave boots in the car when it's going to snow! The northeast wind whipped off the lake so I could hardly stand. It stung my face and iced my glasses. I couldn't find the right key, couldn't find the keyhole and barely found the car. When I made it back in, we shook enough snow from my pocket for three large snowballs. I tried again without glasses, bundled a scarf across my face and got into the car. After we heard the report, we wrapped in blankets like Indian chiefs, ate a cold breakfast and visited. The Scout trip went 12 hours late, but had beautiful skiing snow.

MARCH 15, 1974

Dear Tim,

Grandmother has improved beyond my expectations and is in a nursing home. I hired a physical therapist to set up an exercise program. She scoots all over in her wheelchair, has practiced hard and finally can sign her name. Mike and I challenge her with dominoes and cards as she repatterns brain communications. Even with the big handle I built up on her spoon, she couldn't get it to her mouth without spilling. She tried a thousand times, but never gave up. I brought her clay to strengthen the muscle action in her right hand and large print books, which make it easier when her eyes skip around so much. I placed her on the

State Talking Book program. She has a recording machine and they send books from Milwaukee. Therapeutically it's better if she reads herself, but she gets tired and easily. Everything she does right now is so crucial that I have spent hours working with her. I make her work, scold her, encourage her and try new approaches when she gets tired of trying. What I am expecting from her is almost impossible, but she's doing it. Your Grandmother is made of iron, hope I inherited some of that iron. All the uncertainty and mental anguish must be hard. Uncle Frank and Aunt Lois come every weekend. I go during the week, staying for two or three days in her apartment. She hates the nursing home and is determined to leave it.

Mike installed his VW engine and has started behind-the-wheel training. It's time this budding mechanic learns to drive.

Our Scoutmaster has survived a third surgery. They removed three malignant tumors from his spine and hope that he will regain use of his legs. The Scout charter expires this month and I think your Dad will sign on as new scoutmaster.

We're relieved at Grandmother's progress but the risk of a second stroke is high, so don't put off writing that thank you note. Any time from now on is a gift. She would be thrilled to hear from you on her 82nd birthday next week and continually asks about your business. If you call the Lakeland Nursing Home at Elkhorn, the receptionist will call the floor and take her to an outside phone to receive an incoming call.

March 24, 1974

Dear Tim,

Yesterday was our day in court. If you remember, the city had fined Dad $600 or 15 days in jail because we didn't complete painting our apartment within the time limit on the building orders, and we objected. We took Mike out of school to observe. Two days ago the city attorney called Trevor, our attorney, offering to settle out of court for $150 in lieu of the $600 fine. We had tried repeatedly, both before and after our first court appearance, to get the city to compromise, but they weren't interested then. Now Trevor has turned up a new painting ordinance which covers this period and will affect our case. Our choice was (1) paying the $150 settlement (plus $300 in lawyer fees), 2) refusing the settlement in the hopes that the city would dismiss completely before court, by which time we would chalk up another $100 in fees, or (3) refusing and taking our chances on a dismissal by the judge. If he didn't dismiss, we would be back to the $600 fine or 15 days in jail. We decided on full speed ahead. If this was worth arguing about in the first place, it still is. The city attorney told Trevor yesterday if the case was dismissed they would just find some other cause to prosecute. This angered Trevor and Dad so much they decided to protest no matter what.

March 31 (one week and three trips to Grandma later)

Dear Tim,

The judge expressed many opinions from the bench, saying he hadn't heard the entire case, but he understood the gist of it and at the risk of criticizing a colleague, it seemed a ridiculous fine to him when people guilty of greater crimes go scot free. The city passed a new painting ordinance effective last August 13, (our first court date was September 5) and the judge wanted to know if the city was trying us on the first ordinance, which covers up to August 13th, or on the second ordinance, which covers after August 13th. The city attorney replied, "We want to prosecute on both."

The judge let loose. "You must pick one charge or the other. If you stick to the first ordinance, the time period does not cover. If you pick the new ordinance, then you gave the Willetts no notice, which you must do with a new ordinance. Further, if the original judge was not aware of the change in ordinances, then the city is negligent, because they did not inform him, and if he judged without knowing this he did not have all the facts before him and I can dismiss the proceeding of last September as not being a fair trial." He continued asking the city attorney questions about orders on other buildings. "I feel you are picking on the Willetts. There are obviously many other buildings that need things done whose owners are not being prosecuted."

The city attorney objected, "I work under the direction of the common council and the mayor's office. They pushed me and I had no choice."

But the judge asked, "Have you sent your building inspectors to the houses of all the common council?" This brought uproarious laughter from the spectators. When the city attorney made a remark about bad landlords, Trevor asked to have letters recognized that he knew the city was holding.

The city attorney protested, "This has to be off the record," since in appeal court you can't bring up anything which wasn't brought up in the first court.

But Trevor retorted, "It was you that mentioned bad landlords." The city acknowledged they had received letters from some of our tenants proclaiming what a great landlord Mr. Willett has been. They had written these letters on their own initiative when they discovered the trouble we were in, sending them to the Madison Housing Bureau, who sent them to the City Building Department, who forwarded them to the city attorney's office. As the attorney phrased it, "They actually called us bums for doing this to Mr. Willett."

The judge sat up abruptly. "How interesting. I had surmised all tenants thought all landlords were bums." The judge gave the city two weeks to complete their brief, gave Trevor one week to reply, and after that he will bring down a decision. This has been a worry all winter though I pushed it into one small unused corner of my mind most of the time.

Might you be home for Easter? If Grandma continues to improve, we hope to take her out on a pass for Easter dinner.

April 9, 1974

Dear Tim,

Your birthday call thrilled Grandmother. We arrived soon after and she was still excited. I decorated a cake with yellow jonquils, Uncle Frank and Aunt Lois brought chocolate mint ice cream and we invited the nursing staff, as Grandma knows them all by name. Uncle Frank is trying to get her into a controlled apartment at Fairhaven in Whitewater. Although she would be in her own apartment in a large building, she would have call buttons in each room. Staff would help with baths and medication, make her bed and she could either cook in a tiny kitchen or go to the dining hall. Unfortunately, they have a long waiting list.

Attending winter guide training at the Arboretum keeps me busy. The speaker last week lectured on his grizzly bear research in Yellowstone. He tranquilizes the bears, tattooing them for identification and puts transistors around their necks so their telemetry can follow them. He is studying hibernation and tried to track the females to their dens. As the bears head for the back country, this made rough hiking and they couldn't use snowshoes because they traveled on animal paths. Female #39 treed them for a whole day. When they finally got down, the weather had closed in and they were three days late for a rendezvous with their food supply. By this time the National Park Service rescue operations were out in full force. These are fun classes.

Do you realize how much you are like your Dad? If he were your age during these troublesome times he would probably be exploring independent life styles also. You have his ability to question things, to explore, to jump out of a rut, to work your head off for something you really want, and to realize that personal happiness is all important. Have been meaning to tell you this for months but never have room at the bottom of the page.

P.S. How about a postcard — or something?

April 16, 1974

Dear Tim,

Your phone call reassured us somewhat.

Mike took his VW to school yesterday to paint in the shop. After taking the engine in and out all winter, it now runs in good shape. He sanded and puttied until the little bug looks like a spotted zebra. Dad let him drive it the first time out of the yard, and Jay tailgated with the Fiat. Mike beeped proudly at everybody that he saw.

Waking at 2:30 a.m. this morning, I smelled smoke and woke Dad who rolled out of bed instantly. Jay, who had also awakened, rushed downstairs right behind Dad. We lit a fire in the fireplace on Sunday, didn't realize that it smoldered all day Monday and when Dad went to bed Monday night he closed the damper. In three hours the house filled with so much smoke that it penetrated our closed bedroom, waking me. Dad opened up everything and checked to see that Mike was okay. Using our big window fan, he moved from room to room for two hours before he came back to bed.

April 23, 1974

Dear Mom,

Sorry I can't make it this week as Tim walked in last night, home for Easter. He had a ride from Aspen to Minneapolis and hitchhiked from there. He and his Dad are trying to finance his woodcutting business.

Jay has been accepted at LaCrosse next year so our count will go down one more.

Keep walking, Mom.

May 14, 1974

Dear Tim,

I saved this clipping for you. Dad got congratulatory phone calls all day. It's a grand feeling to beat the city, but it's a victory of principle only. The fine we refused to pay was $600, the lawyer fees were $700. Dad said all along that he'd rather pay our attorney than the city.

Andy graduates from the University on Saturday, but leaves in a month for one more geology summer field course in Utah.

On Mother's Day we took Grandmother back to her apartment for a visit and I fixed dinner. She walked around without her walker, using the wall for support and wants to try apartment living again. I have talked her into a week's visit with us first so we can judge if she can manage by herself.

May 28, 1974

Dear Tim,

Our family has enlarged by nine, all doing fine. Cinnamon considerately managed this on my day off, although I did get up three times during the night to make sure she wouldn't birth them under the woodpile, as she wanted to do.

Dad, Mike and I had a memorable Memorial Day weekend. We took Mike's friend, Kevin and attended the Wolf River

Lodge whitewater canoe school. We sat on the grass Saturday morning while the instructor explained the basics, like friendly rocks and ferrying upstream. I have developed great admiration for the salmon that go upstream to spawn. It took Dad three minutes to break his paddle. We travel with a spare, of course. After we were exhausted, we realized we had to quit paddling straight up and paddle zigzag across the current, resting in the eddies behind all those friendly rocks. After lunch we drove upriver, put in all the canoes and paddled back through three miles of rapids, with the instructor and his son zooming around in their kayaks keeping an eye on their flock. Dad and I must have learned something from the morning, because when we found ourselves in nasty spots, we could recover. When we hung up on boulders the river would swing the canoe around until it slid off, sending us backwards through the rapids.

We didn't see Mike and Kev all afternoon, but when we reached the take-out point, they showed up in different canoes. During the first rapids the two young girls swamped, dumped, and lost their canoe downriver. The girls, in life preservers, walked out of the river with difficulty as the water came to their shoulders. Mike and Kev left their canoe on shore and resurrected the lost canoe. About that time the instructor appeared, taught them how to line it out and then suggested that the boys split up with the girls. Someone commented, "George is playing at matchmaking,"

He replied, "Hell no, that's just common sense." It made the day for Mike and Kevin.

Did you secure the federal permit you need for woodcutting on federal land?

June 5, 1974

Dear Tim,

We enjoyed a good week with Grandmother here. She even walked up and down at the grocery store using her walker. The Nursing Home discharges her this weekend. Uncle Frank will move her back to her apartment until her name reaches the top of the list for Fairhaven. Your cousin, Valerie, will stay with her for a few days and I'll go often. She hates the nursing home, says all those old people make her feel old.

Would you like us to visit in July?

June 10, 1974

Dear Mom and Tim,

We spent a long weekend at the cottage putting on a new roof. I got everyone up at 4:00 a.m. for departure. Jay objected to rising that early so Mike suggested that Jay sleep in the car Thursday night. We arrived at 2:00 p.m. As it was still raining, the boys played cards, Dann fished and I studied for my summer camp. Many of your uncles, aunts and cousins came. The work crew started pounding noisily by 9:15 Saturday morning and didn't quit until 8:00 that night. I kept sending out lemonade and cookies. The crew of eight tore off the roof on the side towards the lake, replaced it and removed part of the other side and a corner of the sleeping porch in preparation for the next day. I studied my weather books and made dire predictions, making myself unpopular. Sure enough, early Sunday morning, I heard a soft pitter-patter on the leaves. Dann and George rushed to cover the unfinished roof. As we lay in bed the night before, the boys had discussed our vulnerability if it rained and had decided Kevin was sleeping under the spot not covered. After a long silence I had heard Kev say, "I don't like this."

Saturday morning I had awakened them with great difficulty. Sunday morning I put my hand on one bare shoulder and muttered, "Time to get up. It's starting to rain," and they were instantly raiding the kitchen for pots to place under the drips. The men on the roof got everything covered and weighted down with logs and rocks, but we had to leave the roof unfinished. We pray for no windstorms until George and Don go back in a week to finish.

The puppies have opened their eyes and are beginning to stagger. We took them with us to the cottage, of course—Spook, Spirit, Sparky, Spunky, Speck, Spike, Sport, Spot, and Spud.

Summer camp started today with strong winds and threatening storms. We walked through the forest and lay down and I told them they might as well get wet and dirty right away.

Mom, we think it's wonderful that you're back in your apartment after living in an institution for four months. The retraining that you faced was gigantic. Perhaps hating the nursing home helped in your determination to do whatever was necessary to get out of there. My Occupational Therapy background made me realize how important it was for you to start moving immediately, but the bottom line was your perseverance. No, I shan't worry about you alone in your apartment as neighbors are close. Whatever the future might hold for you, I realize this is where you want to be. It's been a long winter, but summer is bursting gloriously all around us. Welcome home and I'll be down soon.

12 Scamper Camper

June 21, 1974

Dear Mom and Tim,

I enjoy being outdoors and I enjoy child activities. Madison schools are running experimental day camp in the School Forest so that encompasses both my loves. I have the same 15 kids all week and can keep them absorbed even over three hours of hiking as I work on sharpening their senses. One night they sleep over. Last night tornado warnings, thunderstorms and electricity outages forced us to do our night watch under the shelter. Nature's fireworks all night long kept the kids fascinated. We boiled water in a leaf over our campfire, imitating the story we're reading aloud during morning break in the woods. My weather study produces easy predictions with all this lousy weather.

Our upcoming trip to Colorado looms nearer. We need directions how to find you, Tim. Look for us in a '71 black 3/4 ton Ford truck with dents on the right side, carrying a white and brown paneled Scamper unit piggyback. We can sleep three comfortably, or four uncomfortably and have an icebox, stove, sink and furnace. The top folds down, lessening wind resistance when we're moving but still rises high enough that Mike can sit and play cards, providing Dad doesn't hit any big bumps. This visit is our trial run for an Alaskan trip next summer. Is there a campground nearby or can we park next to your converted school bus?

June 28, 1974
Dear Mom, Tim and Andy,

I just can't write separate letters to all three of you so excuse the carbons. Andy, attending a Geology field course in Utah sounds like a summer vacation. Tim, I hope your woodcutting business keeps you cutting from dawn to dark in the mountains. Mom, visiting with you last weekend was great and you manage wonderfully in your apartment. I'll come back next Wednesday to take you grocery shopping.

Our live-in car dealers outdid themselves. Mike bought a blue '66 VW for $150. Dad says that's a steal. Dad then sold the Toyota which Mike and Kevin had fixed, but took a '63 red junker VW in trade. This one is parts only and Dad gave it to Mike. We came out about even and hope the "curse of the Fastback" is gone. This counts to nine cars again (including yours, Andy.) Mike has four VW's.

I did a night hike with the overnighters at the School Forest. I dropped third graders off at intervals along the path in early dusk so they could experience aloneness in the woods. All sat quietly until I reversed my steps and collected them and we walked out in complete darkness, as I don't allow flashlights.

Last night we lost a boy on night watch. When somebody woke him at 5:00 a.m. for his turn, he realized he had wet his pants, which embarrassed him, so he ran away. I missed him immediately and woke the other naturalists. We searched the trails and then went off the trails, plowing through heavy, soppy brush and found him hiding in the bushes not far from camp.

July 8, 1974

Dear Mom, Andy and Tim,

Got your directions, Tim. We will bring your Coleman oven and quilt. We can't wait to try our Scamper Camper.

It's not surprising that you are having trouble cutting through the red tape to start your own business. Your Dad constantly struggles with those frustrating details. Try not to let it discourage you. Nothing worth doing, comes easily.

We talked Dad out of running for Registrar of Deeds, but Republican Party Headquarters talked him back into it. He has little chance to win against the incumbent. Jay immediately went to the library and registered to vote. The librarian asked him to swear that he was a resident of Madison and over 18. I asked, "How do you check his eligibility?"

"We don't need to check because he has sworn that this is true. If we asked for proof, that would be infringing upon a person's constitutional rights." It's a good thing we had only two minutes left on our meter or I would have argued.

We picked up two loads of sea weed and unloaded it on my garden. Theoretically, this acts as mulch so I don't have to hoe. Jay and Mike shoveled it out of the truck, but Dad had to scrub the truck bed three times before he put on the Scamper and the awful seaweed smell still wafts through it.

Scamper Camper

August 14, 1974

Dear Mom and Tim,

Tim, your converted bus is amazing but that ride to the top of your mountain and driving across the ski slope was pretty scary. Our living quarters in the Scamper are luxurious. We've learned how to live comfortably in each other's pockets and now we're ready to try the Alcan Highway.

We laughed when, several hours after Dad sent the money you needed Tim, we received a long distance call from Andy in Montana. Could we send him $30 because he was down to his last $16? How do guys without families manage? Andy's geology field trip is over. He expects to be home shortly, but doesn't know what he is going to do now.

Mike sold the Volkswagen junker we took in trade on the Toyota, so this is the end of the Fastback. This time he made some profit. About time!

August 20, 1974

Dear Mom,

We had just awakened at 7:00 a.m. when we heard a car door slam and knew Andy had arrived. He and his friend stopped along the way for some spelunking, crawling through narrow apertures in the cave for 50 yards. It sounds awful and his clothes looked awful. Enroute home he backpacked in the Tetons and Glacier National Parks. He came home with a large box of rocks. Fortunately he wasn't hitchhiking. It depresses him not knowing what he wants to do now.

I got your note, Mom, and am expecting Sara and her husband but don't know how to entertain them. I told Jay that since Sara is his cousin and his age, he can entertain her, but he objected. "Oh no, as soon as she got married, that put her into your generation."

If you change your mind and come, you can have Mike's bed and he will sleep in the truck.

Mike and Andy were working on Andy's muffler when a man drove up and asked about the station wagon for sale. Andy came into the kitchen and said, "There's a guy here that wants to know about the wagon."

"Isn't Mike out there?" I asked.

Andy looked blank. "Well, yes."

"There isn't a thing that I could say about that station wagon that Mike can't do better."

Jay added, "You have to understand, Andy, how we operate around here. Mike takes care of all that stuff." Andy looked floored. Mike came in, silently picked up the key and departed to take the prospective buyer for a test ride.

Mike has a girl friend. Her parents established strict hours and Mike got in wrong with the establishment because she was supposed to be home by 11:00. They were, but sitting in the driveway. The garage lights came on and her father came out. On the next date, her parents requested them to double date. Mike is bringing her over here tonight to see the salamanders. Poor Dann! He disappeared into the basement early this morning, frantically trying to clean it.

Andy is looking for a cooking job. I wish we could instill more confidence in all our boys.

August 24, 1974

Dear Mom,

I'm writing from the cottage. I can't remember ever being uncomfortably hot here, but it is and my sunburn hurts.

Last week Dann and Mike puttered with the Fairlane. Mike put on new shocks and they decided the rusty muffler would last another six months. But when we were still 100 miles away, it went clink and the exhaust system fell off. We picked it up, drove on and tried to block our ears. Dann took it to the village of Nebagamon where it sits waiting for parts. Our transportation now is by canoe. We arrived exhausted, both from the heat and working so hard to get ready, so we collapsed for the remainder of Sunday and all day Monday, only to be awakened Monday night by loud pounding at the back door. A neighbor told us that Jay had called and needed us to call home. Our scoutmaster had died and his wife wanted Dann for pall-bearer. The earliest our car would be repaired might be late Tuesday afternoon, which meant we would have to drive all night for a Wednesday morning funeral and then turn around and drive back in the afternoon. Just the thought exhausted me. After much soul searching, we decided the last thing she would want would be for somebody to be on the road for 14 hours. Dann had a long visit with George just before we left so we wrote to his wife saying we would come home a day early and spend the day with her.

After we got back to sleep, Cinnamon kept nudging the bed. I think the thunder and lightning bothered her, but Dann let her out and an overpowering skunk smell filled the cottage, so strong that we could hardly breathe. Dann finally persuaded Cinnamon to come back in and I think the skunk missed, barely!

After getting back to sleep a second time, the storm broke and we rushed to close windows. Everything was wide open because of the heat.

We woke at 4:00 a.m. to the scream of the fire siren in the village and rushed down to the beach where we could see the western sky lit up like a sunset. If one insisted on sleeping around here, one would miss out on most of the excitement. Consequently we've been taking about three naps daily, between swims. Dann caught a 19 1/2" northern. He had forgotten the net so kept urging me to grab the fish when he brought it alongside. I kept asking, "Who, me?" until finally the fish leaped, twisted in mid-air and landed on my lap. Mike said the funniest part was my expression.

We sold seven puppies, but last Saturday Dann and Jay reluctantly took the last two to the pet store. They parked two blocks away and by the time they walked one-and-a-half blocks, they had found homes for both.

SEPTEMBER 3, 1974

Dear Mom,

It's quiet around this empty house. Cinnamon searches in all the rooms and finding nobody, follows me. When I'm cleaning the stairs, she's sleeping on the next one up. When I'm on the phone, she's under it, and she tried to accompany me when I took a bath.

We drove Jay to La Crosse and moved him into the dorm. He has already decided that he signed up for too many classes.

Andy has moved into an apartment. He doesn't have a job but still signed a nine-month lease. We told him this is putting the cart before the horse, but he didn't want parental advice. He sent resumes to oil companies in Houston. His friend sent 150 resumes before he succeeded, so this may take a while.

We've been trying to convince Andy he needs a placard for Dad on his car top, but he said, "You mean drive around with a REPUBLICAN advertisement?"

SEPTEMBER 6, 1974

Dear Mom,

I have enclosed Andy and Jay's new addresses. That leaves just three of us to rattle around in this huge house. Perhaps things will become more "boring and monotonous" now?

We sold the station wagon, we're back to what we want to keep and I can drive the circle drive once more. Mike finished the car that he's been working on for months. They decided to start at top price and advertised in the paper. The first person who came loved it and paid top price with no quibbling and now he has enough money so he can fix one to keep.

Mike is managing our household finances. He was impressed with the $745 per month that he has to spend, until he paid the essential expenses and found that left less than $100 for other things. He objected to our high phone bill and when he finished writing checks, he stretched out to read on the floor near me. I inquired if he'd like his couch back but he remarked nonchalantly, "Oh no, this way we can both use the same light." He also requested that I buy everything in #10 cans to save money.

SEPTEMBER 11, 1974

Dear Mom and Jay,

Election update. Dad attended a Republican rally and a brat roast in Mt. Horeb and the whole village turned out. Today Bill Dyke's press secretary called to see if Dad would like to campaign with him. Impressive to have the mayoral candidate include Dann. People ask me why Dann is running. I often say because he thinks he can do a good job, but he usually says it's important to have a two-party system so that people have a choice. Yes Jay, you can write for an absentee ballot.

Andy has had his ski accident hardware removed. His foot is heavily bandaged and he is back to crutches.

Tim not only got the minimum 20 cords off the mountain that the permit required, but he has a crew of three and they moved 35 extra cords which he had already sold. He was delighted with his first $750 check although it was earmarked for bills.

September 19, 1974

Dear Mom and Jay,

We looked for you this weekend Jay, as we didn't get your letter until Saturday. Memorial lost to West 21-0 and yes, you can have a car on the 26th, providing we have two running. We are beset with problems. I don't know what we are going to do when Mike leaves home as he spends all his free time and school auto lab time just to keep us mobile. He replaced the water hose which broke on the Fairlane. He's been working on the noise in the Fiat, put a muffler on during school shop time but the next day it fell off. Fortunately for me, Dad was driving.

Mike has fixed the damage to the back of the Fiat from last week's accident and last Saturday he had another accident. Turning at an intersection downtown, he hesitated because he didn't know if it was one-way, but then the car ahead turned, Mike followed and it was the wrong way. A car crossed the intersection hitting him in the rear knocking him into another car. He was able to drive that car for only a week and a half and it's probably not fixable. Mike didn't lose points, but felt bad.

On the political front: Dad got so entranced with those little cards that he ordered 4,500. I bundled packages of ten and we're asking all our friends to give away ten. All we need is 450 friends. Dad was a guest of honor at the Republican women's luncheon at the Hilton. We received an invitation to a fish boil for a Democratic candidate. When Dad asked the Republican Women what they thought about our going to Democratic functions, they were delighted. If only 23% of the voters are Republican, they must welcome candidates with Democratic friends.

Mike has a terrible sore throat. Glad you didn't come home, Jay.

September 27, 1974

Dear Mom and Jay,

COPE (Committee on Political Education) made appointments to interview all the candidates at the Labor Temple and Dad didn't want to go because the Union usually endorses Democrats. They did ask a lot of questions: how could he improve on the present office procedure for Registrar of Deeds, how much was the salary (he didn't know), how many girls worked in that office, how did he feel about public employees belonging to a union or going on strike? He told them that the present Registrar has done a good job, added he thought he could speed up procedures, that he thought this should be civil service instead of elective (which shook them up), that he wasn't party-oriented and if a spot had opened on the Democratic side he wouldn't have hesitated to run there, and that he thought it okay for public employees to belong to a union, but not okay to strike without leaving a skeletal force, if it endangered the public. Not all popular answers, I'm afraid.

September 30, 1974

Dear Tim,

Andy secured a job in the camera department at Treasure Island. He expects to learn a lot about photography but it's evenings and weekends only, so he's looking for a regular 40-hour a week job, too. The stitches come out of his leg tomorrow, but he still limps. Two days ago he sent a resume to a Houston firm looking for a geologist and now he waits expectantly for the phone to ring.

Grandmother is here visiting. She asks about you all the time. As she becomes more and more restricted in her activities, she becomes more and more interested in what her grandchildren are doing and loves your letters.

October 8, 1974

Dear Mom,

How wonderful that Fairhaven has an apartment for you and nice that we have some time to help you pack. You could have been saddled with only a week's notice.

Mike started complaining about a sore throat on Thursday and by Sunday wouldn't get out of bed. Monday he was so miserable that I took him to the doctor who confirmed that Mike has infectious mononucleosis. The doctor gave us medicine but said there's not much you can do except sleep, try to eat and just do nothing. He is acutely ill, his throat so sore and enlarged that he can hardly swallow the capsules. He has headaches and a fever and his neck aches so he's always uncomfortable on a pillow. When he announced today that he was hungry, I made a strawberry milk shake. After one swallow he decided this wasn't worth the effort. Other guides took all my tours. I wake Mike every hour for a drink. This means we scrapped our trip to Kentucky, it ends Mike's bow and arrow hunting this fall after only one day out with his new bow and by the time he is well enough to work on his cars, it will be too cold. We will have to leave him home when we move you, a shame as we need his help.

My garden keeps on producing, forcing me to spend time canning. All the green tomatoes ripened, I pick broccoli by the kettleful and I dug three pails of gorgeous carrots.

It's quiet around here with Mike not able to speak.

October 14, 1974

Dear Mom, Tim and Jay,

First the infirmary report: An extreme sore throat, temperature, headaches, neck pains from swollen glands and gums so tender that he can't chew has kept Mike in bed for a week. I push 7-up and eggnog ounce by ounce, but he lost 15 pounds that first week. Yesterday he felt enough better to sit up and beat me at Spite and Malice and Monopoly. You know he's pretty sick when I say that I fixed oatmeal this morning and he thought it tasted good. Recuperation is going to be boring with no brothers in the house.

Jay, the doctor said it was okay for you to come home as Mike is not contagious. The danger is to Mike who is a sitting duck for any germs that you might bring so don't come unless you're healthy. We expect him to be out of school for three months.

Next the political report: we are passing out little green cards like mad, but 4,000 take awhile. Mike has been bundling them from his prone position. We have a car top on the Fiat and the Fairlane, and hope to put one on Andy's, because his car circulates places that ours don't. When you come home, Jay, we'll be happy to let you take the car, providing you circulate it in public places. You have to get used to people staring as you drive. The sign says WILL IT BE WILLETT for Registrar of Deeds? We also have 300 bright orange and black bumper stickers which we're frantically giving away.

When I visited the ladies next door, they asked after all of you. Miss Parsons is interested in your firewood business Tim. Jay, when she heard about the houseplants in your dorm room, she decided to send you one and ordered a Norfolk Island pine which doesn't require much sun. In their native habitat in the South Seas they grow to 100 feet. I hope your room doesn't simulate the South Seas.

Jay, I hope your thumb is okay and that you learned something, like not fighting with drunks.

Andy actually got a telephone call from Houston. They offered a job if he could start work tomorrow. He couldn't, but they said they'd call again.

October 21, 1974

Dear Mom and Tim,

Tim, you should receive your glasses by tomorrow as they did a rush job on the lens. Hope you are managing temporarily with only one lens.

More problems for Mike. On Friday he complained he couldn't blink his left eye or wrinkle his nose on that side. If he laughed, it was lopsided. We sweated out a long weekend waiting for an appointment with the neurologist while Mike got worse every day. We teased him about his crooked grin so when his girl showed up with cupcakes, he was careful not to laugh. The neurologist finally decided this was an emergency and squeezed us in. Mike has a paralysis of the facial nerve called Bells Palsy, an inflammation of the nerve brought on by the mono. He takes cortisone along with eight tablespoons daily of some awful tasting medicine to coat his stomach so that the cortisone won't cause an ulcer. As he can't completely close his left eye, he runs a high risk of picking up dust or other objects which might cause an eye infection. Because that eye won't blink when something floats by, he wears a black patch night and day and has four facial exercises to do every two hours, including smiling and whistling. Try that with only half a mouth. The blood tests show liver involvement so the doctor insisted we must keep him down and quiet. I said, "No problem. After two weeks he still has no desire to get up."

Jay hitchhiked home from La Crosse for the weekend. Holds his cast out and it sticks up in just the right spot for thumbing.

Mike sleeps lots and plays cards every chance he can get. I taught him Canasta and he wins all the time. Must quit as my card shark waits.

October 28, 1974

Dear Mom, Tim and Jay,

Mike appears to be tolerating the cortisone and can now close his left eye. After three weeks in bed listening to TV, playing cards or sleeping, he is reading car ads again and trying to corner his Dad to talk about car auctions. Grandmother sent him a new shirt, Foreyts sent a box of candy which he devoured (appetite is back) and his friend Mary played cards with him all afternoon.

On the political side, we are tired. This campaign has bad sides and good sides. Bad: like the speech that Dad has to give to the Republican Women this morning or bad like the guy who swore at Dad when he stuck a card under his windshield at the Fairgrounds. Good: like when Dad went to McFarland to see the kid who had to give a classroom speech on "Why We should Vote for Dann Willett". The boy was so excited that Dad was coming that he got his classmates to make up an advance list of questions and they taped Dad's answers. Dad presented the kid with a bumper sticker, which made his day. We take the truck out every day and park it somewhere where lots of people will see the cartop sign and we've placed an ad in every county paper. I divided the county into four sections and Dad is taking four afternoons off this week trying to cover every small village and distribute literature.

Jay, Grandma's moving date is the weekend of November 15th. You probably shouldn't try to come as we will move the bulk of her stuff on Friday. Then Dad will return home because of Mike, but I will stay with her, and Saturday Dad will come back to finish.

November 2, 1974

Dear Mom and Jay,

Jay, you get an extra letter this week as I know our absentee campaign manager likes to be in the know. We have trouble distributing materials on the east side because we don't know many people over there. We parked the truck for a day at Hilldale, at Westgate, West Towne, and Middleton Municipal lot. Many people have noticed it. We're taking it to East Towne this weekend which means two long trips. One night as we readied for bed I realized that we hadn't picked it up. Dad said, "Oh yeah, where did we leave it anyway?"

We spent three afternoons driving around the county. During an afternoon we drop about 300 cards and cover 100 miles. Dad, who has always loved beeping at farmers when he is driving along, now does it with a passion and waves at them all. We stop at little crossroads grocery stores and taverns (think we've covered every bar in the county) and leave packets. Dad lost three votes one day when he wouldn't buy drinks, but picked up a vote from that bartender just because Dad wouldn't buy drinks for everybody. Yesterday we stopped for coffee in Cambridge, bought a huge cabbage from a lady in Rockdale and got lost in Albion.

When I attended my Homemakers meeting, a friend fished into my knitting basket, pulled out cards and bumper stickers that I always carry, passed them around and we discussed politics. I find that wherever I go the topic turns to politics, not necessarily only about Dad, although they start with him. Also I find that I am more knowledgeable about all candidates than ever before.

Mike takes his black eye patch off today and we reduce the cortisone. We have decided not to put him on the homebound program.

Jay, why don't you call us collect on election night, but not until after 10:30?

November 8, 1974

Dear Mom and Jay,

Mike returns to school tomorrow after missing six weeks. His face looks fine. Even his ability to wrinkle his nose is coming back.

Jay, I need that string back. Did you lose it or forget? If you've forgotten, the measurement I need is the side seam from underarm to whatever length. How is your Norfolk Island pine doing?

I think you need some professional occupational therapist advice. When that thumb cast comes off, the muscles which have been immobilized need to be exercised so that you don't end up with a weakness, specifically your wrist, which I hope you have been flexing. If you notice any weakness, flex it back and forth and sidewise, every time you sit down. The best exercise is brushing your hair as this uses all the muscles in your wrist.

The big news is that Andy flew to Oklahoma City and has accepted a job working on offshore rigs as a command logger. As soon as they strike oil, they move the geologists to another location. He will attend a short training session after which his parent company rents him out as need arises. He may leave before Thanksgiving, so this might be your last chance to see him.

Jay, we're moving Grandma this weekend, but Mike will be here and Dad at night. Andy said he'd come for supper if you were here. He is looking for a Jeep.

November 11, 1974

Dear Tim,

I am disappointed about our traditional Willett Thanksgivings. Last year I decided that working in the kitchen from 5:00 a.m. to 7:00 p.m. was more than I can handle. I wrote a letter to all your aunts and uncles saying I was tired, and asked if somebody else could carry the ball. I didn't get any response so our big Thanksgivings are finished. We'll miss them.

We lost the election, of course. Dad got 25% of the vote. Everyone tells him he did well, as his opponent was rated to be the best vote getter in the county. We kept thinking there is always one political upset and wouldn't it be nice if it was us?

Mike is back in school. It has been a long haul and he has been the most patient and cheerful patient imaginable. With all the rest of you gone, we suddenly noticed that the kid has a sense of humor.

November 11, 1974

Dear Jay,

I got the string, but it looks long. We should double check when you come home at Thanksgiving. I am working on the sleeves anyway. The sweater went fast because Mike and I spent so much time in the doctor's waiting room. When you didn't come home last weekend we ate the apple pie that I had made in case you came.

Mike has regained 90% usage on that eye. He still does eye exercises as it opens wider than the other when he laughs. So far he hasn't dropped any course. Because he took two Algebra unipack tests at home, he is still with the class, only when he dropped out he was at the top of the class. Now he's on the other fringe.

Tim winterized his bus and expected to move back into it last weekend. As they lost all their ground snow, he is still hauling firewood down the mountain.

Think of all the money Andy's making when he works 12 hours a day. He gets bonus pay when he's on the rig. Oil drills work around the clock as they never lie idle, so often his 12-hour days are nights.

November 18, 1974

Dear Tim and Jay,

I am enclosing Grandma's new address. It makes me terribly sad to move her into an institution. We cut her possessions to a minimum as she doesn't have much space. Each move it gets harder to eliminate things. Her room reminds me of dormitory living with kitchen privileges. Uncle Frank, Aunt Lois, Dad and I moved rapidly all day Friday, confusing Grandma as she couldn't figure out who was where. I had to tell her over and over that I was staying with her Friday night in her new place. Uncle Frank and Dad got exhausted carrying her belongings up one flight of stairs. We filled her room with boxes. Visitors stopped constantly to introduce themselves, but we kept buzzing around them.

Grandma has a full bath with pull bars and she took a bath unassisted. Saturday morning we folded my bed back into a sleeper couch, scrounged up breakfast and went to work on the 14 unpacked boxes. We had to redo the kitchen cupboards and throw out some of the first stuff in order to find room for the last stuff, reminding me of our river float trip in Idaho when they limited us to 10 pounds.

Grandma and I went on a tour of the building as she is afraid of getting lost. We signed the hall checklist. If she hasn't checked it by 9:30 every morning, they will enter her apartment to see if she is okay. We visited the laundry room, her storage bin, the dining room, found her mailbox, the beauty parlor, the main desk, and the library. She will eat her main meal in the dining room and cook the rest herself. I left her awfully tired, but she doesn't realize that yet.

Happy belated Thanksgiving

Dear Tim,

I can't send you blankets until after the Greyhound strike.

Andy is moving his apartment stuff into our attic today, except for a little that goes with him. He will leave Thanksgiving night and will be in Houston for eight weeks of mud school. He bought a '74 Toyota Land Cruiser and if you ever saw a kid playing with a toy, he's it.

Need to go work on my Thanksgiving dinner. It will be strange without you. Jay will arrive home this afternoon and Dad has gone to pick up Grandma. Might you get home for Christmas?

December 2, 1974

Dear Mom,

Enclosed find a clipping, as Dann says we did it again. After a week and a half, the dental lab is back in operation, but still a mess. The fire department called at 5:30 p.m. as Dann was coming up the driveway. "Your building is burning and we need you." Mike and I went along. A phone call like that gives one a gut feeling that doesn't get better when you see four fire engines, a rescue squad, the fire chief's car and two squad cars with flashing red lights. Apparently, faulty wiring caused the fire.

Mike and Dann have been figuring out how to put a wood stove in the garage so Mike can continue to work on his cars. He misses those six weeks of prime weather when he was flat in bed. When they cleared out the garage they found 37 extra tires. No wonder we can't get the second car in.

December 12, 1974

Dear Mom,

Jay is trying to figure out how to water his plants during semester break so I sent him a string. Should the plant be higher or lower than the glass of water?

Tim is struggling with his usual problems. When his truck got stuck, it took two days to find somebody to pull him out and somehow he punctured one eardrum, causing a temporary loss of hearing in that ear.

We made a bedroom switch this weekend, moving Tim's stuff into the hall, Jay's stuff back into his old room, and now Mike has a new bedroom that received two coats of vibrant green paint.

December 23, 1974

Dear Tim,

Hope you have received your Christmas package. All the Christmas stollens have been delivered, the house is decorated, the Christmas cookies are rapidly disappearing, and Jay is home and picks up Grandma this afternoon. I am sewing frantically as my ideas have again exceeded my time. Andy's Christmas package waits to go because he won't be back in Houston for another week.

The Willett mechanics are struggling to heat the garage so that operations can continue through the winter. Yesterday Dad, Mike and Kevin lugged home a burner which they set up in the back corner and piped through one of the window panes in the back door. Mike saws wood frantically to keep the stove fed.

If I could make one wish for you for the New Year, I would wish that all your vehicles would keep running. Merry Christmas.

January 8, 1975

Dear Tim,

We received many Christmas presents to use in our Scamper Camper for our Alaskan trip. Cross your fingers and hope that we really get to go as I won't believe this until departure. Dad gave me an asbestos pad to cover the stovetop to create more work space. He made a cedar sign engraved with our name to hang in our campsite, claiming the spot when we leave temporarily. Jay gave me a welcome mat to throw out the back door so everybody's muddy feet walk across that first. Mike presented us with a book on Alaska that we've all been reading.

I spent days at my sewing machine and produced matching square dance dress and shirt, plus six flannel shirts. Mike habitually complains about store shirts. If we get extra large for length, they flap like tents. I adapted the shirt pattern to Mike and then used it for the rest of you by adding to the length and subtracting from the width. It makes Mike look skinny.

I wrote to Uncle Charles after Thanksgiving and said it might be quiet around his house this year with all of his kids married, we had empty bedrooms, and Grandmother would be here, so why didn't he come? I knew he wouldn't. He did. We told her that one present would be arriving late. On Christmas Eve afternoon, Dad drove out to the airport and coming home, Charles just walked into the living room saying, "Merry Christmas, Mom." She was speechless and nothing could have pleased her more. I invited Uncle Frank and Aunt Lois and Valerie too, giving us a full motel. Dad and I, Jay and Mike all slept in the fireplace room. Grandma kept asking, "Whose idea was this anyway?"

January 22, 1975

Dear Mom,

The Scout winter campout drew okay weather, just below freezing, so they didn't get wet and weren't too cold. Do you remember when Mike and Dann went on the winter campout last year on the Mazomanie Hunting Grounds? Same place this year. Last year Mike lost his billfold. This year Dann found it. No money left, only soggy ID cards and a chewed billfold. You should have seen Mike's face when Dann gave it to him.

I spend all my spare time studying Alaska. We've asked Andy which stopover on the Inside Passage would he recommend and what should we not miss?

January 29th, 1975

Dear Mom,

Andy is considering Foreign Service. At the completion of mud school they offer a two-year international contract trouble-shooting. This includes a bonus, and if you work over 18 months you don't have to pay U.S. income tax. The company pays the foreign tax so the overseas pay comes out double that of domestic. Or he's considering tech pool, another trouble shooting set-up. He would list us as Home Base. They would call and say, "So and so is having trouble. Be on flight #346 at 8:00 a.m. tomorrow." He might stay a day or a month, possibly be sent to Alaska or Saudi Arabia or the Colorado Rockies, as they have lots of trouble in the drills there, then back to home base for days or weeks.

February 15, 1975

Dear Mom,

Andy's letters are like soap operas, each one with a new exciting plan. He says he lies awake nights thinking about where to go?

Another guide and I took advantage of the new snow and went to the School Forest to look for foxes. We pondered where an ideal den location might be and found one. We struggled in the snow to get our footing as we slid up and down the ridges, covered with blackberry bushes. I don't mind sliding down ridges on the seat of my pants but not in the vicinity of blackberry bushes.

Memorial High School is experimenting with an Interim program for semester break. Mike signed up for a work experience class in auto mechanics at Thorstad's Chevrolet and was thrilled when he made it, as they accepted only four. He also signed up for a solar energy class. I volunteered to teach a class on Field Ecology Survey Techniques and am worried about how to teach this. Mike says not to worry as nobody would sign up for a class with that name at that hour (8:00 a.m.) for five days a week.

March 5, 1975

Dear Mom,

We had a great weekend up north. It started to snow shortly after we left home and before long the car danced back and forth on the road and settled into the ditch. That ditch must have been deep and full of snow as the car tilted. It's a funny feeling when the snow depth covers the window and we climbed up and out the top side of the car. We were carrying three snow shovels and put them all to use, but shortly a truck with a plow came along, probably out cruising for people like us so they could pick up extra cash. They had heavy chains and snow tires, but even with four of us pushing, they had a tough time pulling us back to the road. By the time we reached Ashland, the snow had stopped, the moon was out and the night was glistening with diamond-studded snow. We skied on Powderhorn on Friday, White Cap Mountain on Saturday and then drove to the cottage. The plows had thrown up so much snow in the driveway that we couldn't possibly shovel. We walked into the cottage on snowshoes, carrying our gear. The inside thermometer read 12 degrees. After skiing all day, shoveling, unloading, and making fires the boys still had enough energy left to put on snowshoes and cross the lake to town. Sunday we snowshoed in the swamp.

Four kids signed on for my Interim class. We worked in the woods in the middle of a blizzard, the snow clouded our field glasses and soaked all our clipboards. Finally getting wet and cold, we quit.

Dann shadowed Mike to his interim class on Solar Energy.

March 12, 1975

Dear Mom,

We spend all our spare time dreaming about this proposed Alaskan trip. We may leave the middle of June although Dann says if business doesn't pick up, we can't go. I can think of lots of reasons why we shouldn't go!

We are ready for spring, but we keep getting snowstorms every couple days. Just once the driveway didn't get plowed wide enough and now it's getting narrower and narrower.

We spotted an opossum yesterday and Mike followed him to where he apparently lives under Mike's white VW, parked for the winter. The snow depth more than reaches the bottom of the van doors. What could be nicer? Anyway I am thinking spring and have started six dozen plants in Dann's study. Presently we will have only walkways through there.

Dann's Aunt Edna came for dinner and I can't begin to repeat all the super adjectives she used describing Tim. She calls him a great adventurer and thinks he takes after his great Uncle Walter. I just hope our great adventurer is not freezing in that converted bus. Nobody writes and I need cheering up.

March 19, 1975

Dear Mom,

Andy chose the tech pool and is presently in Carlsbad, New Mexico. They sent him to Louisiana twice and recalled him so fast the second time that he left all his clothes at the dry cleaners.

I labeled last weekend as Saturday the Terrible. Mike and Kevin were repairing a VW for a man on the east side. Dann took our truck and the boys, and went to pick up that VW and tow it home. Shortly after they left, I received a call from the Sherman Hall apartments. A tenant had heard a noise in the basement, went down to look and found the basement flooded so deep she couldn't get the basement door open. I tried to trace Dann because I knew his stops, but missed him. Knowing that Dann no longer used the plumber listed on our trouble sheet, I got out the Sherman Hall checkbook, found a plumbing bill he had paid and called. After I explained, the lady responded that everyone was out, but would I please hang up and somebody would call me back? One did and I asked if he had worked at Sherman Hall, told him I thought we had a broken water main flooding the basement and I couldn't locate Dann. He responded, "Lady, I'm on my way."

After 40 minutes Dann turned up at the location of the dead VW where I had left a call-back message. He tried to leave the boys there to work on the VW, but they were afraid they might miss something, so they hastily attached the VW to the back of the truck and towed it along. Two hours elapsed after the break before the men were able to reach the shutoff and turn off the water. The water level in the basement rose to 15 inches. As that is a huge basement, that means an enormous amount of water sloshed through 26 storage cages, submerged the machinery of the washer and dryer, and damaged furniture stored there. The water main had broken underneath the concrete floor and the pressure pushed up three inches of concrete, making a crack 100 feet long which spewed water and mud for two hours. It looks like the front of the building shifted because the drainpipes in the kitchen sinks in the front four apartments broke off and the basement floor has a slant all the way across, highest at the point of the crack. If I stand there, my head touches the ceiling beams. Dann shut off the heat and electricity and hired air hammers and diggers who searched for the break for two days. The basement apartments now have a 15 inch black water line around the walls and on the furniture. Dann ripped up their carpeting, but as it dries it shrinks so we can't reuse it. Worst of all, the insurance company notified us there is an exclusion clause in the policy exempting underground water. I argued that this is not natural underground water, but city water traveling through in the main. We are thankful that we don't own this apartment.

April 7, 1975

Dear Mom,

Easter Sunday was lonesome with the family so far flung. Mike was here in Madison, Andy in Carlsbad, Tim in Colorado and Jay vacationing in Florida. Jay is home already from his Florida spring break. I don't think he had been to bed for two nights. He toured the Space Center and Disney World and lay on the beach. He said I was right about how much money to take, so he did run out.

Three card tables full of nursery plants are housed in Dann's study. We can barely walk through but he doesn't complain much. My saffron plants are dying. I placed them under a light hoping they'll see the light.

April 12, 1975

Dear Mom,

Finally we got a beautiful day, so I quit housecleaning and dug parsnips. The first one measured 23 inches, the record was 27 inches, with the boys standing in line to see who could excavate the longest. I wonder if that's the result of the seaweed we put on last year or from the sand I placed in the furrows of the root vegetables. They stretch down so deep that it's difficult to dig, as when you push the pitchfork down as far as it goes, that's only halfway for the parsnip.

We hope to have that garage sale this weekend so I have dragged all sorts of stuff down to the garage. The trick is not to let any go back after the sale is over.

April 22, 1975

Dear Mom,

We had lots of people at our garage sale and lousy weather (even snow) but made $200 which goes towards the Inland Passage ferry. Dann and Mike sure had fun and I think we're going to end up with a clean garage, which Mike will no doubt fill up again. In the ad Dann listed 80 hubcaps. He has been collecting for years. Mike sold them for $1.00 apiece, and Dann sold one for $5. If I'd been working, they would have been 25 cents.

May 1, 1975

Dear Mom,

You'll never guess what we have in the yard. On second thought maybe you would. We are the proud(?) owners of a malfunctioning, '72, 4-door, orange Fiat. Dann and Mike drove to Mazomanie to see it, drove it around the block and knew the brakes weren't right. Taking it apart, they found locking and overheating brakes. They told the startled lady she shouldn't be driving it. She had been asking $1,700, came down to $1,500, but they found all kinds of stuff wrong with it, offered her $900 and came home empty-handed. She called the next day and accepted $900. Of course, Mike thinks he can fix it.

P.S. The nation's economy is giving Tim trouble as he has no profit from his summer work. The bottom dropped out of wood prices and he has much that he hasn't been able to sell.

P.S.S. Mike can't find a part-time job so he has been fixing cars for cheap, but he is showing a profit.

May 16, 1975

Dear Mom,

Andy called from Carlsbad with a terrifying story. He has been working in an oil field in New Mexico on twelve-hour shifts. His shift finished at 10:00 a.m. but his replacement hadn't showed up yet, so Andy climbed the twenty-foot platform of the drilling rig to watch a procedure. The crew had been having trouble getting a point down and had lowered tools to do a test when the pressure broke the tools. Pounds of mud shot up the tube, pushed by tons of gas pressure erupting and spraying mud and gas over everything. Twelve guys were working on the platform. Those closest took to the stairs, the rest went over the sides and down the rig, sprinting through the sagebrush into the desert. Andy can't remember going down the stairs. As he raced out to the desert, he was startled to see their fifty-five-year-old geologist easily outdistancing him.

A roughneck turned back and plugged the hole. If there had been a spark, it would have taken a year to get the fire out. Andy had opened his office trailer windows because of the intense heat, and mud pouring through the window covered his computer. The bad part is he was scheduled to return to Houston the next day for another eight-week class, but now he can't leave. The good part is that he wasn't hurt. I think he was still shaking when he called us.

June 7, 1975

Dear Mom,

We wrote Tim that his Dad has work for him this summer. As he can't find anything in Colorado, he might come home. We're frustrated waiting for an answer. The work needs to be done soon and we don't know whether he is coming or not. Tim did get a phone call here from a buddy who expected Tim to be home. Tim had told him he had a couple things to do before he left Colorado. If one of those things is to sell that bus, it might well take a long time.

Jay is working night shift at Copps, 9:30 p.m. to 6:00 a.m. One night Jay discovered, to his horror and hers, that one of the cashier girls had been slow and everyone locked up and left while she was in the bathroom. Jay thought she was going to spend the night with him, but then realized that it was only 10:15 and security didn't turn on until 10:20. He unlocked the front door, shoved her out and breathed a sigh of relief when nothing happened. That same night the manager forgot, when leaving, to close the door to a small storage room and so when security did activate at 10:20 the alarm sounded, making a harrowing half-hour before Jay got it stopped. He received constant phone calls from central security telling him what to do, nothing worked and he expected police cars to descend momentarily. They must have been busy elsewhere as a violent windstorm was taking out electricity and uprooting trees all over town.

Mike has been working hard to sell his two VW's before we leave. One is finished and it is beautiful, spray painted with blue shag interior. He priced it at $795 to cover costs of $300.

June 20, 1975

Dear Mom,

What a circus we run! Last weekend Mike sold the Datsun, which he had advertised for one day, and then he and Dann bought the van they had been eyeing for a week. This is an old, malfunctioning, rolling pizza panel truck. Mike went to the used car lot three consecutive days to fix things, in hopes that he could bring it home under its own steam. Tonight he drove in triumphantly with John following in our truck and John's girl riding with Mike, with a pail of water stashed between her legs in case of fire. Mike has big hopes for that van. Besides the motor overhaul, he plans to outfit the back for traveling and will build in a bed, sink and storage.

Don and Norma came out tonight to borrow our trailer, but Mike's van was sitting on the circle drive, plus our truck which Mike has been readying for our trip, plus our Fairlane so it took a lot of maneuvering to pull the trailer out where they could hook it on. Norma and I sat on the front steps and visited while I finished the handwork on the blouse I am taking to camp. A neighbor walked up the drive with cookies she had baked for our trip so she sat down and visited too. The people came to finish paying Mike for the VW and then Chris came to see Mike, had to park on the road, but then he sat on the lawn and visited with us while Mike concluded his other business. It's easy to see why I never get anything done around here in the evening.

It seems like I have been getting ready for this trip for ages.

July 10, 1975

Dear Mom,

Andy is in Teheran. He drove home for a week's vacation, but before he got here, his office called him back. I was counseling at 4-H camp and didn't even see him. He is presently loafing as the monsoons damaged his rig while it was traveling to the Persian Gulf.

We have spent the last two days fully occupied saying goodbye to drop-ins, but now we are off.

July 14, 1975

Dear Mom and Jay,

Late last night we reached the Canadian Rockies and camped outside Banff National Park, with huge rock outcroppings leaning over us.

We drove through a flood in Fargo, North Dakota. We were on I-94, the only road open. Water swirled up to both sides of the highway. We couldn't resist and turned off on an exit. Mike took his Dad's camera and walked down one submerged road, but halted when the water level approached the bottom of his shorts. Cars stopped to take his picture. Water surrounded the sandbagged motels. Piles of mud had been dumped along the shoulders as levees. The radio informed us of a mosquito problem and one look at the front of our Scamper confirmed that. The fields had been submerged for a week and smelled like decaying seaweed. We drove late into the night so we wouldn't have to camp in the area.

We passed customs easily, drawing an immigration official who wouldn't smile even for Dad. She checked every cupboard, missing only our secret food pantry, looked under our sleeping bags and inspected Dad's fishing tackle box piece by piece. She asked if I was carrying a derringer.

Shortly after crossing the border, Mike spotted a building labeled Willett MFG so we walked in asking to see Mr. Willett. This flustered the receptionist. Finally the owner came out and explained, "There is no Mr. Willett. I invented a converter that would change a three phase system to a single phase and patented it. Everybody kept asking—will it do this? Will it do that? So that's what I named the company." Enclosed find a WILLETT pen, compliments of the management.

We stopped at the bank and are carrying lots of what Mike calls funny money. It looks like play money. Mike exchanged his $5 gift from you, Grandmother, and came out $1.36 ahead. Language difficulties plague us in the grocery stores. Mike and I debated a long time over something which looked like wieners and said SAUCISSES FUMEES.

Tomorrow we'll start into the mountains. Will call soon. Hope all your problems maintaining our office are small ones.

July 17, 1975

Dear Mom and Jay,

Talking to you tonight was okay Jay, but that wasn't enough time. We thought we could discuss all your office problems in three minutes, but I guess not. Next time ask your business questions first before our quarters run out.

We spent today on back roads, using shortcuts. Leaving Jasper National Park, we took the Forestry Service road because it was 100 miles shorter. That gravel bumpy road stretched on forever through wild and beautiful country. When we stopped high on a ridge next to a fire observation tower, the ranger invited us in for a cold drink. He must not see people often as he entertained us for hours with stories and pictures of the animals he has trapped in the winter. Wish he had offered a taste of the moose stew bubbling on his stove.

Dad and Mike are preparing the truck for the start of the Alcan Highway tomorrow. They fastened a protective screen over the windshield and headlights. Every night we go to bed in daylight. We have a beautiful campsite on a lake, especially beautiful because we're dusty. Last night was cold and rainy, but we camped next to a hot springs and sat in the pool at 102 degrees until we couldn't stand it any longer. The day before was hot and we camped in the mountains with a swimming hole at our front door. We have seen mule deer, mountain sheep, elk, prairie dogs, coyote, and bear. A bear came into our campground. Mike and I walked over, carefully staying behind a car. The bear sniffed around the bushes and headed towards a pup tent when a man came barreling out of his van screaming, "Beat it, scram. Get out of my tent. I told you that before, now scram bear!" The bear retreated, but continued to circle the campground.

July 21, 1975

Dear Mom and Jay,

We've been on the Alcan Highway for three days. We no sooner started on the gravel section when rain dumped on us. Dad and Mike had secured the screen on the windshield to stop rocks, but the screen plus the downpour made it impossible to see the road so they got out in the rain and removed it. Every truck that passed slurped goopy mud all over us and when we reached a dry section the dust rose in clouds sticking on top of the goopy mud. Mike is trying to talk Dad into coming home without washing the truck. The mud coats our back window solid brown. We have been doing broken headlight statistics. One out of every three cars has lost one or two lights from rocks. Reaching an area of washouts and landslides from the late, heavy spring thaw, we waited two hours while three graders removed a huge landslide. By the time they took a break, 40 cars were waiting. The first six made it up the steep rough road, but the seventh, a small truck pulling a trailer just didn't have enough power to get over the hill. One grader maneuvered down, hooked on and lugged him over the top. The rest of us bumped up at five miles-per-hour with Mike hanging out the window to take pictures.

When we were looking for a campsite, we waited to cross a bridge that was under repair and asked the girl with the STOP flag if she could tell us where the Roaring River Provincial Campground was located. A funny grin crossed her face as she pointed, "It was down there but it washed away last month. Try up the road apiece."

Many interesting wanderers travel this highway and we keep bumping into the same ones. Three times we have camped near a young couple from Michigan who worked and saved, so they could quit their jobs and travel for a year. Two or three times daily we run into a little retired man from Minnesota who toots along on his motorcycle at 30 miles-per-hour in his black rain gear, or we wave at the elderly ladies from Switzerland who flew to Chicago, rented a car and drove from there, or the one-arm guy driving a collapsible unit. Our Scamper creates much curiosity. Dad has just invited a man into our camper who toured Europe in a VW van and wanted to see ours.

We purchased three-day fishing licenses so tonight we ate fresh trout. I caught the first two. Thinking I had a snag, I tried hard to get off, but I caught the fish anyway. Dad and Mike like the great mileage we're getting at this speed. Can you imagine traveling 1,000 miles at 35 miles per hour?

July 23, 1975

Dear Mom and Jay,

We had a terrible time with your last phone call, Jay. We kept feeding quarters in, but apparently the box was full and wouldn't record. Dad kept hitting it and stuffing in more quarters. After we hung up, he hit it one more time and all the coins came tumbling out.

I realized that you would soon run out of the food which I left for you. Suggestions: a roll of Canadian bacon makes an easy meal (cut off a few slices and fry with an egg), or canned hash or a frozen turkey boneless roast can be sliced and warmed. Try ice cream cake roll or some of those blueberry turnovers—all you have to do is roll out and bake. I knew you'd be swamped harvesting our raspberries.

Adjusting to this time schedule and extensive daylight is tough. By the time we get up, you're probably eating lunch. We get twenty-two hours of daylight a day. This morning I watched the sun rise at 4:30 a.m. We are off for three days of backpacking at McKinley National Park. The shuttle bus takes us 83 miles inland and drops us. Our little old truck did great on the Alcan Highway and we came off it undamaged.

July 29, 1975

Dear Mom and Jay,

Jay, I hope you are talking to my garden beans and discouraging them from over-producing until August 11th. Try to squeeze in time to visit Grandmother. I know you're going to be swamped with office problems until after the first of the month. Cheer up. Dad will be home soon and take care of August.

We are headed back to Whitehorse to take the train over the mountains to the Pacific. Dad and Mike are broken-hearted as we picked up a rock in our windshield. After 1,600 miles of gravel roads, one flew up from the blacktop highway as a semi zoomed by us. After a day of driving on gravel, Dad and Mike always pick stones out of the treads with a small tent stake. The gravel is harder on good tires because the tread holds the stones and they work in and cut the tire. Dad and Mike have been watching one tire carefully and yesterday had it turned in an attempt to prolong its life. The frost heaves turn the blacktop roads into washboards. Mike complains that his head keeps hitting the cab ceiling as we traverse the rough roads.

We shortened our time at Mt. McKinley because it rained constantly. We had picked out a back area and secured the two-day permit, packed our backpacks and took the shuttle bus all the way in—all mountain driving, and camped at Wonder Lake Campground, preparatory to hiking the next day. We had planned to cook over campfires until we discovered in horror that we were above the tree line, but a neighborly camper loaned us his extra Sterno. During the night a dreadful storm soaked us so we gave up and caught the 8:00 a.m. shuttle back to the park entrance. I called it the backpackers express because it kept stopping to pick up soggy backpackers coming out of the woods like rats off a sinking ship.

At Dawson City, in the heart of the gold rush country, we panned for gold and attended an old-fashioned vaudeville show depicting the history of the area. We poked around the abandoned log cabins and Mike found a boarded-up building, obviously once a garage, filled with old vintage car parts. We missed Diamond Gerties Gambling Hall because they close on Mondays so we shall have to return someday. We enjoy sourdough pancakes and fresh trout often for breakfast.

August 8, 1975

Dear Mom and Jay,

We crossed the mountains by train and then unloaded our truck off the flatbed car, drove it onto the ferry and sailed down the Inside Passage dwarfed by high mountains on both sides. Students jammed the ferry and at night bedrolls lined the decks. Dad and Mike always put me between them. We planned to be on one of the few runs that stopped at Sitka with a five-hour layover as we wanted to explore the Russian influence in the Eskimo village. Unfortunately, that day we were fogged in and our boat stopped dead in the water until the fog lifted. When we arrived in Sitka, on-going passengers could not disembark as, in order to catch the tide, the boat needed to depart immediately.

We offloaded at Juneau for one night and parked our Scamper in the campground. Juneau is a narrow strip of city bounded by water on one side and mountains on the other. Accessibility is by air or by boat.

The last bit of the trip was open sea. These ferries have rounded bottoms to navigate the shallow parts of the Inside Passage so when they hit the open water they have no stability against swells. Suddenly the cabin boys, who had always been busy rushing around previously, now stood around with brown paper bags. Tomorrow we turn the truck towards you and will be there almost as soon as this letter.

August 18, 1975

Dear Andy and Tim,

Yes, we are home. Our only flat tire occurred as we crossed Montana. After that Mike commented, "I feel insecure traveling with just one spare." We didn't need any of the spare parts that Mike kept stashed under the seat.

On that fabulous ferry trip we saw bald eagles, porpoises and whales. Our boat, the Columbia, with a capacity of 600 people, was the largest on the line. A carpeted solarium covered the rear top deck (this means a roof with heat units on three sides and open back) and as we experienced wind and rain, the carpet soaked up water like a sponge, so most of those people shifted their sleeping bags inside. Those that stayed outside put up tents and tarps. We traveled on the boat for three nights. Our meals cost only $30, $20 for one meal and $10 for the other. The rest of the time we managed with cheese and crackers, Tang and sweet rolls from the backpack. After embarking in Seattle we drove straight home, stopping in Washington State to pick up 33 lbs. of dark sweet cherries and a box of peaches at a roadside stand. Snacking on cherries for 2,000 miles, we rivaled Johnny Appleseed as we spit a trail of cherry seeds out the window crossing the nation.

It's impossible to get anything accomplished now as we've been deluged with friends coming to say welcome home. Quite a few expressed concern over our safety. Grandmother said it was time we came home when she discovered we did things like chartering a four-passenger plane to fly over the glaciers and letting the pilot turn the controls over to Mike. Actually he was a licensed instructor and did an excellent job of teaching, even when his back was turned to Mike as he chatted with us.

Andy, I assume that you are working by now and imagine it has been a long wait for that rig to arrive. Couldn't you do Christmas shopping or something? Jay takes your Toyota out for the requested exercise. Mostly he does it going up and down the driveway because we suspended your insurance.

Dad has his usual vacation beard. He makes a sensation in church when he appears like that. It wouldn't be so bad if he didn't go around kissing everyone.

August 20, 1975

Dear Mom,

You've heard most of our stories, but I thought you might enjoy my WILLETTS' List of 25 Do's and Don'ts for Alaskan Travelers.

1. When traveling in Canada, if you want to know whether you're hot or cold, take the temperature reading (Celsius), double it and add 30 to get an approximate Fahrenheit reading.

2. Always remember Canadian phones don't absorb American coins nor do American phones register Canadian ones. And always give it one last kick after arguing with it, in case it wants to cough up something. The best solution is two change purses—one American, one Canadian.

3. When using Laundromats, pay showers, or phones, if all else fails, try reading the instructions.

4. Either learn to read French or turn the groceries around on the shelves so you can read the English side. Be grateful for international road signs.

5. ON THE ALCAN HIGHWAY: Never believe everything the MilePost book tells you. Expect no facilities until you see them. Learn to live with expectations of washed out campgrounds, burned out grocery stores, abandoned gas pumps and other little problems.

6. Keep insisting you need hot showers, but never expect them.

7. If you're looking for a post office, it's a box someplace with a slit in the top.

8. Insist on the driver parking the truck level at night and above all, never let him get the driver side of the truck, which is the head end of the bed, lower, even if he has to re-park five times.

9. Do not plan on star-gazing in Alaska in the summer. Don't even bother to take flashlights. And face the fact that you have to go to bed before the sun SETS.

10. When anybody asks the time say—do you mean Alaskan time, Yukon Time, Mountain or Central, Daylight or Standard? That way everybody gets mixed up and nobody knows whether it's time to eat.

11. If you have trouble with bears in campgrounds, yell at the top of your lungs, "Scram bear, and get out of my tent". It's a good idea to practice singing when walking in the brush. That way if any bear doesn't care for your voice, he leaves before you get there.

12. Be sparing with your water. Use only for important things like drinking, washing faces at night and washing off the Wisconsin part of your license plate daily.

13. Above all, do NOT wash your car. In addition to conserving water, the thick layer of mud acts as a cushion for flying rocks.

14. Try to keep your accumulation of rocks, driftwood, pine cones, rabbit feet and moose droppings to a pocketful per day.

15. Don't try to get untangled when your line gets snagged, because if it turns out to be a fish, it can be embarrassing.

16. If you have trouble finding ice, try glacier snow. This works great.

17. If you have trouble finding gas, you should have looked sooner and don't let your driver keep driving in and out of stations, because the price is $1.10 per gallon when you can get it at home for $.55 per gallon.

18. If the fishing is poor, try gold-panning. If the panning doesn't "pan" out, the blueberry, strawberry and raspberry picking is great.

19. Don't fall for that old gag, do you want to hear me call a moose? Spoil their fun by saying, "Here moose, here moose" yourself.

20. Do not think you're getting a bargain if you buy "recombined" milk cheaply. Just another word for powdered.

21. If you can't figure out the sign posted on the restaurant wall that says Alaskan BLT's $2.50. It means bacon, lettuce and tomato sandwich.

22. Be sure to ask travelers where they're going as the stories are better than soap opera, ranging from the great-grandmother who had driven her truck 8,000 miles to the long-haired kid, who toured the continent with backpack and 10-speed bike and boarded the wrong boat.

23. WHEN TRAVELING BY CHARTERED PLANE, if your pilot is planning to take you down far enough to see the seals on the icebergs and up the mountains to look for mountain goats, locate paper bags in advance.

24. WHEN TRAVELING ON THE FERRY, try not to be in the shower when the P.A. announces a school of killer whales passing.

25. When coming home through the states, wave frantically at anybody with an unbelievably dirty car because you know exactly where they have been and what a fantastic trip they've had.

We couldn't have picked a nicer way to celebrate our 25th anniversary. We covered many miles: 9,000 by truck and Scamper

Camper, 200 by train, 200 by plane, and 1,000 by ferry. Those miles of memories will last forever. It's great to be home, but it will take me all winter to get reorganized. That pile of papers waiting on my desk when I came home keeps changing, but never diminishing.

This has been an outstanding year. We had a fire in the building we rent to the dental lab, a burst water main in our 26-unit, a tenant who shot himself in one of those apartments, and 70 mile-per-hour winds that brought a huge tree down across an apartment roof. For a change we could use some of that "boring and monotonous" living I once worried about.

13 A Revolving Door

SEPTEMBER 5, 1975

Dear Mom and Jay,

Jay, I can't believe you drove our Fairlane the five weeks we were gone without having trouble. On my first trip out of town, one tire went flat and the car heated up just driving home from downtown. Last Saturday night, when Mike was driving through the Arboretum, somebody fielded a rock breaking the back window to smithereens. Mike stopped the car in the middle of the road, turned on all the lights, locked Sue inside and took off through the bushes, but found nobody. They drove to a nearby house to call the police but the lady wouldn't let them in.

I found the spaghetti left for you in the freezer that you couldn't find. The problem was I had labeled it broccoli. We are enjoying the 60 boxes of raspberries you froze and chuckling over your signature labels.

A Revolving Door

SEPTEMBER 10, 1975

Dear Mom, Tim and Jay,

Today is package day. I am sending a belated birthday package for you, Tim, and for you, Jay, the bedspread I promised for your dorm room. I sent a wedding present to British Columbia for Lisa and I have Andy's birthday package ready to go to Teheran, but yesterday we received a postcard saying, "Here I come westward, in about two weeks." Dad says not to get excited yet. The company may divert him.

When I stopped the Fairlane in the driveway today, it boiled over. Our student mechanic crawled out from where he was working under his VW and crawled under our Fairlane. Before he could find the problem, Dann came barreling up the drive in the Fiat, going like sixty because he'd lost his first and second gear. Mike abandoned the Fairlane and crawled under the Fiat, but then the police called to say that a drunk had broken into our office downtown. Mike quickly reassembled the gears and he and Dann left.

Dann shaved off half his Alaskan beard. He says now he has a "Lincoln."

SEPTEMBER 24, 1975

Dear Mom, Tim and Jay,

Andy came home, talked for hours and left within two days, leaving him two days to drive 700 miles to Houston. He expects to be sent out again right away as everybody else in the Tech Pool is out of the country.

Heavy weather had damaged the rig as it was being towed through the Indian Sea and put them behind schedule. When Andy arrived in Iran, he couldn't get to the rig for weeks. He stayed on it for only a week when his permanent replacement showed up, and they sent Andy home. As the Iranian government paid the Houston office $150 per day for Andy, they were anxious to manage without him.

He says you can't imagine how it feels to land in an airport like Teheran where: no English is posted, he carries none of their currency, is being met by someone he doesn't know who doesn't know him, he can't figure out how to use the phone and has no money to put in it, and can't communicate with the operator. He carried luggage that says IMCO in big letters. He hoisted this high until somebody approached asking, "Are you Andy?" He lived in the company apartment with one of his Houston roommates. I asked if they did their own cooking. They tried, but couldn't read the numbers on the oven.

Taxi drivers confounded them. Andy's linguistic ability stretched only to left, right, or ahead. When they told the driver they wanted to see the Archaeological Museum he said, "Okay," and took them to see the Crown Jewels. They toured that for two hours and then tried for the Museum again. He said, "Okay," and took them to the Government offices so they gave up. Flying home, he stopped in Frankfort for sightseeing, stopped in Pennsylvania to visit a girl and called when he landed in Chicago giving us 40 minutes notice.

The daughter of the people who built our house in 1906 surprised us with a visit. She entertained us with stories about this old house. The huge flat rock in the side yard is a carriage step which used to be alongside the drive in front. This lady was two-years-old when the house was built and her family lived in a tent while it was being finished. She said she had placed her hand in fresh plaster on the attic stairwell. Although we had never noticed before, we went to look and found her handprint in plain sight. She explained that the circular metal plate in the center of the dining room floor had attached to a bulb resting in her mother's lap, to squeeze when she called the maid.

A Revolving Door

Someone broke into our office again. One of our tenants was coming home from work late at night and saw three people breaking the glass in the front door. Dann just got that glass replaced last week. When they realized they were being observed, they walked away, but Dave entered his apartment and called the police. After Dave left, they apparently returned because when Dave went out to talk to the cops in the squad car, he saw people inside the office. The police officer picked up his shotgun, walked into the office and yelled, "freeze". The girl did. The two guys did not, instead they dove head first through the back window. The policeman called for backup and they picked up the burglars a few blocks away.

Sorry I couldn't visit you this week, Mom. I spent lots of time baking while Andy was home. Mike thought this was great, but now we're back to bread and water until the next son shows up. Forty minutes notice is not enough for the chef.

October 3, 1975

Dear Mom, Jay and Tim,

Glad you liked the goodies, Tim. Do the clothes fit? Mom, I bet you've never before received letters from three grandsons in one week. Tim, I have been trying to talk Dad and Mike into a trip to Colorado to apply first aid to your malfunctioning trucks. They assure me this is impossible as they wouldn't have the proper tools and it might be too cold.

Mike just sold his last Volkswagen and is ecstatic. The paint job looked professional and the shag carpeting dressed up the interior. One of our old tenants stopped to pay back rent, fell in love with the car and paid the $695 Mike was asking without even bargaining. Mike didn't have to advertise so he and his partner (Dad) cleared $400. Now Mike can start on his van, beginning with the engine.

Dear Mom

The Alaskan beard is gone. The preacher asked Dann to make an announcement in church last Sunday and commented from the pulpit on the beard. It disappeared the next day.

Because of the encephalitis scare, authorities cancelled all outdoor field trips for 15 days. I have often thought it would be fun for the guides to stay overnight, but our campground facilities are usually full. Although we should have been concerned about mosquitoes, the weather was too gorgeous to waste. So we did it. I posted rules on the kitchen wall: anybody who goes ahead of the naturalist on the trail has to clean the johns, anybody throwing the picnic tables off the cliff has to drag them back up, no feeding the bulls across the back fence, anyone caught talking after 3:00 a.m. has to sit at the salt lick for 15 minutes in absolute silence. My rules really broke them up.

We made stone stew. I purchased meat and everyone brought a vegetable to dump. It looked like enough to feed an army, but after we finished dumping and simmering, our army ate it all. We cranked homemade ice cream and hiked in the woods and did night hikes in the pitch-black woods without flashlights. One simply needs to know the trail and have trained feet. We listened to and answered a barred owl call. Don't know what we said but we answered. Returning for cocoa and ice cream around the campfire, we went to bed at midnight. Two guides arrived just after we had retired, one with a birthday cake for me. I went into the other sleeping cabin and hollered, "Time to eat." They woke up, moaned, groaned and complained that I couldn't have a birthday cake now because it was five minutes after my birthday. One gal, listed on the Caper Chart for morning cabin sweeping, complained that we were strewing crumbs all over. Some of us did a night watch around the campfire, followed by a dawn hike, and completed our overnight with sourdough pancakes and maple syrup. We are grateful to the mosquitoes. We've been trying to do this for years.

A Revolving Door

October 9, 1975

Dear Everybody,

Dann set up his last Boy Scout Court of Honor. The Scouts conferred with Mike and me about a gift for Dann. They wanted to know how many years Dann had been in scouting (16) and asked me to make sure he attended the meeting. As Dann had not the slightest intention of attending, because he had a church Trustee meeting at the same time, I wasn't a happy camper. The Scouts delivered a special invitation for him and at supper I informed him that the church meeting had been delayed an hour. I called the preacher and told him Dann would be delayed an hour. Dann never believed me, (I must be slipping) so with great feelings of apprehension, he attended the Scout meeting. The boys presented him with a good boy award made from a tin can, a cardboard big hand, and a collapsible fly pole.

That man who kicked in the office door last week paid damages of $42, an expensive kick.

October 15, 1975

Dear Mom, Andy and Jay,

Yes, the door kicker was drunk and said he just felt like kicking.

We're thinking about putting the Scamper back on the truck and driving out to see Tim. We would have to drive for two days, visit for two and drive back for two, which would work, barring snowstorms. A year and a half has passed since we've seen Tim, much too long for a mother. He hopes to get a job in the mines, which gives me the creeps. He anticipates hating it but knows he needs that $8 per hour.

Dann brought home a stunning black light poster for Mike, a picture of a plant signed by the artist (Mary Jane) in the corner.

The next night Dann reported, "Tenants in one of our apartments have lined their closet with tinfoil, filled it with plants and installed intense overhead lights." When Dann said he suspected marijuana, Mike proudly dragged out his poster, explaining that Mary Jane is slang for marijuana. The poster and the real plants matched. Those lights created a terrible fire hazard.

I am taking Stretch and Sew classes so that I can learn to sew on knit fabrics. As they expect you to make one project each week, I ought to have a new wardrobe and Christmas presents for everybody.

NOVEMBER 12, 1975

Dear Mom and Andy,

We had a fantastic visit with Tim. He drove us into the canyons and Dann and Tim fished while Cinnamon and I climbed the cliffs. The second day Dann and Tim worked on Tim's truck. The last morning Tim said, "Dad, let's drop a line in the river here before you leave," and they agreed to spend only 10 minutes. They kept to their limit and came back to the truck with a 14-inch trout that Dann had caught and a 16-inch one Tim pulled in on the same pole, as they had only one pole.

Tim can't decide what to do this winter. He doesn't want to stay through another Carbondale winter. He is cutting wood for two men, neither of whom is paying him so he's considering coming home, working or going to Vocational School. Mike wants to get Tim's 1950 Chevy truck back here so he can work on it.

We wanted to drive out of the mountains before the snows and we made it, barely. It snowed Halloween night in Vail Pass, but we went through right behind the snow plows. The Scamper camper works great. Our greatest concern was the holding tank and we worried the water in the pipes might freeze at night. We needed both our furnace and our down sleeping bags.

A Revolving Door

November 18, 1975

Dear Mom and Tim,

We arrived home Sunday night, exhausted. When we drove over Vail Pass, we could see where the snowplows had been, but the pavement was dry and the trees all coated with snowy-white fresh fallen snow. We drove up to Lookout Mountain and coming down that horseshoe bend highway, spotted hang gliders coasting in the updrafts. Further on we spotted a tufted-eared squirrel, a squirrel with the ears of a rabbit, found only in the four corner states. Cinnamon sits on the cab seat and has learned to chase those big two-eyed monsters (vans with lights on) by running from one side of the seat to the other, which makes it tough for the driver.

Jay sounds more and more like a college kid. He wants to move out of the dorm into an apartment and is taking a mini-course in witchcraft.

We have been torn up because we are getting two new bathroom floors installed today. The toilet sat in the corner of the kitchen overnight and I found Cinnamon wistfully sitting in front of the toilet, obviously wondering what happened to her drink.

Wish you were here, Tim. Hope you're keeping warm.

December 1, 1975

Dear Mom and Tim,

Tim, please call so we know how you're doing. Is your truck working? Are you coming home for Christmas?

Andy is still in Montana and has put 10,000 miles on the company car, driving daily to check his wells. The car comes equipped with a down sleeping bag, chocolate bar and a candle. When the weather gets too bad to drive, he is supposed to burrow down in the bag and wait it out. For Christmas last year I gave him a wool shirt like yours, Tim. He says the roughnecks have been accusing him of having lots of money because he wears a $50 shirt. Andy replied, "What do you mean, $50? This didn't cost anything," and he took it off and showed them the 'Made by Mom' label in the back.

Mike hopes to paint his van soon. He installed two heaters in the garage so he can work into the winter. Dann says Mike can't leave home after high school because he will never give up that heated garage.

JANUARY 2, 1976

Dear Mom and Tim,

Happy New Year. We missed you guys on Christmas. Andy didn't make it home either, but he did get an invitation for Christmas dinner. I hope you did, too.

I gave Dann a tandem Schwinn which Mike and I picked up secondhand. Mike cautioned me in advance not to offer the asking price. He forgets I've lived with Dad all these years, too. We found only the old gentleman at home. His wife had decided to sell the bike, but he hated to see it go, as he had given it to her years ago. He enjoyed having an audience and said, "The trouble with people in Wisconsin is that we don't know enough about Indian history and would we like some coffee?" Mike tried to dicker, but couldn't get a word in edgewise and he began to wonder if we would even get it at full asking price. We did. Mike tied it on top of the Fairlane (weather was -20 degrees chill factor) and while he was roping it, the old codger came out three times in bathrobe and slippers: the first time to give us some felt pens with his name on them so we would remember him, the second time to ask our name, "I have to know who gets it, you know, because I feel kinda sentimental about it, you understand," the third time to say he hoped we had as much fun with it as he did. We have been riding around the neighborhood. I'm not sure I like riding rear as the front rider makes all the decisions.

Dann bought himself a Christmas present. He drove by a used car lot before Christmas and spotted a Fiat. He and Mike have been unhappy with our second '72 orange Fiat even after they fixed it, so he traded it in on this bright yellow '74 Fiat.

January 11, 1976

Dear Mom,

One day last week was so awful I wished I had stayed in bed. Our Madison school teachers are striking. I scheduled a naturalist meeting here for the afternoon because I didn't want to hold it at school and cross picket lines, but we woke to a cold house. Dann diagnosed blower trouble, got it going temporarily when it blew a fuse again and quit, so Jay built a fire in the fireplace. Andy interrupted my meeting, calling from Texas, to say that his Christmas packages were lost in transit. Dann and Jay interrupted us when they said goodbye and left to drive Jay and two friends back to school at La Crosse. Dann interrupted again when he phoned from 20 miles away. The transmission was blown on the Fairlane. Could I borrow a car so they could continue? And to please send Mike with our truck and a tow chain. I managed all that by closing the meeting.

I volunteered to go with Mike for the tow. "I'll take you Mom, if I have to, but I'd really rather have Kevin." We picked up Kevin but I stayed to visit with his Mom, as she needed a shoulder to pour her troubles onto.

I walked home, entering the house to a ringing phone to learn that Andy's best chum, aged 24, had been admitted to the hospital the night before and had died of a massive brain tumor. Woody had been like one of our family. My first feeling was concern for his parents, but immediately selfish feelings overwhelmed me as that could have been us. Coming home, after attending my exercise salon, I found Mike dashing around with the fire extinguisher. A butcher knife had slipped in the dishwasher until its plastic handle rested on the heating coil. It smelled awful and it took Mike 15 minutes to find the source. In the meantime we worried. I collapsed on the couch and feebly hoped that Dann would make it home from La Crosse without needing any additional help from us.

Dann took one look at me the next afternoon and called the church choir director. "Jean won't be at practice tonight. She is going to be sick!"

Madison schools remained closed for two weeks. Working mothers became frantic. It worked out well for us as Jay was home on semester break and Dann put both him and then Mike (while school was closed) on the payroll doing apartment repairs. Good for us as we pay them half what we would pay union painters and good for the boys who were short of cash. Occasionally they put in 11-hour work days because after they tore up an apartment, they didn't like to leave it. They came home exhausted every night and even quit asking to use the car in the evenings. One vacated apartment took two days work before they could even start painting. They found 580 empty beer cans, broken furniture strewn all over and a door kicked in. They decided the tenants must have been mad at us. In the next apartment, our apprentice painters grumbled because they had to paint around a kayak in the hall, a bicycle in the dining area and a freezer in the living room. However, in the third apartment, they found two girls who were so delighted with the improvements that the boys put them to work.

I struggle to instill important values in the kids and win some and lose some. We did manage to ingrain a strong work ethic.

They accept the maxim that nothing in this life comes free and working can be fun.

Although we were in sympathy with some of the union demands, we opposed the strike. Fifty percent of the teachers announced a day before Christmas that they were going out sick the next day, although still under contract. What an example! What are mothers going to say when their kids don't want to go to school and would rather stay home and say they're sick? The school board announced that schools would open, but parents should be prepared for kids to return home if the buildings could not be staffed safely. I called a principal and volunteered to help. He asked, "Do you realize that you will have to cross picket lines?"

"That's okay."

"Then I'd be delighted to have your help," he said. I did mind crossing those lines. They scared me, but realizing that I was afraid to enter a public school building made me so angry that I forgot to be afraid.

Mike was aghast (but not opposed) that I would do this and asked, "What will you do if you have to teach a class?"

"Not to worry," I answered. "I have no qualms about disciplining a classroom of elementary kids and, if necessary, I will just teach them what I know best, all about birds and bees and rabbits." Dann went also. The pickets asked our names, which we declined to give, asked us not to cross, which we ignored, and took our license number. Most of the schools did not have enough staff though, so all schools closed after 15 minutes and remained closed for two weeks.

Our washer and dryer perpetuate a constant state of emergency. We couldn't replace them with under-the-counter models because dimensions have increased, so we decided to put the new ones in the basement. Dann tore out the old darkroom in the northwest corner, and remedied the old plumbing. While he was working on that, the old washer kept leaking so he made a small hole in the kitchen floor underneath the washer. Now when something is wrong with the drain, which is usually, the water shoots into the basement instead of rotting the kitchen floor. We put a garbage pail under the hole and we empty it every Monday morning after a veritable Niagara Falls streams through. One week somebody moved the pail two inches. That's all it took! Mike and I hold regular discussions on how much the floor is rotting and whether that washer might drop out of sight some morning. Our discussions speeded up our resident plumber.

Last Saturday we entertained with an Alaskan brunch. So many friends wanted to see our Alaskan slides that we held open house for four hours, repeating the slides over and over with intermissions every 20 minutes for plate refills. I had planned many kinds of sweet rolls and fancy breads, but Mike objected. "You can't show Alaskan slides without serving sourdough pancakes."

When I argued, "No way can I be hostess and cook pancakes, too," he volunteered and cooked for four hours. Guests frequently drifted into the kitchen. As his confidence increased, he flipped higher and higher. Unfortunately, the time he missed was the time he had the biggest audience. He said the hard part was throttling down production when demand lessened without losing heat control and it bored him if he had to slow to one at a time. Some buddies dropped in and he fed them in the kitchen.

I said they were welcome to all they could eat as long as they didn't interfere with the chef.

The next day I came home to find Mike stretched out on the couch watching TV. He had always wanted to eat two Lalapaloozas and he and Kevin had just done it. One lalapalooza equals a triple sundae. The next day he ate nothing at all.

Mike has been sanding and puttying the exterior of his van for months. His girl promised to paint Alaskan mountains on the side panel.

January 16, 1976

Dear Mom,

Dad delivered the kids safely to La Crosse, returning home by midnight. Mike and Kev towed the defunct Fairlane home without difficulty and now we'll have to operate with one less car until they find a used transmission. The furnace blower is operating again, Andy's packages turned up. The only thing damaged in the dishwasher was the ruined knife and the awful smell lessened. Twas a tough day.

Andy returned to Houston for a four-week command school after which he thinks he'll be home. He has a girl in Wolfpoint, Montana and figures the best way to bring Houston and Wolfpoint together is for both to converge on Madison.

We wish Tim would come home. Dann is trying to interest him in some carpentry work he needs done.

January 30, 1976

Dear Everybody,

Andy, your letter impressed Woody's Mom. The church was packed for his Memorial service. I coordinated a dinner for his family for the next day. We'd love to meet your girl, Andy, if you can work out something after command school is over.

Dad and Mike towed our Fairlane to school and put it on the hoist. Mike wants to know what went wrong with the old transmission, but if he takes it apart to see, he can't trade it in to the junkyard. He is planning to put secret hiding places in his van since we've been hearing so many traveling trouble stories.

Our combination tenant/cleaning lady's husband, James, is no longer in city jail, but up the river at Waupun. They had released him for the day on the Huber Law and instead of working, he went to Copp's and lifted more watches. She explained his system. His buddy (a small guy) would enter a department store and put on three pairs of pants beneath his own, tying them around the bottom so they didn't show, and walk out. James would bring them back as returns and receive cash.

February 6, 1976

Dear Andy, Tim and Jay,

Grandmother likes Fairhaven. Monday mornings she attends history class, Tuesday a.m. goes to physical fitness, Wednesday a.m. takes a rosemaling class, Thursday a.m. patronizes the Fairhaven beauty parlor and Friday mornings participates in Bible study.

Mike has been accepted at Vocational School for a two-year body work course.

A Revolving Door

February 9, 1976

Dear Mom,

Tim is home. He will stay if he can find work.

February 13, 1976

Dear Mom, Andy and Jay,

I can't go to bed as a puppy has just arrived five days early and wasn't born in the correct place. When Dad took Cinnamon outside, she ran into her garage doghouse. Getting a flashlight I called her, but no luck. Dad wiggled into the dog house. By that time a puppy had arrived. I wrapped the pup in an old towel and we adjourned to the correct place (whelping bed in the basement) with Cinnamon following anxiously. I can't understand this. Puppies always arrive in 62 days, never five days early.

Kathy arrived yesterday. Today, she collapsed in bed. I suspect she had not been feeling well for several days, but hadn't been where she could collapse. This is the foster girl that we've been talking about. Remember we discussed it when all of you were home. She is a fourteen-year-old 8th grader whose mother told her to get out and for two weeks Kathy has been living with a friend. She would have been on the streets before much longer. Monday a.m. we agreed to take her and she arrived Tuesday. Unfortunately, she was placed by the family psychologist, after which we notified Dane County Welfare that she was here and we needed our license renewed. This is doing it backwards but the psychologist predicted if we had not done it this way, it would have taken a month to license. Kathy couldn't wait. She is one scared little girl.

Jay, your brothers applied to the City Parks for a summer job for you. The two of them had us in stitches just telling about it.

They ad-libbed (*Bulletin*—time out for puppy #2) when they didn't know the answers. Mike listed you with a Math major because he couldn't spell psychology. Where the form asked if you would accept a job lifting 50, 75, or 100 pounds they chose 100 and checked all the available jobs, including zoo cages, because that was the highest paying.

We enjoyed having you all here at the same time and Andy, it was great to meet Laura. Going south as you were, I hope you drove out of that storm quickly.

Bulletin: 11:00 p.m. 3rd puppy... 12:00 p.m. 4th... 3:00 a.m. 5th... 7:00 a.m. total of six.

FEBRUARY 20, 1976

Dear Mom,

I guess you know that Thursday evening Madison declared a state of emergency. On Monday and Tuesday a sleet storm had encased the trees in ice, which never melted. On Thursday a rain storm moved in accompanied by high winds. The trees couldn't take any more weight and crashed onto houses and power lines. Our electricity went out Thursday afternoon: no heat, no electric typewriter, house gets dark by 5:00 p.m., no TV (but they all went off the air anyhow) and no radio. By Thursday night Madison had a water crisis, as 21 of the 24 pumping stations were down and the city reserved the balance for fire calls. Our street closed when a tree fell across it. Downed cables lay all over. When the main station blew, red and blue fireworks shot into the sky. The power company flew in work crews from Missouri. Many people got power back on Friday but 7,500, including us, are still without. The trees on our road leaned over and met in the middle, the driveway closed in overhead and we cut off lower branches to get through. We took brief walks

A Revolving Door

Thursday night until the frequent thunderous crashes around us chased us back home. One of the neighbor's trees came down over the fence, bringing wires down across the Scamper. I needed the cook kit from inside it but Mike said, "No way!" We thought we had lost half our trees, but most were just topped. The house temperature dropped to 44 degrees, even with a roaring fire in the fireplace. One invaluable friend, after their power returned, sent her family over with their station wagon to pick up my 100 houseplants. When the water crises lessened, another friend invited us for pancakes and showers and every night friends invited us for supper. Whenever possible, Kathy and I waited until we were invited out to use the bathroom. Life isn't kind to females using a cold bathroom. Dad closed the dining room by hanging blankets in the archway. If we don't get power by tonight, he may have to drain our water system. We closed the upstairs bedrooms and are sleeping on the living room floor in front of the fireplace. To be without electricity for 72 hours is indescribable. The first night was exciting, the second night we were desperately trying to find ways to manage, by the third night tempers had shortened. We cooked over the fireplace or with the camp stove and were fortunate we didn't lose our phone or our water. We played games by candlelight (tried 24 different games) but could hardly see to read the dice and learned to do what was most important before 5:00 p.m. After that darkness fell inside and out. What a way to break in a new daughter. At least we got acquainted fast and fortunately she was sick only the first day.

Three of the pups couldn't nurse and had to be fed every half hour. We lost the two smallest ones, the remaining four appear okay. They get the prime spot in front of the fire. We had an offer of a hot water bottle for the pups and all supper invitations included the puppies, but we'd rather not move them.

We are worried about the two older ladies next door. Miss Parsons is bedridden and her night nurse has not come for the last two nights. I call over there every two hours. After they ran out of firewood, Mike took over a load. I picked up groceries for them and volunteered to send over our camp stove for their supper, along with somebody to turn it on.

We hope to get electricity by tonight but I heard a nasty rumor that all the main lines in our area have been cut. Power was out at church, necessitating a portable emergency generator for services. Trees are down on two of our apartment buildings. We've added dry ice to the freezer to protect all the raspberries you picked and froze. Tim is out madly snapping pictures.

P.S. Please save this stamp and the ones on your next 49 letters. This is my way of saving 50 state commemoratives.

P.P.S. Cheers! We're holding at 40 degrees, probably because of the fireplace, so Dann doesn't need to drain the water. Those of us with fireplaces and camping experience are in a superior position. I hated to go into the kitchen to cook because my fingers would get so cold. We moved back to our beds last night by adding blankets. Mike piled on six! People are running out of firewood, even we are getting low. The bright side is that everybody has lots of green wood for next year. All the motels are jammed, the restaurants that are open can't keep up. With a batch of new puppies, we didn't feel a motel was an option. The Red Cross Center and West High are open and full of people. Pray for warm weather.

March 16, 1976

Dear Mom,

We are enjoying Kathy. One day last week she ran away instead of going to school but called about 5:30, saying she'd been thinking all day and thought she had made a mistake. Dann picked her up and brought her home. She seems to be awed by all the guys around here, especially Jay who is home on spring vacation. Last night the boys taught her to play 500 as they needed a fourth.

Dad and Tim added a room to the house we bought for investment purposes. They accomplished this in a week and a half working together. Now Tim is painting and then the house goes back on the market. Dad has just purchased a two-apartment on the east side that needs to be fixed, so that's next on Tim's work list.

Andy is teaching mud school.

March 24, 1976

Dear Mom,

The house bursts with activity again. Jay arrived home for spring break, which makes us a family of six and everybody gets up every day. It's been a long time since we had six for breakfast. First, Kathy and Mike tear off to school, next Tim leaves to work on whatever project Dann put him on, usually he and Dann go off together, and Jay rides along with me if I'm going to the office and drops off at the University Library, where he is researching dolphins.

The Board of Education called this week with a nine year-old hard-of-hearing boy to place. With my Occupational Therapy background I could probably handle this more easily than most people. These kids go home on Friday night and come back Monday morning so we would have the weekend free. Our big house plus my medical background intrigued the social worker, but I can't handle any more kids.

I spent an afternoon with Kathy's social worker. Licensing red tape has snarled us up because we placed her before we re-licensed. I phoned them two weeks ago and it's taken that long to send out a worker. She and I shopped for clothes, a treat for both of us. She has bought her own clothes since she was ten years old, with money she earned, so has very few. Today she's baking ice-box cookies. Jay, Mike and Kevin wandered through the kitchen each time a batch came out and she shook her head in disbelief. "I never saw anybody eat like that!"

Would you spend Easter with us? We will have an empty bedroom.

The puppies get cuter daily. One peanut is so much smaller than the rest of the litter that the heavyweights push him aside at feeding time. We administer a shot of eggnog occasionally for an energy booster.

Mike's van came home from school painted midnight blue. He has put in hundreds of hours sanding and now he can move on to the more challenging interior.

Kathy is fun to have around and tops in her class. She has trouble accepting that she cannot live at home as other kids do. Consequently she isn't trying to make friends or find interests at school because she figures she's going home soon. The psychologist told her to plan on at least a year with us and then he would re-evaluate how her mother was managing. She blew up. The problem is that Momma is unstable much of the time.

Yes, the corners of my house finally warmed up, but I am still finding things like the fire extinguisher next to the fireplace and candle wax on the carpet.

March 28, 1976

Dear Mom,

We rented the front office to the Carter for President Headquarters. They run a bank of five yellow phones and 20 volunteers daily, and even Jay volunteered. Yesterday a gal came through our office on her way to the bathroom, stopped, introduced herself and chatted. She is a daughter-in-law of Jimmy Carter, and a first-grade teacher who took off a year to campaign. She and her husband Chip have been on the road nine months. They don't travel together, but she arrived early and she scheduled her husband here so they could have two nights together. Her husband works on the family peanut farm, but his Uncle Billy handles the farm now so that everybody can campaign. At one of Carter's appearances, protesters threw peanuts so the FBI took Carter out through the kitchen entrance. Covering him takes 10 agents. This must cost taxpayers plenty.

Madison staged a Bicentennial celebration and I wore your long centennial dress with hoop and matching bonnet. The arena was so jammed that I couldn't see much and had trouble walking with that hoop. When it gets squeezed on both sides, it jumps out in front. Volunteers set up booths demonstrating bread making, butter making, cheese making, noodle making, and soap making and booths displayed antique cars, a prairie village, printing shop, blacksmith, R.R. station, school, and log cabins.

Wisconsin's covered wagon stopped here. Pennsylvania gave every state a covered wagon, all of which will converge on Valley Forge on July 4th as they work eastward, using five different routes. Our wagon train comes from the Dakotas, Minnesota and

Iowa and the Wisconsin wagon will latch on as it crosses our western border.

Only three healthy pups remain. We suspected that Squawker was either blind or brain-damaged. He had trouble walking and would run into walls. One morning he just sat in the middle of the dog bed crying endlessly and we decided he must be in pain and couldn't let him continue to suffer. Coming five days early must have been hard on the pups. We attribute those five days prematurely to the approaching ice storm which caused a drop in barometric pressure. We may keep one pup. Venus's popularity poll is rising. She has beautiful curly hair, but Peanut's personality has an edge.

Mike ran out of money working on his van and decided he needed more junkers to fix. He put an ad in the paper over the weekend, "*Wanted* VW cheap that needs work". You wouldn't believe how many people in Madison have VW's that don't work. Mike received 15 calls immediately. Sunday afternoon he brought home the first one. He invited Kathy to go along to navigate as she is familiar with the east side where the car was located and Tim went as extra driver. They managed to get home with only two emergency stops for oil. Last night Mike and Tim brought home the second, and they're dickering for three more. Tim has caught the fever as they're working now on a 50/50 basis. They plan on making the next three into two.

We're still having trouble with the Welfare Department. They still insist they can't pay us for the first three weeks because we weren't licensed. My answer to that is, "Why didn't you do it sooner?" They just don't hurry with anything.

A Revolving Door

APRIL 7, 1976

Dear Jay and Andy,

I visited Grandmother on her birthday, taking a daffodil-decorated birthday cake so she could have a party and invite her friends. When I left she was trying to figure out if she asked everybody to bring their own chairs, she could ask everybody living on first floor.

We advertised the pups. Peanut still wins our popularity poll, but only by a hair. Grandmother fell in love with Venus and suggested we hide her behind a basket whenever anybody came to look. Venus cuddles like crazy while Peanut is out tearing through the woods behind her mother. Tim and Mike said of course you guys can't vote on puppies. You're not here.

APRIL 11, 1976

Dear Mom,

Jay sent a puppy vote, but too late. We kept Peanut and she is a little devil on wheels. She needs to be renamed and everyone gets a voice in this. Suggestions were Peanut, Saffron, Samantha, Rumpelstiltskin, Venus, or Ginger.

I am exhausted. I had a two-hour hike in the School Forest this morning, took an hour for lunch followed by a three-hour afternoon hike, an abbreviated supper and another three hour hike after that. I overheard one kid talking to his teacher. "Every time I come here I get a really enthusiastic naturalist!"

My answer to that is, "Is there any other kind?"

Kathy says everyone is over the hill at 39. My feet are over the hill after a day like this.

Summer plans are shaping up. Jay will be home working on the Arboretum crew. Mike fixes cars from dawn to dusk, but has postponed his summer trip as his van is not ready. Tim got a summer job building log cabins in the Wrangell Mountains in Alaska.

I thought last winter would be my "monotonous and boring" one. I don't know what happened. Everybody left, but came right back. Andy came home in February and arranged for his girl to fly in from Montana so we could meet her. Tim, who was working in Arizona for the winter, flew home to see Andy and stayed when he realized that his Dad desperately needed help with remodeling apartments. He seems pleased to be working a 40-hour week and helping his Dad. I have taught Kathy to sew as she needs to enlarge her wardrobe. My problem is to get equal time on the sewing machine for me. She is also our official cookie maker. She told me when she arrived that she didn't like to cook but obviously never had appreciative consumers before.

The changing colors on the kitchen wall reflect from the owl prism that hangs on the window. Our lives seem to be like that prism—always changing, some dark days, some bright but always challenging. We are the proverbial revolving door. Everyone keeps rushing out, but soon comes tripping back.

14 Subtracting or Adding?

April 14, 1976

Dear Mom,

Our never quiet existence has reached a new high. We're going to have a wedding—Andy is engaged. We're subsidizing the telephone company these days. Imagine—a girl in our family!

April 18, 1976

Dear Mom and Jay,

I told Andy your exams last until the middle of May, but he says that the wedding will be after that. He is waiting for a transfer out of the tech pool and this worries him. The company is handling so many trouble spots in the oil fields right now that they've assigned everyone. Even Andy's boss went to Iran and now they are starting to pull instructors so Andy might get shipped out either just before or after his wedding.

April 25, 1976

Dear Jay,

We missed you last weekend. Grandmother came, and many of your aunts, uncles and cousins, making 14 for Easter dinner. On top of a busy holiday weekend, Dad had an accepted offer on a house he had listed for sale and Mike was called for an interview at a new body shop. He is so broke he can't work on his van anymore. Tim answered an ad to build log cabins in the Wrangell Mountains in Alaska, got the job and will be leaving in two weeks.

Andy asked Tim to be best man and when Tim checked into the Alaskan job, he said, "There's no way I'm going to miss my brother's wedding. I'll fly home." He talked to his future boss, who agreed to drive Tim to the Anchorage airport and pick him up there a week later.

About your summer job, you could work for Dad. He had painting work lined up for Tim and Mike. We have city orders on this stuff and it looks like we're losing both of our potential painters.

April 30, 1976

Dear Mom and Jay,

Congratulations, Senator. What does this entail? Mike is waiting to see if you can put through the no-pay deal you used on your platform.

Assume that any wedding news I give you is out-of-date by the time you receive it. This decision-changing around here exhausts me.

Tim leaves tomorrow. Dave, his new boss, has been saving for two years to build a log hunting lodge. He owns land in the

Wrangell Mountain Range, a new truck and all kinds of equipment. They will live in tents while they build. He is paying Tim's traveling expenses, room and board (I think that means a tent, moose meat and fish), $40 a week and a promise of land if Tim stays long enough. Tim says the lousy pay makes it more like a paid vacation, but he loves to do this stuff.

Andy calls often. When he called last night he changed the date to Thursday, June 10th. We groaned. The middle of any week is terrible. This means everybody will have to take off the entire week as we are driving to Montana. Andy called again tonight and changed the date to Saturday, June 12. We're back to taking off only half the week.

April 30, 1976

Dear Andy,

If you don't change your plans again, we are thinking along these lines, Grandmother said "No." I will encourage her, but I suspect it will remain no as she tires easily. Jay, Mike, Dad and I will leave here Wednesday after work, travel in the Scamper Camper and plan to arrive at Wolfpoint Friday morning in time for a Friday evening wedding rehearsal. Please make a reservation for us to take the wedding party out to dinner. Also motel reservations for Dad and me for Friday and Saturday nights. The boys can sleep in the Scamper, but a motel room would give us a dressing room and a bathroom.

We've talked with Tim at great length as he leaves tomorrow for Alaska. Grandmother offered to pay some of his airfare for his birthday present and we'll pay some. We will be out of contact for three weeks, but have asked him to call as soon as he has settled.

May 15, 1976

Dear Mom and Andy,

Tim called. He and his boss had just crossed the Alaskan border and were in Tok. His description of the travel difficulties brought back vivid memories of our trip on the Alcan Highway. They had so many flats on the trailer that they ran out of spares, but were able to repair them. A semi sideswiped their truck, scraping the top rack. It didn't scratch either of the boats they were carrying, but necessitated rebuilding the trailer. Tim still plans to be at the Anchorage airport on the 9th, arriving at Wolfpoint on the 10th. He even got a haircut before he left. I'm not sure whether it was for the Alaskan summer or the wedding.

Mike did not get his summer job, so will be painting for Dad, plus any repair jobs he can line up. His reputation grows. A friend brought his Vega over for Mike to remove rust spots and took it in to a professional garage to have a fender replaced. Now he's telling everybody that Mike did a more professional job than the garage.

What would you think about identical ties? I could make them, either bow ties or conventional. If anybody is disappointed about no formal gear, bow ties will seem dressier.

May 17, 1976

Dear Mom and Andy,

Jay's exams are over and we brought him home. While widening our street, the city messed up our driveway. A ditch stretches across half the width, the other half is steeply uphill and covered with loose dirt. After yesterday's rain, that half was all mud. Dad said no way could we drive through with all Jay's stuff weighing down the rear of the car so, in pouring rain, Dad and Jay carried all his gear from the bottom of the drive up to the house.

When Dad needed to take the truck out today, Dad, Mike and Jay walked down to the end of the drive, laid a dozen steel forms crosswise, corduroyed a section and gingerly drove through. Unfortunately they ran out of gas in the middle of the Willett construction zone. We're going to have unhappy workmen tomorrow when they have to dig their forms out of the rutted mud our truck made.

Questions: When is the big event, afternoon or evening? Can Tim stay with you? Otherwise, he can sleep in the Scamper with Jay and Mike. How much more money should we send? Grandma would be pleased to re-loan you some of what you repaid. Do you have a phone yet?

May 19, 1976

Dear Mom and Andy,

We have changed Tim's reservations. Instead of flying down the west coast, he will fly to Minneapolis and we'll pick him up on our way. Otherwise he would have to transfer four times and if he missed connections, there are no alternate flights, but we need him to call home so we can tell him about the change.

May 21, 1976

Dear Andy,

We are sticking with your yellow and blue color scheme. I found some neat crushed velvet wide bow ties in blue or gold and will make the shirts, blue for you and yellow for your brothers. I went shopping this week and found a two-piece goldenrod dress for me. Tim will pick up his ticket and reservations at Anchorage, except he hasn't called yet and we need desperately to tell him the change in plans.

May 22, 1976

Dear Mom,

I relaxed in bed yesterday morning, reflecting on this hectic spring. Our family is closely bonded and yet right now so far apart in miles. My schedule is so jammed this week that even survival looks tough. In two weeks we will drive into Big Sky country into the back lands of Montana to a tiny town surrounded by Indian reservations. I had planned on doing many things yesterday: calling to see if the kids' silverware order was in, checking the Scamper and adding food supplies for a two-day trip out and two back. I have finished four shirts for four boys in the wedding party except for 36 buttons and 36 buttonholes. I need to pick up my goldenrod dress and to put the back on the lavender log cabin quilt I am making for an additional wedding present. As I lay in bed I wondered how to manage all that?

Worse, Tim still hasn't called. When they came out of the bush for supplies, he was supposed to call and verify his flight plans. We have changed them and he doesn't know this.

Obviously I needed to stop thinking and start doing and rolled over, doing a couple back stretches while running my fingers over my breasts. I felt a small lump so I did it again, and again. The lump remained. I tried a different angle but it stayed the same. I slid out of bed and stood tall but the small hardness, that I had never noticed before, remained. As I dressed my mind raced back to a single thought. I have no time for this.

At breakfast Dann and I discussed our options. There were none. He insisted that I phone immediately for an appointment and when the receptionist put my call through to the doctor, he said, "Come in now."

As he's not only my doctor, but also a friend, I argued, "Can't. I don't have time."

"Now," he insisted. He examined me while asking questions and called in a surgeon who repeated the exam. Leaving the room briefly, he came back in and said, "I have arranged for you to be admitted next Wednesday for a biopsy."

"That's a problem," I mumbled. "I have no time because Andy is being married in two weeks."

"If all goes well, you can go home the next day."

When I reached home, our weekend company had already arrived and I had no opportunity to talk with Dann. I didn't need to say a word as two tears slid silently down my face. Now we have to wait through this awful weekend until next Wednesday.

Thursday, May 27, 1976

Dear Mom,

It was a long weekend, an even longer Monday and Tuesday. The buttonholes got done. The backing for the quilt did not. I picked up the goldenrod dress, the gift of silverware came in, but no call came from Alaska.

I held Dann's hand Wednesday morning and worried, not about my life span, but about an empty seat in the front pew at Andy's wedding. I signed the slip giving permission for an immediate mastectomy if they found malignancy. My last thought as I drifted through space was to wonder, "Will all of me be here when I wake, or will there be parts missing?"

Struggling to regain consciousness later, I dragged one hand slowly across my chest. Soft breasts—still there! I surely was one of the lucky ones.

I had worried how Kathy would cope with me in the hospital. Her Mother had been sick often and she had always blamed Kathy by saying that worrying about her daughters caused her illnesses. How would Kathy react to mine? I alerted her social worker that trouble loomed and we needed help, but no help was forthcoming. I left Kathy with cooking responsibilities and called home frequently and she coped for the 24 hours I was gone.

Returning home, I was so delighted with my restored world that I walked outside marveling at every detail: the splattering of crimson and yellow in the tulip beds, teardrops of dew hanging like sparkling diamonds at the drip-points of every leaf, the circular spider web in the forsythia bush, orange daylilies lined up like soldiers on parade under the cedars. I listened to the blue jays scolding and to the catbird on the wire singing a dozen different songs. The smell of the black locust blossoms was overpowering, as if the tree was drenched with French perfume. The wind gently blew on the blossoms and cumulus clouds scooted across the sky, dark and gray as if predicting a storm. When I re-entered the kitchen, I found a message that Dr. Max had called asking Dann to return his call. Why Dann? Why not me? When Dann came home he read the message and silently left the room. After an eternity of waiting, he came to the supper table and explained to the kids and me simultaneously. "During a biopsy one section is tested immediately. This test is 98% accurate. Another section is frozen and tested after 24 hours. Two percent of the time this second test shows malignancy. Your Mom is among that 2%. She needs more surgery."

"I'll go now," I panicked, "there is no time to waste with Andy's wedding so close." But it was Friday. The operating rooms were not only closed for the weekend, but for the Memorial Day holiday. Visions of an empty pew at Andy's wedding flit through my mind now all the time. We face another long weekend. Why is so much of life made up of waiting?

Subtracting or Adding?

June 2, 1976

Dear Mom,

Over last weekend the quilt back got cut, but not quilted. I sewed on 36 buttons to match the 36 buttonholes and because I had to wait for the surgery date, I attended Mike's high school graduation. Still no phone call from Alaska.

On June 1, the hospital re-admitted me. I told everybody who would listen that I had a wedding in Montana on June 12 and they wrote that in big letters all over my medical records. Dann left the house unlocked on Tuesday and during the surgery my sewing club friends came with their quilting frame. When Dann returned home after a long day of waiting rooms and hand-holding, the house was empty and quiet, but the neatly folded lavender quilt lay ready for gift-wrapping.

I had a double simple mastectomy. Simple means they do not remove as many muscles, making it easier to get back full range of motion in your arms. My doctor told me if I would wait to leave until the last moment, I could go to the wedding. The Reach for Recovery volunteer from the American Cancer Society answered questions and showed me finger and arm exercises so those aching muscles would not stiffen.

Although Kathy and I muddled through my first hospitalization, we didn't make it through this one. Today she ran away. We have decided that we just can't cope with the extra problems that she entails when we don't know what lies ahead for us and Dann has asked the Department of Public Welfare to place her elsewhere. I feel awful. I know she needed us.

Tuesday, June 8, 1976

Dear Mom,

I am home. Our house resembles Grand Central Station. Dann hooked up a 50-foot line so I could use the telephone from the couch. My day's activities consist of soaking baths, arm exercises, endless phone calls, many visitors, and general supervision from the couch. My Homemaker and Scouting buddies have taken over. Each night four people bring in dinner. I finally asked them to stop so we could eat leftovers.

Three women cleaned, ironed, and shopped for groceries. When Michael came home and walked through the kitchen, a lady yelled, "Hey, you can't walk on that wet floor." He offered her cold lemonade and fled. When Jason arrived home from work hot and tired, he collapsed in the living room and visited with everybody. When the minister called, it startled him to see women, carrying brooms and scrub pail, walking through continually.

I don't know how we would have managed this week without those gratis meals. Dann says he would have done the cooking, but he couldn't do everything. It was a big help to all my men to have me home to answer the phone.

We plan that Jay and Mike will leave tomorrow after work (Wednesday) in the Scamper Camper and pick up Tim at the Minneapolis airport. Dann and I have to wait for the surgeon's okay on Friday and then we'll fly. The problem is we still don't know where Tim is and he doesn't know that we've changed his flight plans and that tickets to Minneapolis are waiting for him at the Anchorage airport. Now I not only worry about an empty pew where the groom's mother should be, but also about a missing best man. Andy is distraught worrying about things beyond his control.

Subtracting or Adding?

Thursday, June 10, 1976

Dear Mom,

Jay and Mike left at 8:30 p.m. last night with still no word from Alaska. We delayed the boys' departure as long as we dared hoping to hear from Tim but still allow time for them to reach Wolfpoint by Friday morning. We asked them to call home when they reached the Twin Cities.

In the stillness of the night, four hours after they had left, the telephone shrilled and it was Tim. He had been unable to reach a phone earlier, had finally arrived in Fairbanks, purchased his own ticket through to Wolfpoint and was about to board. He said that this job had not worked out, he had all his gear with him and was coming home to work for his Dad. Lastly he said, "Don't worry. I'll make it by rehearsal time."

Thirty minutes later, at 1:00 a.m., Jay and Mike checked in. With a sigh of relief we could tell them that Tim was enroute flying in from the west. "Just keep on rolling," we said. All this was not conducive to a good night's sleep.

Kathy and her social worker came and packed up her stuff. We asked her about the money we know she took from my purse while I was in the hospital but she stubbornly denied it. We had decided that if she admitted the theft we would try again, but she wouldn't. I had some special birthday funds in my purse with doodling on the outside of the envelope and we found that empty envelope in her bureau drawer. I feel bad because we thought she was special. I am going to have to do something to that empty bedroom quickly so I don't have to look at it.

Are weddings always filled with turmoil?

Dear Mom

June 14, 1976

Dear Mom,

Dann and I left Friday on schedule. We took off and landed six times during the 1200-mile flight. Each time we landed I went to the ladies' room and did my finger-walking exercises. I walked both hands up the wall until my shoulders hurt, pushed them a bit higher and walked them down again.

The last leg of the journey was aboard a small Frontier prop plane with no stewardesses or drinks, a gorgeous view of the desolate terrain below and a thunderstorm hovering about us. I gave a great sigh of relief when I spotted all four boys waiting at the Wolfpoint Airport. Because it is so close to the Canadian border, it has a big sign International Airport even though the terminal is smaller than our garage and sits isolated in a windswept field. Andy told us later that arriving at Wolfpoint is easy. Departing is difficult because there is no ground-to-air communication. When someone wants to fly out, they send up balloons signaling for the aircraft to land.

The wedding took place on schedule with no empty place in that front pew. While getting dressed in our motel room, the boys teased a lot. Tim remarked, "I look pretty nice but I don't look like me."

It was a simple, beautiful ceremony. I stared at the groom, the best man, and the two groomsmen. Momentarily my vision wavered and I saw only four grinning, mischievous, barefoot little boys, with patched faded blue jeans and wild cowlicks, faces covered with dirt and grime. But those little boys disappeared and four young men reappeared, handsome in their suits with velveteen bow ties and blue and yellow shirts that collectively had 36 buttonholes. Again my vision wavered and I saw another wedding 26 years ago when Dann and I, hand in hand, oblivious to the hot, packed congregation behind us, spoke our vows wondering what the future held for us.

Subtracting or Adding?

I take back the comment I made to you, Mom, that being a housewife must be "boring and monotonous." I remember how you chuckled. Now I know why. Somehow, over the years we've managed to raise a rambunctious, close-knit, loving family of four boys. Your influence has helped. I don't feel regrets that the first one is moving on to a family of his own. That makes our extended family larger. Mothers often cry at weddings and I did. Twenty-six years ago I wondered what the future held. I still do. What comes next?

Love from all of us, Jean.

Epilogue Ten Years Later

That "boring and monotonous" existence of married life never caught up to us. The boys repeatedly left and repeatedly returned. Their growing families and their successes and failures filled our lives with inspiration and satisfactions.

The trouble-shooting kid continued to work for oil companies, graduated to teaching the trouble-shooters and eventually left the pressure of the oil fields for Mathematics, his other love, as a C.P.A.

The one who came home from the mountains because his Dad needed him, discovered that need continued endlessly and gradually took over the family business.

The son who questioned everything turned his curiosity towards computers, the environment and finally finance.

The kid attached to the legs always sticking out from under a car, who took cars apart and put them back together before he ever reached driving age, started his own auto body shop and dreams of designing solar cars.

And our first girl, whom we loved but were not able to hold on to, settled down in Washington state with her husband and daughter in a two story log cabin, which they built themselves chink by chink.

Ten Years Later

The Willett family cottage remains a Willett family cottage after 81 years—now encompassing fourth generation cousins. Mom lived to the age of 94 and her interest in our family remained a big part of her life to the end.

On December 30, 1986, Fairhaven advised me to come and I sat holding her hand through that last, long night. As the hours slowly passed I recalled all that she had meant to me over the years.

Hands Across the Bed

Mom, I'm here
the day is fast departing for darkness has long since fallen.

Let me hold your hand
as you have often held mine.
The time has passed for words between us
only thoughts scooting through our clasped hands
like voices sliding down a phone wire.

My mind is filled with visions of you
dogging your father's steps through the old barn
determined to show him a mere girl could do anything a boy could.
I know how he would let you ride old Jo bareback
if no one was around.

Dear Mom

Flying through the fields with pigtails flat out
He objected though, didn't he,
when you walked the high crossbars on the silo
just because you wanted to be on the other side.
Somehow I get the feeling that you were special to him
as he was special to you.

I need to hold your hand tighter, Mom.
I hear the night noises of people in the next beds
and I am frightened.
I have visions of you as teacher
How could you do that?
How could you handle
that one room schoolhouse
when you were only just out of school yourself?
How could you teach boys who were as old as you were?
Perhaps
disciplining mischievous children came natural to you even then.
How could you drive yourself to school
with horse and sleigh
and not get upset when you tipped into the snowbank

Your small hand completely enclosed in mine grows cooler yet.
Oh that I might warm it for you.

Your day was full of challenges, wasn't it?
During those dark times of the depression
we ate
we loved
we experienced family togetherness
and I never knew that one of those special Christmases we shared,
you did it all for $.50.
Nobody told me that until later.

Ten Years Later

I see your eyes flicker.
You're asking me to help, aren't you?
I'm trying Mom,
through our hands.

I wonder how you felt when we all spread our wings and departed.
But I never really left, did I?
You still held my hand and cried with me
or laughed
but most of all you always kept listening.
You listened when I flippantly said college is exciting
but being a housewife must be "monotonous and boring"
and you knew
and laughed to yourself.

As I am listening to you now
only to you.

And listened when I called you four times from my hospital
bed saying
"It's a boy"
and remarked "if your boys cause you any trouble
just remember you deserve that for all the hard times you gave me."
But Mom,
how could I be other than stubborn
or curious
or a daredevil?
I was your daughter.
You listened when tearfully I told you I had a malignant tumor
and you counted with me those mythical five years
until my odds improved.

Dear Mom

You made such a wonderful Grandmother
You were always there
with hugs and kisses or scolds
With fresh cookies and stories to tell.
I think you must have enjoyed being a Grandmother
because you always talked about us
to everybody.

You leave 23 parts of you behind forever
and they all send you their love
through me
to warm you this last time.

Your day was long, Mom,
very long and full.
But the day is done.
I grieve
but am glad.

The darkness is lifting
and a new day is here.

Jean and Dann Willett

If you enjoyed this book, feel free to send any comments to Jean Willett through the publisher or directly at jwillett@chorus.net.

A portion of the proceeds of the sales of this book will be donated to the University of Wisconsin Comprehensive Cancer Center.